Child Safety

A Pediatric Guide for Parents, Teachers,
Nurses, and Caregivers

G.W. Medical Publishing, Inc.
St. Louis

This book is dedicated to Frances Pinnel, the librarian at the Margery H. Nelson Medical Library at St. Christopher's Hospital for Children, who spent many hours helping the contributors to this book find the articles and resources they needed to produce valuable chapters, and to Jeannie Hernandez, who consistently kept the project organized while juggling many other responsibilities as executive assistant to the senior author.

Child Safety

A Pediatric Guide for Parents, Teachers, Nurses, and Caregivers

Angelo P. Giardino, MD, PhD, MPH, FAAP
Medical Director
Texas Children's Health Plan
Clinical Associate Professor of Pediatrics
Baylor College of Medicine
Attending Physician
Children's Assessment Center
Texas Children's Hospital
Houston, Texas

G.W. Medical Publishing, Inc.
St. Louis

Publishers: Glenn E. Whaley and Marianne V. Whaley

Design Director: Glenn E. Whaley

Managing Editors: Megan O. Hayes
               Karen C. Maurer

Associate Editors: Robert Lewis
               Christine Bauer

Book Design/Page Layout: G.W. Graphics
               Charles J. Seibel, III
               Sudon Choe

Print/Production Coordinator: Charles J. Seibel, III

Cover Design: G.W. Graphics

Color Prepress Specialist: G.W. Graphics
               Charles J. Seibel, III

Copy Editor: Anne Wenzel

Developmental Editor: Kimberly McClelland

Proofreader: Michael S. McConnell

Indexer: Robert A. Saigh

Printed in Canada.

Publisher:
G.W. Medical Publishing, Inc.
77 Westport Plaza, Suite 366, St. Louis, Missouri, 63146-3124 U.S.A.
Phone: (314) 542-4213 Fax: (314) 542-4239 Toll Free: 1-800-600-0330
http://www.gwmedical.com

Library of Congress Cataloging-in-Publication Data

Child safety : a pediatric guide for parents, teachers, nurses, and
    caregivers / [edited by] Angelo P. Giardino.
        p. ; cm.
    Includes bibliographical references and index.
    ISBN 1-878060-67-8 (perfect bound book)
    1. Child welfare. 2. Children's accidents--Prevention. 3. Child
abuse--Prevention. 4. Safety education.   I. Giardino, Angelo P.
    [DNLM: 1. Child Welfare. 2. Adolescent Psychology.
    3. Caregivers. 4. Child Psychology. 5. Safety Management
--methods.   WA 320 C534955 2007]
HV715.C54 2007
362.7--dc22

                                                    2006028637

ASSOCIATE AUTHORS AND CONTRIBUTORS

Cynthia W. DeLago, MD, MPH, FAAP
CARES Institute
Assistant Professor of Pediatrics
Department of Pediatrics
School of Osteopathic Medicine
University of Medicine and Dentistry of New Jersey
Stratford, New Jersey

Eileen R. Giardino, PhD, RN, CRNP*
Associate Professor of Nursing
The University of Texas School of Nursing at Houston
Department of Acute and Continuing Care
Houston, Texas

Hans B. Kersten, MD, FAAP
Assistant Professor of Pediatrics
Drexel University College of Medicine
Division of Ambulatory Pediatrics
St. Christopher's Hospital for Children
Philadelphia, Pennsylvania

Paul S. Matz, MD, FAAP
Assistant Professor of Pediatrics
Drexel University College of Medicine
Attending Physician
Division of Ambulatory Pediatrics
St. Christopher's Hospital for Children
Philadelphia, Pennsylvania

Maria D. McColgan, MD, MEd, FAAP*
Director, Child Protection Program
St. Christopher's Hospital for Children
Assistant Professor
Drexel University College of Medicine
Philadelphia, Pennsylvania

Robert S. McGregor, MD
Professor of Pediatrics
Associate Chair for Education and Operations
Drexel University College of Medicine
Director, Pediatric Residency Program
St. Christopher's Hospital for Children
Philadelphia, Pennsylvania

Laura E. Smals, MD
Assistant Professor of Pediatrics
Drexel University College of Medicine
St. Christopher's Hospital for Children
Philadelphia, Pennsylvania

Nancy D. Spector, MD, FAAP
Assistant Professor of Pediatrics
Drexel University College of Medicine
Associate Residency Program Director and Attending Physician
St. Christopher's Hospital for Children
Philadelphia, Pennsylvania

Tahniat S. Syed, MD, MPH*
Assistant Professor of Pediatrics
Drexel University College of Medicine
Division of Adolescent Medicine
St. Christopher's Hospital for Children
Philadelphia, Pennsylvania

* Contributor

FOREWORD

Children and adolescents need multiple layers of adult support if they are to stay safe and thrive. Families are clearly the most important forces in children's lives. Parents convey the values and skills that will prepare children to navigate the world and monitor them to be sure they do so safely. Teachers have an immeasurably important role as they transfer the knowledge that will give children the opportunity to contribute to our society. We also count on teachers to watch over our children and to notice when they seem to be in trouble. Health professionals too have a special role. Beyond just caring for the health of our children, they are trusted advisors to parents. Further, health professionals are the only adults who see young people repeatedly and confidentially throughout adolescence, serving as important reinforcement in an overall strategy to keep them safe and moving away from risk behaviors and toward a productive future.

One of the things that makes *Child Safety: A Pediatric Guide for Parents, Teachers, Nurses, and Caregivers* unique is that it recognizes that we each have a role and speaks to all who care for children. It provides us with the information we need to become aware of problems and motivates us to tackle them. Most importantly, it offers us the skills so that we can become comfortable taking the necessary action to protect children.

If we are to have our greatest impact on the health of children and youth, we simply must focus on prevention. It is important to recognize that much of what harms adolescents is also preventable, including injuries from accidents and violence, the devastation caused by drugs, alcohol, and other illicit substances, and sexually transmitted diseases.

What can we do to protect our children and youth? First, we should continue to do what we already do for children, and we should do it well. We should be the most attentive and loving parents, the best teachers, and the most effective health professionals we can be. Second, we all need to learn to assess young people for risk before crises strike. The challenge is to remain open and available to children so they always have a safe refuge and a sounding board, and to ask the right questions in advance of crises.

Third, we have to talk to kids in a way that might change their behavior. This means that we have to turn away from lecturing and just telling kids what not to do. We have to learn to engage them and put them in the driver's seat as they wisely choose to make safer choices. When we approach young people to teach them about dangerous choices or to suggest ways they can navigate around risk, we must do so in a way that will support their attempts to do the right thing rather than undermine their confidence. Too often, adults attempt interventions that backfire or inadvertently instill shame. The key is to speak in a language that young people understand and to help them recognize that they have existing strengths that can be built upon.

Fourth, we must all be advocates for social policies that support the health and well-being of all children, not just our own. This means we need to advocate for the policies that support the integrity of families, effective schools, and the reduction of the social inequities that create so much stress in children and families' lives. Finally, we all need to work to make sure that parents feel supported to do the critically important job of raising children.

As we put into place strategies to keep children safe, we must be very clear that our efforts to support children do not end with protecting them from risk. It is not good enough to raise children free of abuse and resistant to violence, drugs, and the early initiation of sexual activity. It is not adequate for our children to not be depressed or delinquent. We need them to thrive, to grab the torch from us and repair our world.

It is far too common for adults who serve youth to be focused on the cessation or avoidance of risk behaviors. We need to think long and hard about the message we send when we focus on what youth should not do. Remember that children live up to . . . or down to…our expectations of them. When we focus only on risk, we subtly send the message that we expect youth to engage in problem behaviors.

The risk-based model of child development is seriously limited. If we only think about prevention, then we send youth the very dangerous message that it is good enough for them to avoid problem behaviors. We have to articulate what we hope they will achieve with as much passion and precision as we use when telling kids what to avoid. We need to raise children and adolescents who are resilient—youth who can confront challenges and rise above them while learning the important life lessons that prepare them for leadership.

The prevention messages in this book are a critical first step. Safety first, always. If we follow the prevention messages and strategies offered here, we will protect many children and teens from the traumatic life experiences that would impede their healthy development. Not even the most resilient children are invulnerable, and we must do everything in our power to prevent children from needing to test the limits of their resiliency. The most important factor that determines whether or not young people will thrive is the presence of adults who believe in them unconditionally and hold them to high expectations. High expectations in this context neither means perfect grades nor the most touchdowns, it means that we expect our youth to be fine, decent people with integrity who will contribute to our families and our world. Young people only need this deep connection with 1 adult to support them to meet and rebound from challenges, but young people surrounded by caring adults are even more fortunate. Of course, parents are ideally the people to convey these messages of acceptance and high expectation, but when parents are unable to do this, other relatives, clergy, teachers, and health professionals can fill this role.

Growing up in today's world is not easy. Terrorism, war, violence on our streets, and school shootings permeate the media. Sex can kill. Pressures exist to look this way, feel that way. Messages not so subtly sent to some of our children state that we have no expectations that they will ever succeed and are not worth an investment of resources. Messages to others say a B+ is a failure and that the only worthwhile definition of success is acceptance at an elite college. They better prove they can succeed . . . or else. We, the caring adults in the lives of children can, and must, choose to make a difference by offering meaningful connections to our young people, loving guidance, consistent support, and a safety net that protects them from harm.

Kenneth R. Ginsburg, MD, MSEd, FAAP
Associate Professor of Pediatrics
Craig Dalsimer Division of Adolescent Medicine
The Children's Hospital of Philadelphia
University of Pennsylvania School of Medicine
Health Services Director
Covenant House Pennsylvania
Philadelphia, Pennsylvania

FOREWORD

Those who care for children, either personally or professionally (or both) can greatly benefit from a resource that addresses the issues that threaten the physical and emotional safety of our youth. In *Child Safety: A Pediatric Guide for Parents, Teachers, Nurses, and Caregivers*, a variety of topics are discussed in practical terms for all of us who regularly interact with children. Classic subjects such as substance abuse and emergency medical situations are interspersed with more current issues like branding and the increasing defiance of many children and adolescents. Chapters on other areas of concern will be greatly appreciated by the reader, such as the matter of discipline versus corporal punishment.

The words "child safety" bring to mind lessons taught to us by adults years ago. As children, we were admonished to look both ways before crossing the street, to avoid playing with matches, and to never talk to strangers. We were oblivious to general dangers. It was a time when we could trust that we would be taken care of and that the grown-ups could keep "bad things" away.

In many ways, the simplicity of the past is gone. Children of today have a great number of lessons to learn in order to stay safe. For instance, the age of technology has brought us great innovations, like the personal computer. But this modern convenience has a sinister side, such as the perils lurking in cyberspace from both bullies and predators. There is a barrage of media violence that was never a concern for youngsters in previous generations. Then there are the unseen toxic threats in our environment. Children today are not shielded from knowledge of these dangers. Instead, one needs only to turn on the television and hear about the "bad things" that surround our world. Certainly, the challenge of protecting children seems daunting.

Weary parents have often turned to professionals in heath care and education to assist and further reinforce issues of prevention and safety, but even these institutions have been affected by the times we live in. The health care professional has limited appointments with patients in the clinic and often picks a certain topic to discuss with the family, leaving other issues for the next visit. Teachers are faced with overcrowded classrooms and diminished resources, making it difficult to assist the child who is being bullied. In many schools the nurse has been replaced by "health aids" who possess minimal, if any, backgrounds in health care, placing our children in potential danger in emergency medical situations.

As a pediatric nurse practitioner, I see this book as an important reference to assist me in counseling my young patients regarding the issues confronting them today. As a parent, these topics will serve to better prepare me for the conversations I will be having at home. The subject matter of each chapter is followed by questions commonly asked by parents and caregivers, along with a number of charts and graphs for illustration. I am pleased to recommend this text to those who are committed to the care, education, and safety of our children and feel confident that it will be a valuable resource for you.

Sandra L. Elvik, MS, RN, CPNP
Associate Professor of Pediatrics
UCLA School of Medicine
Assistant Medical Director
Child Crisis Center
Harbor-UCLA Medical Center
Torrance, California

PREFACE

The goal of this book is to provide parents, caregivers, and any professionals that work with children with the practical information they need to understand the forces that shape child behavior, predict the risks to which children are vulnerable at various ages, take preventive actions, help children learn to make responsible decisions, and respond calmly and confidently when safety issues arise. This book began life as a second edition of *A Parent's & Teacher's Handbook on Identifying and Preventing Child Abuse*, by James A Monteleone, MD. However, as we researched the topic and began collaborating, the group of authors who contributed to this book came to the conclusion that the threats to the health and well-being of children are around us all the time. Although some situations related to violence and unsafe conditions result in child abuse and neglect, all families confront issues of child safety. With education and attention, these threats to health and well-being are preventable. The project quickly evolved to a broader project that addressed child safety as well as abuse. Special additions to this text include chapters on the effects of media violence, environmental health, body art, and, in light of September 11, concerns that caregivers and children have about the threat of terrorism.

The thread that binds all of the chapters together is *communication*. Child safety, when children are young, relies on constant dialogue between caregivers as well as between caregivers and the environment. When children are older, safety relies on communication between caregivers and the children themselves. More childhood crises occur due to miscommunication, omission of information, and social or familial isolation than from unavoidable events. When those unavoidable events strike, it is communication that can bring everyone through, safely. Finally, it is communication that will influence social and educational policy changes that will make the country a safer, more nurturing environment for our children.

I wanted, more than anything, for this book to be practical and easy to use. It is organized in an easy-to-reference format and uses tables and figures to direct attention to important information. The contributors come from an assortment of medical backgrounds, and each offers unique insights into and opinions on the subjects they address. On their behalf and mine, I would like to thank Joanne Schwab and Laurel Smith, the parent advisory board members who reviewed the book. It is our hope that readers will hear the variety blend into one authoritative, comforting voice, and that, as a result, they will feel confident using this text as their primary child safety reference.

Angelo P. Giardino, MD, PhD, MPH, FAAP

Reviews

Child Safety *is a well-written, readable guide for parents and caretakers, educators, and health care professionals, providing an outstanding overview of timely, important, complex problems that confront us and our children. It reminds us that our children are challenged everyday and must meet critical decisions related to substance use, sexuality, violence, and development of their self-image, among others, head-on. The authors offer practical, usable advice and educational information, including tips on how to respond and guide children through these turbulent issues.*

Michael L. Haney, PhD, NCC, CCISM, LMHC
Division Director for Prevention and Intervention,
Children's Medical Services
Florida Department of Health

This book is an excellent resource for anyone concerned with keeping children physically and psychologically safe and free from harm in an ever more complex world.

Chapters related to the Internet and threats of terrorism give valuable and up-to-date information about the risks of living in today's highly complex world. The checklists offer easy-to-follow tips for parents and caregivers, allowing for the most difficult subject matter to be dealt with in an effective and informed manner.

Nancy Chandler
Executive Director
National Children's Alliance

As the types and scope of influences on our children continue to mushroom at warp speed, parents and those who advise them are rightly feeling overwhelmed and uncertain about how and when they should intervene, draw the line, or pull the plug. Dr. Giardino and his asso-ciates provide a solid book, grounded in the most current research and understanding of these complex issues. The text educates us about the issues but, more importantly, provides concrete advice about what really matters. From child abuse to interpersonal violence to substance abuse and the Internet, this is a powerful tool for everyone involved with raising children in a world where young people are bombarded with media, hype, and marketing from the moment they can sit up and watch television.

Sherryll Krazier, PhD
Founder of the Safe Child Program & author of
The Safe Child Book *and* Bully Proof Your Child

With an emphasis on current research findings, this book provides great insight into some of the pressures and challenges facing today's youth, including bullying, drugs, sexual activity, media violence, and parental divorce. Peppered with case examples from the authors' clinical work, this resource will help parents, educators, and clinicians develop a clearer understanding of the impact of these and other risk factors on children's mental health.

Having a heightened awareness of these issues will also enhance readers' personal and professional relationships with children and adolescents.

Catherine Bradshaw, PhD
Assistant Professor,
Department of Mental Health
Associate Director, Johns Hopkins Center for the Prevention of Youth Violence
Johns Hopkins Bloomberg School of Public Health

This book is a commonsense, easy-to-understand but thorough approach to child safety. As a former medical consultant to a day care center, I know there are many health-related issues that face those who provide day-to-day care and education to children. Having a reliable source to clarify the issues surrounding common health concerns will not only decrease anxiety and worry, but also help utilize the health care system more effectively. Of note is the book's coverage not only of traditional topics such as poisonings, tobacco use, and sexual activity, but also of very modern concerns such as tattoos, terrorism, and the risks of Internet use. The authors are to be commended for their approach to these new morbidities.

Dipesh Navsaria, MPH, MS(LIS), MD
Pediatric Resident Physician & Occasional Children's Librarian
University of Wisconsin Hospitals & Clinics

G.W. Medical Publishing, Inc.
St. Louis

Our Mission

To become the world leader in publishing and

information services on child abuse, maltreatment,

diseases, and domestic violence. We seek to

heighten awareness of these issues and provide

relevant information to professionals and consumers.

A portion of our profits is contributed to nonprofit organizations
dedicated to the prevention of child abuse and the care of victims of abuse
and other children and family charities.

CONTENTS

Child Safety

A Pediatric Guide for Parents, Teachers, Nurses, and Caregivers

G.W. Medical Publishing, Inc.
St. Louis

Chapter 1

BULLYING

Nancy D. Spector, MD

Josh, a 7-year-old boy, is forced to give up his lunch money every day; Abigail, a 13-year-old girl, is ignored by a group of her classmates in the school hallway, and other girls frequently pass notes about her during class; Jake, a small, quiet 14 year old, is forced into a locker by a 16-year-old boy while a group of students looks on.

These children are all victims of bullying. Although it is often accepted as a normal part of childhood, bullying behavior should not be tolerated. The social and psychological consequences of bullying are vast and affect not only the victim and the bully, but also other children who observe the bullying. Bullying is a common and serious problem affecting thousands of children and adolescents every day. It is defined as an act of aggression with 3 key components: an imbalance of power, an intention to harm, and events repeated over time. The imbalance of power between the bully and the child being bullied may be real or perceived, and it is often secondary to the relative age, size, or strength of the bully and the victim.

Bullying is a willful, aggressive activity. The intention of the bully or bullies is to harm and induce fear in another through the threat of further aggression. It is important to differentiate bullying from teasing (**Table 1-1**). *Teasing* is something fun to do with friends, and both people should be able to find humor in the experience. Unlike with bullying behavior, no harm is intended, and there is no imbalance of power. The roles of the teaser and the teased are traded easily.

SCOPE OF THE PROBLEM

Bullying is a common problem throughout the world. Countries including the United Kingdom, Ireland, Norway, Australia, Spain, and Japan have reported bullying rates that range from 6% to 46% of children and adolescents. A recent national survey of children in grades 6 through 10 highlights the seriousness of the problem in the United States. Approximately 10% of youths attending public, private, or Catholic schools reported bullying others "sometimes," a term that the authors of the article discussing the survey did not define, and nearly 9% reported bullying others once a week or more. These statistics mean that more than 2 million youths are estimated to be involved in moderate bullying and more than 1.5 million in frequent bullying. Because episodes of bullying are often underreported, actual rates may be even higher.

Table 1-1. Bullying Versus Teasing			
	INTENT TO HARM	IMBALANCE OF POWER	REPETITIVE
Bullying	Yes	Yes	Yes
Teasing	No	No	Maybe

Bullying occurs with the highest frequency among elementary school students. In fact, in *Bullying at School: What We Need to Know and What We Can Do*, Dan Olweus reports that surveys have shown that the percentage of bullied students is highest at 7 years of age and steadily declines until 15 years of age. At present, there are no data to show how commonly bullying occurs among preschoolers, kindergarteners, or first graders.

TYPES OF BULLYING

There are 3 traditional types of bullying: *verbal*, *physical*, and *psychological*. Each type may occur individually or in combination with another type. Examples of verbal bullying include name-calling and verbal threats. Physical bullying can involve hitting, punching, or taking another's belongings. Psychological bullying may be gossiping, spreading rumors, manipulating social relationships, engaging in social exclusion, and intimidating others. Boys tend to use physical bullying most often, whereas girls tend to use verbal and psychological bullying. Boys may target acquaintances or strangers, whereas girls, in contrast, tend to target close friends within a group. Because our culture prohibits girls from using open aggression, the bullying behaviors girls usually use are distinctive. For them, social exclusion, shunning, rumors, name-calling, and manipulation are methods employed to inflict psychological pain on victims. This targeting makes the effects of the bullying more intense and more devastating. To further exacerbate the problem, these bullying behaviors are difficult for parents, teachers, and other adults to detect. Boys and girls are reported to use verbal bullying equally. Overall, boys bully significantly more than girls.

A new form of bullying is becoming increasingly common: *cyberbullying*. Cyberbullying is defined as bullying via information and communication technologies such as email, text messages on cell phones and pagers, instant messaging, personal Web sites, and personal polling Web sites. Recent estimates suggest that 5% to 25% of children have been victims of bullying via the Internet. Reliable estimates on the incidence of all types of cyberbullying do not exist because it is often not reported. One reason for this underreporting is that victims worry that their parents will revoke their Internet privileges if they discover the problem.

Cyberbullying occurs primarily among middle and high school adolescents, but children in elementary school have also been reported as victims. Cyberbullies may use e-mail and instant messaging to spread rumors and make derogatory statements about another child. The e-mail messages may go directly to the victim or may be sent to the victim's peer group. In another method of cyberbullying, the bully obtains the e-mail password of the victim and sends inappropriate material to others using the victim's account. A third method of cyberbullying involves the perpetrator posting an unflattering photo or story about a victim on a Web site. These forms of bullying are particularly dangerous for victims because information distributed on the Internet is so widely accessible. Instances of cyberbullying should be reported to schools or to local law enforcement. These entities will engage experts to combat the problem. There are also many Internet resources available for children, parents, and teachers that provide advice on the issue (see "Where To Turn for Help" below and also Chapter 9, Risks of the Internet).

CHILDREN AT RISK

Children who are at particular risk of being bullied are girls who mature early and boys who mature late. In addition, homosexual boys and girls are at significantly increased risk. In 1 survey Barbara Coloroso mentions in *The Bully, the Bullied, and the Bystander*, it was determined that 80% of gay/lesbian youths had been taunted about their sexual orientation, and more than half had been physically assaulted or ridiculed by peers or teachers. Verbal sexual bullying is different for boys and girls. For boys, it may involve derogatory terms or phrases that make the victim feel less masculine. For instance, "You run like a girl," or "wimp," may be used, as well as homophobic terms such as "gay" or "queer." For girls, verbal sexual bullying involves the use of phrases that objectify their bodies, or demean their sexuality. Girls may also receive threats of sexual violation. Physical sexual bullying may range from touching in a sexual way to overt sexual assault (see also Chapter 7, Sexual Abuse).

EFFECTS OF BULLYING

Bullying can adversely affect normal child and adolescent psychosocial development. Children who are bullied are more likely to develop psychosomatic problems such as headaches, abdominal pain, poor appetite, bed-wetting, and sleep problems, as well as anxiety and feelings of unhappiness or depression. According to a study by Dutch researcher Minne Fekkes and colleagues, children who are bullies and/or victims of bullies experience similar psychological health problems, including psychosomatic symptoms and depression. It is also very common for a child who is being bullied to try to avoid potential situations in which they may come in contact with the bully. Children may avoid going to school or other social activities, or change their usual walking or biking routes. Bullies often demand money from their victims; bullied children may come home from school hungry because they have lost their lunch money, or they may secretly take money from their parents in order to have money to give to the bully. Children who experience physical bullying may come home with torn clothes or physical injuries. Girls, because they are more likely to be victims of verbal or psychological bullying, are less likely to have obvious physical signs of bullying. Girls are more likely to suddenly become uninterested in school or exhibit changes in grades or school performance. They may also appear to be sad or scared after receiving phone calls or e-mail. Finally, children may withdraw from family or school activities and may stop talking about peers and everyday activities.

It is likely that a child who is being bullied will be reluctant to discuss the situation with his or her parents. These children feel humiliated and ashamed, and they often have a difficult time believing that adults are willing to and capable of providing help. Victims of bullying also frequently fear that if they report the bullying to an adult, the bully will retaliate further. Girls may be particularly reluctant to tell their parents for fear that their parents will minimize the problem (eg, by stating "It happens to everyone") or intervene in a way that will make things worse ("I'm calling the principal right away").

WHAT PARENTS AND CAREGIVERS CAN DO

IDENTIFYING CHARACTERISTICS OF CHILDREN INVOLVED WITH BULLYING

Because bullying is such a common problem, parents and teachers need to be aware of common characteristics of the children who are potential bullies, as well as of the potential victims of bullies. **Table 1-2** summarizes these characteristics.

The Bully

Bullies place their own wants, needs, and pleasures above those of others. They often use others to obtain their goals and have difficulty seeing situations from anyone else's vantage point. Bullies like to dominate other people and often hurt other children when adults are not present; they tend to use blame, criticism, and false allegations to project their own inadequacies onto targets. Bullies refuse to accept responsibility for their action and are incapable of seeing the effects of their behavior. It is important to realize that a child or adolescent who is a bully may also be the victim of bullying in other social or home situations.

Table 1-2. Characteristics of Bullies and Victims of Bullying	
BULLIES	VICTIMS OF BULLYING
— Selfish	— Sensitive
— Manipulative	— Shy, timid
— Domineering	— Quiet
— Blame and criticize	— Submissive and eager to please
— Often lie	— Lack self-confidence
— Never accept responsibility for own actions	— Distinctive from peers physically, mentally, or intellectually
	— May have a homosexual orientation
	— New to school or neighborhood

The Victim

Specific characteristics place a child at an increased risk for bullying. These at-risk youths are often sensitive, shy, quiet, timid, submissive, and demonstrate a lack of self-confidence. They are eager to please and placate others. If a youth has been a victim in the past, he or she is usually acquiescent and unwilling to fight. The bullied children are frequently younger than their bullies and have physical characteristics that distinguish them from their peers—for example, being taller, shorter, thinner, overweight, wearing glasses, or having acne. The child or adolescent victim may have a mental or physical disability; he or she may even exhibit an annoying habit or behavior such as a tic or a stuttering problem. Other potential victims are youths who stand out from their peers because of their intelligence, academic achievement, or particular talent. A child might also be a potential victim because of his or her sexual orientation. In addition, a child who is new to a school or neighborhood may be at particular risk. In the end, the reason for the bullying may not be this obvious—the victim might simply be in the wrong place at the wrong time.

The Bystanders

It is estimated that peer witnesses observe 85% of bullying episodes. Children present during an episode of bullying have several choices: to stand by idly, turn away, actively encourage the bully, participate in the bullying, or actively intervene to stop an episode of bullying. One study discussed in Olweus's book found that 85% of peer observers actually support the bully. Of these children, approximately half became active participants in the bullying. Only 13% of peers intervened. In this study, peers were more respectful of and friendly toward the bullies than the victims.

ROUGH PLAY VERSUS AGGRESSIVE ACTIVITIES

Not only is it important to identify potential characteristics of bullies, victims, and bystanders, it is also important to differentiate between types of play in children. Adults frequently confuse aggression and play fighting. Caregivers need to be aware of the features of aggressive versus rough-and-tumble play and intervene when elements of aggression appear. In aggressive play, 1 child usually forces another child to participate, whereas in rough-and-tumble play, the second child will choose to participate. Also, children do not use full physical force in rough play, and they are more likely to alternate their roles. For instance, children will take turns being the "chaser" and the "chased." In aggressive events, however, roles will often stay constant. Generally, children involved in rough-and-tumble play will have positive or neutral expressions on their faces, whereas victims of aggression will appear angry, hurt, afraid, or anxious. Finally, children involved in play fighting will want to stay together and continue to play, but victims of aggressive episodes will want to leave. **Table 1-3** addresses questions parents and caregivers often have about how to recognize and intervene in situations of bullying.

Table 1-3. Frequently Asked Questions

How do I recognize if my child is bullying other children?

If your child is aggressive with peers and adults, it is likely that he or she is also aggressive in situations with other children. Additionally, if your child comes home from school with extra money or other possessions, consider that he or she may be a bully. Listen carefully if another adult suggests that your child is a bully.

How do I recognize if my child is being bullied by another child?

The signs that a child is being bullied are often subtle. Consider that your child may be the victim of a bully if his or her interest in school or other activities suddenly changes, or if he or she changes the route he or she normally takes to school. Victims of bullies may also develop headaches, stomachaches, sleep problems, or anxiety; come home with torn clothes or physical injuries; or return home missing money or other possessions.

How do I ask my child if he or she is being bullied?

If you suspect that your child is being bullied, it helpful to start by asking indirect questions about bullies: "Is there a bully on the bus?" Then follow up with more specific questions about your child's own experiences. If your child discloses that he or she is a victim, remain calm, listen carefully to the story, and reassure your child that he or she is loved and that the bullying is not his or her fault. Develop a plan with your child to solve the problem. Make sure to give him or her the tools to handle the next bullying encounter. Remain patient, supportive, and reassuring.

If my child is being a bully, what are the first steps I should take?

If you discover that your child is being a bully, listen carefully to the description of the actions of your child. Take the news seriously. Let your child know that his or her behavior is unacceptable, and help your child to understand what consequences bullying actions have on others. Develop a plan for appropriate negative consequences for your child. Help your child develop the tools for positive problem-solving and negotiation skills.

If my child is being bullied, what are the first steps I should take?

First, help your child develop a plan for the immediate future. He or she should know what to do next time he or she is confronted by the bully. You should then consider discussing the problem with your child's teachers and school administrators. Don't confront the bully or the bully's parents alone because this may cause the problem to escalate. It may be helpful to discuss the problem with your pediatrician or another health care professional. If your child shows symptoms of depression and anxiety, seek the assistance of a mental health professional.

PREVENTING BULLYING

The primary way for parents and teachers to prevent bullying is to create positive home and school environments promoting caring, respect, and acceptance of others. Bullying, harassment, intimidation, and social exclusion should not be tolerated. Children are not born bullies. The temperament with which a child is born may contribute to his or her potential to be a bully, but important environmental influences such as home life, adult role models, and the media will alter that temperament. Children should be taught how to interact socially, resolve conflicts, deal with frustration, and cope with anger and stress. See **Table 1-4** for strategies for preventing children from becoming bullies or victims of bullying.

Table 1-4. How to Keep Children From Bullying and Being Bullied

— Provide effective discipline as a parent.

— Teach children how to be a good friend.

— Teach skills of conflict resolution.

— Create opportunities to do good things.

— Nurture empathy.

— Teach children to accept diversity.

— Monitor television, computer, video games, and music.

— Ask children about their relationships with other children.

— Especially for girls: Speak openly to daughters about quiet aggression.

Parents who suspect that their child is a bully need to take the problem seriously. Look for underlying problems that may cause the child to feel angry or frustrated, and consider the possibility that he or she may also be a victim of bullying. Also, make sure that children understand that bullying behavior will not be accepted or tolerated. Discuss and emphasize the consequences of the bullying on the victim, and establish and carry out negative consequences to make it clear that bullying is unacceptable behavior. Children who bully need to be firmly discouraged and made aware of the consequences of their actions because they are at an increased risk for violent behavior and social problems later in life.

Encourage positive interactions and relationships with others. Teach children non-violent problem-solving and negotiating skills. Parents may look to children's teachers and schools for recommendations for programs that teach problem solving and relationship building. Many schools promote the concepts of character education and pro-social skills, which focus on character, respect, and cooperation. It is also imperative that parents and caregivers serve as a positive role model and recognize and reward good play and conflict resolution techniques.

INTERVENING IN BULLYING

Parents who suspect that their child is being bullied need to be sensitive to the fact that being a victim of bullying is a humiliating experience. Children may be reluctant to reveal that they have been bullied, so start by asking indirect questions about how they spend time at lunch and recess or how the trip to school has been, regardless of whether children walk or take the bus. Parents should ask if there are bullies in the neighborhood, on the bus, or at school. If a child does not acknowledge to someone that he or she has been bullied but there is reason to suspect otherwise, parents and caregivers should contact the school and discuss concerns with the child's teacher or seek advice from the family physician or another health care professional.

When a child reveals that he or she has been bullied, listen to him or her without being judgmental or blaming. It is important to remain calm and not show anger. Children need to have the opportunity to share their feelings in a safe environment, and simply allowing them to speak of their experiences can help lift the burden from them. It is also important to emphasize that it is not the victim's fault, but rather it is the bully's behavior that is the problem. Make sure that you reassure the child that you will support and help him or her through the problem.

If a child has been the victim of bullying, assess the real physical risk to the child and carefully evaluate the context of the bullying. For instance, a child is probably in greater physical danger from a bully using physical force to extort money than from a bully verbally tormenting him or her over a physical attribute such as height or weight. It is also essential for parents and caregivers to consider all of their options for action carefully. For example, first decide whether to notify the child's teachers and school administration. Then, decide whether to contact the bully's parents directly and consider the possibility that doing so could escalate the situation, especially if the bully learned the behavior from his or her parents. Consider how risky each option is to the child being bullied before taking any action.

In addition, review with the victimized child all of his or her options. Discouraging the child from responding to the bullying behavior with aggression or from going along with the bullying behavior is recommended. He or she might also temporarily avoid the situations that place him or her at risk of bullying, stand up to the bully and calmly request that the bullying behavior stop, or stay in the company of others when possible. Parents and caregivers should remember to encourage children to build friendships with others and to involve children in activities that will promote friendships. Finally, be sure to show love and support for the child and praise him or her for confronting his or her fears.

It is important to discuss a child's victimization with his or her teachers and school administration officials. Many schools have active programs that discourage bullying behavior. When an intervention plan is created, it is extremely important to emphasize that it is the behavior of the bully that should be altered, not the behavior of the victim.

Adult supervision is a key element in the prevention of bullying behavior. Bullying is more likely to occur in circumstances in which there are many children congregated and only a few adult supervisors. Examples of high-risk areas include school playgrounds, cafeterias, hallways, and school buses. Because bullying behavior occurs so frequently, it is important to give children the appropriate tools to disclose such conduct to an adult. All children should be taught how to distinguish between *tattling* and *telling*. Children who know when it is appropriate to tell an adult about an episode of bullying are more likely to step forward and help another child or themselves. One way to differentiate tattling from telling is to say, "Tattling will only get another child *in* trouble, so don't tell me. Telling will get you or another child *out* of trouble, so do tell me." This type of explanation helps children to discern what situations warrant adult involvement. **Table 1-5** lists dos and don'ts for parents and caregivers to remember when helping a victim of bullying.

Table 1-5. Dos and Don'ts of Intervening With Bullying

— Do discuss bullying and the episodes with your child.

— Do discuss the bullying with your child's teachers and school administrators.

— Do distinguish *telling* from *tattling*.

— Don't minimize, rationalize, or explain away the bully's behavior.

— Don't rush in to solve the child's problem.

— Don't tell your child to avoid the bully.

— Don't tell your child to fight back.

— Don't confront the bully or the bully's parents alone; after all, the bully learned his or her behavior from someone.

PROFESSIONAL STUDY AND CONTROVERSY

SURVEY ON BULLYING

Although bullying is a very prevalent behavior in the United States, the amount of literature available on bullying pales in comparison to that available in other countries. One of the first US studies highlighting the national prevalence of bullying and its psychosocial consequences was published in a 2001 *Journal of the American Medical Association* article by Tonja R. Nansel, a researcher from the National Institute of Child Health and Human Development, and colleagues. This article brought significant national media attention to the subject of bullying. Despite increasing national efforts to educate the public about the significant negative consequences of bullying, it is still not uncommon to hear people talk about bullying as a normal and expected part of growing up.

BULLYING AND OTHER VIOLENT BEHAVIORS

Nansel lead another study published in 2003 that refuted the idea of bullying as being a benign part of child and adolescent development. Nansel and her colleagues looked at data from a nationally represented survey conducted in 1998 of youth in grades 6 through 10. The National Institute of Child Health and Human Development sponsored the survey, and 17 000 students (83%) responded to it. The goal of the study was to determine the relationship between bullying, being bullied, and other violent behaviors. Specifically, the researchers looked at behaviors that are thought to be important indicators of violence because of their potential risk for resulting in serious physical harm: weapon carrying, involvement in frequent fighting, and injuries resulting from fighting.

Overall, boys were more likely than girls to engage in violent behaviors. Students were most likely to carry weapons (gun, knife, or club) if they had engaged in bullying behavior or if they had been bullied in school. In fact, 70% of boys and 30% to 40% of girls involved in bullying on a weekly basis reported carrying a weapon in the past month. The authors concluded that bullying is likely to occur concurrently with more serious aggressive behavior, and, therefore, should not be accepted as normative behavior.

PSYCHOLOGICAL COSTS OF BULLYING

Recent literature highlights mixed evidence on the psychological cost of bullying. A 2003 study by Jaana Juvonen, a UCLA professor of psychology, and colleagues surveyed nearly 2000 Latino and African American children in the sixth grade, predominantly in low socioeconomic neighborhoods. The researchers reported that 22% of the children surveyed had been perpetrators of bullying, 7% had been victims of bullying, and 6% had been both a perpetrator and a victim. Studies before this one relied mainly on self-reporting to evaluate bully/victim groups and the adjustment problems of each group. Because of the concern that youths involved in bullying will not identify themselves, this study assessed the students' experience as a bully, a bully victim, and as an observer. The teachers in the school were also surveyed. The researchers hoped that the classmates could correctly identify the bullies and their victims and that the teachers could accurately identify psychosocial adjustment problems such as depression and psychosomatic complaints.

The study revealed that children who are bullies but not victims of bullying manifest the fewest number of adjustment problems. In fact, bullies were psychologically stronger than their classmates and enjoyed high social status among them. The victims of bullying, in contrast, demonstrated emotional difficulties and have significant social problems. The children who were both bullies and bullying victims had the most problems with socialization, conduct, depression, and loneliness. These findings differ from previous studies, which have shown that bullies tend to suffer from psychological problems, especially depression, for developmental research shows that in early adolescence, social status is one of the strongest predictors of positive self-images and psychological well-being and as a consequence, bullies should not suffer from depression, anxiety, or loneliness to as great a degree as victims. However, this study also showed that even though bullies have a high social status, classmates would rather not spend time with them, at least in part because they fear them.

Dr. Juvonen's study again stresses the significant negative consequences of bullying. Because bullying most often occurs at school, on the playground, and on the bus, it is extremely important that schools implement and use prevention and intervention programs. A comprehensive, school-wide program should help to identify instances of bullying by raising the awareness of teachers, students, and parents. Teachers, in particular, play a vital role in preventing bullying and should be adequately trained to recognize, prevent, and intervene in these situations. Programs should also empower classmates and bystanders to end bullying by encouraging them to intervene in bullying episodes and to report these episodes to an adult.

BULLYING AND WEIGHT
School programs may need to pay particular attention to a high-risk group whose numbers are on the rise—overweight and obese children and adolescents. The prevalence of obesity is increasing at an alarming rate in both Canada and the United States. It is estimated that at least one third of Canadian and US youths are overweight or obese. Ian Janssen, a professor of physical health and education at Queen's University in Canada, and colleagues published a study in 2004 demonstrating a link between the epidemic of obesity and bullying. They looked at the associations between bullying and weight status for 5749 Canadian boys and girls ages 11 to 16 years. Findings showed that overweight and obese children are more likely to be the victims and perpetrators of verbal, physical, and psychological bullying than are their normal-weight peers. Because overweight and obese youths are at an increased risk of bullying, parents, teachers, and physicians need to be aware of this particularly vulnerable group.

CONCLUSION
Bullying is a conscious, willful, and deliberate act of aggression that may be inflicted verbally, physically, or psychologically. It is not the same as teasing, nor should it be dismissed as a normal part of childish behavior. Bullying has significant psychological

effects on all the children involved. Parents and caregivers need to be aware of the characteristics of children who are potential bullies or victims, and by creating positive home and school environments and encouraging children to be tolerant, understanding, and to interact positively with others, parents can teach children that bullying is wrong and that submitting to bullies is unnecessary. Schools can be sources of programs that raise awareness of and prevent bullying, and teachers and school officials can institute social practices that discourage it.

WHERE TO TURN FOR HELP

BOOKS

American Academy of Pediatrics. *Caring for Your School-Age Child: Ages 5 to 12*. New York, NY: Bantam; 2003.

American Academy of Pediatrics. *Caring for Your Teenager*. New York, NY: Bantam; 2003.

Coloroso B. *The Bully, the Bullied, and the Bystander*. New York, NY: HarperResource; 2002.

Olweus D. *Bullying at School: What We Know and What We Can Do*. Malden, Mass: Blackwell Publishers; 1993. Understanding Children's Worlds series.

Simmons R. *Odd Girl Out: The Hidden Culture of Aggression in Girls*. Orlando, Fla: Harcourt; 2002.

WEB SITES

American Academy of Child and Adolescent Psychiatry: Facts for Families

http://www.aacap.org/publications/pubcat/facts.htm

American Academy of Pediatrics

http://www.aap.org

American Medical Association

http://www.ama-assn.org

Federal Bureau of Investigation: A Parent's Guide to Internet Safety

http://www.fbi.gov/publications/pguide/pguidee.htm

iSafe: Internet Safety Information

http://www.Isafe.org.

National Education Association

http://www.nea.org/index.html

Online Safety 4 Kids

http://www.onlinesafety4kids.com

Safe Schools Fact Sheets: Bullying—An Overview of Bullying

http://www.colorado.edu/cspv/publications/factsheets/safeschools/pdf/FS-SC07.pdf

Stop Bullying Now!

http://www.stopbullyingnow.com/research.htm

Chapter 2

MEDIA VIOLENCE

Laura E. Smals, MD

No one living in the United States today can escape the media revolution. Over the last few decades, the explosion of technology has allowed all aspects of our daily lives to literally be run by technology. Americans use technology as a key resource for information gathering, acquisition of products, financial services, and, of course, entertainment. The youths of the new millennium are some of the largest consumers of television, radio, computers, and video games. This technology is readily available, affordable, portable, and increasingly unavoidable. According to American Academy of Pediatrics (AAP) reports, US children spend an average of 3 hours per day watching television, and if the time they spend using other media such as computers and video games is added, the total rises to over 6 hours of media exposure per day—more time than children spend in school, with their families, or involved in any activity other than sleeping.

One of the reasons for this increased media use is its availability. A 1999 Kaiser Family Foundation survey showed that 99% of US households had at least 1 television and 88% had 2 or more. The same survey showed that 53% of children had a television in their bedroom and 89% of households had computer or video game equipment. In addition to having saturated the lives of Americans, media have changed significantly since the 1950s. With the invention of digital technology, media images are now more vivid, more graphic, and more realistic than ever before. All of these factors make media a very powerful influence in our children's lives—an influence that is not frequently recognized.

EFFECTS OF MEDIA VIOLENCE

The link between media violence and aggressive behavior in children is well established. The AAP has record of more than 3500 research studies that have looked at the association between media and violent behavior, and 99.5% of these studies have shown a clear association between media violence and increased aggression. This correlation is stronger than the link between tobacco use and lung cancer. Various media formats model violence—cartoons, sitcoms, reality shows, video games, and music videos—and children are especially vulnerable to media's influences because they lack the ability to distinguish fantasy from reality. Heroic figures frequently use violence to resolve conflict, and negative consequences are rarely portrayed. This leads children to think that violence is an effective way to resolve problems and that there are no long-term or negative consequences. In the book *Deadly Consequences: How Violence is Destroying Our Teenage Population and a Plan to Begin Solving the Problem*, Deborah Prothrow-Stith tells the story of a gunshot victim who was surprised and angry that being shot was painful because it never really seemed to hurt the characters on television. Also of concern is the fact that violence in media is often glamorized. Commonly, heroes or heroines initiate the violence and are praised and rewarded for their behavior. In a recent AAP review of various media, one fourth of the music videos portrayed overt violence and weapon carrying. Furthermore, these videos frequently portrayed violence and sexual content in the same video, adding to the titillating quality of the violence. The message is clear: Success, beauty, sex, and violence go hand in hand.

In addition to illustrating and modeling violent behavior, violent media desensitizes children. Repeated images of characters being killed or maimed elicit decreased responses with each exposure. Eventually, children become insensitive to the gruesome nature of the violence and see it as normal or commonplace. Violent video games, in which players are asked repeatedly to destroy objects, creatures, or even humans in a graphic and violent manner, are especially desensitizing. Frequently, players receive extra points for shooting opponents in the head or maiming them in an especially gruesome manner. An ideal way to teach aggression is to have children repeatedly commit violent virtual acts, receive rewards for these acts, and entice them to spend hours in this activity each day. Video games have an almost addictive quality; children and adolescents seem to want to spend more and more time playing them in an attempt to beat their last score.

Initial studies have shown that after exposure to violent video games, young people exhibit fewer cooperative social interactions and helping behaviors and more aggressive thoughts and violent retaliation. The AAP media review found that aggressive behavior increased in approximately 13% to 22% of adolescents who played violent video games. Although not all children playing video games became aggressive, repeated exposure and desensitization to violent acts can clearly lead to increased hostility and aggression and decreased empathy. The engaging nature of video games makes them a potentially effective vehicle for teaching these behaviors.

Violence in the media portrays the world in a scary and unrealistic way, and television viewers frequently see the world as more dangerous than it truly is. This "mean world syndrome" often leads youths to think that they need to carry a weapon to defend themselves or to have a "get them before they get me" mentality. Some children have developed anxiety, depression, posttraumatic stress disorder, or sleep disturbances from exposure to media violence.

The media also misrepresent the identities of those who perpetrate violence. The AAP review noted that on US television, a disproportionate number of perpetrators are African American, a typecasting that promotes prejudice and stereotyping. In music videos, a beautiful hero or heroine typically commits the majority of the violent acts, and reviewers observed that the victims are most often women and blacks. These portrayals glamorize violence and perpetuate the feelings of victimization in these groups.

Defending the effects of media violence is the argument that media merely reflect our culture. The "art reflects life" argument is not accurate when interpreted in such a way. According to US crime report statistics reported in the journal *The American Psychologist*, only 13% of crimes are violent, and 0.2% of crimes are murders. On television, 87% of the crimes portrayed are violent and 50% of the crimes are murders.

It is estimated that the average US child will have viewed 200 000 acts of violence on television by the age of 18 years. Even in the worst neighborhood in the United States, it is unlikely that a child will view that many acts of "real life" violence.

EFFORTS TO LIMIT THE EFFECTS OF MEDIA VIOLENCE

Although the association between media violence and aggression in children and adolescents is well established, there is still much debate as to what can be done about it. Despite abundant scientific studies addressing media violence, the consequences of this research are widely unknown, and educating parents and caregivers about the effects of media violence should be a priority. Screening media for violent content is also a way to curb its effect. Most people are familiar with the movie industry rating codes; there are also rating codes designed for screening violence in television shows and video games (**Table 2-1**).

Table 2-1. Rating Codes for Television, Video Games, and Movies

MEDIA	AGE-SPECIFIC CODES		CONTENT CODES	
Movies	G	General audience	None	
	PG	Parental guidance suggested		
	PG-13	Parents strongly cautioned		
	R	Restricted. Under 17 years of age requires accompanying parent or adult guardian		
	NC-17	No one 17 years of age and under admitted		
Television: broadcast	TV-Y	All children	FV	Fantasy violence
	TV-Y7	Directed to children over 7 years of age	V	Violence
			S	Sex
	TV-G	General audience	L	Coarse language
	TV-PG	Parental guidance suggested	D	Suggestive dialogue or innuendo
	TV-14	Parents strongly cautioned		
	TV-MA	Mature audience only		
Television: premium channels	None		MV	Mild violence
			V	Violence
			GV	Graphic violence
			AL	Adult language
			GL	Graphic language
			BN	Brief nudity
			N	Nudity
			AC	Adult content
			SC	Strong sexual content
			RP	Rape
Video games	eC	Early childhood, ages 3+ years	Animated violence	
	E	Everyone, ages 6+ years	Comic mischief	
	T	Teenagers, ages 13+ years	Strong language	
	M	Mature, ages 17+ years	Mature sexual themes	
	Ao	Adults only		
Arcade games	None		Animated violence	
			Lifelike violence	
			Sexual content	
			Language: green, suitable for everyone; yellow, mild; red, strong	

The Telecommunications Act of 1996, in the section titled "Communications Decency Act," established rating codes for all network television programs. These age-specific and content-specific codes were implemented in 1997 and appear in the upper left-hand corner of the screen during the first 15 seconds of the television show. They are designed to work with the V-chip, a computer chip required in all televisions manufactured after January 1, 2000, that allows parents to block all programs that have codes unacceptable to them. A similar system was designed for computer and video games, using age-based codes. There are also parental advisory systems for coin-operated video games, music CDs, and videos. With the exception of the movie industry, all of these rating systems "self-assign" their code, having the producer of the product decide what rating a product should have. This self-assignment is clearly fraught with flaws, as there is no incentive to rate a product as moderately to highly violent if doing so will negatively affect sales. In addition, these systems are poorly understood by consumers and, therefore, are poorly utilized. A Kaiser Family Foundation survey tested parents on their familiarity with the rating codes. Eighty-four percent of parents showed an awareness of the movie ratings, 56% of television ratings, 59% of video game ratings, and 50% of music ratings. A review article by Brad Bushman, associate professor of psychology at Iowa State University, reported that of the parents familiar with the systems, understanding of the codes ranged from 7% to 74%, depending on the code.

WHAT PARENTS AND CAREGIVERS CAN DO

Parents and caregivers can take certain steps to limit the adverse effects of media violence on their children (**Table 2-2**). For example, the AAP Media Education Committee recommends that parents restrict children's "screen time" to no more than 1 to 2 hours per day. Screen time includes computer or video games and television. Encouraging children to read, involving them in after-school clubs, and promoting outdoor activities are other things that parents can do to decrease media time. A National TV-Turnoff Week, which challenges families to do without any television for an entire week, occurs every spring and frequently opens family members' minds to other individual and family activities that they might enjoy. In order to prevent children from watching television unsupervised, the AAP Media Education Committee also recommends not allowing children to have televisions in their bedrooms. Children are much more likely to watch shows in the late hours than at other times of the day.

Table 2-2. Dos and Don'ts of Regulating Media Exposure

— Do restrict "screen time" to 1 to 2 hours per day, including television shows, videos, and computer and video games.

— Do come up with recreation alternatives to audio and visual media. Possibilities include board games, books, active outdoor play, sports, and arts and crafts.

— Don't allow televisions, computers, or video game systems in children's bedrooms.

— Don't let children watch television, play video games, and/or use the computer without supervision. Make sure you know the content of these items or programs before purchasing them for your child or allowing your child access to them.

— Do discuss "fantasy violence" (eg, cartoons and animated films) with children. Ask them what they think the people or characters are thinking or feeling when someone hurts them and explain that real-life violence, unlike cartoon violence, really hurts people.

— Do become familiar with the rating codes and V-chip technology. Utilize them, but be aware that they do not screen out all violence.

— Do participate in the annual TV-Turnoff Week.

— Do model responsible media usage: Children learn most from parents and caregivers.

Parents should watch television with their children and actively screen movies, games, and programs for violent content. Although rating systems are flawed, parents and caregivers can use them to avoid some of the more violent content to which children could be exposed. If children do see a violent program or movie, parents should explain that the events are not real and do not accurately reflect what the violent act would be like in real life. Initiate discussion with children about the television shows. Finally, parents and caregivers need to be models of responsible media usage for their children by avoiding violent programming. Children will be more likely to comply with rules if parents also use media responsibly. Parents and caregivers need to be aware that media and their influences are not going away. **Table 2-3** addresses questions that parents and caregivers commonly have about children and media violence.

PROFESSIONAL STUDY AND CONTROVERSY

Concern about media violence and its influence on children began in the 1950s, shortly after the invention of television. As early as the 1960s, Albert Bandura and colleagues demonstrated that children would imitate violent behavior seen on television, especially if the behavior was either rewarded or ignored. Increasing concern over media violence led to a 1972 US Surgeon General's report showing a clear link between increased aggression in youth and violence on television. One study that examined this link was called the "Notel" study. In it, Tannis MacBeth Williams and colleagues investigated 3

Table 2-3. Frequently Asked Questions

How can I know if media violence is having a negative effect on my child?

Many children will not exhibit obvious negative effects from media violence. It is often years of cumulative exposure that have this effect. Immediate effects, however, include children having nightmares about what they have seen in the media or growing more aggressive, often imitating the "fighting" that fictional characters do.

How can I limit the effects of media violence on my children?

The best way to limit the effects of media violence on children is to monitor what children watch as much as possible. You are best equipped to counteract violent content if you really know what your children are being exposed to. Children, for the most part, should be protected from exposure to violent content as much as possible.

What do I do once I realize that my child is already affected by violence in television or video games?

If you feel your child is showing a negative response to something he or she has seen in the media, the best response you can have is to discuss it with your child. Explaining how the violence is not real or explaining how those behaviors do not work well in real life can help to counteract its effects. Often, it is necessary to repeat conversations, and parents and caregivers need to be open to having continual discussions on the matter.

Is there an age at which a child can "handle" violent content?

Children younger than 7 years have a hard time differentiating reality from fantasy and are especially vulnerable to the effects of violent media. However, children of all ages can suffer the effects of violence in the media. As children age, they begin to learn the difference between reality and fantasy, but the repetitive nature of media violence makes violent content dangerous to children of all ages. Even if children understand the violence they can still be affected negatively by it.

small, demographically similar towns in Canada. The only difference between the 3 towns was that at the start of the study, one—the "Notel" town—lacked access to any form of television. Television was then introduced, and researchers monitored the effects of this change on the town's children for 2 years. Aggression was one of the characteristics they observed. They then compared these observations with those of the similar towns in which television already existed. Although aggression levels increased in all 3 towns, the researchers saw a much more significant increase in aggression among the Notel children as television was introduced. This study and others have shown a link between television viewing and increased aggression in children.

In 1982, the National Institute of Mental Health issued a report stating, "After 10 years of research, the consensus among most of the research community is that violence on television does lead to aggressive behavior by children and teenagers who watch the programs." There have been subsequent reports from the American Psychological Association, the AAP, and many other child advocacy groups reviewing decades of research clearly linking media violence to increased aggression in youth. Despite overwhelming evidence and growing concern, the amount of violence in media continues not only to be present, but also to grow.

The National Television Violence study was performed from 1995 to 1997 and evaluated over 10 000 hours of broadcast television programming. This report found that 61% of US programming portrayed interpersonal violence, and the majority of this violence was portrayed in an entertaining or glamorous manner. The highest proportion of violent content was found, interestingly, in children's shows. Although the amount of violence on television was not measured 30 years ago, most people would agree that "Gilligan's Island," "Mission: Impossible," and even "Bonanza" do not compare with the graphic images of television today.

CONCLUSION

Technological media has become an integral part of life in the United States. Television, computers, and video games have the potential to influence children's fundamental conceptions of violence, their response to both real and fictional violence, and their willingness to use violence or aggression in everyday life. Studies have shown an association between violent media consumption and acts of aggression in children. They are not as able as adults to distinguish reality from fantasy, and it is up to parents and caregivers to protect children from violent media. Rating codes can help parents screen out inappropriate television programs and avoid buying violent video games, but the most important step parents can take is to preview computer and video games and to watch television and movies with their children so that they can teach children the difference between reality and fantasy, and right and wrong.

WHERE TO TURN FOR HELP

The American Academy of Pediatrics Media Matters Campaign

http://www.aap.org/advocacy/mediamatters.htm

Kaiser Family Foundation

http://www.kff.org

LimiTV, Inc.

http://www.limitv.org

— Provides tips for decreasing time families spend watching TV.

The National Institute on Media and the Family: Mediawise

http://www.mediafamily.org

TV Parental Guidelines

http://www.tvguidelines.org

— Provides guidelines for interpreting the television rating codes.

TV Turnoff Network

http://www.tvturnoff.org

Chapter 3

ALCOHOL, DRUGS, AND ILLICIT SUBSTANCES

Robert S. McGregor, MD

Parents have, historically, been concerned about their children's use of alcohol, drugs, and other illicit substances. Today, according to the 2004 National Survey on Drug Use and Health (NSDUH), 50% of 12th graders report having used an illicit drug at least once. Although drug and alcohol use among teenagers and preteenagers remains a problem, the groups of drugs most commonly used change from time to time. Illicit drug use is less common today than in the early 1980s, but it has been increasing over the last 10 years—for example, marijuana, the most widely used illicit drug, has demonstrated long-term trends, showing, in the findings for the 2002 NSDUH, an increase in use during the 1960s and 1970s, a decline in the 1980s, and a subsequent increase in the 1990s (**Figure 3-1**).

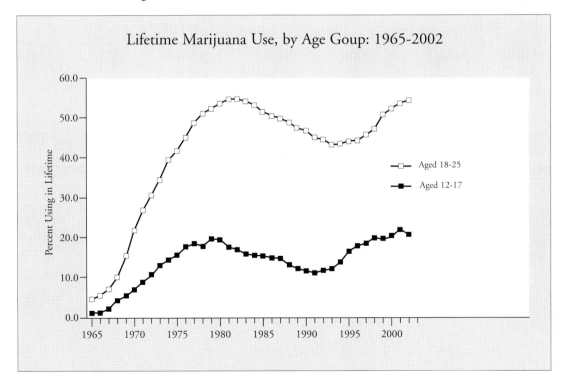

Figure 3-1. *The percentage of young adults aged 18 to 25 years who had ever used marijuana was 5.1% in 1965 but increased steadily to 54.4% in 1982. Although the rate for young adults declined somewhat from 1982 to 1993, it did not drop below 43% and actually increased to 53.8% by 2002. Reprinted with permission from the Substance Abuse and Mental Health Services Administration (SAMHSA).*

The NSDUH began in 1971 as the primary source of statistical information on substance use and abuse by the US population. The survey was constructed in 1971 to respond to a growing concern over drug abuse, and it collects information from US citizens through face-to-face interviews. According to 2004 data, an estimated 19.1 million Americans aged 12 years or older were currently engaged in illicit drug use in the month prior to the survey. This estimate represents 7.9% of the population aged 12 years or older (**Figure 3-2**). Rates of drug use showed substantial variation by age (**Figure 3-3**). The use of hallucinogens such as ecstasy, LSD, and PCP was also examined in this survey and exhibited 2 distinct periods of increase—in first-time users of LSD during the early 1970s and in first-time users of ecstasy in the late 1990s (**Figure 3-4**). Alcohol, the substance most commonly abused by teenagers and adults alike, showed an increase in use with older drinkers, peaking at 69.8% of people aged 21 to 25 years in 2004 (**Figure 3-5**).

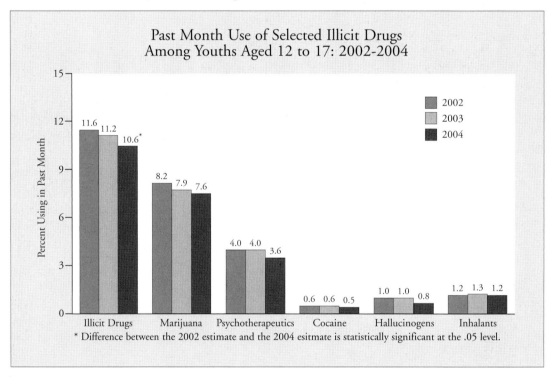

Figure 3-2. *The rate of current illicit drug use among youths gradually declined between 2002 and 2004. The rate was 11.6% in 2002, 11.2% in 2003, and 10.6% in 2004. This represents a statistically significant change between 2002 and 2004. Reprinted with permission from SAMHSA.*

Monitoring the Future is an ongoing study of 8th, 10th, and 12th graders that looks at attitudes and behaviors related to alcohol and other drugs. So far, alcohol is used more than any other substance, and marijuana is the most used illegal drug. More high school seniors use illicit drugs than 8th or 10th graders (**Figure 3-6**).

Most information regarding the recognition of and intervention in adolescent drug and alcohol use is essentially the same, regardless of the type of drug used. Some common drugs of abuse include alcohol, acid (lysergic acid diethylamid, abbreviated LSD), club drugs, cocaine, crack cocaine, ecstasy (3, 4-methylenedioxymethamphetamine, abbreviated MDMA), heroin, inhalants, marijuana, methamphetamines, PCP (phencyclidine), prescription medications (typically narcotic pain medicines or Valium-like drugs), nicotine, over-the-counter medicines, and anabolic steroids. See **Appendix 3-1**

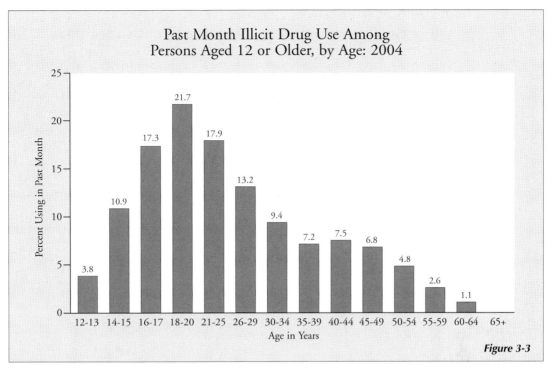

Figure 3-3

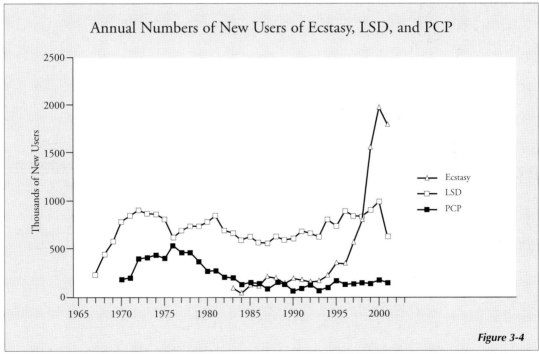

Figure 3-4

Figure 3-3. *Rates of drug use showed substantial variation by age. For example, 3.8% of youths aged 12 or 13 reported current illicit drug use in 2004. Drug use peaked among 18 to 20 year olds, who made up 21.7% of users; 32% of users were youths aged 12 to 17 years; and 39.6% of users were young adults aged 18 to 25 years. Reprinted with permission from SAMHSA.*

Figure 3-4. *Initiation of ecstasy use has been rising since 1993, when there were 168 000 new users. LSD incidence dropped from 958 000 new users in 2000 to 606 000 new users in 2001. Reprinted with permission from SAMHSA.*

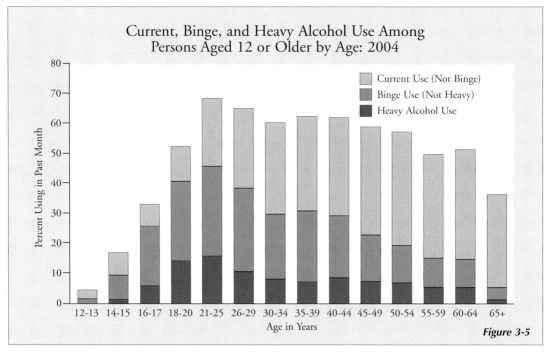

Figure 3-5

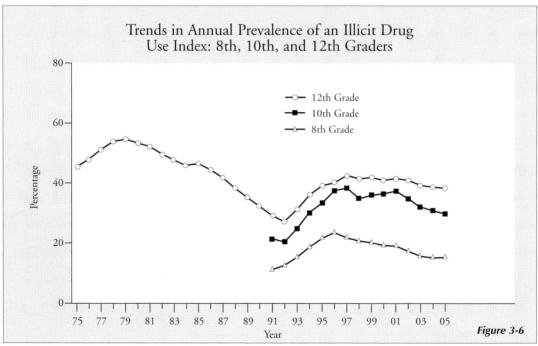

Figure 3-6

Figure 3-5. *Among young people, the prevalence of current alcohol use in 2004 increased with age, from 2.3% at age 12 to 69.8% of persons at age 21. Overall, about 10.8 million underage persons aged 12 to 20 (28.7%) reported drinking alcohol in the past month. Nearly 7.4 million (19.6%) were binge drinkers, and 2.4 million (6.3%) were heavy drinkers. Reprinted with permission from SAMHSA.*

Figure 3-6. *Illicit drug use is more pervalent in older youths; high school seniors consistently use at a higher rate than high school sophomores and 8th graders. The low point of use was observed in the early 1990s for all age groups and appears to have increased and somewhat leveled off in the early 2000s. Reprinted with permission from Monitoring the Future.*

for basic information on commonly used drugs, including their effects, warning signs, and slang terms.

Because alcohol is the substance most commonly used and abused among teenagers and preteenagers, this chapter focuses on the prevention, recognition, and intervention of alcohol use. One important difference, however, is that alcohol rehabilitation remains less successful than rehabilitation for other commonly abused drugs. Until recently, many intervention and treatment approaches were not based on scientific studies.

According to 2002 data from the National Clearinghouse for Alcohol and Drug Information, the average age of alcohol initiation is 13 years. More than half of all 8th graders and 80% of all 12th graders have used alcohol. Sixty percent of high school seniors have been drunk at least once before graduating. In 1998, more than 10 million US teenagers consumed alcohol. Such startling statistics imply that adolescent drinking in the United States is the norm; however, research published in the *Journal of Marriage and the Family* and elsewhere reveals that almost two thirds of parents are not aware that their children drink.

When discussing risk-taking behaviors in adolescence, one must recognize that adolescents are not all developmentally equal. During early adolescence (typically ages 12 to 14 years), children tend to think in concrete terms and are very concerned with the immediate present, with little regard for future consequences. In adolescence (ages 14 to 18 years), thoughts become more abstract and idealized. Adolescents are more aware that their actions do have consequences—today, tomorrow, and in the future. The establishment of independent living and responsibility characterizes late adolescence and early adulthood (ages 18 to 23 years). Various factors can prolong this independence stage; for instance, formal education or chronic illness can require adolescents and young adults to be financially, emotionally, or physically dependent on parents for an indefinite time period. Parents need to adapt their approach to discussing and preventing alcohol use and abuse to the developmental stage of their adolescent. For example, young adolescents may not be dissuaded from using alcohol because early usage increases their risk for alcoholism in the future, but they may be persuaded by the immediate loss of Internet privileges if caught drinking.

DEFINITIONS

Before discussing risks, recognition, prevention, and intervention, it is important to define some basic terms related to alcohol use. A *drink* is 12 ounces of beer, 5 ounces of wine, or 1.5 ounces of distilled spirits or "hard" liquor—whiskeys, vodka, tequila, rum, gin, or liqueur (**Figure 3-7**). Clinical experience shows that adolescents and parents frequently fail to recognize the equivalency, thinking that beer and wine are somehow less of a risk. *Binge drinking* is having multiple drinks on a single occasion—5 or more drinks for men, 4 or more drinks for women. *Heavy drinking* is binge drinking every 2 weeks. Episodic heavy drinking is drinking associated with amnesia for the events during the drinking period, typically the previous night.

Figure 3-7. *Comparison of standard alcoholic drinks.*

EFFECTS OF ALCOHOL USE

There are many reasons not to view adolescent alcohol use as innocent experimentation. The most immediate and graphic risks are illustrated by the remarkable decrease in the motor vehicle fatalities when the drinking age was raised from 18 to 21. Combining alcohol use with driving, boating, and other water recreation contributes significantly to deaths among teenagers. In trauma registries, 50% of fatal teenaged accidents and 38% of drownings involve alcohol use. Also, use of alcohol during adolescence is associated with a 4-fold increased likelihood of alcoholism in adulthood. The exact cause is unclear, but evidence indicates that the progression from initial alcohol exposure to regular usage to true dependency/addiction is accelerated in teenagers. Some researchers suggest that teenagers experience a higher intoxication effect per drink because of a relative lack of the liver enzymes needed for the breakdown of alcohol.

Heavy users or abusers of alcohol place themselves at risk every time they drink. Alcohol can cause life-threatening poisoning, alter emotions and perceptions, impair judgment, and cause sensory distortion, blackouts, mood disturbances (especially depression), hangovers, gastritis, and even heart rhythm problems. Chronic use of alcohol among adolescents can lead to impaired relationships with family, peers, and teachers and to decreased school performance. Alcohol use is often associated with other risk-taking behaviors such as increased sexual activity and multiple sexual partners. Alcohol is also involved in 30% to 60% of date rape cases. The long-term effects of alcohol use on individual health may include cirrhosis, nutritional and vitamin deficiencies, nerve problems, memory loss, impotence, and heart and brain damage. These effects are well established but rarely manifest in the teenage years.

When surveyed as to why they use alcohol, most adolescents answer that they use it for enjoyment, peer acceptance, problem avoidance, and reduction of stress and boredom. Similar answers have been noted for other drugs. Media messages that portray alcohol use in a positive light also contribute to an increased likelihood that teenagers will drink.

WHAT PARENTS AND CAREGIVERS CAN DO

PREVENTION

Adolescence is complicated and involves establishing a personal identity while undergoing a period of rapid physical, emotional, and hormonal growth. Parenting an adolescent is as involved as—and in many ways more challenging than—parenting an irrational preschooler. On the surface, teenagers may seem self-sufficient and happier when parents stay out of the way, but in reality, they need and crave parental guidance and support. The challenge for caregivers is to recognize when adolescents are deviating from normal, inherently chaotic adolescent development. Clinical experience indicates that the first drink may well occur at age 12 or 13 years, so the time to discuss drinking is before children reach that age. Well before adolescence, parents should start having frank, open discussions about alcohol, drugs, and their parental expectations. Parental attitudes and behaviors surrounding alcohol use establish important views for the preteenager and teenager, and parental attitudes and behaviors do, in fact, influence teenagers' decisions to drink. Studies have shown that teenagers are 60% less likely to drink if they know their parents disapprove, and it is caregivers' role to remain available and vigilant of their children's behaviors. In order for adolescents to know parents' stance on alcohol, parents must communicate effectively and be available for their teenagers. **Table 3-1** lists ways parents can discourage underage alcohol use.

Poor parenting skills, especially in a family in which antisocial behavior has been modeled, can increase the risk of adolescent drug and alcohol use. Teachers, coaches, and other care providers may need to supplement or replace parental efforts to identify at-risk youths. In the ideal setting, parents may opt to recruit teachers or other school officials to monitor an adolescent and to alert the family if absences or other signs of

Table 3-1. Dos and Don'ts of Preventing Underage Alcohol Use

— Do talk to your child about alcohol and clearly express your position on adult and underage consumption.

— Do help your child develop aversion strategies to use in social situations.

— Do set a good example of responsible alcohol consumption.

— Don't be uninvolved in adolescents' lives. Know their friends, and ask questions about where they go and what they do.

— Don't hesitate to check on questionable parties or to set rules.

— Do remain open and approachable so that your adolescent feels comfortable coming to you with questions or problems.

substance use occur. The American Academy of Pediatrics (AAP), in 1998 and 2001 policy statements regarding tobacco, alcohol, and other drugs, identifies the risk factors listed in **Table 3-2** with increased substance use among children.

Parents who consume alcohol have an extra challenge to setting a good example. If parents choose to continue drinking while they have adolescents in the home, parents should always try to model responsible drinking behavior. Although most teenagers

Table 3-2. Risk Factors Associated With Childhood Substance Abuse

— Family history of alcoholism

— Parental alcohol, tobacco, or other drug use

— Family history of antisocial behavior

— Child abuse and neglect, poor parenting skills, poor parental relations

— Sibling drug use, drug use by a best friend, perceived peer drug use

— School failure, low school interest and achievement

— Rebellion and alienation

— Low self-esteem

— Early antisocial behavior

— Depression or other psychopathology

— Negative character traits such as lying, lack of empathy, a need for immediate gratification

— Low religiosity

— Early initiation of sexual activity

Data from "Alcohol Use and Abuse: A Pediatric Concern" by the AAP.

quickly dismiss most double standards, adolescents are capable of understanding that some things are more appropriate for adults than for teenagers. It may be culturally acceptable to have adolescents drink wine with dinner; however, the distinction between adult and adolescent behavior should remain clear. This means not allowing children to mix or taste cocktails, serve drinks to their parents, or sip from a parent's glass.

Provide children with a way out of difficult social situations. Role play how to say no when offered alcohol or drugs: "Thanks, but that's not my thing" or "My parents will ground me forever if I get caught—no thanks!" Discuss strategies in advance of how to contact a parent, caregiver, or another adult to get a ride home if alcohol or drugs are being used by drivers or at a party. Cell phones are extremely useful in these situations. Also discuss utilizing the "no yelling, no questions asked that night" strategy should teenagers find themselves in a risky situation.

RECOGNIZING WARNING SIGNS

Although prevention is the best strategy, recognizing the warning signs of alcohol use is an important step for parents, teachers, and health care providers. Some of the warning signs associated with alcohol and drug use are listed in **Table 3-3** and **Appendix 3-1**. Realizing the extent of teenaged substance use and being open to considering it a potential issue will begin to empower responsible adults to resolve problems.

Table 3-3. Warning Signs of Adolescent Alcohol Use
— Odor of alcohol on clothes or breath
— Strong odor of eucalyptus cough drops or mouthwash, which are commonly used to cover up the smell of alcohol
— A sudden change in attitude or mood, or withdrawal from family and friends
— Unexplained disappearance of money or alcohol from the home
— Loss of interest in activities of school
— Changes in school performance or sudden discipline problems
— Increased secrecy, a desire to stay away from home for prolonged periods, or sudden changes in plans to return home in the evening
— Suddenly associating with a new group of friends

INTERVENTION

Illicit substance and alcohol use is, unfortunately, very common among adolescents, and it frequently occurs at home or in friends' homes (**Figures 3-8** and **3-9**). Parents who suspect that it is happening in their home should not panic. Never confront an adolescent who is intoxicated; postpone it until the teenager is appropriately recovered. If it is a constellation of behavior changes that raises caregivers' suspicions, they should sit down with the child and talk openly about their worries. In either situation, caregivers should ask adolescents about the extent of their use. Was it a 1-time experiment, or has a pattern developed? Inquire as to why the teenager is using. This conversation will hopefully provide a forum in which ground rules and consequences can be developed—communication is key. Unfortunately, it is exceedingly challenging to establish communications during a crisis if communication has not been fostered before the point of confrontation. If parents or caregivers are unable to engage adolescents in a discussion, they should seek outside resources such as an addictions counselor, pediatric specialist, adolescent medicine subspecialist, school counselor, clergy member, or other professional used to dealing with teenagers and/or substance abuse. **Table 3-4** contains important points to remember when trying to intervene in situations of adolescent alcohol use or abuse.

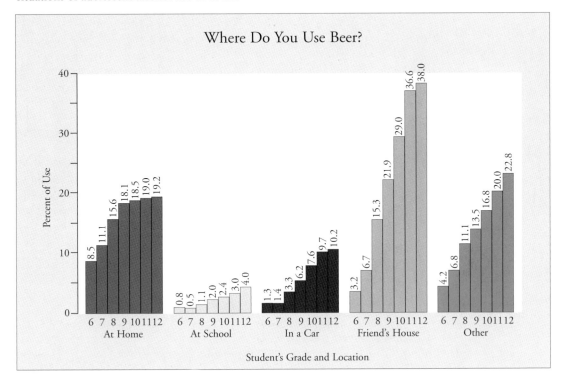

Figure 3-8. *From grades 6 through 12, students consistently use beer at a friend's house followed by their own home. Percentage of use steadily increases as the youths grow older, and 11th and 12th graders are the highest users. Use of beer in cars increases steadily and rises as driving age approaches, and use of beer at school remains comparatively low, indicating that supervision is most needed at the homes of peers. Reprinted with permission from Pride Survey.*

Parents and caregivers should assess their own behaviors to make certain that they do not enable the adolescent experimenter or user. Substance abuse problems can grow when adults ignore or minimize the risks of using. Even if keys are confiscated and guests are required to sleep over, enabling behaviors like supplying alcohol are never helpful. Less obvious enabling behaviors include writing excuses to legitimize alcohol or other drug-related school absences, finishing the teenager's homework, or meeting other failed commitments of the adolescent. Parents who find themselves in the role of an enabler need to stop and seek help from a substance abuse counseling center.

If the adolescent states that alcohol is not the problem, describe the behaviors that are worrisome and await an explanation. Although alcohol is the most commonly used substance, consider other substances as well. Adolescents may lie by omitting facts, so ask explicit questions about specific legal and illegal drugs. Alternative explanations for the behaviors generating concern may well include mental health issues, most commonly depression. Many depressed adolescents turn to alcohol and other drugs to self-medicate when they experience problems. Sudden failure in school, for example—perhaps resulting from previously unrecognized learning disabilities—can damage self-esteem and encourage adolescents to turn to alcohol to feel better or try new

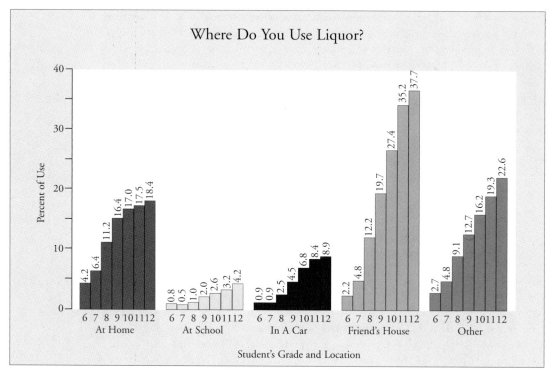

Figure 3-9. *The pattern of this graph for use of liquor closely follows the patterns for beer use in the same age groups. Reprinted with permission from Pride Survey.*

Table 3-4. Dos and Don'ts of Intervening With Underage Alcohol Use
— Don't deny or ignore signs indicating that your child drinks or has a problem with alcohol.
— Do choose appropriate moments to talk about problems with alcohol. Trying to speak with an adolescent who has been drinking or is intoxicated will not be successful.
— Do set rules regarding alcohol use and firm consequences for breaking them.
— Don't be afraid to involve children in the rule-making process. It can help.
— Don't be an enabler: Don't supply alcohol to underage drinkers or make excuses for adolescents who miss school, work, or fail to meet obligations because of drinking.
— Do seek outside help or advice when necessary. Sources include counselors, doctors, and literature.

behaviors/recreations in an attempt to find a niche among peers. Also, the onset of schizophrenia or bipolar disorders often begins in adolescence. Both of these mental health conditions can mimic the symptoms indicating drug use. Concerned caregivers should consult the teenager's physician. Additionally, parents can access a fair amount of useful information via the Internet. A list of Internet resources can be found at the end of this chapter.

In discussions about alcohol, most teenagers prefer parents to be direct. Ask teenagers whether alcohol or other drugs are ever an issue in their circles of friends. Let them know you are aware that many teenagers do experiment with alcohol and drugs and discuss why you think they should not participate. Discuss the dangers of alcohol and drug use. Parents and caregivers should make certain that expectations and rules are very clear and that teenagers understand them. Explain the reasons behind the rules and delineate the consequences for breaking them. For adolescents in the early adolescent stage, emphasize that actions will have real and concrete consequences: For example, alcohol use at friends' houses will make sleepovers at those houses off limits. As with toddlers, remember that variable reinforcement encourages acting out or breaking of rules, and thus it is imperative to be consistent. No teenaged drinking means no alcohol at any time in any place—at home, in a friend's home, at a graduation party, anywhere. As adolescents move toward more formal thought processes, discussions about values such as honesty and responsibility are important.

Parents and caregivers should know adolescents' friends and their friends' parents. Open discussion with the friends' parents about their views on supervising teens and alcohol/drug use is important. Ideally, parents will agree to forbid others' children from consuming alcohol or drugs in their homes and to notify one another if adolescents become high or drunk at their home. However, alcohol-related parties often occur when parents are away. It is not unreasonable to call parents whose home is being used for a party. Do not be "too cool" to actually check out questionable parties. **Table 3-5** answers questions parents and caregivers frequently have about and alcohol and related drugs.

PROFESSIONAL STUDY AND CONTROVERSY

PREVENTION

Prevention is the best strategy for avoiding problems related to adolescent alcohol use. The only proven preventive method is for parents and caregivers to maintain open communication and set overt expectations with clear-cut consequences for when teenagers breech the rules. Some evidence exists indicating that teenagers want to discuss alcohol and other risk-taking behaviors with their health care provider; however, medical professionals do not always initiate such discussions. Parents should encourage

---

Table 3-5. Frequently Asked Questions

Are beer or wine coolers safer than hard liquor?

They are "safer" only in the sense that hard liquor has a higher percent of alcohol by volume than beer or wine. Approximately 12 ounces of beer and 1.5 ounces of hard liquor contain equivalent amounts of alcohol. Some argue that a wine-cooler type of drink places a teenager at risk for intoxication because the taste of the alcohol is often disguised in a soft drink or fruity flavor.

If my teenger's friends drink or experiment with drugs, should I be worried?

Worried? Yes. Panicked? Not necessarily. Data indicates that peer behavior is linked to an individual adolescent's risk-taking behaviors, especially in early or middle adolescence. Parents need to keep dialogue open and discuss openly with teenagers how they feel about their friends' behavior and what they think about the risks they take.

(continued)

Table 3-5. *(continued)*

Does peer pressure play a role in elementary school?

Unfortunately, peer pressure is a strong influence on behavior even in elementary school. In a report from a 1995 *Weekly Reader* survey, 30% of children in fourth through sixth grade reported that they had received pressure from their classmates to drink beer. However, a strong parental presence with clear-cut expectations about alcohol and drug use should be more of an influence at this age.

How do I handle the fact that his father and I drink socially?

As with any other behavior, parents are subject to scrutiny by a challenging adolescent, a fact that has led to many parents to suspend their own use of alcohol. If you opt to continue to drink, always model responsible drinking behavior: Never driving under the influence and never becoming obviously intoxicated. With alcohol use, you can discuss the fact that mature adults can make informed legal choices; however, with other parental drug use, you should at least practice abstinence at home.

Does alcohol use affect adolescents differently than adults?

Yes, Factors increasing the risk of adolescent substance abuse may in fact be increased because of the potentially vulnerable nature of a developing nervous system and an endocrinologic system. Studies are now demonstrating physical differences in the part of a teenager's brain that controls drug reinforcement after early exposure to alcohol. This difference may help explain the increased risk of alcoholism given exposure before age 15 years.

Is marijuana a "gateway" drug leading to more frequent drug use and the use of more powerful drugs?

Marijuana does not by itself create a physiologic need for more powerful drugs; however, depending on the underlying reasons for an adolescent's use, marijuana smoking may reinforce the relaxation and escape features that make drug use attractive. In the effort to buy any illicit drug, youths gain access to those who deal with multiple drugs, so adolescents who use marijuana constantly face the opportunity to expand their usage.

teenagers to initiate discussions and ask questions during visits to the health care provider and consider offering to give them privacy with the provider so that they can question freely.

Behavior-based prevention strategies include the use of behavioral contracts (**Appendix 3-2**). Critics of this approach say that the contract condones and expects experimentation, but supporters suggest that a proactive approach is best and leads to improved adolescent safety. No critical data exist to definitively support or refute these claims. However, clinical experience does indicate that actively involving adolescents in prevention strategies—allowing them to draft the contract and negotiate the consequences of a breech—may be more effective than subjecting them to a fixed set of rules.

Broader preventive strategies have had mixed results, but they may still be useful. These approaches include school-based strategies, such as educational curricula about alcohol and drug use prevention and extracurricular activities offering life skills training, family-based strategies, and public policies. Alcohol and drug education, when paired with preseason medical examinations, has shown some success with junior-high athletes, though not for college athletes. Younger adolescents may respond better to education and advice than older adolescents, who appear to respond better to messages delivered during interactive, feedback-based interventions.

A 5-year study called the Adolescent Alcohol Prevention Trial observed 11 995 students and revealed that educational interventions significantly delayed the onset of alcohol use among public school students in the 8th, 9th, and 10th grades. Public efforts have also succeeded in increasing the legal drinking age from 18 to 21 years of age in all states, a public policy change that has resulted in a significant decrease in motor vehicle fatalities. Some novel approaches, such as using interactive computer programs dealing with drug and alcohol use in the waiting rooms of emergency departments, have undergone preliminary study but need more trial before being implemented.

Physicians can successfully identify teenagers at risk for substance abuse problems using screening tools like the CRAFFT tool shown in **Table 3-6**. Some physicians have suggested that these types of tools may help teenagers to self-screen; however, data are not currently available to support self-screening as a reliable method for identifying risks or problems.

When an adolescent responds positively to a screen, physicians should assess the extent of his or her use, the effects of the use on school and family, and the extent of associated risk-taking behaviors such as driving while intoxicated, suicidal ideation, or expanding drug types. The diagnosis of substance use problem should be confirmed by a mental health professional with expertise in adolescent substance use and abuse.

Table 3-6. CRAFFT—Questions to Identify Adolescents With Alcohol Abuse Problems*	
C	Have you ever ridden in a **c**ar driven by someone (including yourself) who was "high" or had been using alcohol or drugs?
R	Do you ever use alcohol or drugs to **r**elax, feel better about yourself, or fit in?
A	Do you ever use alcohol or drugs while you are by yourself, or **a**lone?
F	Do you ever **f**orget things you did while using alcohol or drugs?
F	Do your family or **f**riends ever tell you that you should cut down on your drinking or drug use?
T	Have you ever gotten into **t**rouble while you were using alcohol or drugs?

* Two or more "yes" answers indicates that the adolescent has a serious problem with alcohol abuse.

© Children's Hospital Boston, 2001. Reproduced with permission from the Center for Adolescent Substance Abuse Research, CeASAR, Children's Hospital Boston. For more information, contact info@CRAFFT.org, or visit www.crafft.org.

NEW RESEARCH INVOLVING NEUROLOGICAL AND HORMONAL EFFECTS

Little controversy exists about the risks of alcohol use among adolescents and its relation to the coexisting risk-taking behaviors, such as sexual activity and other substance abuse. Suicide and accident association has been fairly well established. New research is looking at possible unique features of the adolescent brain that may predispose teenagers to risk-taking behaviors or make adolescents more vulnerable to addiction once they begin using. Research focusing on the structural and functional consequences of alcohol use on the developing brain demonstrates actual brain volume loss in the hippocampus—the part of the brain involved with memory, learning, and emotion. These brain changes are not normally seen in adults. Other studies have examined hormonal communication between the brain, the pituitary or master gland, and the ovaries of adolescent girls. Data suggest that there may be a direct link between alcohol consumption and interference with ovarian function. There may be many more physiological effects of early alcohol and drug use than previously thought, making prevention even more of a priority.

CONCLUSION

Underage alcohol use is very prevalent in US culture. Familial risk factors for underage use include having an alcoholic or drug-abusing parent or sibling, and having parents or caregivers who are uninvolved or express favorable attitudes toward alcohol or drug consumption. Other risk factors include having a learning disability or experiencing academic failure, suffering from anxiety or depression, and exposure to peer drinking. Strong connections between the parents and children, clearly communicated parental expectations to avoid alcohol, and parental involvement in children's lives can help prevent alcohol use and abuse. Other factors that promote responsible attitudes toward alcohol consumption include academic success, having strong connections with a church group, school activities, or families, and having parents that drink responsibly or do not drink at all.

WHERE TO TURN FOR HELP

FOR CRISIS

Seek out expertise from a physician or addictions counselor, or call a drug abuse hotline.

National Alcohol/Drug Abuse & Referral Hotline

800-662-HELP

National Alcohol and Substance Abuse Information Hotline

800-784-6776

FOR CONCERNS
National Clearinghouse for Alcohol and Drug Information

800-729-6686

http://www.health.org

The US Department of Education Partnership for a Drug-Free America

800-624-0100

— Offers free copies of *Growing up Drug Free: A Parent's Guide to Prevention*.

WEB SITES
Al-Anon/Alateen Family Group Headquarters Inc

http://www.al-anon.alateen.org

American Academy of Pediatrics

http://www.aap.org/healthtopics/subabuse.cfm

— Offers parents information about drug use and underage drinking.

American Council for Drug Education

http://www.acde.org

American Medical Association Office of Alcohol and Other Drug Abuse

http://www.ama-assn.org/ama/pub/category/3337.html

FACE Truth and Clarity on Alcohol

http://www.faceproject.org

Kids Health

http://www.kidshealth.org

— Medical information from the Nemours Foundation.

Marijuana: Facts for Teens

http://www.nida.nih.gov/MarijBroch/Marijteens.html

Monitoring the Future Study: A Continuing Study of American Youths

http://www.isr.umich.edu/src/mtf

Mothers Against Drunk Driving

http://www.madd.org

National Council on Alcohol and Drug Dependence, Inc.

http://www.ncadd.org

— Information and advice for parents.

National Institute of Drug Abuse

http://www.drugabuse.gov

National Office of the Robert Wood Johnson Foundation

http://www.rwjf.org

Partnership for a Drug-Free America

http://www.drugfree.org

Rutgers University Center of Alcohol Studies Library

http://www.alcoholstudies.rutgers.edu

Substance Abuse and Mental Health Services Administration Center for Substance Abuse Prevention

http://www.samhsa.gov

Talking With Kids About Tough Issues

http://www.talkingwithkids.org

APPENDIX 3-1: ILLICIT DRUG GUIDE*

GENERAL WARNING SIGNS OF SUBSTANCE USE

General warning signs include unusual odors on clothing such as alcohol, burned leaves, chemicals, or paint. Physical symptoms include bloodshot eyes and loss of appetite or weight. Other signs are a sudden change in attitude or moods, loss of interest in school or extracurricular activities, withdrawal from family and friends, and the unexplained disappearance of money or alcohol from the home. Finally, concern is warranted if the teenager has new friends but is reluctant to introduce them to his or her family. Warning signs associated with specific drugs follow.

MARIJUANA

Marijuana is the most commonly used illicit drug (**Appendix Figures 3-1, 3-2,** and **3-3**); at least one third of Americans have used marijuana sometime in their lives. It is usually smoked as a cigarette (joint) or in a pipe or bong. Prices for commercial-grade marijuana have remained relatively stable over the past decade, ranging from approximately $400 to $1000 per pound in the southwest border areas of the United States to between $700 and $2000 per pound in the Midwest and northeastern United States. The national price range for sinsemilla, a highly potent form of marijuana usually grown domestically, is between $900 and $6000 per pound. Marijuana produced in Mexico and smuggled into the United States remains the most widely available form. High-potency marijuana also enters the US drug market from Canada. Marijuana can be grown easily, and there is an increasing supply of domestically grown marijuana. The availability of marijuana from Southeast Asia generally is limited to the West Coast.

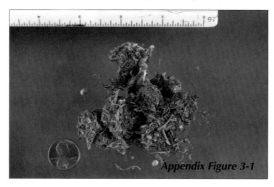
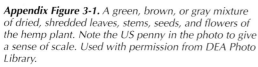

Appendix Figure 3-1. *A green, brown, or gray mixture of dried, shredded leaves, stems, seeds, and flowers of the hemp plant. Note the US penny in the photo to give a sense of scale. Used with permission from DEA Photo Library.*

Appendix Figure 3-2. *Loose marijuana looks like dried plant material and is easy to conceal. Used with permission from DEA Photo Library.*

Appendix Figure 3-3. *Plant appearance of marijuana. Used with permission from DEA Photo Library.*

Data from the US Drug Enforcement Administration and the US Department of Health and Human Services Substance Abuse and Mental Health Services Administration.

Effects

May cause frequent respiratory infections, impaired memory and learning, increased heart rate, anxiety, panic attacks, tolerance, and physical dependence. Chronic smokers may have many of the same respiratory problems as tobacco smokers including daily cough and phlegm, chronic bronchitis symptoms, and frequent chest colds; chronic abuse can also lead to abnormal functioning of lung tissues.

Warning signs

Unexplained dizziness or trouble walking, unexplained giddiness, difficulty remembering things that just happened, excessive sleepiness, binge eating (called colloquially "the munchies")

Slang

Weed, smoke, pot, herb, grass, dope, indo, hydro, boom, Mary Jane, bud, gangster, chronic (there are more than 200 slang terms for marijuana)

Blunts, reefer, joint (specifically for marijuana cigarettes)

Other forms

Sinsemilla (sin-seh-ME-yah), hashish ("hash" for short), and hash oil are highly potent forms of marijuana.

COCAINE

Cocaine is the second most commonly used illicit drug in the United States and is typically snorted or dissolved in water and injected (**Appendix Figures 3-4-a** and **b**). About 10% of Americans older than 12 years have tried cocaine at least once in their lifetime, and nearly 1% are currently using cocaine. The US-Mexico border is the primary point of entry for cocaine shipments being smuggled into the United States. Organized crime groups based in Colombia control the worldwide supply of cocaine. Cocaine prices depend on the purity of the product. In 2001, cocaine purity declined by 8%, from 86% pure in 1998 to 78% pure in 2001. The decrease in purity indicates a decrease in the supply of cocaine in the United States. Nationwide, prices ranged from $12 000 to $35 000 per kilogram.

Appendix Figure 3-4-a

Appendix Figure 3-4-b

***Appendix Figure 3-4-a** and **B.** White crystalline powder cocaine is generally snorted or dissolved in water and injected. Used with permission from DEA Photo Library.*

Effects

Cocaine is powerfully addictive. The mixing of cocaine and alcohol create coaethylene and increases the risk of sudden death. Cocaine-related deaths are often a result of cardiac arrest or seizures followed by respiratory arrest. Users may also suffer irregular heartbeat, increased heart rates, permanent damage to blood vessels in the brain, and, from shared needles, AIDS or hepatitis.

Warning signs
Anger, hostility, anxiousness, confusion, violent behavior, paranoia, hallucinations, increased physical activity, loss of appetite, weight loss, inability to sleep

Slang
Blow, nose candy, snowball, tornado, wicky stick, coke, dust, snow, toot, line

Crack Cocaine

Crack is cocaine that has not been neutralized by an acid to make the hydrochloride salt (**Appendix Figure 3-5**). This form of cocaine comes in a rock crystal that can be heated and its vapors smoked. The term "crack" refers to the crackling sound heard when it is heated. About 2% of Americans older than 12 years have tried crack.

Appendix Figure 3-5

Appendix Figure 3-5. *Crack is an off-white, chunky material. Used with permission from DEA Photo Library.*

Effects
Smoking crack can cause severe chest pains with lung trauma and bleeding.

Warning signs
See Cocaine

Slang
Rock

Inhalants

Inhalants include a large group of chemicals that are found in household products such as aerosol sprays, cleaning fluids, glue, paint, paint thinner, gasoline, propane, nail polish remover, correction fluid, and marker pens.

Effects
None of the inhalants mentioned above are safe to inhale—they all can cause death. In addition, chemicals such as amyl nitrite, isobutyl nitrite ("poppers"), and nitrous oxide ("whippets"), often sold at concerts and dance clubs, can cause permanent damage to the body and brain.

Warning signs
Slurred speech; drunk, dizzy, or dazed appearance; unusual breath odor; a chemical smell on clothing; paint stains on body or face; red eyes; runny nose

Slang
Glue, kick, bang, sniff, huff, poppers, whippets, Texas shoeshine

LSD
LSD is produced from lysergic acid, a fungus that grows on grain plants such as rye, and the primary distribution location within the United States is San Francisco, California. It is an odorless, colorless, tasteless hallucinogen that alters a person's mood and comes in tablet, capsule, and liquid form; it is also often added to absorbent paper and divided into squares that equal one dose. Effects begin within 60 to 90 minutes and can last up to 12 hours.

Effects
Users hallucinate and experience feelings of losing control, depression, insanity, or dying. Flashbacks of an LSD experience can persist months or days after the last dose.

Warning signs
Excessive sweating, loss of appetite, sleeplessness, dry mouth, tremors; depression, anxiety, fear, panic, rapid mood swings, lack of muscular coordination, incoherent speech, feeling isolated or alone

Slang
Acid, blotter acid, windowpane, microdots

METHAMPHETAMINE
Methamphetamine is made in illegal laboratories and has a high potential for abuse and addiction. It typically appears as a white powder that easily dissolves in water (**Appendix Figure 3-6**). Methods of usage include injecting, snorting, smoking, and oral ingestion.

During 2000, 4% of the US population reported trying methamphetamine at least once in their lifetime. Abuse is concentrated in the western, southwestern, and Midwestern United States. Illegal laboratories in California and Mexico are the primary sources of supply for methamphetamine available in the United States. Domestic labs that produce methamphetamine are dependent on supplies of the precursor chemical pseudoephedrine. Pseudoephedrine is sometimes diverted from legitimate sources but is

Appendix Figure 3-6. White powder methamphetamine. Used with permission from DEA Photo Library.

Appendix Figure 3-6

also smuggled from Canada and, to a lesser extent, from Mexico. Prices for methamphetamine vary throughout different regions of the United States. At the distribution level, prices range from $3500 per pound in parts of California and Texas to $21 000 per pound in southeastern and northeastern regions of the United States. Retail prices range from $400 to $3000 per ounce.

Effects
Addiction, psychotic behavior, and brain damage are all possible. Withdrawal symptoms include depression, anxiety, fatigue, paranoia, aggression, and intense cravings. Chronic use can cause violent behavior, anxiety, confusion, insomnia, auditory hallucinations, mood disturbances, delusions, and paranoia. Damage to the brain caused by methamphetamine usage is similar to Alzheimer's disease, stroke, and epilepsy.

Warning signs
Anger, hostility, anxiousness, confusion, violent behavior, paranoia, hallucinations, increased physical activity, loss of appetite, weight loss, inability to sleep

Slang
Speed, meth, poor man's cocaine, crystal meth, ice, glass, speed, chalk

METHAMPHETAMINE HYDROCHLORIDE
Methamphetamine hydrochloride is another form of methamphetamine. It appears in clear chunky crystals, resembling ice, which can be inhaled by smoking (**Appendix Figures 3-7-a** and **b; Figure 3-8**).

Effects
See Methamphetamine

Warning signs
See Methamphetamine

Slang
Crystal meth, ice, crystal, glass, tina

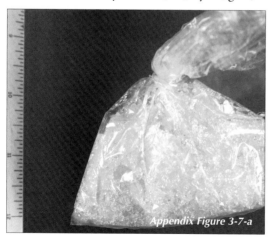

Appendix Figure 3-7-b

Appendix Figure 3-7-a

Appendix Figures 3-7-a and **b.** *Methamphetamine hydrochloride, or crystal meth. Used with permission from DEA Photo Library.*

Appendix Figure 3-8. *Pipe used for smoking of methamphetamine. Used with permission from DEA Photo Library.*

Appendix Figure 3-8

NARCOTICS

The term *narcotic* refers to opium, opium derivatives (morphine, codeine), and their semisynthetic substitutes (heroin). Opium is obtained from poppy plants (**Appendix Figure 3-9**). Narcotics are used medically to treat pain, suppress coughs, relieve diarrhea, and induce anesthesia, and it can be injected, taken orally, or absorbed through the skin. There are state, federal, and international laws governing the production and distribution of narcotic substances. Commercial opium is standardized to contain 10% morphine. In the United States, a small amount of the morphine obtained from opium is used directly (about 15 tons); the remaining is converted to codeine and other deriv-

Appendix Figure 3-9. *A dried poppy that is the source of opium and a variety of narcotics that have medical and illicit uses. Used with permission from DEA Photo Library.*

atives (about 120 tons). Morphine is one of the most effective drugs known for the relief of severe pain and remains the standard against which new analgesics are measured. Like most narcotics, the use of morphine has increased significantly in recent years. Since 1990, there has been about a threefold increase in morphine products in the United States. Treatment for narcotic addiction can involve the use of detoxification drugs such as methadone, LAAM, and Buprenorphine.

Effects
Narcotics produce a general sense of well-being and reduce tension, anxiety, and aggression.

Warning signs
Drowsiness, inability to concentrate, confusion, apathy, decreased physical activity, flushed complexion, constipation, nausea, vomiting, decreased breathing, constricted pupils, clammy skin

Slang
— Heroin: sugar hill, smack, dope, gumball, tootsie roll, black tar, H

— Heroin/Morphine: doogie, Dr. Feelgood, Good and Plenty, hard candy, Miss Emma, racehorse charlie, sweet dreams, sugar, unkie

— Opiates/Narcotics: dopium, dreams, dream stick, goma, hard stuff, gum, hop, joy plant, Indonesian bud, midnight oil, O, Ope, pin yen, ze

CLUB DRUGS
Club drugs refer to a wide variety of drugs often used at all-night dance parties ("raves"), nightclubs, and concerts. The most common club drugs are listed below, along with their common slang names. LSD is also a member of this group.

Effects
Club drugs are used to enhance the party environment by changing the sensory experience, having extra energy, or being able to stay awake longer. Side effects can include seizures, coma, and even death.

Warning signs
Feelings of euphoria and well-being; confidence; lack of inhibition; aggression; abnormal alertness; nausea; vomiting; sweating; jaw clenching; teeth grinding, anxiety, paranoia; loss of appetite; hallucinations; confusion; changes in mood, memory, sleep patterns, sexual function

Slang
— Ecstasy: E, X, XTC

— GHB: Liquid ecstasy, liquid X, grievous bodily harm, Georgia home boy

— Ketamine: K, Special K, Ket, vitamin K, Kit Kat

— Rohypnol: Roofies, R-2

APPENDIX 3-2: BEHAVIORAL CONTRACTS

GENERAL RULES

Contracts should be mutually developed by the parent and the teenager and contain the following:

— Specific behaviors that are not to occur

— Consequences if behaviors do occur and possible rewards if the behavior is avoided

— Specific situations to which the contract applies

— Signature of both the parent and the teenager

Some contracts include behavior modification for both adolescents and parents. There are often 2 parts: 1 for the teenager and 1 for the parent or caregiver. See below and http://www.sadd.org, the Web site for Students Against Destructive Decisions, for samples.

Family Contract

I respect my family's values and rules about alcohol and drug use, and I want to maintain a safe and healthy lifestyle. Therefore, I agree to the following:

1. I will not smoke cigarettes.

2. I will not drink alcohol or make a decision about drinking alcohol until I am 21.

3. I will not use or experiment with any drugs.

If I break this contract:

Discuss consequences together and fill in below. Consider seeking professional advice if consequences are not effective.

    First offense:

    Second offense:

    Third offense:

Signed,

_____   _____

Son or Daughter   Date

_____   _____

Parent/Caregiver   Date

This contract is adapted from "Commonsense: Strategies for Raising Alcohol- and Drug-free Children." National PTA and GTE Corporation (1998).

Chapter 4

TOBACCO AND SMOKING

Tahniat Syed, MD, MPH
Cynthia DeLago, MD, MPH

Tobacco affects children of all ages, even the unborn. Fetuses, infants, and young children suffer indirect health effects from second-hand smoke, and older children suffer direct effects if they smoke or use spit tobacco (dip, chew, smokeless, or snuff). If you are involved in the care of anyone in this age group, this chapter is for you.

Each year, tobacco kills more people than car accidents, alcohol, drug abuse, murders, suicides, fires, and AIDS combined! Despite this staggering statistic, many people think that tobacco will not affect them or their children. The effects of smoking are so subtle that it is hard to think of it as a threat until a close friend or family member dies of a tobacco-related illness like lung cancer. Even then, parents or caregivers may continue to believe it will not affect their children because those who die from tobacco tend to be older adults. In reality, most adult tobacco users started when they were children and realized only too late how difficult it was to quit. A study in *Preventive Medicine* reported smoking initiation in significant numbers for children as young as 10 years. The rate of lifetime cigarette use among youths aged 12 to 17 years has averaged between 29% and 39% every year since 1965 (**Figure 4-1**). As children become older, the amount of tobacco use generally increases (**Figure 4-2**). **Figures 4-3-a** through **4-4-c** show various trends and attitudes among adolescents regarding tobacco use. The tobacco industry is well aware that the future generation of smokers becomes hooked before the age of 18 years. It is for this reason that tobacco is marketed toward children. **Table 4-1** lists other statistics on smoking in the United States.

So how can parents and caregivers protect children from the direct and indirect effects of tobacco? This chapter provides information on the harmful effects of smoking and exposure to tobacco smoke, the different factors involved in smoking initiation, and practical strategies for preventing smoking and helping someone quit.

Table 4-1. Brief Statistics on US Smoking

— 22.2% of teenagers aged 16 to 17 years smoke.

— Among youths aged 12 to 17 years, more girls smoke than boys.

— 3000 people start smoking every day. Approximately 49.5% of these people are younger than 18 years.

— Average age of first cigarette use is 16.7 years.

— Average number of cigarettes smoked per day by current smokers was 13; the number increased steadily from 2 (among 12 year olds) to 18 or 19 (among 50 to 64 year olds).

— 35.5 million persons aged 12 years or older (representing 14.7% of US population) meet criteria for nicotine dependence.

— Rate of nicotine dependence is higher among adults who started smoking as youths.

— Smoking is less common among persons with more education.

— Use of illicit drugs and alcohol is more common among smokers than nonsmokers.

Data from the Results of the 2004 National Survey on Drug Abuse and Health *by the US Dept of Health and Human Services.*

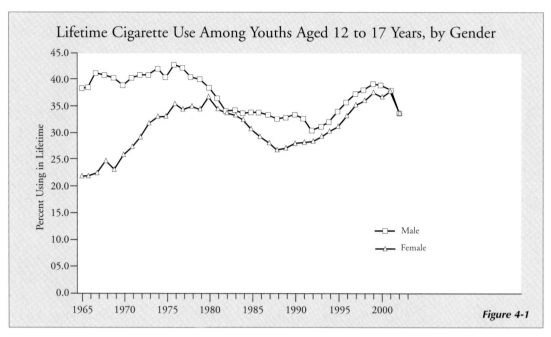

Figure 4-1

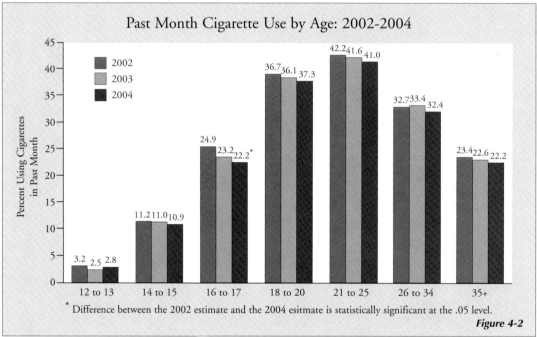

Figure 4-2

Figure 4-1. *Although the rate of cigarette use among youths aged 12 to 17 years increased during the 1990s from 30.3% to 37.8%, there was a significant decline from 2001 to 2002 (37.3% to 33.3%). From 1965 to 1980, the rate among adolescent girls increased from 21.7% to 36.2%. Since 1980, rates for girls have been nearly the same as the rates for boys. Reprinted from the Substance Abuse and Mental Health Services Administration (SAMSHA).*

Figure 4-2. *Current cigarette use peaked at 41.0% in 2004 among young adults aged 21 to 25 years. Less than a quarter (22.2%) of persons aged 35 years or older in 2004 smoked cigarettes in the month prior to the survey. Rates of cigarette smoking were mostly stable across the 3 survey years within these age groups, with 1 exception. Among youths aged 16 or 17, the rate of current cigarette smoking declined from 24.9% in 2002 to 22.2% in 2004. Reprinted from SAMHSA.*

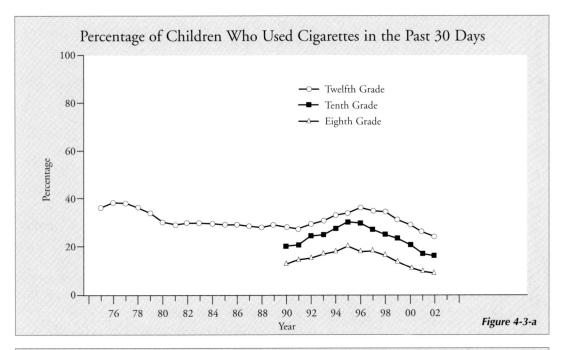

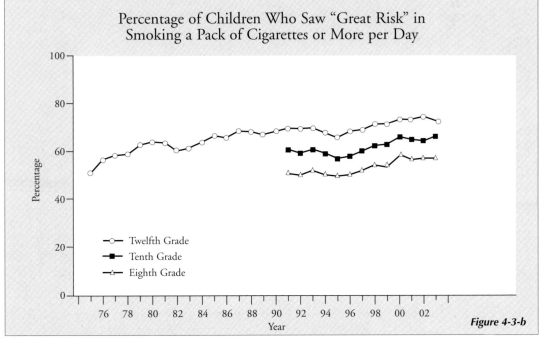

Figures 4-3-a *through* **d.** *Looking at trends for 8th, 10th, and 12th graders, one sees encouragement in that all groups have decreased in cigarette use over the 30 days before the survey (**a**); all increasingly see risk to smoking (**b**); all increasingly disapprove of smoking a pack or more of cigarettes, though seniors are more accepting, followed by sophomores, with the 8th graders being the most disapproving (**c**); and all decreasingly think it is easy to get cigarettes (**d**). Reprinted from Monitoring the Future.*

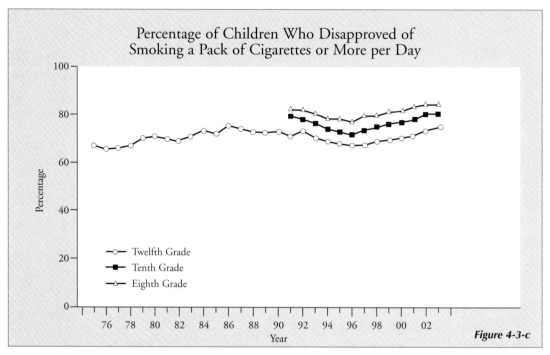

Figure 4-3-c

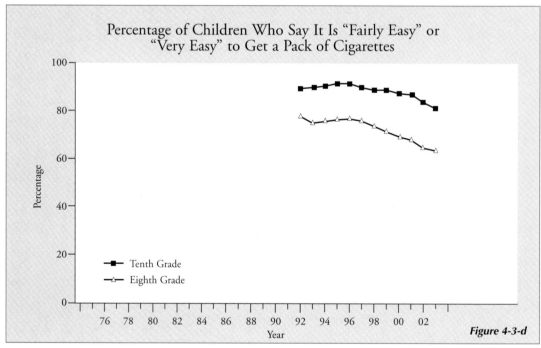

Figure 4-3-d

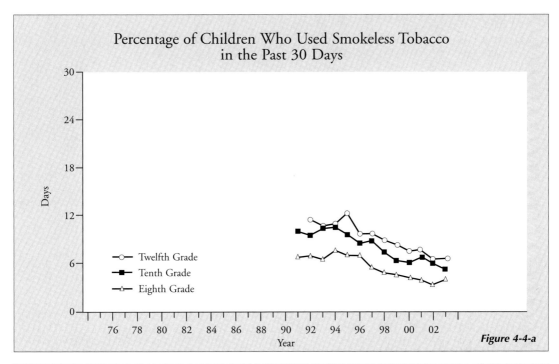

Figure 4-4-a

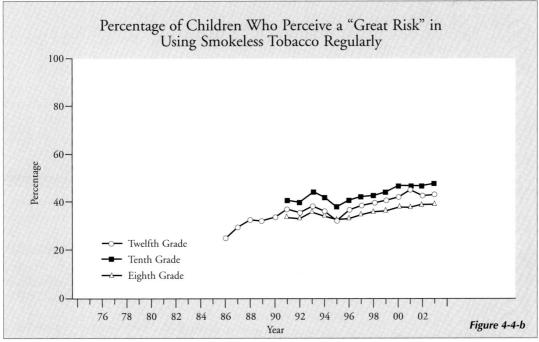

Figure 4-4-b

Figures 4-4-a through **c.** With regard to smokeless tobacco, the trend for use over the 30 days before the survey is declining and at a rate of use much lower than cigarette use for 8th, 10th, and 12th graders (**a**). All 3 groups also increasingly see a health risk to smokeless tobacco but at a lower rate than the perception of risk seen with cigarette use (**b**). Eighth and 10th graders increasingly disapprove of regular use of smokeless tobacco (**c**). Reprinted from Monitoring the Future.

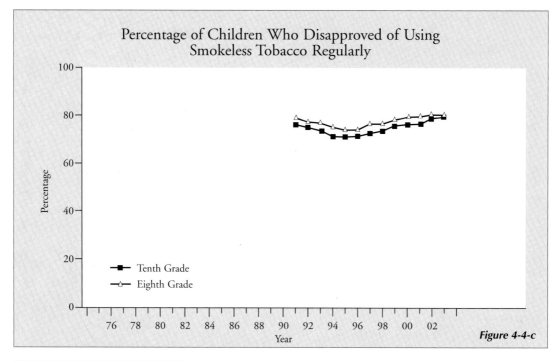

Percentage of Children Who Disapproved of Using Smokeless Tobacco Regularly

Figure 4-4-c

Table 4-2. Harmful Effects of Tobacco on Adult Health

— Atherosclerosis

— Cardiovascular disease (heart attacks, chest pain)

— Lung cancer

— Other cancers

— Cataracts

— Wrinkles

— Yellow teeth

— Poor dentition

— Decreased oxygen supply to the body, especially fingers and toes

— Emphysema

— Chronic bronchitis

— Stroke

— Poor exercise tolerance

Data from The Health Consequences of Smoking: A Report of the Surgeon General.

EFFECTS OF TOBACCO AND EXPOSURE TO SMOKE

SMOKING

Tobacco smoking has been linked with health problems, such as emphysema, chronic bronchitis, and lung and other cancers (**Table 4-2**). These health problems result from direct exposure to the more than 3000 chemicals that make up a cigarette. One of these chemicals, nicotine, is both poisonous and addictive, and it is the substance primarily responsible for making it difficult for people to quit smoking. Tobacco-related illnesses, which occur mostly in adults, develop after years of smoking. However, according to data from the Surgeon General, most adults who develop these illnesses start smoking before the age of 18 and form their attitudes about smoking at an even younger age. This is one reason why tobacco is a pediatric concern. Research from the Surgeon General report *Preventing Tobacco Use Among Young People* indicates that if children see parents, siblings, or other people that they greatly admire smoke, they are more likely to smoke in the future. In fact, data from the Centers for Disease Control and Prevention (CDC) show that children are twice as likely to start smoking if their parents smoke.

ENVIRONMENTAL TOBACCO SMOKE

The most serious tobacco-related illnesses generally tend to develop in someone who has been smoking a long time. However, ***environmental tobacco smoke*** (ETS), which is also known as second-hand smoke or passive smoke, has well-studied negative health effects even on people who do not smoke. Infants and children are most affected because they cannot easily remove themselves from their environment. Environmental tobacco smoke is a mixture of over 3000 chemicals, many of which cause cancer, and is composed of 2 types of smoke: *side-stream smoke*, which is given off from a burning cigarette, cigar, or pipe; and *mainstream smoke*, which is exhaled by the person smoking. Side-stream smoke is more dangerous than mainstream smoke because it burns at a lower temperature, which means that it contains higher concentrations of toxins.

Environmental tobacco smoke causes a range of health problems for infants and children, including more frequent ear infections (which sometimes require ear tube placement) and chronic respiratory problems (**Table 4-3**). Also, ETS is associated with more than one third of all sudden infant death syndrome cases, also known as "crib death." **Table 4-4** lists ways to protect children from ETS exposure.

Table 4-3. Effects of ETS on Children's Health	Table 4-4. Dos and Don'ts of Protecting Children from ETS
— Sudden infant death syndrome — Respiratory infections — Asthma attacks — Ear infections — Respiratory complaints: cough, phlegm — Asthma — Bronchitis — Tonsilitis — Pneumonia — Low exercise tolerance *Data from* The Health Consequences of Smoking: A Report of the Surgeon General.	— Do quit smoking. If you continue to smoke, keep it outside. — Do realize that smoking outside does not completely eliminate smoke particles, which stick to your hair, skin, and clothes and are inhaled by your child. — Don't create a "smoking room" in your house because it may not help; the smoke will still circulate throughout the house. — Don't let anyone smoke in your home or in your car. — Do make sure the child's childcare provider does not smoke. — Do choose to do activities in nonsmoking public areas or nonsmoking sections in places that allow smoking. — Do go only to restaurants that are completely nonsmoking.

WHEN TOBACCO-RELATED HEALTH EFFECTS START

Some health problems resulting from smoking and ETS exposure can start very early. **Table 4-5** summarizes the physical effects that tobacco has on a young person, which include delayed lung growth, chronic respiratory complaints such as coughing or phlegm production, and long recovery times for illnesses—even a simple cold. Even newborns are affected by maternal smoking; a study recently published in the journal *Pediatrics* observed that newborns whose mothers who smoked as few as 7 cigarettes per day had gastrointestinal symptoms and neurobehavioral changes similar to those seen in drug-addicted infants.

The behavioral effects of smoking on teenagers are just as severe. The Surgeon General reports that teenagers who smoke have a much higher chance of performing poorly in

Table 4-5. Direct Effects of Tobacco on Children's Health

— Delayed lung growth

— Chronic respiratory complaints (coughing, phlegm)

— Halitosis (bad breath)

— Dental cavities and gum disease

— Poor nutritional intake

— Long recovery times for illness

— Low exercise tolerance

Data from The Health Consequences of Smoking: A Report of the Surgeon General.

school or dropping out, using other drugs like marijuana or alcohol, and suffering from stress, sadness, or nervousness. Because cigarette smoking can be retraced as the first event in many other high-risk behaviors, cigarettes have come to be known as a "gateway drug."

Adolescents seem to know about the dangers of smoking, but because they often perceive themselves as invulnerable, they think that tobacco will not have any effects on them. They also underestimate the power of nicotine addiction, believing that quitting will be easy. Research for the Surgeon General has found that even adolescents who smoke as few as 3 to 5 cigarettes per day have a high likelihood of becoming regular smokers. Nicotine is more addictive than other drugs—even more so than cocaine. In 1 study from the Surgeon General's report, high school students who were regular smokers were asked whether they thought they would still be smoking in 5 years. When those 5 years had passed, 73% of those who said they would not be smoking still were. Data from other research reveal that teenagers who smoke as few as 5 cigarettes a day display withdrawal symptoms or experience unpleasant effects from lack of nicotine. **Table 4-6** contains frequently asked questions related to adolescents and tobacco use.

WHAT PARENTS AND CAREGIVERS CAN DO

PREVENTION

Knowing about the process of addiction allows parents and caregivers to help children avoid dependence. The process starts during early childhood, or the "preparatory stage," when children form their beliefs, perceptions, and expectations about smoking. This is the time when parents and caregivers need to teach children that smoking is dangerous, that most people do not smoke, and that it is not an effective way to solve problems. Even before doing this, parents and caregivers who smoke should try to quit as soon as possible. Until they quit, they should smoke outside and out of view of children. Most importantly, they should make sure not to involve children in their smoking habit by, for example, asking children to get their cigarettes or to light a cigarette for them. It is difficult for smokers to teach their children about the negative aspects of smoking because children see inconsistencies between adults' words and actions.

Even if children are not in daily contact with people who smoke, they will encounter smoking on television, in movies, and at restaurants, bus stops, or other public places. G-rated movies like *101 Dalmatians* (the last G-rated movie allowed to show smoking), popular teenage movies, and prime-time television shows often have characters who portray smoking as cool, glamorous, and helpful in stressful situations. Tobacco companies distribute promotional items such as backpacks, T-shirts, and free cigarettes to young people. With an annual budget of over $5 billion set aside for marketing cigarettes to young people, tobacco companies are well equipped to advertise their product. In promotional media, people who look healthy, thin, and popular portray cigarette smoking as socially attractive, exciting, and cool. It is important to talk to children about what they see in media and in public forums in order to dispel media myths and make them aware of the truth.

Table 4-6. Frequently Asked Questions

Can teenagers become addicted to nicotine?

Absolutely. Not only do teenagers become addicted to nicotine, but also it is often as hard for them to quit as it is for adults.

How can adults initiate a discussion about smoking with adolescents?

Try the following questions:

— How do you feel about smoking?

— Do any of your friends talk about smoking? What do they talk about?

— Do any of your friends smoke?

— Do any parents of your friends smoke? How do you feel about that?

— What do you know about smoking?

— Has anyone ever asked you to try smoking?

— What would you do if someone asked you to try smoking?

— Have you ever smoked cigarettes before?

What immediate side effects do people have when they quit smoking?

People who quit smoking often experience irritability, anxiety, frustration, trouble concentrating, and weight gain. Despite these effects, ex-smokers will almost immediately experience the health benefits of improved respiratory function, better sense of taste and smell, and improved cardiovascular status.

Is it a good idea to use spit tobacco to help quit smoking?

Even though spit tobacco has been promoted as a safer alternative to smoking and has been used as an aid to quit smoking, it is not a good idea. First, it contains variable amounts of nicotine, a highly addictive drug, as well as several known carcinogens and irritants. Second, many who try this method to quit smoking end up using both cigarettes and spit tobacco. Third, it is just as dangerous and addictive as cigarettes. Users are a greater risk of developing cancers such as oral, stomach, esophageal, or bladder cancer instead of lung cancer. Finally, it is associated with other serious health effects such as discolored teeth, bad breath, gum disease, tooth decay, cracked and bleeding lips and gums, increased blood pressure, increased heart rate, and white patches or leukoplakia on the oral mucosa, gums, or tongue. Spit tobacco use also interferes with the sense of smell and taste.

The next stage of nicotine addiction is the "trying stage," which occurs during the older childhood/young adolescent years. During this stage, children may try taking a few puffs from a cigarette. If parents have an open relationship with their children, children will be more likely to discuss their experiences. If they do, encourage them to share thoughts about smoking and help them understand why smoking is not good for them.

The early to mid teenage years are the "experimentation stage." Children in this stage may begin to smoke cigarettes or use spit tobacco repeatedly, but not regularly. They usually will limit their tobacco use to certain situations or events such as parties or walking to school with their friends. Again, if parents or caregivers have an open relationship with adolescents, they may feel comfortable enough to tell them what they are doing. Encourage them as much as possible to choose not to smoke; parental disapproval is a strong deterrent. Also, parents should know their children's friends and the friends' parents. They should know where their children are and what they are doing. Parental involvement can help discourage children from participating in dangerous activities and habits.

Public efforts can help deter smoking during the "experimentation stage" by decreasing access to cigarette and tobacco products. These efforts include making sure that stores are not selling cigarettes to minors and removing cigarette vending machines from public places. Rising cigarette taxes have helped to reduce access to tobacco; however, some stores have continued to sell affordable cigarettes to minors by selling them individually rather than in packs.

Eventually, adolescents may progress to the "regular-use stage," when they smoke almost daily. Teenagers are more tempted to smoke regularly if they think it will help them in some way—for example, with losing weight, making or keeping friends, coping with stress, or improving their concentration or mood. Research has shown a strong link between smoking and depression. Young people with depression may use cigarettes as a "medication" to improve their mood. Although the good feelings that young people initially find in cigarettes encourage them to smoke, it is actually nicotine addiction that gets them hooked. Adolescents experience the unpleasant feelings caused by nicotine withdrawal if they stop smoking—even if, as previously mentioned, they smoke as few as 5 cigarettes per day. Withdrawal symptoms may include cravings, anger, irritability, sadness, frustration, and nervousness. As with any habit, a person goes through a series of gradual developmental stages, and there are opportunities for intervention at each stage. **Table 4-7** contains dos and don'ts to help parents and caregivers trying to keep children from smoking or using other tobacco products.

Table 4-7. Dos and Don'ts of Preventing Tobacco Use

— Do talk to children about tobacco use and the negative effect it has on health. Make your position on tobacco use clear.

— Do discuss media and advertising portrayals of smoking or other tobacco use with children.

— Be mindful of what children are watching and reading. Avoid TV programs and movies that have characters who smoke.

— Don't smoke or use tobacco products in front of children. Quit if you can.

— Don't involve children in your habit by asking them to retrieve or light your cigarettes.

— Do remember that children want to be like the people around them and set a good example. Siblings are also very strong influences, so if 1 starts smoking, make sure he or she is not affecting the others.

— Do avoid being around tobacco products whenever possible.

— Do encourage children to discuss experimentation with you and remain open to hearing to their thoughts and experiences.

— Do support public actions that make tobacco products less available to children and adolescents.

INTERVENTION

Despite all prevention efforts, some young people will still start smoking. When that is the case, there are some ways to help. First, converse with children to find out if they want to quit. Remember that parents who smoke will seem hypocritical if they tell their children not to smoke; quitting together may be the answer. If children want to quit, help them set a quit date. Remind them that quitting will be hard, especially if they are addicted. Many people will attempt to quit 2 or 3 times before actually succeeding. Remain supportive throughout the entire process. Avoid comments that seem condescending, argumentative, or negative. Reinforce any successes positively, no matter how small they seem. For example, if a child does not smoke after eating but has not quit completely yet, that small step can be a big deal. He or she will appreciate it if parents and caregivers acknowledge this as an accomplishment.

Next, have children identify important people in their lives who can support them as they quit smoking. These people should be those who will not nag and will help children stay on track with the decision to quit. Also, help children come up with alternative ways of keeping busy during times that they would normally smoke. Teenagers often say they smoke because they are "bored." Encourage adolescents to engage in alternative activities—playing a sport, getting a job, volunteering, or spending time with a parent or other family member. Other things that have helped smokers to quit are chewing gum, drinking water, or sucking on hard candy when they feel an urge to smoke, enlisting support people to distract them, exercising, and avoiding smoking areas.

Most teenagers try to quit many times on their own before seeking help from parents, teachers, or school nurses. Asking children how long they went without a cigarette will help them realize that they are capable of quitting and that past methods have helped. Have them identify events or situations that lead them to smoke so that these situations can be avoided in the future. Recommend that adolescents purge their environment—home, car, locker, and book bag—of tobacco-related products such as ashtrays, lighters, and cigarettes. Lastly, advise them to quit for good, reminding them that it takes just 1 puff to start a relapse. Smoking cessation medications such as the nicotine patch have not been tested adequately on children and may be appropriate only for certain individuals. See **Table 4-8** for a list of these medications, most of which are available over the counter and may be covered by insurance. Talk to children's doctors before using any of these products, and be aware that candidates for nicotine replacement therapy should always receive the behavioral guidance mentioned above as well.

WHEN KIDS DON'T WANT TO QUIT

What if a child says that he or she does not want to quit using tobacco? Although this is not the answer concerned adults want to hear, it is important to realize that no one can force another person to change. Quitting is a personal decision. Parents can help by letting their children know that they still care for them, but that they do not approve of their behavior. Setting rules such as no smoking in the house or car can be helpful. Contracts that prohibit spending allowance money on cigarettes or spit tobacco can also be effective. Acknowledge children's desire to smoke, and help them find ways to address this desire without smoking cigarettes or using spit tobacco. Lastly, expect some resistance—parents and caregivers should try not to let children's attitudes about quitting upset them to the point of arguing. **Table 4-9** summarizes important points for parents to remember when trying to help children who smoke.

WHAT TEACHERS AND NURSES CAN DO

Teachers, school nurses, and youth-group leaders are invaluable resources for tobacco prevention programs. Several curricula have been developed to teach "life skills" such as

Table 4-8. Smoking Cessation Aids

	How It Works	Precautions	How to Use It	How Long Does It Take to Work?
Nicotine patch	Nicotine is slowly absorbed through the skin over 16 or 24 hours, which helps decrease withdrawal symptoms	Pregnancy, cardiovascular disease	Attach a patch first in the morning.	10 minutes and lasts 16 or 24 hours
Nicotine gum	Nicotine is slowly absorbed through the skin inside the mouth	Pregnancy, cardiovascular disease	Bite into the gum until there is a bitter taste, then keep it inside the mouth between the lip and gum. When it loses its taste, bite on it again and repeat.	<5 minutes
Nicotine nasal spray	Nicotine is absorbed from the skin inside the nose	Pregnancy, cardiovascular disease	Tilt the head back slightly and allow one spray to enter each nostril. Do not sniff, swallow or inhale through the nose while administering the spray.	<5 minutes
Nicotine lozenge	Nicotine is absorbed from the skin inside the mouth	Pregnancy, cardiovascular disease		<5 minutes
Nicotine inhaler	Nicotine is absorbed from the skin inside the mouth	Pregnancy, cardiovascular disease	Puff frequently, up to 80 times from each cartridge.	<5 minutes
Bupropion (Zyban)	Affects places in the brain that control withdrawal symptoms	Seizure disorder, eating disorder	Set a quit date within 2 weeks of starting the pills.	<5 minutes

cigarette refusal tactics, alternative ways to cope with and solve problems, and how to interpret media messages. These techniques can reduce the number of children who start smoking. The Minnesota Smoking Prevention Program has all these components and is designed for children in the fourth through eighth grades. The American Lung Association also has a curriculum for smoking cessation for adolescents called N-O-T on Tobacco. Additionally, the CDC offers free smoking prevention materials and provides parents, educators, and youth group leaders with links to other useful Web sites, along with information on interpreting media messages and materials on the

---

Table 4-9. Dos and Don'ts of Intervening in Underage Tobacco Use

— Don't expect children and adolescents to overlook their parents' tobacco use. Keep this in mind when encouraging them to quit.

— Don't force children to quit. It must be their decision.

— Do give support and respond positively to all successes.

— Don't be condescending when discussing tobacco use with children.

— Don't be afraid to set rules that make it difficult for children to smoke or to restrict allowances and spending money.

— Do expect resistance to the efforts you make to encourage children to quit using tobacco.

---

logistics and benefits of quitting smoking. The American Heart Association and the American Lung Association offer fact sheets about tobacco and the dangers of smoking. Teachers and nurses are in ideal positions to teach these curricula and advocate tobacco use prevention, especially if they are nonsmokers or ex-smokers.

PROFESSIONAL STUDY AND CONTROVERSY

Researchers are actively studying various aspects of tobacco use. Areas of study relevant to children include how tobacco images in the media affect children's introduction to smoking; the effects of maternal smoking on infants' lungs and brains; the combination effects of in utero exposure of nicotine and other air pollutants on infant mortality, preterm births, and infant health; and the effects of ETS on children and how to protect them from it. This section will focus on studies of how parents and media influence children's decision to use tobacco. However, tobacco advertising and its effect on children is just one of the many issues of tobacco use being researched and debated. These issues need interested citizens to get involved, speak out, and make the environment healthy for our children.

PARENTAL DISAPPROVAL, PARENTING STYLE, AND MEDIA

Parental disapproval of smoking and parenting style can influence children's decisions on whether to start smoking. Madeline Sargent and James Dalton studied the effects of viewing smoking in movies on middle school students and their smoking initiation rates. Children who reported viewing movies with more smoking scenes were found to have higher rates of smoking initiation than children who watched movies with few or no smoking scenes. However, they also demonstrated that children in 4th to 11th grades were less likely to become established smokers if they felt that their parents strongly disapproved of smoking, regardless of their parents' smoking status. The effect was greatest if they felt that both parents disapproved.

Another study published in the *Journal of the National Cancer Institute* identified 2 influential factors associated with a greater likelihood of smoking by teenagers: having friends or family members who smoked and scoring highly on the Index of Receptivity to tobacco marketing. This 5-point index was based on the number of positive responses to tobacco survey questions on "recognition of advertising messages, having a favorite advertisement, naming a brand he/she might buy, owning a tobacco-related promotional item, and willingness to use a tobacco-related promotional item." Of the 2 factors, the adolescents who scored highly on the receptivity index were more likely to smoke than those who had friends or family members who smoked. On a related note, Drs. Alison Albers and Lois Biener, of the Boston University of Public Health and University of Massachusetts in Boston, respectively, have found that adolescents more receptive to tobacco marketing are more disengaged from school than their peers. Students who were more receptive to tobacco advertising and who believed they could quit at any time were more likely to progress from tobacco experimentation to becoming regular smokers. Although both media and parental disapproval are influences, it is still not clear which is stronger.

Parenting style also seems to modify the effectiveness of tobacco advertising on children. Dr. John Pierce and his colleagues from the Cancer Center at the University of California–San Diego looked at the effects of tobacco advertising and parenting style on 12- to 14-year-old adolescents who had never smoked. They assessed parenting styles and the children's receptivity to tobacco advertising and surveyed the children 3 years later to see which ones had started smoking. The researchers found that teenagers who had more authoritative parents were less likely to smoke than teenagers who had less authoritative parents. The teenagers with both authoritative parents and high receptivity to tobacco advertising were more likely to smoke than those who had authoritative parents and low receptivity to advertising. Pierce and colleagues concluded that tobacco industry advertising undermines a parent's ability to prevent their children from smoking.

Despite new laws prohibiting tobacco companies from advertising to teenagers, smoking appears more frequently in movies, and brand names are displayed. Anti-tobacco advertisements sponsored by the tobacco industry prominently display their company logos and are placed in retail and convenience stores, 2 venues frequented by youth. In a 1998 report titled "Beyond Prevention: Helping Teens Quit Smoking," the World Health Organization stated:

In many countries, cigarette advertising links smoking with being cool, taking risks, and growing up. At the same time, the tobacco industry insists that it does not want children to smoke. These statements have recently been backed up with campaigns, which are supposedly designed to discourage young people from smoking. But programs like "Tobacco: Helping Youth Say No" are not only slick public relations efforts designed to bolster industry credibility; they may actually encourage youth tobacco use. By leaving out the health dangers, ignoring addiction, and glamorizing smoking as an "adult custom," these campaigns reinforce the industry's advertising theme presenting smoking as a way for children to exert independence and be grown up.

The tobacco industry's anti-tobacco campaign advertisements legally appear on television, billboards, and radio and in print. They advertise the tobacco industries' names and Web sites, knowing full well that the Internet is a direct line to adolescents. The RJ Reynolds Web site has a section called Tobacco Issues in which it presents its business philosophy. The last item states:

We do not want children to smoke, not only because it is illegal to sell cigarettes to minors in every state, but also because of the health risks and because children lack the maturity of judgment to assess the risks.

The bottom line is for parents to voice disapproval, set house rules about tobacco use, and be vigilant of the sources of information children are exposed to on a daily basis.

FILTERING TOBACCO-RELATED MEDIA

Children can be exposed to tobacco industry information and promotions on the Internet. The ability of parents and caregivers to block the information on the Internet is limited. The Center for Media Education examined filtering and rating technologies for the Internet. Researchers found that a variety of technologies are available for parents, including stand-alone and server-based filters, filtered Internet service providers, filtered and restricted browsers for children, filtered and child-friendly search engines, PICS (Platform for Internet Content Selection)-based rating systems, and monitoring software. They also determined that stand-alone filtering devices were not very effective. The best program was Surf Watch, which was able to block access to more than half of the tobacco and alcohol promotional sites. For more discussion on this topic, refer to the resource list at the end of the chapter.

CONCLUSION

Tobacco is a highly addictive substance and can cause serious health and behavioral effects for smokers and those around them, especially children. The key to minimizing or avoiding these effects is to keep children from smoking and away from ETS. Talking to children about tobacco, its effects, the difficulty of quitting, and the way tobacco is portrayed in media and advertising will help them make informed decisions. Parents need to make sure that children know why they disapprove. Media that glamorizes tobacco use may challenge parents' prevention efforts, and parents or caregivers who smoke and cannot or will not quit face even greater challenges. Public support of policies that make public areas such as restaurants smoke free and decrease tobacco advertising will reinforce parents, and caregivers' efforts at home.

WHERE TO TURN FOR HELP

ARTICLES

US Department of Health and Human Services (USDHHS). *You can Quit Smoking: Smoking Cessation and Consumer Guide*. Washington, DC: USDHHS, Public Health Service; 1996.

WEB SITES

American Heart Association

http://www.americanheart.org

American Lung Association

http://www.lungusa.org

Campaign for Tobacco-Free Kids

http://www.tobaccofreekids.org

Centers for Disease Control and Prevention

http://www.cdc.gov/tobacco/edumat.htm

— Provides educational programs, information, and links to other Web sites for parents, teachers, and youth group leaders.

— See specifically:

1. *Reducing Tobacco Use: A Report of the Surgeon General—Education Fact Sheet.* Washington, DC: US Dept of Health and Human Services, Centers for Disease Control and Prevention; 2001. Available at: http://www.cdc.gov/tobacco/sgr/sgr_2000/factsheets/factsheet_education.htm. Accessed June 8, 2006.

2. *Reducing Tobacco Use: A Report of the Surgeon General—Historical Fact Sheet.* Washington, DC: US Dept of Health and Human Services, Centers

for Disease Control and Prevention; 2001. Available at: http://www. cdc. gov/tobacco/sgr/sgr_2000/factsheets/factsheet_historical.htm. Accessed June 8, 2006.

Foundation for Smoke-Free America

http://www.notobacco.org

National Center for Chronic Disease Prevention and Health Promotion

http://www.cdc.gov/tobacco/how2quit.htm

— Provides smoking cessation resources

Office of the Surgeon General: Tobacco Cessation Guidelines, 2003

http://www.surgeongeneral.gov/tobacco/default.htm

— Provides links to resources and programs, available in both English and Spanish.

The Quit Smoking Company

http://www.Quitsmoking.com

— Provides products and information to aid smoking cessation.

Quitnet

http://www.quitnet.com

— Provides smoking cessation resources, tips, and support.

Smoke-Free Movies

http://www.smokefreemovies.ucsf.edu

— Provides information on locating movies that do not depict smoking.

Smoke Screeners

http://www.cdc.gov/tobacco/smokescreen.htm

— An educational program that helps teach media literacy skills to young people.

Chapter 5

INITIATION OF SEXUAL ACTIVITY

Robert S. McGregor, MD

Early initiation of sexual activity is of concern for the mental and physical well-being of our preteenagers and teenagers (and their parents). First, the good news: In recent years, the teenaged birth rate in the United States has decreased—by 22% between 2001 and 2003, according to data from the Alan Guttmacher Institute (AGI). The bad news is that our teenaged pregnancy rate is still twice that of Canada, 4 times that of France, and 5 times that of Germany. Over 900 000 teenaged girls become pregnant each year in the United States, but pregnancy is only 1 of many consequences of adolescent initiation of sexual activity. In addition to having the highest pregnancy rate among teenagers in developed countries, US adolescents also have the highest rates of abortion and sexually transmitted diseases (STDs).

Thirty-five percent of US girls become pregnant at least once by their 20th birthday. However, this statistic may be skewed, depending on the demographics of the study populations. One AGI study states that Hispanic girls are particularly at risk, with 3 of 5 becoming pregnant before reaching 20 years of age. However, the AGI also reports that the recent worldwide decrease in pregnancy rate reflects the increased motivation of youths to achieve higher levels of education and employment training; lifecourse goals beyond wanting to become a parent; the provision of comprehensive sex education, leading to youths' greater knowledge about contraception, more effective contraception use, and improved ability to negotiate contraception practice; and the greater social support for services related to both pregnancy and disease prevention among adolescents and young adults. Twenty-five percent of this decrease in pregnancy rate is related to an increase in abstinence practice, and 75% is related to behavioral changes of those teenagers who are already sexually experienced.

EFFECTS OF EARLY INITIATION OF SEXUAL ACTIVITY

Of all adolescent risk-taking behaviors, sexual activity is the most "natural." Sex hormones are the normal physiologic consequence of puberty, and sex drive follows suit. Sexual experimenting and the establishing of a sexual identity are an important part of normal adolescence. The main focus of this chapter is opposite-sex sexual activity. There is not much information about same-sex experimentation among preteenagers and adolescents. What is known is that many heterosexual teenagers experience same-sex experimentation, and many homosexual or bisexual teenagers experience opposite-sex experimentation. Both types of sexual experimentation should be considered normal, and it is important for both parents and teenagers not to label sexual orientation on the basis of an experimentation episode.

By the time they turn 15 years of age, one third of today's teenagers have had sexual intercourse, an increase from 5% in 1970. According to youth risk behavior surveillance data from the Centers for Disease Control, 62% of girls and 61% of boys report having had intercourse by the age of 18 years. Recent trends indicate that between 45% and 50% of 9th- through 12th-grade students have had sexual intercourse (**Figure 5-1**). Regardless of how common it becomes, early initiation of sexual activity should be considered "risky business." If preteenagers or teenagers younger than 15 years become sexually active, their health risks are similar to those of any sexually active adult, including pregnancy and STDs, but these risks may also be associated with increased feelings of guilt and shame and with damaged self-esteem. Damaged self-esteem is never timely, but when combined with all the other potential developmental risks of adolescence, it can be especially disruptive and problematic. Adolescent parenthood carries its own list of consequences. In addition, the likelihood of having multiple sexual partners is directly related to the age of onset of sexual activity: The earlier adolescents start sexual activities, the more lifetime partners they will often have. The more partners, the higher the risks—particularly, for girls and young women, there is an increased risk of cervical cancer.

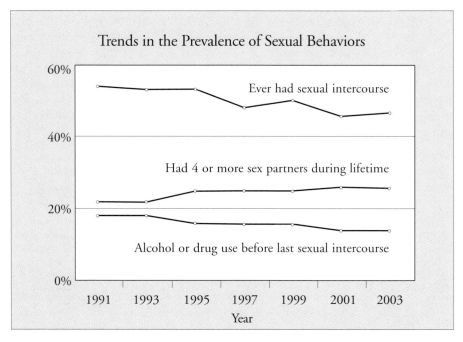

Figure 5-1. *Results of the National Youth Risk Behavior Survey from 1991 through 2003, as reported by the Centers for Disease Control, indicating the percentage of teenagers per year who have ever had sexual intercourse, teenagers who have had 4 or more sexual partners in their lives, and those who used alcohol or drugs before their last experience with sexual intercourse.*

ADOLESCENT VIEWS OF SEX

Some literature suggests that teenagers may be focusing more on the sex act than the concept of sexuality as an emotional, committed, or spiritual experience. The concept of "friends with benefits," or of having acquaintances with whom you "hook-up" in the absence of a traditional relationship like dating, is chronicled in a recent *New York Times* article titled "Friends, Friends With Benefits and the Benefits of the Local Mall" as being an exciting, sexually validating, sexually gratifying, efficient relationship that involves no responsibility. Just how prevalent these attitudes are among teenagers is tough to quantify; however, a study by the Manhattan Institute for Policy Research indicates that suburban teenagers are more likely to have had sex outside of a romantic relationship than their urban counterparts. Estimates are that 43% of US high school seniors have had sex outside of a traditional relationship. These numbers might have been even higher if the study had addressed oral sex.

The challenge of studying adolescent sexual activity is complicated by the lack of consensus as to what constitutes sexual activity. See **Table 5-1** for important terms related to sexual activity among adolescents. The spectrum of heterosexual sexual activity ranges from hand-holding and hugging to penile penetration of the vagina. The "in-between" activities are viewed differently by many populations. This is especially true of oral-genital contact. Reports are largely anecdotal and appear in the popular press, but estimates are that from 10% of middle schoolers to 55% of early high school students engage in oral sex; in one survey, more than 55% of teenagers aged 13 to 19 years say they have had oral sex. Twenty-four percent of self-proclaimed "virgins" admit to participating in oral sex. Many teenagers and preteenagers view oral sex as abstinence or non-sex because they maintain their "virginity" and do not risk pregnancy. An increasing number of adults view oral sex as consistent with abstinence behavior, and a smaller number of teenagers profess similar views with respect to anal intercourse. Two thirds of the 15- to 19-year old boys surveyed by authors of a 2000 *Family Planning Perspectives* article reported having experience with nonintercourse sexual behaviors such as oral sex, anal intercourse, or masturbation by a female partner. Even though not thought of by some respondents as sex, oral-genital contact is considered intimate by almost all surveyed and is not free of risks. Risks of oral-genital sex include multiple bacterial and viral STDs, including gonorrhea, syphilis, chlamydia, herpes simplex virus, hepatitis B, and human papillomavirus. In fact, many more of the recent isolates from genital herpes lesions implicate the type of herpes virus most commonly associated with oral cold sores (herpes simplex virus type I). Although oral sex and other noncoital behaviors are a significant part of adolescent sexuality, the existing research is focused almost exclusively on penile-vaginal intercourse. Therefore, most of the comments to follow in this chapter deal with limited heterosexual activities—specifically, penile-vaginal intercourse.

WHAT PARENTS AND CAREGIVERS CAN DO

Given the sexually charged environment to which US teenagers are exposed, including exposed and bejeweled navels and low-rise-style jeans, the increasing popularity of coed sleepovers, the sexual innuendos of commercial marketing (eg, naked models on the shopping bags and in the catalogs of popular clothing stores), and the graphic lyrics of many popular songs, can parents, educators, and other concerned adults have an effect on their teenagers' decisions? Through knowledge and frank communication, they certainly can.

AWARENESS

Similar to any other potential problem, it is necessary to be aware of the issue before trying to solve the problem. A University of Minnesota study of parental influence on adolescent sexual initiation tracked more than 3000 students in 8th through 11th grades. Parents were queried as to whether they thought their children were having intercourse. For those students who began having intercourse during the time in which this study was performed, more than 50% of the parents questioned incorrectly stated that their child was not sexually active.

PREVENTION

The literature reflecting noncoital sexual activities indicates an increasing prevalence of this behavior in the middle school population. The best way to delay initiation of sexual activities is to begin discussing parental views of risky behavior and expectations early. **Table 5-2** lists dos and don'ts for parents to remember when talking to their children about sex. Prevention or delay is the best strategy, but if teenagers have already engaged in sexual activity, ask them to clarify their reasons for experimenting. Many adolescent girls report that they do not want or enjoy sexual activity but think it is necessary to get or maintain the interest of a member of the opposite sex. The University of Minnesota study mentioned above looked at decreasing risk-taking behaviors by simply coaching mothers to communicate openly with their teenagers regarding any specific issue. What was found is that even with no reference to sexual activities or delay thereof, the communication group was far less likely to engage in sexual intercourse than the control group. So parents should open the lines of communication early (before middle school)—and keep talking! **Table 5-3** lists some questions and answers that parents and caregivers commonly have about the initiation of sexual activity.

Table 5-1. Important Terms

Premature sexual activity. Penile-vaginal intercourse before the age of 15 years. This is the definition currently used by researchers, but keep in mind that with the increasing incidence of noncoital experimentation in middle school, perhaps the definition should expand to include all noncoital oral-genital-anal contact before the age of 15 years.

Abstinence. Refraining from having vaginal sexual intercourse. It is not uniformly agreed upon whether other sexual behaviors such as oral sex, anal intercourse, and mutual masturbation are considered abstinent behavior.

Secondary abstinence. Refraining from vaginal intercourse for some defined period of time, usually until marriage or becoming involved in a serious, committed relationship, after having had a period of sexual activity.

Youth development programs. Programs that foster independent decision-making among youths and promote communication and connectedness between youth and their families and schools.

Coed sleepovers. A recent phenomenon in which preteenagers or teenagers have a sleepover involving members of the opposite sex, with or without parental knowledge.

Hooking-up. An imprecise term that refers to activities ranging from open-mouth kissing to girls performing oral sex on boys to penile-vaginal intercourse (often used reflecting the nonrelationship sex described in the introductory text above).

Friends with benefits. A phrase that implies casual sexual activity, oral-genital, penile-vaginal intercourse, or anal-genital sex, with someone outside of a romantic relationship.

Player. Typically refers to a male adolescent who has relations with multiple girls at a time or in rapid succession, somewhat akin to the old term "playboy."

Skank. Refers to a girl with a reputation for being promiscuous. Synonyms are slut and ho.

Being "together." Suggests casual dating or relationships.

Going out. Implies exclusivity in a relationship, similar to the old term "going steady."

Head. Slang reflecting fellatio, or oral sex.

Serial monogamy. A myth teenagers hold in which they believe they are indeed at lower risk for sexually related diseases because they have sex exclusively with one partner for some period of time until the relationship ends and they move on to the next exclusive (monogamous) relationship.

Table 5-2. Dos and Don'ts of Talking to Children About Sex

— Don't wait for a "big sex talk" to discuss sexual values and expectations; establish open communications about sexual issues well before children reach puberty.

— Do watch television with your teenager. Be aware of television and other media exposure to sex and use them to neutrally discuss sex-related values.

— Do openly discuss expectations regarding sexual activity, the consequences of adolescent parenthood, and contraception; clearly state your own sexual values and attitudes and explain the thought process behind your decisions.

— Do be a role model of responsible sexual behavior and promote self-esteem.

— Don't avoid talking about contraception for fear that you will promote sexual activity.

— Don't assume that if adolescents want to discuss contraception, they must be having sex.

— Do be a good listener and an approachable parent; try not to lecture or preach.

— Don't ridicule or disrespect adolescents for their sexual thoughts, beliefs, or experiences.

Table 5-3. Frequently Asked Questions

When should I have the "sex talk" with my child?

The "sex talk" is as dreaded by kids as it is by their parents. Make sexual issues an open topic of conversation beginning when sexually related questions are asked, regardless of your child's age. Watching television with your preteenager or teenager can provide plenty of opportunities to explore how your adolescent views sexually oriented subjects such as casual sex, serial monogamy, and teenaged pregnancy. This activity will give you a chance to explain your views and concerns about safer or less emotionally charged topics.

Can parents really influence their teenagers' decision-making regarding sex?

The answer is an unqualified yes. Studies show that parents are the single most influential force considered when adolescents contemplate initiating sex. Let your views on sexual topics be known without preaching. The most important role a parent can play is to establish a close bond early in the preteenager years and to continue to foster that "connectedness" throughout the teenage years.

Won't talking about contraception make my teenager more likely to have sex?

No. Studies show that teenagers whose parents spoke openly about contraception waited longer to start having sex, used contraception once they became sexually active, and ultimately had fewer sexual partners by the time they reached young adulthood when compared with peers who did not speak with their parents about contraception.

(continued)

Table 5-3. *(continued)*

What if my teenager doesn't like me when I say no or set limits?

It does not feel good, but get over it. Although teenagers might never tell their parents, they feel more secure and better grounded when behavior limits and curfews are in place and enforced. Making overly harsh or restrictive rules can backfire and promote rebellion, but setting no limits is a recipe for disaster.

Aren't after-school hours the time teenagers are most likely to have sex?

Surprisingly, no, despite the limited availability of many parents from 3 PM to 6 PM. Most teenagers (42%) have their first sexual encounter between the hours of 10 PM and 7 AM, typically in their partner's home (29% for boys, 39% for girls). Supervision is, therefore, essential.

Can schools play a role in delaying sexual activity?

Yes. They can provide meaningful activities to promote connectedness between the student and the school community. Youth development programs geared toward owning responsibility for decision-making and promoting autonomy can help delay sexual activity.

Interestingly, although adults perceive peers as the ultimate influence for teenagers having sex, less than one third of teenagers surveyed identified peers as the number one influence. More than 50% of teenagers surveyed by the Commonwealth Fund identified parents as being the most dominant influence. The 2 most important deterring features for teenagers' sexual activity are the perception of a strong maternal-child relationship independent of sexual discussions and the perception that parents value education. Also proven is the need for supervision. A study published in the *Archives of Pediatric and Adolescent Medicine* by Dr. Richard Crosby and colleagues reported that in a city population, STDs were much more likely in teenagers who perceived that their parents did not know or care about their activities and locations. See **Table 5-4** for suggestions on discouraging early sexual activity.

Table 5-4. Dos and Don'ts of Discouraging Early Sexual Activity

— Do monitor activities and set reasonable curfews and restrictions early on.

— Do act consistently toward your teenager.

— Do make yourself present in your adolescent's life and know his or her friends and their families.

— Don't be afraid to ask about where your teenager goes with friends or what they do.

— Do discourage early, serious, exclusive dating and encourage group dating.

— Do discourage your teenager from dating partners more than 2 years older.

— Don't be timid about asking where, when, and with whom children have had sex if you know that they have had sex or if they tell you about sexual experiences.

— Don't try to be your adolescent's friend: Be a parent.

The school's role includes supplying multiple supervised activities available to appeal to all students. Teacher training in classroom management to assist in the creation of an environment for cooperative learning has been helpful to promote student connect-edness. General youth development programs that emphasize autonomy in decision-making also have been helpful in increasing social competency. Content-based sexual education has not proven to be as effective as one might think. Results of "abstinence-only" educational programs have especially been disappointing, despite the increased federal interest in such funding.

The other consideration should be to find a resource for promoting open discussion as to what having sex means to teenagers and which options to consider for future behavior. Resources for parents to consider include their clergy, private counselor, trusted teacher, or physician. Again, an adolescent medicine or family planning clinic may be a resource.

Finally, setting a good example is key. Parents, especially single parents, and other caregivers need to consider their own sexual behavior as a role model. Any parent involved in blatant sexual activity, ranging from serial monogamy to a multiple-partner or partner-swapping lifestyle, needs to reflect on what this behavior suggests or condones for his or her adolescent. Consider changing this lifestyle or increasing discretion.

IDENTIFICATION AND INTERVENTION

It is not easy to identify sexually active adolescents without signs such as pregnancy or the presence of an STD. A more practical strategy may be to identify those who may be at risk and to invest more efforts to support those individuals. Low self-esteem seems to be a common risk factor. Children from abusive families and academically struggling students may be at risk secondary to poorer self-esteem. Role models also play an important part; students with older siblings who are sexually active, especially if the sibling has already been pregnant or fathered a child, are at risk. Crosby and colleagues found that a teenager's perception of having little parental supervision has been associated with an increased STD incidence and presumably with increased sexual activity. This association may contribute to the finding that children of single parents appear to be at higher risk for early sexual activity. "Early bloomers," or adolescents who physically develop earlier than peers, seem to be at risk perhaps as a result of a physical and mental maturity mismatch and an increased vulnerability to approaches from older, physically mature members of the opposite sex. According to AGI studies, a large age difference between teenagers and their partners increases the likelihood of sexual activity. Thirteen percent of couples comprising youth 12 to 14 years of age, in which the partners are the same age, have intercourse. If 2 years separate the partners, the incidence is 26%, and if more than 3 years separate them, the incidence is 33%. Recognizing that it is easy to overgeneralize, some populations do stand out in epidemiology research. Culturally, as a group, young Hispanic women seem to be at higher risk for teenage pregnancy, but it is unclear whether this implies more sexual activity or less use of contraception.

Signs or symptoms that a child may be engaged in risky behavior are not specific for sexual risk taking. Some studies indicate that sexual risk taking occurs independent of other adolescent risk taking behaviors; however, drug and alcohol use are often associated with the initial sexual act and with increased sexual activity. Signs or symptoms associated with premature sexual activity are listed in **Table 5-5**. Such signs may suggest sexual exploration but just as likely represent acting out, testing limits, or trying out new identities. Withdrawal from existing peer groups should trigger the consideration that depression or other psychological problems may occur. These

Table 5-5. Signs Indicating Adolescent Sexual Activity

— The introduction of a new friend, especially one 2 or more years older

— Social withdrawal or a change in a child's usual social circle

— Tearfulness or mood swings

— Wearing provocative clothing or makeup

— Drug or alcohol use

changes should invoke a thoughtful discussion between a parent and child as to why the change occurred or what it signifies to the child. Popular culture related to youth and adolescent behavior is prone to trendy fads and fashion. Become aware of the most current fads by browsing through teen magazines and watching adolescents' favorite television shows with them. By staying in touch with teenagers' interests, parents may be privy to fads like "sex bracelets," which the media covered recently. Sex bracelets are inexpensive, brightly colored, flexible, plastic bracelets linked to color-coded sexual acts. Wearing one of these jelly bracelets can signal willingness to perform a certain sexual act, and they are sometimes used in games in which sexual favors are exchanged. However, there are no scientific surveys or studies supporting the notion that sex bracelets are being used by the youth culture, and the vast majority of those wearing jelly bracelets do not consider them sexual. Parenting Web sites and resources related to raising teenagers are good sources for keeping up with these fads as they develop; see also "Where to Turn for Help" at the end of the chapter.

If a teenager is identified as being sexually active, a supportive exploration of motivation and intent, along with pregnancy and STD protection strategies, is a good idea. The younger the teenager, the less likely the sexual activity was voluntary, the less likely the teenager used contraception, and the more likely he or she is to use it inconsistently in the near future. Many younger adolescents may not have wanted to initiate sexual activity and may be receptive to the concept of secondary abstinence, or "secondary virginity." This concept refers to a sexually experienced teenager deciding to stop having sex and abstaining from future sexual activity for some period of time. The idea of secondary virginity receives a lot of press and is attractive to parents, but little fact-based information is available to indicate whether it is effective in decreasing sexual activity or teenaged pregnancy.

Parents need to at least protect their child from unwanted consequences of premature sexual activity; namely pregnancy and STDs. With this in mind, resources could include the adolescent's primary health care provider or a reproductive health center. Many educationally-oriented medical centers have adolescent medicine specialists with expertise in dealing with adolescent sexual issues.

PROFESSIONAL STUDY AND CONTROVERSY
"ABSTINENCE ONLY" EDUCATION

Depending on the measurable outcomes used, "abstinence only" education has questionable efficacy. Limited studies exist as to whether this counseling decreases sexual activity, pregnancy, or STDs. Existing studies indicate that such a strategy is not effective, despite a federal mandate that 30% of funded research for reducing adolescent pregnancy be used for such an approach. Proponents for "abstinence only" strategies cite outcome measures such as number of attendees and parental acceptance to indicate that this is a successful strategy. Because of the polarized nature of the sexual education debate, there have been questions raised about these success measures as well as other approaches as well. More research focusing on meaningful outcomes should happen before further restricting spending of the limited dollars available for teenaged pregnancy prevention.

CONTRACEPTION COUNSELING

Although intuitively a message to youths about abstinence coupled with contraceptive information sounds mixed at best, data exist indicating that teenagers should be given more credit in understanding the link. When adolescents receive such combined counseling, they do delay sexual activity, and when they later do initiate sexual activity, they are much more likely to use contraception and prevent unplanned pregnancies as well as STD transmission. Information is imperative, and research indicates that teaching about sex does not promote sexual activity. Preteenagers and teenagers in today's society know that contraception exists. Some health professionals raise the concern that if parents and professionals focus solely on "abstinence only" education, they will appear to be communicating in an uninformed voice that may harm their creditability with adolescents and which, in the end, may confirm to youths that adults do not want to share the whole story with them. Studies emerging from organizations such as the National Campaign to Prevent Teen Pregnancy are calling for balanced education that incorporates parental values as well as available information on responsibility, disease risk, and contraceptive options. The idea behind this approach is that it will provide credible information that adolescents and young adults will take seriously.

COED SLEEPOVERS

The last 5 to 10 years have witnessed many disagreements within popular literature as to whether coed sleepovers promote healthy ideas of equality between male and female adolescents and limit emphasis on looking good, with the added efforts of makeup and hair looking "just so," or whether they set up an unnecessary temptation or peer pressure-filled setting for preteenagers and teenagers to experiment sexually. Although adolescents want to be trusted, it is the authors' experience that many parents of sexually active teenagers wrongly predict that their children are inexperienced with vaginal sexual intercourse. No studies exist delineating the incidence of sexual experimentation at coed sleepovers, but many counselors and pediatricians have gone on record to state that these parties are not a good idea. Anecdotally, teenagers have stated that sexual experimentation does occur at such activities and that parental supervision is often lacking and inconsistent, to say the least.

CONCLUSION

Although we cannot make young peoples' decisions for them regarding sexual activity, high-quality relationships with responsible adults do matter. Communication is key, whether it is an open family dialogue or within a school community. Involved parents, caregivers, and teachers can make a difference. Evidence proves that teenagers want to know what their parents think and why. In multiple surveys, teenagers say they could more easily postpone initiation of sex after an open and frank discussion with a parent. However, what you do is as important as what you say. Set a good example, and youths will follow.

WHERE TO TURN FOR HELP

Alan Guttmacher Institute

http://www.guttmacher.org

Child Trends

http://www.childtrends.org

Henry J. Kaiser Family Foundation

http://www.kff.org

National Association of State Boards of Education: Safe and Healthy Schools Project

http://www.nasbe.org/healthyschools

National Campaign to Prevent Teen Pregnancy

http://www.teenpregnancy.org

ReCAPP: Resource Center for Adolescent Pregnancy Prevention

http://www.etr.org/recapp

Sex Bracelets

http://www.sex-bracelets.com

University of Minnesota Department of Pediatrics

http://www.allaboutkids.umn.edu

Chapter 6

PHYSICAL ABUSE AND NEGLECT

Angelo P. Giardino, MD, PhD, MPH
Laura E. Smals, MD

"What It Takes to Be a Mom or Dad"*

Read to your children. Keep your promises. Go for walks together. Let your children help with household projects. Spend time one-on-one with each child. Tell your children about your own childhood. Go to the zoo, museums, and ball games as a family. Set a good example. Use good manners. Help your children with their homework. Show your children lots of warmth and affection. Set clear, consistent limits. Consider how your decisions will affect your children. Listen to your children. Know your children's friends. Take your children to work. Open a savings account for college education. Resolve conflicts quickly. Take your children to your place of worship. Make a kite together. Fly a kite together. You get the idea.

Physical abuse is most generally defined as the form of child abuse seen when children sustain injury at the hands of caregivers—namely, parents, babysitters, teachers, or others who have responsibility for children. If someone not in a caregiving role injures a child, the injury is considered *physical assault*. Child abuse–related or child maltreatment–related injuries also are referred to as inflicted or nonaccidental injuries. More specifically, the methods for inflicting injuries seen in physical abuse include hitting with a hand, stick, strap, or other object; punching; kicking; shaking; throwing; burning; stabbing; or choking to the extent that it causes harm. Definitions of physical abuse focus on the presence of the injury rather than on the perceived intention of the caregiver; with regard to perpetrators of physical abuse, most do not initially intend to injure the child.

Neglect, in contrast, can be generally defined as the failure to meet a child's basic needs. Whereas physical abuse is defined as the presence of injury, neglect is better defined as risk that results from caregivers' carelessness or failure to meet a child's needs adequately. Children have basic needs that include food, warmth, clothing, shelter and protection, grooming and hygiene, activity and rest, prevention from illness and injury, continuous care, affection, security, sense of self-esteem, and an opportunity to learn.

SCOPE OF THE PROBLEM

Child abuse and neglect remain a big problem facing children and families to this day. Approximately 900 000 to 1 000 000 children are known to be maltreated each year in the United States, according to a report by the US Department of Health and Human Services Administration for Children and Families. About 25%, or about a quarter

---

*Adapted from What it Takes to be a Dad. *Printed with permission from the National Fatherhood Initiative, www.fatherhood.org.*

million, of these cases are identified as physical abuse, and about 50%, or half a million cases, are identified as cases of child neglect. **Figure 6-1** lists a breakdown of the rates of the various subtypes of child abuse and neglect, comparing the rates for the years 1998 through 2002.

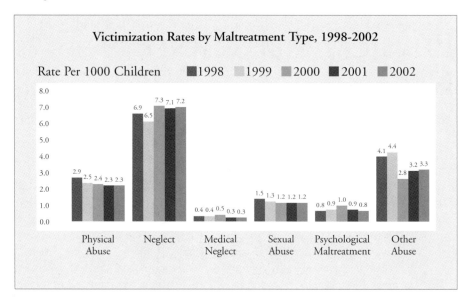

Figure 6-1. *Rates of physical abuse declined slightly from 1998 to 2002. Overall, more children experience neglect than any other form of maltreatment. Adapted and reprinted from* Child Maltreatment 2002: Summary of Key Findings *by the US Dept of Health and Human Services.*

Different forms of injury have different risks for the child's health and well-being. Bruises may be superficial or may indicate more serious deeper injury. A study by Dr. Carol Berkowitz found that in physical abuse cases, bruises are the most common injury, accounting for about 40% of cases. Bone fractures are seen in 30% of cases, and burns are involved in about 10% of cases. In child maltreatment cases, burns tend to be severe because of the loss of control and the frustration involved. Bone or skeletal injuries may be single or multiple in nature and may be associated with other serious injuries. Very serious injuries to internal organs and the brain are less common but are potentially life-threatening. These injuries are among the most lethal, especially for very young children and infants. Brain injury in younger children is particularly serious and more likely to result in a chronic disability and death than a similar injury in older children. According to Duhaime and colleagues, each year an estimated 1300, and probably closer to 2000, children are killed in the United States as a result of maltreatment.

Physical abuse affects children across all races, genders, ages, and income groups. No significant difference in the occurrence of physical abuse is noted in studies of victims by racial background; though boys are at higher risk for serious injury. With regard to age, the occurrence of physical abuse was highest for children aged 5 to 6 years, followed by those aged 12 to 14 years, and lowest in children younger than 2 years. However, this low occurrence rate for children younger than 2 years may reflect a detection problem, as children who are too young to attend school are less observable to community professionals. Children younger than 2 years of age are most at risk for serious and lethal physical abuse.

A special population of children that must be considered when discussing child abuse and neglect comprises those with special health care needs. These include children with disabilities (blind, deaf, wheelchair bound, or mentally retarded), chronic illnesses, developmental disorders, or emotional disorders. The increased health care needs of these children frequently add stress to the family structure. Such needs may represent a financial burden for the family and often limit flexibility for the caregivers with regard to babysitting, school placement, and even locations of vacations. Special needs children also are more difficult to discipline because of their cognitive and com-municative deficits. Some studies, such as *A Report on the Maltreatment of Children With Disabilities* by the National Center on Child Abuse and Neglect, have indicated that children with disabilities are 1.7 times more likely to be physically abused than children without disabilities (**Table 6-1**). Caregivers of these children must have a heightened awareness of the children's vulnerability to physical abuse and work carefully with families to provide respite, coping mechanisms for stressful times, and tools for effective discipline that does not involve corporal punishment.

Table 6-1. Risk of Abuse for Children With Special Needs

TYPE OF MALTREATMENT	FREQUENCY OF MALTREATMENT		RATIO*
	Children With Disabilities (per 1000)	Children Without Disabilities (per 1000)	
Any maltreatment	35.5	21.3	1.67
Physical abuse	9.4	4.5	2.09
Sexual abuse	3.5	2.0	1.75

Adapted and reprinted from A Report on the Maltreatment of Children With Disabilities *by The National Center on Child Abuse and Neglect Information. More up-to-date information may be available at http://nccanch.acf.hhs.gov/pubs/prevenres/focus/.*
*Rate at which children with disabilities are more likely to be maltreated than children without disabilities in a sample of 1000 children.

ORIGIN OF THE PROBLEM
RISK FACTORS
No single cause has been identified that explains the occurrence of all cases of physical abuse and neglect. The many factors associated with situations leading to physical abuse and neglect require an amalgam of models and conceptual frameworks to account for the heterogeneous set of cases classified as physical abuse. Circumstances that may give rise to the occurrence of physical abuse or inflicted injury can be organized into the categories highlighted in **Table 6-2**.

The human ecological model of development and interaction generally is regarded as an ideal conceptual framework that helps organize the complex interactions among the caregiver, child, family, social situation, and cultural values which lead to a child's inflicted injury or physical abuse. Although most people think of "ecological" as referring to trees, rivers, and climates, the human ecological model is applied to people and describes a child functioning within a family (microsystem), a family functioning within a community (exosystem), and various communities linked together by a set of sociocultural values that exerts an influence on them (macrosystem). These systems within systems interact and exert effects on each other (eg, the child interacts with and

Table 6-2. Situations That Can Lead to Physical Abuse

— A caregiver's angry and uncontrolled disciplinary response to a child's actual or perceived misconduct

— A caregiver's involvement in a domestic violence situation in which a child may become injured, either intentionally or unintentionally

— Leaving a child in the care of another caregiver who is physically abusive

— A caregiver's use of alcohol or drugs, causing a disinhibition that leads to abuse

— Psychological impairment of a caregiver that causes him or her to resent, reject, or perceive a child as different or provocative

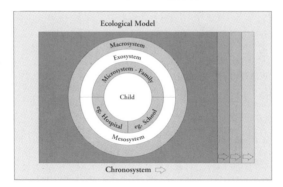

Figure 6-2. Schematic of the ecological model. Adapted from the work of Dr. Urie Bronfenbrenner.

has an effect on the family, the family influences the child, and the neighborhood has an effect on the family and child). See **Figure 6-2**, which graphically represents the systems-within-systems view of human ecology.

From this human ecological viewpoint, physical maltreatment may arise when a caregiver and a child interact around an event (such as a misbehavior or an accident) or in a given environment (eg, the family setting within the home), with the end result being the injury of the child (ie, child abuse occurs). Viewing maltreatment in this way allows one to consider the factors that parents or caregivers, children, and an environment contribute to creating a situation of risk. Parents and caregivers have personal developmental histories, unique personality styles, psychological functioning and coping strategies, expectations of a child, and a level of ability to nurture that child's development in a way that meets the child's developmental needs. A child may have a number of caregivers throughout the day or week. **Figure 6-3** identifies caregivers who perpetrated abuse or neglect in cases reported in 2002.

Children may have certain personal characteristics that make providing care more complex; however, caution must be used in considering a child's contribution to the abusive interactions because all children need and deserve safe, nurturing care, regardless of any characteristics that they may possess. According to a study by Dr. James Garbarino and colleagues, specific factors that may place a child at higher risk for physical abuse include prematurity, poor bonding with a caregiver, various special needs, and a caregiver's perception that a child is different or difficult, especially with regard to temperament.

Finally, the environment may contain stressors that may overextend the coping abilities of the caregiver (eg, losing a job, financial pressures around credit card bills, poor health). Not all stressed caregivers respond by inflicting harm on the children in the environment. However, some human beings have a capacity for violence, and if a

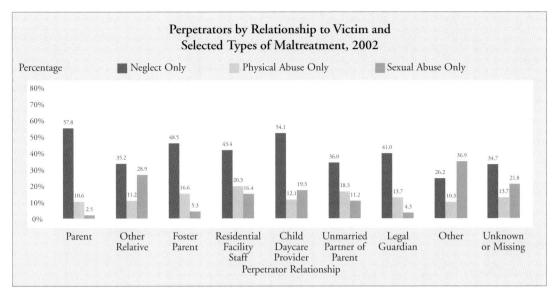

Figure 6-3. *Most parents who maltreat their children neglect them. Perpetrators of sexual abuse tend to be more distant relatives or "others," such as neighbors or family friends. Adapted and reprinted from* Child Maltreatment 2002: Summary of Key Findings *by the US Dept of Health and Human Services.*

specific home situation already has some form of violence within it—a parent spanking his or her children, or one parent pushing or slapping the other—then the environment is more likely to give rise to physical abuse if the amount of stress rises to a level beyond that with which parents or caregivers can effectively cope. Dr. Garbarino and Dr. Anne Crouter found that the level of social connectedness to relatives and nonrelatives is related to a child's risk for physical abuse. With family members nearby and ready to assist, stressed caregivers can get help navigating through difficult situations. In addition, caregivers under high degrees of stress who participate in clubs, unions, and other organizations are better able to ask for help from others and to get help to those who are socially isolated.

INTIMATE PARTNER VIOLENCE, CORPORAL PUNISHMENT, AND CHILD MALTREATMENT

The relationship between *intimate partner violence* (IPV), also called *domestic violence*, and child maltreatment is receiving increasing attention from a variety of professionals and governmental agencies. Statistics from the National Clearinghouse on Child Abuse and Neglect Information show that each year, 3 to 10 million children witness episodes of family violence, and 30% to 59% of mothers of abused children are victims of domestic violence. Dr. Sandra Graham-Bermann, a researcher and clinical psychologist, has found that children whose mothers are victims of intimate partner violence are 6 to 15 times more likely to be maltreated than children living in families in which the mothers are not being battered. Children may receive injuries either indirectly, such as by trying to protect the parent who is being hurt or becoming involved in an altercation between the adult caregivers, or directly. See Chapter 8, Intimate Partner Violence, for more information on how IPV affects children.

The relationship between the use of corporal punishment and maltreatment is also an area of concern that is now getting attention in professional literature. Corporal punishment is defined as a discipline method that uses physical force as a behavioral modifier. Corporal punishment in the United States is nearly universal—90% of US families have used spanking as a form of discipline at some time, according to the responses of primary care physicians to one survey on corporal punishment. Corporal punishment is rooted in personal, cultural, religious, and societal views of children and how they are to be disciplined. Forms of corporal punishment include pinching, spanking, paddling, shoving, slapping, shaking, hair pulling, choking, excessive exercise, confining children in closed spaces, and denying children access to a toilet.

No credible evidence exists in medical literature to support the use of corporal punishment. Spanking is no more effective at decreasing undesired behavior in children than consistently applied time-outs or removal of privileges. Appropriate discipline sets limits, teaches right from wrong, assists children in decision making, and helps children develop a sense of self-control. When physical force is used as a disciplinary technique, the concern is that a parent or caregiver may become angry and frustrated and reapply the physical force excessively if misconduct continues even after the discipline has been applied. In such a situation of escalating anger, the risk of parents or caregivers losing control and injuring the child is very real.

Caregivers who use corporal punishment often are angry, irritable, depressed, fatigued, and stressed. They apply the punishment at a time that they are at risk of losing control of their emotions, and they frequently express remorse and agitation while punishing their children. Approximately half of US pediatricians have reported being opposed generally to the use of corporal punishment; one third are completely opposed to its use. Three fourths of the pediatricians reported having been spanked when they were children. Many health care professionals advocate time-outs, loss of privileges, grounding, and expressions of parental disappointment as alternatives. See Chapter 17, Discipline and Corporal Punishment, for more information on time-outs and other methods of discipline.

Neglect

Neglect can also be understood in the framework of the human ecological model. Neglectful caregivers are typically seen as unable to access the basic family support systems in their family setting, neighborhood, or community. Although they are unable to meet children's basic needs for a variety of reasons, these caregivers are often seen as isolated and perceive their extended families, neighborhoods, and communities as more socially cold than do nonneglectful caregivers. What is not clear is whether this perception is a sort of self-fulfilling prophecy in which perceptions of social isolation lead to behavior patterns that cause caregivers to be further socially isolated—eg, their neighbors perceive them as unappreciative of help and stop offering it, only making the caregivers feel more isolated and less likely to ask for help.

Effects of Physical Abuse and Neglect

Physical abuse and neglect may affect children physically, psychologically, and emotionally. Immediate physical consequences vary depending on the type and severity of the injury; both immediate and long-term physical consequences are often obvious. Psychological and developmental effects may be less noticeable, more complex, and more difficult to comprehend. For example, if the abusive environment interferes with the achievement of an internal sense of safety and trust, children may, as a result, have difficulty attaining developmental tasks related to cooperation and interactive play. The anticipated negative effect of child maltreatment on a child's psychological functioning and developmental trajectory may be lessened by mediating factors that include the child's coping strategies and personality characteristics, supportive people in the child's environment, and the level of response the child perceives once the abuse or neglect is recognized. Typical negative consequences that may be seen in cases of physical abuse

---

Table 6-3. Consequences of Child Abuse and Neglect

GENERAL HEALTH

Immediate effects

— Bruises, burns, lacerations, broken bones

Longer-term effects

— Brain damage, hemorrhages, permanent disabilities

— Negative effects on physical development from physical trauma

BRAIN DEVELOPMENT

Reactions to persistent stress associated with child abuse and neglect

— Brain may strengthen the pathways among neurons that are involved in the fear response

— Brain may become "wired" to experience the world as hostile and uncaring

Inhibited development in certain regions

— Inactive regions wither away in situations of neglect because children lack exposure to stimuli that would strengthen cognitive pathways

— Regions responsible for regulating emotion may not function appropriately, leading children to exhibit impulsive behavior, lack empathy, or experience difficulty interacting with others in social situations

MENTAL AND EMOTIONAL HEALTH

Behavior effects

— General state may range from passivity and withdrawal to aggression

— Can include low self-esteem, depression, anxiety, and posttraumatic stress disorder

Effects on adolescent and adult survivors

— Depression, attachment disorder, poor peer relations

— Tendency toward overeating, smoking, alcohol or drug use

— Eating disorders, self-injurious behaviors (such as suicide attempts)

Data from A Coordinated Response to Child Abuse and Neglect: The Foundation for Practice *by Goldman et al and "Recognizing Child Abuse: What Parents Should Know" by Prevent Child Abuse America.*

and neglect include behavioral difficulties related to self-control such as aggression, violence, and juvenile delinquency; psychosocial and cognitive problems such as decreased academic and vocational achievement; and psychological disorders such as poor attachment formation, lack of empathy, and low self-esteem. **Table 6-3** lists some of the consequences abuse and neglect have for children.

Physical abuse and neglect can have profound effects on children's mental as well as physical well-being. A small number of children will have minimal mental health impairment resulting from abuse or neglect, the majority will experience a moderate effect, and a few will experience severe effects, such as posttraumatic stress disorder and dissociative syndromes, that significantly impair their mental well-being. Maltreated children who developed insecure attachments to caregivers may become more mistrustful of others and less ready to learn from adults. They also may experience difficulties understanding the emotions of others, regulating their own emotions, and forming and maintaining relationships with peers.

Psychologists and psychiatrists conceptualize the mental effect of child maltreatment in 3 phases. In the first phase, initial reactions to the abuse are seen and may include anxiety, stress reactions, alterations in developmental functioning (eg, regressing to an earlier stage), withdrawal, aggressive affect, and cognitive distortions. In the second phase, if the abuse is ongoing in nature, a type of "accommodation" of the ongoing abusive or neglectful environment is potentially visible, which may include forms of learned helplessness or minimization of the pain being experienced (both physical and emotional). Finally, the third phase involves what would be termed *long-term effects* that negatively affect functioning in future adult life and are related to relationship formation and the ability to work and achieve.

Whether children who are abused and neglected are more likely to become abusers themselves is a subject of concern. Dr. Cathy Widom's review of studies on violence illustrates that the evidence that has amassed over 2 decades of professional study clearly shows that the majority of children who are abused and neglected do not grow up to become delinquent, criminal, or violent. Although being exposed to a violent or neglectful environment is certainly a risk factor for the development of adult criminality and abusive parenting, it is certainly not an inevitable outcome. Only one quarter to one third of children exposed to child maltreatment go on to abuse their own children. Thus, the majority of the abused and neglected children are not predisposed to be abusers.

WHAT PARENTS AND CAREGIVERS CAN DO

PREVENTION

The Office on Child Abuse and Neglect issued *Emerging Practices in the Prevention of Child Abuse and Neglect* in 2003, which reviews various prevention efforts that have been undertaken over the years since society has confronted the abuse and neglect of children. This report describes the various programs that are currently underway to prevent maltreatment in today's society. The prevention approach is hinged on 3 components: public awareness activities, skills-based curricula of child-parent–focused programs, and educational group–type and support group–type formats.

The public awareness aspects to the prevention efforts attempt to reach diverse communities and focus on public service announcements, posters, information kits, and the production of documentaries. An example of a public awareness campaign aimed at preventing child maltreatment is "Don't Shake the Baby," which alerts professionals and the public about the dangers associated with shaking babies and provides information to parents on positive coping skills to use when caring for crying infants. Another campaign that shows how corporate partners can be invaluable is the collaboration between Prevent Child Abuse America and Marvel Comics, which produced Spider-Man comic books that address child sexual abuse and other safety issues related to children.

Schools and local community groups that teach children about safety and protection typically provide skills-based curricula. Most of the programs to date have been centered on preventing sexual abuse and teaching children to distinguish appropriate from inappropriate touch. See also Chapter 7, Sexual Abuse.

Parent-focused interventions fall into 2 categories: those primarily oriented toward education programs on parenting, which structurally have a curriculum directed at a target audience, and those that are more oriented toward a support group format and focus on strengthening family functioning. The parent education programs vary from a series of short-term classes that meet over several months to more intensive initiatives that meet frequently over a longer period of time. **Appendix 6-1** lists some of the more common parenting education initiatives.

The international network of accredited organizations that delivers free community-based Parents Anonymous® groups, which are lead by both a parent and a trained group leader, exemplifies parent support groups. These groups create a mutually supportive environment in which parents and caregivers may learn strategies to have long-lasting, positive effects on their families' functioning. The parent support group is complemented by a children's program that aims to help children develop positively via the Parents Anonymous® approach. The other well-known program is Circle of Parents, a parent/caregiver self-help support group sponsored by Prevent Child Abuse America and the National Family Support Roundtable, which sets out to help anyone in a parenting role have a place to discuss the positives and negatives involved with raising children, share mutual support among others experiencing the same successes and challenges, and learn coping and parenting skills. Other strategies that are supportive of family functioning include home visitation programs, respite care programs, and family resource centers. Each is described in **Appendix 6-1**.

Preventing the abuse of children is a major public health goal. The knowledge gained from the scholarly study of children and families dealing with child maltreatment is used to inform those who design and implement prevention programs. Dr. Howard Dubowitz reported in an article published in the journal *Child Abuse and Neglect* that for every dollar spent on effective child abuse prevention efforts, society saves several dollars over the long term when the overall costs associated with child abuse and neglect—the funds spent on health care, education, social services, law enforcement, the court system, and the adult prison system—are considered.

Prevent Child Abuse America challenges everyone to play a role in building strong communities that value children and families and that keep children safe from child abuse. This group promotes the "Five R's" of child abuse prevention, which are designed to assist all to better understand the role that individuals, both lay people and professionals, can play in keeping children safe, as shown in **Table 6-4**.

REPORTING PHYSICAL ABUSE AND NEGLECT

Cases of possible child abuse should be reported to the local child protective services (CPS) agency or police department. Professionals working in a specific community typically are aware of the various hotlines used for such reports. Other interested community members, however, may be less familiar with these resources, and to receive information on where to make a report, they are encouraged to call the National Child Abuse Hotline at 1-800-4-A-Child. The typical information that a person would be expected to provide when reporting a case of child maltreatment would include:

— The child's name and address, if known

— The suspected perpetrator's name and address, if known

— A description of the suspicion and what may have been seen or heard

— Other details such as additional people who may have relevant information related to the possible abuse

— Name and phone number of the reporting person, if the report is not anonymous

---

Table 6-4. Five R's of Child Abuse Prevention

— **R**aise the issue. Stay informed and encourage politicians, your school district, and your faith community to sponsor prevention efforts such as classes and support groups for families.

— **R**each out to children and families in the community. Support children and families by being a good neighbor, helping where you can by babysitting and donating resources such as clothing, furniture, and toys to those who need them, especially young families.

— **R**emember the risk factors. Child maltreatment crosses all groups in society, but certain risk factors are recognized as increasing the risk for the possibility that children might be harmed, such as if the parents

— Abuse alcohol, drugs, or other substances

— Are isolated from family and neighbor support

— Are angry and/or have poor coping strategies

— Appear uninterested in the child's care, eating, and safety

— Have serious economic, housing or other personal problems

— **R**ecognize the warning signs. Potential signs that may warn of possible child abuse are recognized when the child displays

— Excessive anxiety when around adults

— Aggressiveness toward others

— Restlessness, difficulty concentrating

— Sudden or dramatic changes in behavior

— Excessive interest for age in sex, or sexually acting out

— Unexplained or excessive bruising or other injuries

— Low self-esteem

— Poor hygiene, clothing inappropriate for climate, or undernutrition

— **R**eport suspected child abuse or neglect. See the Reporting Physical Abuse and Neglect section (on the Prevent Child Abuse America Web site) for further information

---

Data from "What You Can Do" by Prevent Child Abuse America. Available online.

All 50 states require professionals to alert authorities of suspicions of potential child abuse and neglect. Although child abuse and reporting laws vary from state to state, each state legislature defines mandated reporters as those professionals who by virtue of their work with children are obligated to make reports to the CPS agency and, in some cases, to law enforcement. Physicians, nurses, and teachers are consistently included in the list of mandated reporters. Items such as time parameters for reporting, the format of the report, and how and when to contact the police vary quite a bit from state to state; these details can be checked using the resource lists provided in **Appendix 6-2**.

Recognizing abuse and neglect in children is essential to offer help and for the appropriate authorities to be informed and take steps to protect them. **Table 6-5** suggests signs that may help concerned adults or professionals determine whether to take action on behalf of a child.

What Health Care and Other Professionals Can Do

Injured children require medical evaluation and care. The medical evaluation for physical abuse and neglect is fairly standardized and follows the typical health care evaluation format; namely, history or interview from child and caregiver, complete head-to-toe physical examination of the child, appropriate laboratory/diagnostic studies, consideration of diagnostic possibilities consistent with the findings in the case (the differential diagnosis), and the formulation of a diagnostic impression and treatment planning. Whenever a child is injured, a complete history of the circumstances surrounding the injury is essential. Typical questions are noted in **Table 6-6**.

Table 6-5. Signs of Physical Abuse or Neglect		
Signs of	Signs in	
	Child	**Parent or Caregiver**
Physical Abuse	— Has unexplained burns, bites, bruises, broken bones, or black eyes	— Offers conflicting, unconvincing, or no explanation for the child's injury
	— Has fading bruises or other marks noticeable after an absence from school	— Describes the child as evil or in another very negative way
	— Seems frightened of the parents and protests or cries when it is time to go home	— Uses harsh physical discipline with the child
	— Shrinks at the approach of adults	— Has a history of abuse as a child
	— Reports receiving injury from a parent or another adult caregiver	
Neglect	— Is frequently absent from school	— Appears to be indifferent to the child
	— Begs for or steals food or money	— Seems apathetic or depressed
	— Lacks needed medical or dental care, immunizations, or glasses	— Behaves irrationally or in a bizarre manner
	— Is consistently dirty and has severe body odor	— Is abusing alcohol or other drugs
	— Lacks sufficient clothing for the weather	
	— Abuses alcohol or other drugs	
	— States that there is no one at home to provide care	

(continued)

Table 6-5. *(continued)*

SIGNS OF	SIGNS IN	
	Child	**Parent or Caregiver**
Abuse or Neglect	— Shows sudden changes in behavior or school performance	— Shows little concern for the child
	— Has not received help for physical or medical problems brought to the parents' attention	— Denies the existence of (or blames the child for) problems in school or at home
	— Has learning problems (or difficulty concentrating) that cannot be attributed to specific physical or psychological causes	— Asks teachers or other caretakers to use harsh physical discipline if the child misbehaves
	— Is always watchful, as though preparing for something bad to happen	— Sees the child as entirely bad, worthless, or burdensome
	— Lacks adult supervision	— Demands a level of physical or academic performance the child cannot achieve
	— Is overly compliant, passive, or withdrawn	— Looks primarily to the child for care, attention, and satisfaction or emotional needs
	— Comes to school or other activities early, stays late, and does not want to go home	
	Parent and Child	
	— Rarely touch or look at each other	
	— Consider their relationship entirely negative	
	— State that they do not like each other	

Data from A Coordinated Response to Child Abuse and Neglect: The Foundation for Practice *by Goldman et al and* "Recognizing Child Abuse: What Parents Should Know" *by Prevent Child Abuse America.*

Indicators for possible neglect are at times less obvious than are those seen in a child with an obvious injury. Situations that raise the concern for possible neglect include: an excessively hungry child who reports not having eaten for an extended period of time; children who appear unkempt, with dirty, excessively soiled clothing or dirt in their skin creases; children wearing improper clothing for seasonal conditions; young children left alone without adult supervision; children left in the care of siblings who are young and in need of supervision themselves (even considering cultural variations in child supervision practices that are common among different ethnic groups); children shuttled excessively between related and unrelated caregivers who often do not know where the primary caregivers are for extended periods of time; children who go without necessary medical and mental health services; and children who fail to attend school and/or display a pattern of unexplained and excessive absences. **Table 6-7** lists histories that raise concerns for possible physical abuse or neglect.

Table 6-6. Questions to Ask When Evaluating an Injured Child
— What was the date and time of the injury, and when was it first noted?
— Where did the injury occur?
— Who witnessed the injury?
— What was happening before the injury?
— What did the child do after the injury?
— What did the caregiver do after the injury?
— How long after the injury did the caregiver wait until seeking care for the child?

PHYSICAL EXAMINATION

Physical examination findings that should raise suspicion for possible maltreatment include:

— Injury pattern inconsistent with the history provided.

— Multiple injuries/multiple types of injuries.

— Injuries at various stages of healing (**Figure 6-4**)

— Poor hygiene, clothing inappropriate for climate, and evidence of poor nutrition.

— Presence of very specific patterns of injury that are almost diagnostic of abuse if found (referred to as pathognomonic injuries), including loop marks (**Figure 6-5**), burn pattern from being forcibly immersed in hot water, and classic findings that may be seen in shaken baby injuries such as bleeding around the brain (subdural hematoma), bleeding in the back of the eye (retinal hemorrhage), and skeletal injuries such as rib fractures.

— Burn patterns that have geometric shapes and that may resemble an object used to burn the child (patterned burns); those that resemble the classic forced immersion burn pattern with sharp stocking and glove demarcations on the extremities (indicating a water line with little splashing) (**Figure 6-6**), and those with the sparing of flexed, "protected" areas (indicating a flexed, protective response to being held in a hot liquid); and those that have a splash/spill burn pattern not consistent with history or developmental level.

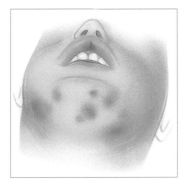

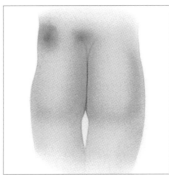

Figure 6-4. *Child with multiple bruises involving multiple surfaces in relatively inaccessible places, and in various stages of healing.*

Table 6-7. Child Histories That Suggest Abuse or Neglect

PHYSICAL ABUSE

— Details are inconsistent and change over time (evolving history).

— Caregivers give implausible details not congruent with the trauma observed on examination.

— Caregivers describe minor trauma, but the child displays major injury on examination.

— No history of trauma is offered (so-called magical injuries).

— Injury is said to be self-inflicted but is not compatible with the age or developmental abilities of the child.

— Caregivers demonstrate a significant delay in seeking treatment for the child (longer than most caring adults would consider reasonable).

— Serious injury is blamed on a younger sibling/playmate.

— Frequent changes in site of care have occurred; that is, the child has been to many different pediatricians or emergency rooms. This is referred to as "doctor shopping" and is done to elude suspicion.

NEGLECT

— Evidence indicates that basic needs are not being met (general appearance, signs of unmet needs, risks present in environment).

— The caregiving pattern suggests neglect (lack of adherence to routing health care recommendations, past episodes of neglect, previous CPS reports).

— Caregiver factors that may contribute to the neglect are apparent (ineffective coping strategies, sense of isolation, presence of domestic violence).

— Assessment of caregiver strengths and potential resources available to the family indicates a lack of parental interest in the child's well-being, family members who are ready and willing to help, and available community-based caregiver support programs.

— Previous interventions have been attempted. (What was helpful? What succeeded? What failed? Why?)

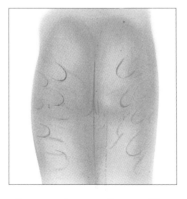

Figure 6-5. *Loop marks caused by whipping with an extension cord.*

— Cigarette burns, bilateral or mirror-image burns, and localized burns to genitals, buttocks, and the skin between the genitalia and anal area (especially at toilet-training stage) also indicate possible physical abuse.

— Evidence for excessive delay in seeking treatment, and the presence of other forms of injury.

— Bruising over prominent bony areas, such as the chin and shins, are common in childhood (**Figure 6-7-a**), but patterns of bruising that that involve multiple areas of the body beyond bony prominences (**Figure 6-7-b**), bruises at many stages of healing (**Figure 6-8-a** and **b**), bruises in nonwalking children, markings resembling objects or indicative of restraint (**Figure 6-9**), grab marks, slap marks, bilateral black eyes (**Figure 6-10**), human bites, and loop marks should all raise concerns about possible physical abuse.

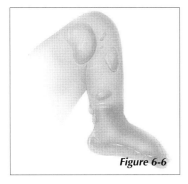

Figure 6-6

Figure 6-6. *Stocking immersion burn of the foot. The sole is spared because it was in contact with the bottom of the tub. There are also splash burns on the upper leg.*

Figure 6-7-a. *Areas where accidental injuries generally occur.*

Figure 6-7-b. *Areas where abusive injuries generally occur.*

Figure 6-8-a and **b.** *Injuries to the ear, both old (a) and recent (b), caused by a blow to the side of the face. When this type of injury heals without medical intervention, it leaves a distortion of the ear's cartilage often called "cauliflower ear."*

Figure 6-9. *Circular bruising of the wrist caused by restraints.*

Figure 6-10. *Bilateral black eyes, when there is no broken nose, must be caused by at least 2 blows and cannot be explained by a single incident.*

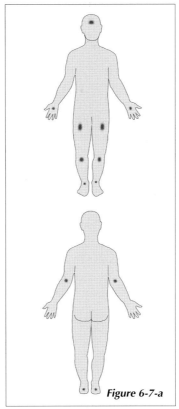

Figure 6-7-a

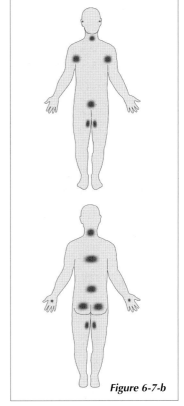

Figure 6-7-b

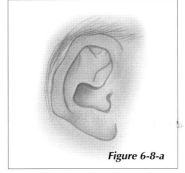

Figure 6-8-a

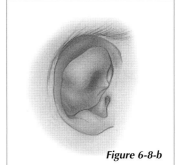

Figure 6-8-b

Figure 6-9

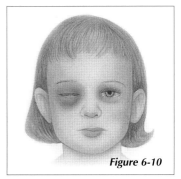

Figure 6-10

LABORATORY AND IMAGING STUDIES

The history and the physical findings determine which laboratory or diagnostic imaging studies are necessary to the diagnosis of physical abuse and neglect. Blood tests may be necessary to identify bleeding problems or a chemical ingestion, and serum tests may be ordered to determine the presence of liver, pancreas, or urinary tract injuries. Skeletal injuries in children younger than 2 years may not be obvious, so when physical abuse is a possibility, a standard set of X-rays that looks at each bone in a child's body, called a skeletal survey, is generally taken in order to rule out both new and old skeletal injuries. Depending on the history and physical examination, other diagnostic and imaging tests may be done, including a computed tomography (CT) scan of the head, which is necessary in any case suggestive of inflicted head trauma; a CT scan of the thorax and abdomen, which may be helpful to view the organs in the chest and abdomen if injury is probable; and a magnetic resonance imaging (MRI) scan, which can be a valuable adjunct to the head CT scan because it can further define an injury and identify different ages of blood contained in a subdural hematoma surrounding the brain.

INITIATION OF MEDICAL TREATMENT

Treatment for physical abuse is a complex endeavor involving an interdisciplinary team approach. The nature of the injury determines the form of medical therapy; the details of the caregiving environment determine the psychosocial supports needed to keep the child safe. For medical issues, skeletal fractures of the long bones may require casting. Burns vary in severity, and treatments range from cleansing the area to skin grafting. The most severely injured children may require resuscitation and will need intensive care. A number of specialists may need to be involved to correctly examine and treat these seriously ill children.

Interventions directed at neglectful caregiving need to be tailored to the capabilities of the caregiver, the needs of the child, and the available resources in the extended family, neighborhood, and community. Taking an approach that begins with any demonstrated strengths that the caregivers possess has the best chance for success because such an approach allows one to begin with something that is positive and constructive. Unfortunately, this is not always possible. In more difficult cases, in which very few strengths are present within the child's caregivers at the outset, close follow-up and a fair amount of support are required, provided that the child is felt to be safe from excessive risk to health and well-being. If substantial risks exist, CPS may need to intervene more forcefully to ensure that child's safety, well-being, and development remain the focus of any treatment plan, regardless of the caregivers' statements about their interest in meeting their child's needs.

MAKING THE DIAGNOSIS

Determining whether an injury was inflicted or accidental is extremely important in the evaluation of possible maltreatment and can significantly affect the well-being of the child and family. In addition, there are medical conditions whose symptoms may mimic signs of physical abuse. Mongolian spots, for example, can look like bruises, and a vitamin D deficiency can make a child's bones abnormally susceptible to breaks. Folk healing practices in some immigrant communities can also look like abuse. The process of working through this clinical reasoning is what is meant by forming a differential diagnosis, and in cases of possible inflicted injury is essential for the health care provider to consider all possibilities. By being thorough and considering both inflicted and noninflicted causes, one can be confident about the diagnostic impression and avoid inappropriately accusing parents and caregivers of abuse.

OTHER COMPONENTS OF RESPONDING TO POSSIBLE PHYSICAL ABUSE OR NEGLECT

Psychosocial management that requires a significant amount of coordination among various services providers, including the physician and other health care providers, complements medical management.

The CPS agency in each community is responsible for performing investigations following suspicion of physical abuse and relies on the physician to provide the details of the medical evaluation. In addition, CPS assesses the caregivers' background, caregiving abilities and potential, environmental safety, risk for repeat abuse, and risk to other siblings. A variety of treatment options are available, ranging from periodic contact with the child and family to removal of the child from the home, either temporarily or permanently, with termination of parental rights. The CPS process for child maltreatment cases typically involves the following steps:

— *Intake.* Screening of reports and acceptance of case.

— *Initial risk assessment.* Caregiver interviews, medical information gathering, home evaluation, and possibility of contact with law enforcement.

— *Case planning.* Determination of safety for the child with essentially 3 options:

1. The child goes home with the caregiver with or without services, depending on the circumstances.

2. The child is removed from home and family with caregivers' consent, and caregivers are offered services to assist them in working toward reunification.

3. The child is removed from the home and family without the caregiver's consent, involving court action and incorporation of legal steps and processes to determine the ultimate plan for the child.

Once a report of possible abuse or neglect is made by someone who is concerned, usually in the form of a call to the state or county hotline followed by some form of written documentation, the state's laws outline a timeline for subsequent evaluation. CPS screens the information, conducts an investigation, and provides supportive services for the child and family. Law enforcement may become involved, depending on the circumstances of the case. Under state statute, the people making the report in good faith may claim immunity from criminal and civil liability should an angry caregiver file a lawsuit against them for making the report even if, ultimately, it is determined that no maltreatment has occurred. For certain professionals, such as physicians, failure to make a report of possible abuse may result in them being held liable for failing to report the case under the state's laws.

PROFESSIONAL STUDY AND CONTROVERSY

CORPORAL PUNISHMENT

Caregiver reliance on corporal punishment is a risk factor for physical abuse. Despite this risk, corporal punishment remains a socially acceptable form of punishment; in a study of students in Washington State schools, over 90% of college students reported being spanked at least once in their childhoods and over 60% stated that the effects were helpful. Discipline is essential to child rearing. However, many national organizations have taken a strong stand that though discipline is essential to raising children, corporal punishment does not need to be part of that essential discipline process. At present, little in professional literature supports corporal punishment over consistently applied, nonphysical interventions. See also the "Professional Study and Controversy" section in Chapter 17, Discipline and Corporal Punishment.

CHILDREN APPEARING IN COURT

Child testimony in court proceedings is an area of special concern to child abuse professionals because the court represents a formal adult setting and handles often-contentious adult arguments. There are unique stresses that the courtroom may cause to children who are called to testify in court proceedings regarding their own maltreatment. Appearing in court creates anxiety in both adult and children, and no agreement exists about whether it is positive or negative for children to face their alleged abusers in the court setting. Children may be called to testify in court if they are developmentally able to relay and receive information accurately, know the difference between telling the truth and telling a lie, and understand the need to tell the truth in court. If a child is asked to testify, everyone working with the child needs to be aware of the high levels of anxiety that inevitably will arise and to assist the child and family in anticipating and planning around this effect. Some communities have developed "court schools" akin to the preoperative visit that some children's hospitals have implemented to address the anxiety of a surgical procedure. In the typical court school, professionals familiarize the child with the courtroom, the procedures that will be followed, and the roles of people who will be present and asking them questions.

CONCLUSION

Parents and caregivers have a responsibility to protect children from physical abuse and neglect. The most important steps are becoming educated about how to prevent abuse and recognizing the signs that a child may be in danger. There are a number or resources available to all members of the community to facilitate involvement in preventing abuse and neglect. These organizations present an opportunity to protect children from violence while preserving family ties and promoting children's well-being.

WHERE TO TURN FOR HELP

CHILD ABUSE

Childhelp USA

800-4-A-CHILD (800-422-4453)

http://www.childhelpusa.org

— Helps child abuse victims, parents, and concerned individuals.

Child Welfare Information Gateway (formerly The National Clearinghouse on Child Abuse and Neglect Information)

800-394-3366

http://www.childwelfare.gov

— Provides access to timely, essential information to help protect children and strengthen families.

Prevent Child Abuse America

http://www.preventchildabuse.org

— Works with chapters in 39 states and the District of Columbia to provide leadership to promote and implement prevention efforts at both the national and local levels.

— Holds many local programs, prevention initiatives, and events to help spread the word in communities, creating awareness that prevention is possible.

National Fatherhood Initiative

301-948-4325

http://www.fatherhood.org

— Provides helpful information to fathers on how to meet their parenting responsibilities in a manner that is sensitive to the developmental needs of their children.

Youth Crisis Hotline

800-HIT-HOME

— Helps individuals reporting child abuse and youth ages 12 to 18 years.

Family Violence
National Domestic Violence Hotline

800-799-SAFE (800-799-7233)

http://www.ndvh.org

— Helps children, parents, friends, and offenders.

Relief for Caregivers
National Respite Locator Service

http://www.respitelocator.org

— Helps parents, caregivers, and professionals at risk for abuse or neglect and those caring for children and adults with disabilities and terminal illnesses.

Victims of Crime
National Center for Victims of Crime

800-FYI-CALL or 800-211-7996 (TTY)

http://www.ncvc.org

— Helps individuals, families, and communities that suffer from crime.

Appendix 6-1: Educational and Support Resources Especially for Parents*

Appendix 6-1: Table 6-1. Education	
Parents as Teachers http://www.patnc.org	— A universal access model providing early childhood parent education and family support programs — Targets parents with children ages birth to 5 years — Comprises monthly, biweekly, or weekly personal visit and periodic developmental and health screenings — Missouri Department of Elementary and Secondary Education found that Parents as Teachers children are more advanced at age 3 years in certain areas than other children and that Parents as Teachers parents are more confident in their parenting skills and more involved in their children's schooling

(continued)

*Data from Emerging Practices in the Prevention of Child Abuse and Neglect by Thomas et al and "What Everyone Can Do to Prevent Child Abuse" by the US Dept of Health and Human Services Administration for Children and Families.

Appendix 6-1: Table 6-1. *(continued)*

National Parent Aide Network (NPAN) http://www.preventchildabuse.com/parent.htm	— Focuses on parents needing extra support, role modeling, and friendship
	— Supports a national network of parent aide programs while stimulating program development in communities not currently being served
	— Parents benefit by understanding the developmental needs of their children while learning how to manage their home environment more effectively
Meld http://www.meld.org	— Works to reduce family isolation by helping incorporate parents, including noncustodial fathers and immigrant parents, into the lives of their children and their communities
	— Serves all families, especially those parents at high risk for possible abuse or neglect
	— Parents with common needs meet with group facilitators over a 2-year period
	— Eighty-seven percent of participating teenaged mothers did not become pregnant again, 77% of age-appropriate participants were enrolled in middle or high school, and 100% of the parents of special-needs children indicated that their problem-solving skills had improved as a result of participation
Every Person Influences Children (EPIC) http://www.epicforchildren.org	— Helps to develop parenting skills, parent advocacy in education, and parent leadership in the community
	— Implemented in 16 states and the Virgin Islands, EPIC has 6 parent resource centers in New York State
	— Eighty percent of parent participants report improved relationships with their children, better communication with children's teachers, and reduced risk factors for abuse and neglect
Parents and Children Together (P.A.C.T.) http://www.pacthawaii.org	— Targets parents with young children
	— Parents and children participate in playtime, build family skills, and connect emotionally
	— P.A.C.T. encourages parents to focus on child development and communication; individualized programs have been instituted at some schools, bringing parents to the classroom and integrating learning with parenting

(continued)

Appendix 6-1: Table 6-1. *(continued)*	
Nurturing Program http://www.nuturingparenting.com	— Fifteen Nurturing Programs focus on specific populations — Programs are home or group based and range from 9 to 45 weeks for 1.5 to 3 hours per week — Programs, manuals, and activities are available for purchase on the Web site; many local communities offer free of subsidized Nurturing Programs

Appendix 6-1: Table 6-2. Support	
Parents Anonymous® http://wwwparentsanonymous.org	— An accredited international network that provides a mutually supportive environment in which parents can learn new parenting strategies — The Adult Group is available to any individual in a parenting role — The Children's Group is available to any child whose caregiver participates in a Adult Group; it is designed to respond to the needs of children with emotional, behavioral, educational, or physical challenges — Group meetings are weekly and free of charge — National research studies definitively confirm the effectiveness of Parents Anonymous in diminishing the effects of risk factors while dramatically increasing the resiliency of parents and children, thereby helping prevent child abuse and neglect
Circle of Parents http://www.circleofparents.org	— Aimed at anyone in a parenting role — Most established groups offer a free program for children — Provides parent self-help support groups in which the challenges of parenting can be discussed in an environment that offers a free exchange of ideas — Prevent Child Abuse America and the National Family Support Roundtable established network standards requiring weekly meetings

Appendix 6-1: Table 6-3. Home Visitation Programs

Nurse-Family Partnership http://www.nursefamilypartnership.org	— Targets low-income first-time mothers from pregnancy (ideally before the 20th week) through the child's first 2 years — Focuses on preventing unintended subsequent pregnancies, school drop out, failure to find work, and welfare dependence while strengthening parenting skills and increasing knowledge and self-confidence — Weekly, monthly, and bimonthly home visits from nurses are keyed to the developmental stages of pregnancy and early childhood — Program research shows 79% reduction in rates of child maltreatment among at-risk families from birth through the child's 15th year, 54% fewer arrests among the 15-year-old children of mothers enrolled in the program, and a 25% reduction in cigarette smoking during pregnancy among women who smoked a the time of registration
Healthy Families America (HFA) http://www.healthyfamiliesamerica.org	— Targets families facing multiple challenges such as single-parent status, low income, substance abuse, and abusive victimization — Services are initiated prenatally or at birth and are offered at least once per week and have well-defined criteria for increasing of decreasing frequency of service over a 3- to 5-year period — Modeled after Hawaii's Healthy Start Program
Early Head Start http://www.ehsnrc.org	— Aimed at low-income families; each program is responsible for determining its own eligibility criteria — Programs welcome and fully include children with disabilities and will support the child and family's full participation in community activities — Home visits are a component of community-based and integrated program promoting healthy child development and healthy family functioning — Early Head Start is an outgrowth of Head Start, which has a long history of providing services to infants and toddlers

(continued)

Appendix 6-1: Table 6-3. *(continued)*

Home Instruction for Parents of Preschool Youngsters (HIPPY) http://www.hippyusa.org	— Helps parents prepare their 3 to 5 year old for success in school
	— Home visits occur at least twice per month and must be at least 45 minutes long
	— Group meetings occur twice per month and are overseen by a coordinator
	— Studies on participants in the United States, Israel, Australia, Canada, New Zealand, the Netherlands, Turkey, and South Africa have shown improved school readiness, improved academic performance, and strengthened parent-child relationships
Parent Child Home Program (PCHP) http://www.parent-child.org	— Serves families with 2 and 3 year olds
	— Paraprofessionals visit homes twice per week for 2 years
	— Has 148 sties worldwide, encourages site replication, and conducts research
	— Research shows that 2 years after completing the program, participants' verbal responsiveness to their school-aged children correlated with how well children scored in reading, arithmetic, task orientation, social responsibility, self-confidence, and cognitive skill evaluation
	— A study of long-running PCHP replication found that low-income children who had completed the program graduated from high school at higher rates than similarly aged children who had not completed the program, and at rates equal to those of middle-class students
Hawaii's Healthy Start Program	— Aggressive outreach tartets children and families at high risk for abuse and neglect
	— Trained paraprofessionals visit families weekly for 6 to 12 months after the borth of a child and 1 to 2 times per month thereafter
Project 12-Ways http://www.p12eays.siu.edu	— Provides a comprehensive approach to abuse prevention, using an ecobehavioral model to teach parents new skills and to provide information on parenting safety and child development
	— Families are referred through local Department of Children and Family Services offices and must meet specific guidelines
	— Project counselors meet with each family 1 to 2 times per week
	— Has been helping families in rural Illinois since 1979 and has since been replicated in California and Oklahoma

APPENDIX 6-2: MANDATORY REPORTERS, STATUTES AT A GLANCE

MANDATORY REPORTERS OF CHILD ABUSE AND NEGLECT* (Current through June 2003)

State	PROFESSIONS THAT MUST REPORT					OTHERS WHO MUST REPORT			
	Health Care	Mental Health	Social Work	Education/ Childcare	Law Enforcement	All Persons	Other	Standard for Reporting	Privileged Communications
ALABAMA §26-14-3(a) §26-14-10	X	X	X	X	X		– Any other person called upon to give aid or assistance to any child	– Known or suspected	– Attorney/client
ALASKA §47.17.020(a) §47.17.023 §47.17.060	X	X	X	X	X		– Paid employees of domestic violence and sexual assault programs and drug and alcohol treatment facilities – Members of a child fatality review team or multidisciplinary child protection team – Commercial or private film or photography processors	– Have reasonable cause to suspect	– Not granted in statutes reviewed
ARIZONA §13-3620(A) §8-805(B)-(C)	X	X	X	X	X		– Parents – Anyone responsible for care or treatment of children – Clergy/Christian Science practitioners – Domestic violence victim advocates	– Have reasonable grounds to believe	– Clergy/penitent – Attorney/client
ARKANSAS §12-12-507(b)-(c) §12-12-518(b)(l)	X	X	X	X	X		– Prosecutors – Judges – Department of Human Services employees – Domestic violence shelter employees and volunteers – Foster parents – Court-appointed special advocates – Clergy/Christian Science practitioners	– Have reasonable cause to suspect – Have observed conditions which would reasonably result	
CALIFORNIA Penal Code §11166(a),(c) §11165.7(a)	X	X	X	X	X		– Firefighters – Animal Control Officers – Commercial film and photographic print processors – Clergy – Court appointed special advocates (CASAs)	– Have knowledge of or observe – Know or reasonably suspect	– Clergy/penitent

*Readers should not rely on this summary for legal advice.

National Clearinghouse on Child Abuse and Neglect Information, May 5, 2005

MANDATORY REPORTERS OF CHILD ABUSE AND NEGLECT*

(Current through June 2003)

State	Health Care	Mental Health	Social Work	Education/ Childcare	Law Enforcement	All Persons	Other	Standard for Reporting	Privileged Communications
	PROFESSIONS THAT MUST REPORT						OTHERS WHO MUST REPORT		
COLORADO § 19-3-304(1), (2), (2.5) § 19-3-311	X	X	X	X	X		– Christian Science practitioners – Veterinarians – Firefighters – Victim advocates – Commercial film and photographic print processors – Clergy	– Have reasonable cause to know or suspect – Have observed conditions which would reasonably result	– Clergy/penitent
CONNECTICUT § 17a-101(b) § 17a-101(a)	X	X	X	X	X		– Substance abuse counselors – Sexual assault counselors – Battered women's counselors – Clergy – Child advocates	– Have reasonable cause to suspect or believe	– Not addressed in statutes reviewed
DELAWARE Tit 16 § 903 Tit 16 § 909	X	X	X	X	X		– Not addressed in statutes reviewed	– Know or in good faith or suspect	– Attorney/client – Clergy/penitent
DISTRICT OF COLUMBIA § 4-1321.02(a),(b), (d) § 4-1321.05	X	X	X	X	X		– Not addressed in statutes reviewed	– Know or have reasonable cause to suspect	– Not granted in statutes reviewed
FLORIDA § 39.201(1) § 39.204	X	X	X	X	X	X	– Judges – Religious healers	– Know or have reasonable cause to suspect	– Attorney/client
GEORGIA § 19-7-5(c)(1), (g) § 16-12-100(c)	X	X	X	X	X		– Persons who produce visual or printed matter	– Have reasonable cause to believe	– Not granted in statutes reviewed
HAWAII § 350-1.1(a) § 350-5	X	X	X	X	X		– Employees of recreational or sports activities	– Have reason to believe	– Not granted in statutes reviewed
IDAHO § 16-1619(a), (c) § 16-1620	X	X	X	X	X	X	– Not addressed in statutes reviewed	– Have reason to believe – Have observed conditions which would reasonably result	– Clergy/penitent – Attorney/client

*Readers should not rely on this summary for legal advice.

National Clearinghouse on Child Abuse and Neglect Information, May 5, 2005

MANDATORY REPORTERS OF CHILD ABUSE AND NEGLECT* (Current through June 2003)

State	Health Care	Mental Health	Social Work	Education/ Childcare	Law Enforcement	All Persons	Other	Standard for Reporting	Privileged Communications
	PROFESSIONS THAT MUST REPORT					OTHERS WHO MUST REPORT			
ILLINOIS 325 ILCS§5/4	X	X	X	X	X		– Homemakers – Substance abuse treatment personnel – Christian Science practitioners – Funeral home directors – Commercial film and photographic print processors – Clergy	– Have reasonable cause to believe	– Clergy/penitent
INDIANA §31-33-5-1 §31-33-5-2 §31-32-11-1	X	X	X	X	X	X	– Staff member of any public or private institution, school facility, or agency	– Have reason to believe	– Not granted in statutes reviewed
IOWA §232.69(1)(a)-(b) §728.14(1)	X	X	X	X	X		– Commercial film and photographic print processors – Employees of substance abuse programs – Coaches	– Reasonably believe	– Not granted in statutes reviewed
KANSAS §38-1522(a), (b)	X	X	X	X	X		– Firefighters – Juvenile intake and assessment workers	– Have reason to suspect	– Not addressed in statutes reviewed
KENTUCKY §620.030(1), (2) §620.050(3)	X	X	X	X	X	X	– Not addressed in statutes reviewed	– Know or have reasonable cause to believe	– Attorney/client – Clergy/penitent
LOUISIANA Ch Code art: §603(13) §609(A)(1) §610(F)	X	X	X	X	X		– Commercial film or photographic print processors – Mediators	– Have cause to believe	– Clergy/penitent – Christian Science practitioner/penitent
MAINE Tit 22, § 4011-A(1) Tit 22 § 4015	X	X	X	X	X	X	– Guardians *ad litem* and CASAs – Fire inspectors – Commercial film processors – Homemakers – Humane agents – Clergy	– Know or have reasonable cause to suspect	– Clergy/penitent

*Readers should not rely on this summary for legal advice.

National Clearinghouse on Child Abuse and Neglect Information, May 5, 2005

MANDATORY REPORTERS OF CHILD ABUSE AND NEGLECT*

(Current through June 2003)

State	Professions That Must Report					All Persons	Others Who Must Report	Standard for Reporting	Privileged Communications
	Health Care	Mental Health	Social Work	Education/ Childcare	Law Enforcement		Other		
MARYLAND Family Law § 5-704(a) § 5-705(a)(1)	X	X	X	X	X	X	– Not addressed in statutes reviewed	– Have reason to believe	– Attorney/client – Clergy/penitent
MASSACHUSETTS Ch 119, § 51A Ch 119, § 51B	X	X	X	X	X		– Drug and alcoholism counselors – Probation and parole officers – Clerks/magistrates of district courts – Firefighters – Clergy/Christian Science practitioners	– Have reasonable cause to believe	– Clergy/penitent
MICHIGAN § 722.623 (1), (8) § 722.631	X	X	X	X	X		– Clergy	– Have reasonable cause to suspect	– Attorney/client – Clergy/penitent
MINNESOTA § 626.556 Subd 3(a), 8	X	X	X	X	X		– Not addressed in statutes reviewed	– Know or have reason to believe	– Clergy/penitent
MISSISSIPPI § 43-21-353(1)	X	X	X	X	X	X	– Attorneys – Ministers	– Have reasonable cause to suspect	– Not addressed in statutes reviewed
MISSOURI § 210.115(1) § 568.110 § 210.140	X	X	X	X	X		– Persons with responsibility for care of children – Christian Science practitioners – Probation/parole officers – Commercial film processors – Internet service providers (ISPs) – Clergy	– Have reasonable cause to suspect – Have observed conditions which would reasonably result	– Attorney/client – Clergy/penitent
MONTANA § 41-3-201(1)-(2), (4)	X	X	X	X	X		– Guardians *ad litem* – Clergy – Religious healers – Christian Science practitioners	– Know or have reasonable cause to suspect	– Clergy/penitent
NEBRASKA § 28-711(1) § 28-714	X	X	X	X		X	– Not addressed in statutes reviewed	– Have reasonable cause to believe – Have observed conditions which would reasonably result	– Not granted in statutes reviewed

*Readers should not rely on this summary for legal advice.

National Clearinghouse on Child Abuse and Neglect Information, May 5, 2005

MANDATORY REPORTERS OF CHILD ABUSE AND NEGLECT*

(Current through June 2003)

State	PROFESSIONS THAT MUST REPORT					OTHERS WHO MUST REPORT		Standard for Reporting	Privileged Communications
	Health Care	Mental Health	Social Work	Education/ Childcare	Law Enforcement	All Persons	Other		
NEVADA §432B.220(3), (5) §432B.250	X	X	X	X	X		– Religious healers – Clergy/Christian Science practitioners – Alcohol/drug abuse counselors – Probation officers – Attorneys – Youth shelter workers	– Know or have reason to believe	– Clergy/penitent – Attorney/client
NEW HAMPSHIRE §169-C:29 §169-C:32	X	X	X	X	X	X	– Christian Science practitioners – Clergy	– Have reason to suspect	– Attorney/client – *Clergy/penitent privilege denied*
NEW JERSEY §9:6-8.10	X					X	– Not addressed in statutes reviewed	– Have reasonable cause to believe	– Not addressed in statutes reviewed
NEW MEXICO §32A-4-3(A) §32A-4-5(A)	X		X	X	X	X	– Judges – Clergy	– Know or have reasonable suspicion	– Clergy/penitent
NEW YORK Soc Serv Law §413(1)	X	X	X	X	X		– Alcoholism/substance abuse counselors – District Attorneys – Christian Science practitioners	– Have reasonable cause to suspect	– Not addressed in statutes reviewed
NORTH CAROLINA §7B-301 §7B-310						X	– Any institution	– Have cause to suspect	– Attorney/client – *Clergy/penitent privilege denied*
NORTH DAKOTA §50-25.1-03 §50-25.1-10	X	X	X	X	X		– Clergy – Religious healers – Addiction counselors	– Have knowledge of or reasonable cause to suspect	– Clergy/penitent – Attorney/client
OHIO §2151,421(A)(1), (A)(2), (G)(1)(b)	X	X	X	X			– Attorneys – Religious healers – Agents of humane societies	– Know or suspect	– Attorney/client – Physician/patient
OKLAHOMA Tit 10, §7103(A)(1) Tit 10, §7104 Tit 10, §7113	X			X		X	– Commercial film and photographic print processors	– Have reason to believe	– Not granted in statutes reviewed

*Readers should not rely on this summary for legal advice.

National Clearinghouse on Child Abuse and Neglect Information, May 5, 2005

MANDATORY REPORTERS OF CHILD ABUSE AND NEGLECT*   (Current through June 2003)

| State | PROFESSIONS THAT MUST REPORT | | | | | OTHERS WHO MUST REPORT | | Standard for Reporting | Privileged Communications |
	Health Care	Mental Health	Social Work	Education/ Childcare	Law Enforcement	All Persons	Other		
OREGON §419B.005(3) §419B.010(1)	X	X	X	X	X		– Attorneys – Clergy – Firefighters – CASAs	– Have reasonable cause to believe	– Mental health/patient – Clergy/penitent – Attorney/client
PENNSYLVANIA 23pa §6311(a), (b)	X	X	X	X	X		– Funeral directors – Christian Science practitioners – Clergy	– Have reasonable cause to suspect	– Clergy/penitent
RHODE ISLAND §40-11-3(a) §40-11-6(a) §40-11-11	X					X	– Not addressed in statues reviewed	– Have reasonable cause to know or suspect	– Attorney/client – *Clergy/penitent privilege denied*
SOUTH CAROLINA §20-7-510(A) §20-7-550	X	X	X	X	X		– Judges – Funeral home directors and employees – Christian Science practitioners – Film processors – Religious healers – Substance abuse treatment staff – Computer technicians	– Have reason to believe	– Attorney/client – Clergy/penitent
SOUTH DAKOTA §26-8A-3 §28-8A-15	X	X	X	X	X		– Chemical dependency counselors – Religious healers – Parole or court services officers – Employees of domestic abuse shelters	– Have reasonable cause to suspect	– Not granted in statutes reviewed
TENNESSEE §37-1-403(a) §37-1-605(a) §37-1-411	X	X	X	X	X	X	– Judges – Neighbors – Relatives – Friends – Religious healers	– Knowledge of/ reasonably know – Have reasonable cause to suspect	– Not granted in statutes reviewed
TEXAS Family Code §261.101(a)-(c) §261.102	X	X	X	X		X	– Juvenile probation or detention officers – Employees of clinics that provide reproductive services	– Have cause to believe	– *Clergy/penitent privilege denied*

*Readers should not rely on this summary for legal advice.

National Clearinghouse on Child Abuse and Neglect Information, May 5, 2005

MANDATORY REPORTERS OF CHILD ABUSE AND NEGLECT*   (Current through June 2003)

State	PROFESSIONS THAT MUST REPORT					OTHERS WHO MUST REPORT		Standard for Reporting	Privileged Communications
	Health Care	Mental Health	Social Work	Education/ Childcare	Law Enforcement	All Persons	Other		
UTAH § 62A-4a-403(1)-(3) § 62A-4a-412(5)	X					X	– Not addressed in statutes reviewed	– Have reason to believe – Have observed conditions which would reasonably result	– Clergy/penitent
VERMONT Tit 33, § 4913(a), (f)-(h)	X	X	X	X	X		– Camp administrators and counselors – Probation officers – Clergy	– Have reasonable cause to believe	– Clergy/penitent
VIRGINIA § 63.2-1509(A) § 63.2-1519	X	X	X	X	X		– Mediators – Christian Science practitioners – Probation officers – CASAs	– Have reason to suspect	– Not granted in statutes reviewed
WASHINGTON § 26.44.030 (1), (2) § 26.44.060(3)	X	X	X	X	X		– Any adult with whom a child resides – Responsible living skills program staff	– Have reasonable cause to believe	– Not granted in statutes reviewed
WEST VIRGINIA § 49-6A-2 § 49-6A-7	X	X	X	X	X		– Clergy – Religious healers – Judges, family law masters or magistrates – Christian Science practitioners	– Reasonable cause to suspect – When believed – Have observed	– Attorney/client – *Clergy/penitent privilege denied*
WISCONSIN § 48.981(2), (2m)(c)-(e)	X	X	X	X	X		– Alcohol or drug abuse counselors – Mediators – Financial & employment planners – CASAs	– Have reasonable cause to suspect – Have reason to believe	– Not addressed in statutes reviewed
WYOMING § 14-3-205(a) § 14-3-210						X	– Not addressed in statutes reviewed	– Know or have reasonable cause to believe or suspect – Have observed conditions which would reasonably result	– Attorney/client – Physician/patient – Clergy/penitent

For a complete listing of individuals mandated to report suspected child maltreatment, see Department of Health and Human Services, Child Abuse and Neglect State Statute Compendium of Laws: Reporting Laws: Mandatory Reporters of Child Abuse and Neglect (2002).

National Clearinghouse on Child Abuse and Neglect Information, May 5, 2005

*Readers should not rely on this summary for legal advice.

Chapter 7

Sexual Abuse

Angelo P. Giardino, MD, PhD, MPH
Laura E. Smals, MD

Child sexual abuse refers to the involvement of children in sexual activities by an older or more powerful person who is in a caregiving role, such as a parent, relative, babysitter, teacher, or coach. It differs from *sexual assault* only in that the perpetrator of an assault is someone not in a caregiving role. According to a report by the US Department of Health and Human Services Administration for Children and Families, approximately 100 000 children are known to be sexually abused each year in the United States. Numerous surveys of adults agree that approximately 20% of women and 8% to 10% of men experienced some form of sexual abuse before reaching the age of 18 years. When the broadest noncontact forms of sexual abuse activities (eg, exhibitionism by the perpetrator) were removed from analyses, the estimates of adults who were sexually abused before the age of 18 years dropped to approximately 14% for women and 7% for men. Even these lower numbers are too high—one sexual abuse victim is one too many.

Other categories of sexual abuse include intrafamilial abuse and pedophilia. *Intrafamilial abuse*, sometimes referred to as *incest*, is sexual activity between individuals who are not permitted to marry, including steprelatives. In the cases involving stepfamilies, the presence or absence of blood relationship is not as important as the kinship role the abuser has in relation to the child. *Pedophilia* is defined as the preference of an adult for sexual contact with children. Pedophiles are typically skilled at ingratiating themselves with children and are likely to target the most vulnerable children in a given group for sexual contact. Vulnerable children are easier to manipulate and trick into keeping the inappropriate activity secret.

The sexual activities that occur in abuse or assault cases are imposed on the child and represent an abuse of the caregiver's power and trusted position. Because of their immaturity, children cannot give informed consent to sexual activities. *Rape*, which applies to both sexual abuse and assault, is a technical, legal term that refers to forced intercourse. Involvement of children in prostitution or in the production of pornography is a form of child sexual abuse frequently referred to as *child sexual exploitation*. The Internet, with its phenomenal ability to connect people, now poses a potential risk to children if used by those who would harm them.

Children with developmental disabilities or special needs are at increased risk for child sexual abuse. Research and clinical experience demonstrate that these children are nearly 2 times more likely to be sexually abused than children without physical or cognitive disabilities. Reasons include the fact that special-needs children frequently require more assistance with their physical needs, providing increased opportunity for abuse; they are often seen as vulnerable and therefore as easy, available targets; and they may have severe cognitive and linguistic impairments which interfere with their ability to communicate, leading the perpetrator to think that they are unlikely to be caught. Children living in residential facilities may not have a specific adult caregiver with whom they bond, making disclosure less likely. Children with special needs are at great risk for sexual abuse, and it is especially important to be aware of signs and symptoms of abuse in these children.

The Process of Grooming and Sexual Abuse

Certain preconditions are typically present in cases of child sexual abuse. First, perpetrators are motivated to act on impulses that stem from sexual arousal to children. Next, perpetrators overcome any internal and external barriers they face to sexually abusing a child. Internal barriers include conscience, superego, or feelings perpetrators have against sexually abusing children, and external barriers are those laws or social rules that exist to protect children—for example, school rules prohibiting adults from being alone with children in private locations. Perpetrators find ways to bypass the typical protections in the caregiving environment that normally serve to prevent the sexual misuse of children. Finally, they manipulate a child, overcome the child's resistance, and involve the child in inappropriate sexual activity. This manipulation typically relies upon the use of fear to control the child and keep the sexual activities secret.

An early study of sexual abuse by Dr. Suzanne Sgroi and colleagues identified several typical seduction patterns. First, perpetrators engage children in nonsexual activities. This engagement helps form a relationship with the child in which trust may be established. Perpetrators interact with children around activities such as games, hobbies, or other interests, or spend time talking with or listening to children. Once trust and confidence are established, perpetrators introduce sexual content into the relationship. The nature of this inappropriate sexual content tends to evolve over time, beginning with forms of noncontact activities and progressing to contact activities. Noncontact activities may include perpetrators exposing their genitalia to a child, inappropriate observations of a child's genitalia—when the child is dressing, using the toilet, bathing, and so forth—and allowing a child to view pornography. Contact activities typically become more invasive over time and may include sexualized kissing, fondling, masturbation, and various forms of genital or anal contact.

Dr. Sgroi's research has also illustrated that secrecy is always a component of child sexual abuse. Perpetrators maintain access to children by coercing them to keep the inappropriate activities secret. This coercion is either direct and explicit (eg, threatening the child or the child's family's safety) or indirect and implicit (eg, manipulating the child's trust in such a way that creates a fear of potentially losing the relationship or attention if the secret comes to light).

At some point, at least in the sexual abuse cases that are reported, disclosure to an outside party occurs. This disclosure can come about either accidentally, when the sexual abuse is suspected or witnessed leading to an evaluation, or it can be purposeful, when the child reaches out and tells someone that abuse is taking place. As one can imagine, a child and family's world is turned upside down once the abuse comes to light. The home environment may no longer be a supportive environment. Regretfully, the family and/or caregivers may even pressure children to retract the allegations so that the home situation will go back to the perceived normal, or stable, condition that it was in before the disclosure. Initial disclosures are retracted in some cases of sexual abuse.

Effects of Sexual Abuse

Sexual abuse may have both short-term and long-term effects on a child's health and well-being. These effects are variable, and no universal set of physical (medical) or behavioral (mental) health effects has been defined. Children's responses to sexual abuse are influenced by their innate coping abilities, the support they receive from family once the abuse becomes known, the types of sexual activities in which they were involved, and the nature of the relationship they had with the perpetrator. Long-term effects may not be obvious for many years. Some children seem to come out of the abuse relatively unscathed, while others suffer serious physical and mental health effects.

PHYSICAL EFFECTS

Medical effects related to child sexual abuse could include a number of medical conditions. As described by Dr. Carol Berkowitz, these effects can include:

— Abdominal or gastrointestinal disorders such as irritable bowel syndrome, heartburn, and chronic abdominal pain.

— Genital (gynecologic in girls) and anal disorders such as chronic pelvic pain, genital or anal tears, and sexually transmitted diseases.

— Pregnancy, in postpubertal girls.

— Various forms of somatization (physical symptoms existing without a correlating medical condition), including headaches and pain syndromes.

It is important to remember that children who are sexually abused will exhibit physical and medical effects much less frequently than they will behavioral effects. This is true in both the short and long term.

BEHAVIORAL AND MENTAL HEALTH EFFECTS

The possible psychological and behavioral health effects of child sexual abuse are, like the physical effects, variable. According to research by Dr. Lucy Berlinger and colleagues, possible mental health effects of child sexual abuse fall into 3 descriptive ranges of experience:

1. Severity, categorizing symptoms and conditions as mild to severe

2. Time course, describing effects as short-term to long-term, and sometimes even lifelong

3. Internal/external symptom patterns, which range from children who internalize feelings and respond to stress by withdrawing and becoming depressed to children who externalize feelings and respond to stress by becoming aggressive and disruptive

A child's sense of self-worth, development, and adjustment are all placed at risk by a perpetrator's actions, and the abuse can significantly alter the way a child develops and interacts with others.

Children who are sexually abused are usually exposed to a set of sexually traumatizing events. These incidents may shape what children learn about sexual behavior and may lead children to exhibit sexual preoccupation and repetitive sexual behavior. Developmentally inappropriate knowledge of sexual activity, often in extensive detail, is a hallmark of traumatic sexualization and can result in misconceptions of sex and healthy sexual relationships. Sexual abuse is also a betrayal. Children who recognize that a trusted individual has caused them harm, misrepresented moral standards, or failed to protect them properly may react to the loss of this trusted figure with strong grief or sadness. Disappointment and an ongoing desire for trusting relationships may place abused children in vulnerable positions in future relationships with peers and adults.

In addition, children often experience a sense of disempowerment when they realize that they have been coerced, manipulated, and physically violated by the perpetrator and the abusive behaviors and activities. Children may manifest symptoms of fear and anxiety and demonstrate impaired coping strategies as a result of feeling powerless. Symptoms associated with fear and anxiety may include nightmares, phobias, hypervigilance, clinging behavior, and various somatic complaints. Signs of impaired coping abilities are despair, depression, learning problems, running away, and difficulties in school activities or, if old enough to be employed, job performance.

Finally, the traumatic sexualization may also be associated with feelings of stigma, and children's self-images may be shaped by the negative words often used to describe the sexual abuse—bad, awful, shameful, or guilty. Children can feel isolated and respond by associating with other stigmatized individuals or groups or becoming involved with drugs, alcohol, or other criminal types of activity. Others may become depressed, attempt suicide, or engage in self-destructive behavior. Many victims of sexual abuse experience high degrees of guilt and shame and manifest low self-esteem. Other serious mental health disorders associated with child sexual abuse are listed in **Table 7-1**. Posttraumatic stress disorder and its relationship to sexual abuse are of special note because of the considerable attention they have received in the press. The diagnosis of posttraumatic stress disorder in the context of sexual abuse requires the following: the existence of abuse and reliving the abusive events via frequent intrusive thoughts or nightmares, avoidance behavior, a sense of numbness toward common events that may or may not be originally related to the actual abuse, and increased symptoms of anxiety, such as jumpiness, sleep disturbance, or poor concentration.

WHAT PARENTS AND CAREGIVERS CAN DO

RECOGNIZING PHYSICAL WARNING SIGNS

Specific physical findings related to sexual abuse are relatively uncommon and are found in the minority of cases. Identification of child sexual abuse is difficult because the majority of cases display only nonspecific behavioral changes that could be associated with other pediatric issues. However, physical evidence does occasionally exist, and those signs that should prompt a parent to bring a child in for a complete health care examination are listed in **Table 7-2**. When physical signs and symptoms are present, physicians, nurses, or other clinicians generate an extensive list of diagnostic possibilities, called differential diagnoses. They then progress through a careful "work-up" to eliminate diagnostic options and eventually arrive at a diagnosis. A number of medical conditions can mimic the physical evidence of sexual abuse.

Table 7-1. Mental Health Disorders Associated With Child Sexual Abuse

— Depression

— Eating disorders

— Anxiety disorders

— Substance abuse

— Somatization

— Posttraumatic stress disorder

— Dissociative disorders

— Psychosexual dysfunction in adulthood

— Interpersonal problems, including difficulties with issues of control, anger, shame, trust, dependency, and vulnerability

---

Table 7-2. Physical Signs of Sexual Abuse

— Genital or anal pain

— Genital or anal bleeding

— Genital or anal discharge

— Genital or anal redness

— Genital or anal bruising

— Genital or anal injury, such as tears

— Signs of sexually transmitted diseases

— Pregnancy

RECOGNIZING BEHAVIORAL WARNING SIGNS

Nonspecific behavioral complaints are commonly the initial or manifest symptoms that prompt consideration and evaluation of possible child sexual abuse. Because the behavioral signs of sexual abuse (**Table 7-3**) can be observed in other situations, these signs do not alone identify child sexual abuse but should warrant its consideration.

Not all sexually abused children exhibit increased sexualized behaviors, and it is important to remember that all children exhibit sexual behaviors at one time or another. Some behaviors are natural developmental events—children are curious beings. However, aggressive sexual behaviors and imitations of adult sexual behaviors tend to be relatively rare in children who have not been sexually abused. For example, Dr. Miller Heiman and colleagues found that among children aged 2 to 12 years, the most common sexual behaviors are interest in the opposite sex, watching people undressing, touching others' breasts, kissing children or adults who are not relatives, sitting with an exposed groin area, scratching their groin, undressing in front of others, and touching their genitalia in privacy. The study also reported that least common sexual behaviors among children in a similar age group included children putting their mouths on genitalia, asking to engage in sex acts, masturbating with objects,

Table 7-3. Behavioral Signs of Sexual Abuse
— Sexualized behaviors, especially if adult in character
— Phobias
— Sleep disturbances
— Poor school performance
— Running away
— Truancy
— External behaviors such as aggressiveness or acting out
— Internal behaviors such as symptoms of depression or withdrawal

inserting objects into their vagina/anus, imitating intercourse, imitating sexual sounds, French kissing, undressing other people, asking to watch explicit television, and imitating sexual behavior with dolls. Parents or caregivers of children exhibiting these behaviors should be reasonably concerned.

In an observational study by Dr. Frank Lindblad and colleagues of the sexual behaviors of preschoolers in Sweden aged 2 to 6 years, and in another study of English preschoolers by Dr. Davies and colleagues, behaviors that were observed in less than 1% of the children include touching an adult's genitals; attempting to make an adult touch the child's genitals; using objects against own or other child's genitals/anus; and masturbating obsessively, without pleasure or in a way that caused pain. Such behaviors may be considered red flags for parents and caregivers.

Research in the area of normal child sexual behaviors has identified consistent observations around the "sexual" content in children who have not been abused. Children are naturally curious about their own bodies as well as the bodies of those around them, but their exploration of their bodies and of those around them is usually limited to looking and noninvasive touching. As children grow older, they learn social mores, and observed sexual behaviors markedly decrease in frequency. Simulation of adultlike sexual actions and adult knowledge of a sexual nature are fairly uncommon among children, and children who have not been abused display significantly fewer sexual behaviors when compared to their abused peers. In fact, nonabused children typically do not have knowledge beyond what would be expected for a child at a given age and developmental level.

Although no single isolated behavior is evidence of sexual abuse, a pattern of behaviors, especially if adult in nature, or behaviors associated with sexual abuse along with a report of increased sexual behaviors should prompt a thorough sexual abuse evaluation.

Communicating With Children and Health Care Professionals

Open communication is essential. Any physical health symptoms need to be discussed and evaluated. Behavioral changes also require exploration, as does knowledge of detailed information about sexual behavior that is adult in nature, explicit demonstration of sexual play, compulsive masturbation or masturbation in public spaces, and excessive sexual curiosity for the age and developmental level of the child. Nonspecific behavioral changes that do not necessarily have sexual content also require consideration as well. **Table 7-4** contains a list of dos and don'ts for parents and caregivers to consider when trying to protect children from abuse or when responding to an abusive situation.

Why Sexual Abuse Can Go Unrecognized

Reasons why caregivers and professionals fail to recognize child sexual abuse are many and include taboos around the notion of adults sexually exploiting children, personal anxiety surrounding discussion of sexual topics in general, collective and personal denial that sexual victimization of children occurs at all, and relative lack of knowledge about the victimization of children. As openness in society around the discussion of sexually related topics increases, and as awareness and understanding of child sexual abuse continue to grow, professionals and the general public are developing ways to identify children who may have been sexually abused, evaluate them, and work with those who have in order to help them overcome the effects of such a traumatic experience. **Table 7-5** addresses questions parents frequently have about child sexual abuse.

Table 7-4. Dos and Don'ts of Preventing or Intervening in Child Sexual Abuse

— Do be attentive to children's normal behavior and investigate changes, especially if children are also complaining of physical discomfort of some type.

— Do know the adults and older children with whom a child spends time, especially if a child has special needs. Pay attention to how the child talks about these individuals and the role these relationships play in the child's life.

— Don't immediately react if a child exhibits sexual behavior. Some sexual behaviors are normal; take time to analyze the behavior and determine its origin.

— Do make the safety of abused children your first priority. Immediately remove them from the environment in which they were abused and the company of the perpetrator, regardless of who the perpetrator is.

— Do seek medical evaluations for children who may be or are victims of sexual abuse.

— Do support children who have been victimized and seek appropriate psychological therapy.

— Don't use adjectives that will make children feel guilty or stigmatized when talking about the abuse or the perpetrator.

— Do be aware that sexual abuse can have both long-term and short-term effects, and be patient with children as they heal.

Health Care Evaluation

In cases of possible sexual abuse, it is necessary for children to have a complete health care evaluation because there may be other causes for a child's physical and behavioral symptoms. The evaluation consists of 5 standard components that most parents will find familiar (**Table 7-6**). If the health care evaluation indicates that sexual abuse is a real possibility—not necessarily firmly diagnosed but highly possible—the pediatrician or nurse practitioner is required under state-mandated reporting laws to contact the local child protective services agency to file a report and initiate an investigation. The health care evaluation and the medical report will become a part of the investigation.

Table 7-5. Frequently Asked Questions

How does sexual abuse happen?

Typically, a set of conditions are present in which a perpetrator gains access to vulnerable children, overcomes any internal or external barriers that might protect children, and then engages children in nonsexual and finally sexual activities that become progressively more invasive. The child is typically coerced into keeping the sexual contact a secret through direct or indirect threats that sufficiently scared the child into keeping the secret.

If children display "sexual behaviors," are they being abused?

Not in all cases, but caregivers should be concerned and consider the possibility. Children are naturally curious about their own bodies as well as the bodies of others. So childlike or "curiosity-related" exploration of their own bodies and the bodies of similarly aged playmates is typically normal. However, if the behaviors have an aggressive or adultlike character to them, then this is cause for increased concern and should prompt an evaluation by a health care professional.

If the physical exam is normal, does that mean that sexual abuse did not occur?

A normal examination is expected in approximately 90% of examinations for alleged sexual abuse. It is common that these examinations, in actual cases of sexual abuse, will not have any specific findings and that the physical examination in a case of sexual abuse will be classified as "normal" or "nonspecific." Therefore, a normal examination without findings is more the expectation than not in actual cases of sexual abuse.

Is the child somehow responsible for luring the adult into sexual contact?

Children, by virtue of their development and age, are not able to "consent" to sexual activity. Therefore, the adults in the situation are responsible for any activity that occurs, not the children on whom this activity is imposed.

Table 7-6. Components of a Health Care Evaluation for Sexual Abuse

1. History	Obtained by interviewing children and/or caregivers
2. Head-to-toe physical examination	Includes inspection of external genital and anal structures (internal examination is rarely required)
3. Laboratory testing	Depends upon the time a child last had contact with the abuser
4. Preliminary diagnosis	Based on review of the history and symptoms
5. Final diagnosis	Based on review of laboratory test results and all information collected during the examination

HISTORY AND INTERVIEW

In cases of child sexual abuse, the history elicited during the interview with the child is typically the most valuable component of the medical evaluation because it is often the only diagnostic information uncovered. In addition, if performed in a sensitive and knowledgeable manner, the history-taking process can be a first step in the healing process for the sexually traumatized child.

During the initial meeting, physicians or nurse practitioners should introduce themselves and other members of the team who will work with a child. Caregivers who accompany children should be given the opportunity to privately describe their concerns, provide information about their child's health, and outline any information they have related to the possible abuse. Interviewing caregivers first, while children are in a separate room or play area, allows children some extra time to become more comfortable with the clinical setting. Clarifying the limits of confidentiality in cases suggestive of child sexual abuse is paramount to avoid feelings of betrayal later on if and when information is shared between the various agencies (eg, child protective services, police) that might become involved.

After caregivers are privately interviewed away from children, the health care provider, usually a pediatrician or nurse, begins interviewing children with unthreatening topics such as favorite activities, school subjects, and personal interests. The interviewer will use a sensitive approach and build on what he or she learned from the caregiver interview. Once a rapport has been established, interviews can then proceed to asking children why they have come to the pediatrician or nurse practitioner's office. Asking simply-worded, open-ended questions such as "can you tell me more?" followed by "and then what happened?" will allow an interviewer to progress through the standard what, when, where, and how questions, which are central to the medical evaluation for child sexual abuse. Skilled interviewers use a developmentally sensitive approach to the questioning in order to help children understand what is being asked and answer questions as accurately as possible. Using open-ended questions as much as possible permits children to relate information in a credible framework. Interviewers should support children for working hard to answer the questions but not, in order to maintain the credibility of the information elicited, for the content of the answers.

To make children more comfortable with the difficult task of speaking about sexual activities, interviewers will use the children's words for body parts. They also use drawings to help the children describe where they may have been touched and with what. After the interview concludes, caregivers can be invited back in the room to help facilitate the transition to the physical examination.

PHYSICAL EXAMINATION

In contrast to cases of sexual assault, victims of child sexual abuse will lack definitive signs of abuse in over 90% of examinations and so, according to research by Dr. Astrid Heger and colleagues, the physical examination will be normal or nonspecific in the overwhelming majority of actual cases. A number of reasons account for this lack of physical examination findings. First, children and their families typically know the perpetrators, and so the perpetrators—who want to avoid detection—will avoid using physical force strong enough to leave marks on their victims. Second, disclosure of the sexual abuse is frequently delayed, and evaluations may take place weeks to months after the abusive contact, when superficial injuries have healed. Finally, the genital structures are composed of mucous membranes similar to the tissue that lines the inside of our mouths, which heal rapidly and often without obvious scarring.

The general approach to the physical examination follows the standard techniques for a comprehensive head-to-toe physical examination. However, for cases suggestive of child sexual abuse, the examination will place particular emphasis on the genital and anal examination. Children should experience this more thorough inspection of their genital and anal anatomy only in the setting of a complete examination. In this way, children receive the message that their whole body and health are important and avoid experiencing any undue focus on their anal and genital areas.

LABORATORY TESTS AND FORENSICS

Child abuse victims may have contracted sexually transmitted diseases, as indicated by vaginal discharge, signs of vulvovaginitis, and characteristic lesions, such as the viral lesions observed in genital herpes or the warts indicating a human papilloma virus infection. Rapid tests are not appropriate for prepubertal children, especially in the context of a child sexual abuse evaluation, because they have a higher potential for false positive results. Culture tests remain the most accurate method of testing and the most valuable to law enforcement and legal personnel. Recommended tests may include cultures for gonorrhea, chlamydia, syphilis, and herpes, and a serology for HIV.

The collection of forensic evidence by means of a "rape kit" may be indicated if a child is taken for medical attention within 72 hours of the last sexual contact. The perpetrator may have left seminal products or other identifying material on the child's body, clothing, bed linens, or upholstery that can be tested for DNA. In the vast majority of cases, the disclosure occurs long after the 72-hour time frame, so forensic evidence collection would not be valuable in these cases. However, when possible, evidence that may be collected includes the following:

— Child's clothing that was worn at the time of the sexual contact

— Swabs for semen, sperm, and acid phosphatase

— Fingernail scrapings from underneath the child's nails

— Pubic hairs found on the child's body

— Debris found on the child

— Samples of the child's saliva and blood to determine blood type

— Bed linens or other fabric related to the abuse (collected in a paper bag to allow for drying)

The collection of forensic evidence and specimens for STD testing depends both on the symptoms of a specific case and are most useful soon after an abusive incident.

PROFESSIONAL STUDY AND CONTROVERSY

LACK OF PHYSICAL FINDINGS

The absence of physical findings during the physical examination goes against the conventional beliefs popular in the lay public that indicate that if sexual abuse has occurred, then physical findings should be found on examination. However, a growing number of reliable studies make it clear that the presence of specific physical findings is the exception, not the rule. Physical findings overall would be expected in less than 10% of sexual abuse cases, as indicated by the research by Heger and colleagues.

POTENTIAL FOR FALSE ALLEGATIONS DURING CUSTODY BATTLES

In custody battles between parents who are divorcing, false allegations of sexual abuse are sometimes made. Although it is true that contentious custody battles may create a charged environment in which a child could be coached to make a false allegation, it is also true that children whose custody is being challenged may in fact be victimized sexually. All allegations must be taken seriously and investigated fully so that cases are not missed and excused because of the possibility that a false allegation may be made.

NEED FOR COORDINATED INVESTIGATIONS

Repeated interviews of children who may have been sexually abused are of significant concern because children are forced to relive their story each time they tell it.

Professionals and lawmakers have voiced the need for a more coordinated response to sexual abuse allegations—a cooperative investigation that would require children to be interviewed only once. All professionals involved in the case would use this single interview. Child advocacy centers (sometimes called Children's Alliances) have emerged as a best-practice model for this type of investigative questioning.

Conclusion

Children are vulnerable to sexual abuse and assault, and they are usually victimized by adult caregivers or friends. Pay attention to how children relate to and talk about the adults in their lives, when they voice medical complaints that do not seem to have identifiable causes, or when they exhibit sexual behaviors that are unusual for their age. Sexual abuse and assault has serious short-term and long-term effects on children's social and psychological development, and victims need to have patience and support from their parents, caregivers, teachers, and health care providers while recovering. The best way to prevent child sexual abuse and assault is to recognize that such situations exist, know the adults in your children's lives and how the children regard them, and work to increase social awareness of the causes, signs, and effects of sexual abuse and assault.

Where to Turn for Help
Web Sites
Channing Bete Company

http://www.channing-bete.com

— Has produced readily accessible materials (primarily written) that communicate practical and targeted messages on a wide range of health and development issues for over half a century.

— Channing Bete Company and Prevent Child Abuse America have collaborated to produce booklets and workbooks that offer guidance to parents about how to prevent and recognize child sexual abuse.

— 6 recent titles are: *Basic Facts About Child Sexual Abuse; Internet Safety and Your Child—A Guide For Parents; Know What?® Your Body Is Yours!; My Body Belongs To Me; The Hidden Hurt—Child Sexual Abuse;* and *We Wonder®—Keeping My Body Safe!*

Child Welfare Information Gateway

http://www.childwelfare.gov

— Established to collect, organize, and disseminate information on all aspects of child maltreatment, family welfare, and adoption.

— Formerly the National Clearinghouse on Child Abuse and Neglect Information and the National Adoption Information Clearinghouse.

Comments: There is a wealth of highly credible and well-researched material on this Web site.

Pandora's Box

http://www.prevent-abuse-now.com

— Highly informative Web site maintained by child advocate and health care consultant Dr. Nancy Faulkner.

— Dr. Faulkner advocates for the protection of children and prevention of child sexual abuse, serves as National Board President of Safeguarding Our Children–United Mothers (SOC-UM), and is board member of P.A.R.E.N.T.

Comments: Web site is user-friendly and contains a wealth of parent-oriented material that deals with child abuse and neglect, and specifically with child sexual abuse.

Prevent Child Abuse America

http://www.preventchildabuse.org

— Has led the way in building awareness, providing education and inspiring the public in pursuing efforts to prevent the abuse and neglect of our nation's children.

— Works with chapters in 39 states and the District of Columbia, providing leadership to promote and implement prevention efforts at both the national and local levels. These chapters engage communities nationwide around prevention initiatives and events, spreading the word within the community that the prevention of child abuse and neglect is possible.

PREVENTION PROGRAMS
Child Sexual Abuse: A Solution™

http://www.stanfield.com/sexed-1.html

— Targets parents, teachers, and children separately.

— Includes six videos, starring Chester the Cat, and a comprehensive teacher's guide.

— Includes parents and teachers to create a consistent message and a larger network of support, which helps protect children better.

Circles II®

http://www.stanfield.com/sexed.html

— Addresses special needs students in a wide range of ages and functioning levels.

— Program comes with 3 videotapes, a wall graph, and a teacher's guide.

— Illustrates step-by-step strategies to recognize abusive behavior and teaches appropriate protective behaviors to use against unwanted advances.

— Circles II® is 1 part of a 3-part system teaching about intimacy, relationships, and AIDS and communicable disease prevention.

Good Touch/Bad Touch

http://www.goodtouchbadtouch.com

— Teaches children in preschool through sixth grade what abuse is and provides them with preventive tools.

— Kit provides age-appropriate lessons with a variety of aids.

— Empowers children to speak out against abusers, understand their own bodies better, and understand that abuse is never the victim's fault.

— The program is trademarked and accredited by the Georgia Department of Education and has been implemented in 34 other states.

Illusion Theater

http://www.illusiontheater.org

— Uses formal theater and a peer education format, where schools and other groups perform Illusion's educational plays, to address difficult and controversial social issues such as sexual abuse and violence prevention.

— Peer education sites receive scripts, training, direction, evaluation, and technical assistance from the theater's professional staff.

— Addresses issues to an audience of ages ranging from elementary school children to adults.

— TOUCH, the nationally acclaimed sexual abuse prevention play, was created in 1978. TOUCH pioneered the concept of education and prevention plays and led to the development of Illusion's education and outreach program.

Kids on the Block (KOTB)

http://www.kotb.com

— An educational puppet troupe offering programs on disabilities, differences, and social concerns, including sexual abuse and alternatives to violence.

— Teaches children how to speak up and, through plot and character biographies, provides an understanding that the victim is not at fault.

— Curriculum includes puppets, scripts, audiocassettes, answers to questions children ask, follow-up materials, resource suggestions, a training video and workbook, and continued KOTB support.

No-Go-Tell!™

http://www.stanfield.com/sexed-1.html

— A child protection program for children with special needs aged 3 to 7 years.

— Package includes 2 dolls and a unique system of teaching panels.

— Teaches children to distinguish between friends, family, and strangers and between good and bad touch; to identify what parts of the body are private; and who and how to tell about abuse.

Safe Child

http://www.safechild.org

— Teaches children in preschool to third grade that they have some control over what happens to them.

— Includes role-play to help children understand what it feels like to be assertive.

— Helps children to speak up effectively and in a way that is appropriate, using their own actions and feelings.

Talk About Touching

http://www.cfchildren.org/tat_detail.shtml

— Teaches about inappropriate touching through the context of personal safety and how to ask for help.

— Uses story and discussion, teacher modeling, and skill practice.

— Includes teacher training, parent involvement, and self-assessment tools.

— Program aligns with guidelines for personal safety programs established by the National Center for Missing & Exploited Children.

Chapter 8

INTIMATE PARTNER VIOLENCE

Eileen R. Giardino, RN, PhD, CRNP
Angelo P. Giardino, MD, PhD, MPH

Domestic violence between adult caregivers in the home seems to be the most toxic form of violence for children. Children are at risk as well when a parent or caregiver is abused. [*]

For many children, the first lessons about violence are from their parents, not from television or the streets. In households where violence occurs, the child learns early that it is acceptable to use threats or force to get one's way, that violence has a place in an intimate relationship, that adults can hurt one another and not apologize or take some responsibility for their actions. [†]

Intimate partner violence (IPV) is also referred to as *domestic violence*. It is the actual or threatened physical, sexual, psychological, or economic abuse of an individual by someone with whom they have or have had an intimate relationship. This includes spouses, ex-spouses, girlfriends, or boyfriends. Physical abuse is often preceded by emotional abuse. Although definitions of IPV vary within professional literature, the unifying concept in most credible definitions is the presence of physical, sexual, or emotional harm along with behaviors that intimidate, control, or dominate another person in a relationship. Other forms of aggression considered to be IPV include date rape, dating violence, and spousal abuse.

When sexual contact is involved in an interaction, the abuse may be referred to as sexual misconduct, sexual assault, or rape. The use of physical contact may include the terminology of battering—that is, wife-beating, wife-battering, spousal-battering, or partner-battering. Patterns of behaviors in IPV go beyond physical force to include situations such as verbal abuse, imprisonment, consistent humiliation, stalking, or denial of access to financial resources, shelter, and family or social contacts.

Forms of violence used to control another person include actions such as intimidation, instillation of fear and shame, and physical force. Perpetrators may also deliberately isolate partners from family and friends and prohibit victims from speaking out to others about the situation. This leaves the abused person without emotional or physical supports and resources.

In years past, violence within the house and family was often accepted as a private matter that those outside of the household were not to address. However, violence perpetrated within a family system is as illegal as violence that occurs on the street. No class, race, religion, or age group is exempt from IPV. According to a 2001 federal report titled *Intimate Partner Violence*, women are generally victims of IPV at a rate of about 5 times that of men (767 versus 146 per 100 000 persons, respectively). There are no specific characteristics, signs, or symptoms that identify all victims or perpetrators.

---

[*] *Straus and Gelles,* Physical Violence in American Families: Risk Factors in 8145 Families.
[†] *Groves,* Children Who See Too Much: Lessons From the Child Witness to Violence Project.

The most unlikely person is potentially a victim, and an apparently kind person may be an abuser.

Research on the occurrence of IPV shows that the longer a relationship continues, the more violent it becomes. There is an increasing frequency, duration, and intensity of physical, sexual, and emotional abuse. Factors within families that create situations in which IPV is more likely to occur include family members who are mentally challenged or physically ill, the birth of a child, substance use or abuse, separation, divorce, financial stress, and job loss. Legislation in each state provides the police and courts with procedures and sanctions to protect victims of IPV, but such laws vary widely, as do the resources and supports available to victims within a given community.

Table 8-1. Households That Experienced Intimate Partner Violence

Characteristic Household	Percentage of Households That Experienced IPV, 2000
Race/ethnicity	
Caucasian	0.4
African American	0.5
Hispanic	0.5
Other	0.5
Metro status	
Urban	0.5
Suburban	0.4
Rural	0.4
Region	
Northeast	0.3
Midwest	0.7
South	0.4
West	0.5
Household size	
1 person	0.4
2 to 3 persons	0.4
4 to 5 persons	0.5
6 or more persons	1.0

Data from Crime and the Nation's Households, 2000, *a Bureau of Justice Statistics bulletin.*

STATISTICS
ADULTS AND IPV

The US Department of Justice Bulletin *Crime and the Nation's Households* states that in the year 2000, about 1 in every 200 households experienced intimate partner violence. There is little variation in abuse rates among women when compared by education level, race or ethnicity, or geographic location. **Table 8-1** describes households in which violence has been committed by a current or former spouse, boyfriend, or girlfriend. Violence measured by the National Crime Victimization Survey (NCVS) used to make this report includes rape/sexual assault, robbery, and aggravated and simple assault.

Statistics from *Intimate Partner Violence* showed that women accounted for 85% of IPV victims while men accounted for about 15%. Women between the ages of 20 and 24 years showed the highest rate of victimization by an intimate partner (21 per 1000 women; 3 victimizations per 1000 men ages 25 to 34 years). This rate was about 8 times the peak rate for men. For both women and men, rates of violence by an intimate partner were below 3 victimizations per 1000 persons younger than 16 years or older than 50 years (see **Table 8-2**).

National Violence Against Women telephone surveyed a sample of 8000 women and 8000 men with the following results:

— Nearly 25% of women and 8% of men reported they were raped or physically assaulted by a current or former partner

— 1.5% of women and 0.9% of men reported being raped or physically assaulted by a partner in the previous 12 months (for an estimated total of 1.5 million women and 835 000 men)

— Almost 5% of surveyed women and 0.6% of surveyed men reported being stalked by an intimate partner (spouse, cohabiting partner, or date) at some time in their life.

Survey results demonstrated that both higher and lower socioeconomic communities experience levels of IPV. It is a myth that IPV does not exist in communities of higher socioeconomic status. However, women in households with lower annual household incomes did experience significantly higher rates of IPV than women in households with higher annual incomes. The victimization rate of women within the lowest annual household income range was nearly 7 times that of women living in households with the highest annual household income (20 versus 3 per 1000). This survey showed no discernible relationship between IPV against men and household income.

ADOLESCENTS AND IPV

Dating violence is particularly prevalent in high school and post high school and college years. A study published in the *Journal of Interpersonal Violence* estimated that dating violence among middle school and high school students ranges from 28% to 96%, and another study in the *Journal of the American Medical Association* stated that approximately 1 out of 5 female high school students reports being physically and/or sexually

Table 8-2. Intimate Partner Violence, by Age, 1993-1998

Rate of Nonlethal Intimate Partner Violence (per 1000 males and females)*

AGE OF VICTIMS	FEMALE VICTIMS	MALE VICTIMS
12-15	2.5	0.6
16-19	17.4	1.7
20-24	21.3	2.4
25-34	15.5	2.6
35-49	8.1	1.5
50-64	1.5	0.4
65 or older	0.2	—[†]

Reprinted from Intimate Partner Violence, *a report by the US Department of Justice.*
* Note: The difference between male and female intimate partner violence rates is significant at the 95% confidence interval for every age group.
† Based on 10 or fewer sample cases.

abused by a dating partner. According to the Commonwealth Fund Survey of the Health of Adolescent Girls, 8% of high school age girls responded "yes" when asked if a boyfriend or date ever forced sex against their will. Unfortunately, teenaged victims rarely ask others for help. The pervasive "boys being boys" mentality permits, and may promote, aggressive and coercive male behavior in a dating context. The causes of dating violence are complex, but each situation has an element of power and control that manifests itself as coercive behavior by the violent partner.

EFFECTS OF IPV ON CHILDREN

There is a strong relationship between the occurrence of IPV and child maltreatment, as statistics from the National Clearinghouse on Child Abuse and Neglect Information indicate a 30% to 60% overlap within families between violence against women and child abuse by the same perpetrator. In the 8145 familes Dr. Murray Straus and Dr. Richard Gelles studied, 50% of the men who repeatedly assaulted their wives also physically abused their children. Children who live in homes where violence occurs face the risk of observing disturbing events, being physically injured, and being neglected.

Approximately 43% of female victims of IPV live in households with children younger than 12 years, according to research by victim rights consultant Christine Edmunds and colleagues. Study findings indicate that between 3.3 and 10 million children annually witness some type of IPV. Children who witness IPV may be physically injured during the parental assault. Dr. Greg Parkinson, in one study, reported that children of abused women were 57 times more likely to be harmed because of IPV than children of nonabused mothers. This may happen in a variety of ways, such as being hit in the crossfire when attempting to protect the adult being harmed, being the primary target for violence by the perpetrator (child abuse), and being punished for transgressing a rule when caregivers are tense or irritated as a result of the violence.

EFFECTS OF WITNESSING ABUSE

Evidence indicates that witnessing IPV and abuse may be harmful to a child's emotional well-being. Children are more likely to exhibit behavioral and physical health problems such as anxiety, depression, and violence towards peers. The *American Journal of Orthopsychiatry* published a study of 160 preschool-aged children from low-income Michigan families that found that children exposed to violence in their family setting suffered symptoms of posttraumatic stress disorder (PTSD). Symptoms included nightmares and bed-wetting, and they were at greater risk than their peers of having asthma, allergies, headaches, gastrointestinal problems, and flu. This study also looked at differences between children aged 3 to 12 years who observed domestic violence (nonabused witness) and who had both observed and been a victim of domestic violence (abused witness). Findings showed a significantly greater distress (behavior problems, anxiety, and depressive symptoms) in the abused-witness children than in the comparison group, with non-abused-witness children falling between the 2 groups. Finally, Dr. Sandra Graham-Bermann's research on violence and PTSD indicates that children experiencing PTSD are 4 times more likely to have asthma and gastrointestinal problems than their peers.

Some think that infants and young children are too young to process IPV. However, young children can be overwhelmed by such exposure to violence, particularly because the child knows both the perpetrator and the victim. Betsy McAllister Groves wrote of lessons she learned through the Child Witness to Violence Project at the Boston Medical Center, commenting that dealing with violence seen on the streets is easier than facing the horrors of seeing what people who ostensibly love one another could do to each other in their homes. Yates and colleagues found that in the group of people they studied, behavior problems for boys in middle childhood were most strongly related to contemporaneous partner violence whereas behavior problems among both boys and girls at the age of 16 years were most strongly related to partner violence exposure during the preschool years. Furthermore, Straus and Gelles found that between 53% and 70% of men who assaulted their wives were also known to abuse their children and that men who witnessed IPV as children were twice as likely to be abusive in their adult relationships than those who did not. Therefore, it is important to protect the abused parent so that the parent can work to ensure the safety of the children.

WHAT PARENTS, CAREGIVERS, AND TEACHERS CAN DO

RECOGNIZING SIGNS OF DISTRESS IN CHILD WITNESSES OF IPV

The signs and symptoms of IPV vary depending on the child's age and developmental level (**Table 8-3**). Children younger than 5 years who have witnessed violence in their homes may exhibit separation anxiety, bed-wetting, sleep disturbances, or failure to thrive. Toddlers and young school-aged children may exhibit periods of increased restlessness and whining that sometimes culminate in crying, yelling, and temper tantrums. Children aged 6 to 12 years may show signs of manipulative behavior, fears of abandonment or loss of control, or eating problems. Also, children who have learned that using violence is a productive way to meet their needs may begin using violence in their everyday lives and engage in more delinquent types of behaviors. Adolescents who

---

Table 8-3. Possible Warning Signs of IPV, by Developmental Levels

BIRTH TO 5 YEARS	6 TO 12 YEARS	ADOLESCENTS
— Separation anxiety — Bed-wetting — Sleep disorders — Failing to thrive — Periods of increased restlessness — Whining — Crying, yelling — Temper tantrums	— Seductive or manipulative behavior — Fears of abandonment — Loss of control — Eating problems — Periods of increased restlessness — Whining — Crying, yelling — Temper tantrums	— Using violence — Engaging in delinquent behaviors — Abusing drugs or alcohol — Becoming pregnant — Thinking about suicide or homicide — Being anxious or withdrawn — Running away from home — Lying — Stealing — Engaging in truancy from school — Being sexually promiscuous — Attempting suicide — Committing sexual assault crimes

Data from "Effects of Domestic Violence on Children" by Margolin and Effects of Domestic Violence on Children and Adolescents: An Overview *by Volpe.*

---

live in a tumultuous environment may exhibit disruptive behaviors such as engaging in drug or alcohol abuse, sexual acting out, or thoughts of suicide or homicide. These children are more likely to be anxious or withdrawn, run away from home, lie, steal, and engage in activities such as truancy or promiscuity. Such behaviors can result in other deleterious consequences in the home and community. Negative behaviors often increase in intensity over time as the child continues to live in an environment that involves IPV. Children from violent homes often perform considerably below their peers in organized sports, school performance, and social activities.

RECOGNIZING SIGNS OF IPV IN ADOLESCENT DATING RELATIONSHIPS

The warning signs for dating violence among adolescents may include nonspecific behavioral signs. These may include sudden changes in clothing or makeup, avoiding friends, failing grades, dropping out of school activities, sudden changes in mood or personality, crying spells, or hysterical episodes. Physical signs of actual violence or battering may include unexplained or suspicious bruises, scratches, or other injuries. Parents and adolescents need to be able to recognize characteristics of potentially abusive partners (**Table 8-4**).

BARRIERS TO REPORTING IPV

Many factors discourage victims from reporting IPV. Victims may not desire to disclose the truth of abuse within an intimate relationship or family situation. They often want to avoid embarrassment and protect their own reputation as well as the

Table 8-4. Characteristics of a Potentially Violent Partner

— Wants to get serious quickly and will not take NO for an answer

— Often loses his or her temper

— Is possessive or jealous, wanting to choose the partner's friends and activities and to know where the partner is at all times

— Blames the victim: "You make me get so mad"

— Apologizes for outbursts, promising never to do it again

— Drinks, uses drugs, or shows violent tendencies outside the relationship

Table 8-5. Why IPV Victims Fail to Seek Help
— View IPV as a source of shame
— Are in denial about the IPV
— Concern that the abusive partner may become more violent, placing the victim or other family members at risk for further danger
— Fear that they will not be believed
— Economic or emotional ties to the abuser
— Feel a lack or control and believe that there is no way out of the situation

reputation and social standing of others involved. See **Table 8-5** for other reasons that people do not ask for help. **Table 8-6** provides answers to 2 questions people frequently ask about IPV.

There are barriers to reporting abuse that stem from the inadequacies of others. Some people are never asked if they experience abuse so therefore never disclose or discuss it. Studies, like the one Linn Parsons and colleagues performed of obstetrics and gynecology patients, have found that some health care providers do not believe their clients are affected by IPV and therefore do not ask about it. Other reasons health care providers do not ask questions include lack of formal training about abuse issues and fear of offending patients with uncomfortable questions. Some health care providers, according to the American Medi-cal Association report *Violence Against Women: Relevance for Medical Practitioners*, believe they lack the time to deal with the actions that they would need to take if IPV or abuse were revealed. These barriers can be addressed in professional and lay public educational programs, making it easier for those affected by IPV to ask for and receive help.

Table 8-6. Frequently Asked Questions
Why doesn't she just leave if he is hitting her?
Conventional beliefs are that it is easy for a victim in a IPV situation to remove oneself from the dangerous circumstances. Research has shown that leaving such a dangerous and dysfunctional relationship is anything but easy. First, there is a relationship with many emotional ties that require reflection and can affect the victim's emotional well-being, especially if children are involved. Second, economic factors may very well play an important part in the decision to leave. Alternatives may not exist or may be quite inadequate. Finally, in extreme cases with immigration issues, the abused partner may have no options short of being deported. Deciding to leave is less than easy.
During what times are people at highest risk for IPV?
Times of high stress for the perpetrator typically are seen as the most dangerous period. Women are at higher risk of abuse from partners during pregnancy; and pregnant teens appear to be at particularly high risk for IPV. Dating violence among adolescents reaches its peak during the first few weeks of a female college student's freshman year. This peak is thought to be associated with factors related to alcohol use on college campuses, lack of familiarity with the physical environment, and lack of an established network of friends who could assist with protection and safety. Another especially dangerous period for IPV is when the person being victimized attempts to end or leave the relationship. Crime statistics confirm that the highest risk for IPV to turn murderous is at the time of departure, and this is why appropriate safety planning is so essential.

What Communities Can Do

Community-based services and initiatives are focused on the strengths and needs of the entire family. They can provide a coordinated response to IPV and child abuse. The goals of most efforts are to provide safety planning and protect abused parents and their children from further injury or harm. Public awareness campaigns can also promote a vision for community involvement that takes what was once viewed as a private family matter and makes it a community concern and responsibility.

Communities need to understand the problems associated with IPV and provide the resources and tools to help people address their problems. Collaboration between community members, child abuse advocates, and IPV advocates can then help victims know what protective and psychological services are available to them. In order to effectively address IPV issues within a household, it is important that coordination exists between individuals and organizations that help families in crisis. Successful services and supports will develop coordination among child protective services, law enforcement, IPV advocates, and the courts to ensure the safety of the children and the integrity of the nonoffending caregiver's relationship with the children. Prioritizing victims over bureaucratic processes will encourage more to seek and accept help.

The Health Care Encounter: An Example of an Evolving Response to IPV and Child Maltreatment

Adult Settings

The identification of IPV begins with the health care provider asking questions about a client's relationships and home environment. It requires a consistent and direct approach to the issues every time a person is seen. Routine screening for IPV is the first line of defense for detecting abuse. Therefore, it is important to learn how to ask questions about interpersonal violence. Specific questions regarding IPV are becoming more widely accepted as part of the history-taking process. Uncovering additional information about a person's social situation may give additional clues on how to best assist adults and children who are at risk or who are being harmed.

Building a safe and trusting environment is important and can take place even in a short time period. It requires the basics of rapport building—showing an interest in the person, listening to his or her concerns, and creating an atmosphere of openness. Disclosure occurs more often when the interviewer asks questions face to face. The health care provider should ask difficult questions directly, taking care to remain nonjudgmental, empathetic, and nonthreatening to all responses and in all interactions. For example, if the woman is pregnant, making statements such as "Pregnancy can be a time of added stress to a relationship, and it is not uncommon for people to experience increased tension or abuse during this time. I will ask you questions about your physical and emotional well-being at each visit because it is important for your health and that of your baby" may effectively elicit information. In 2 well-known studies, one led by Judith McFarlane and one by Rosalind Wright, women said they would have disclosed abuse if the health care provider had asked them about it.

It is important for the health care provider to ask all questions related to safety and abuse when the person is alone and away from significant others, children, family members, or support persons. The interview environment should be a safe place where no one can walk into the room or overhear what is said. In the event that an interpreter is needed, it is imperative that the interpreter not be related or connected to the patient in any way. This ensures greater safety for the person to be free to disclose information that could put him or her in danger. It is appropriate to ask at least 1 or 2 specific screening questions even though there are a multitude of areas that can be covered. Having a repertoire of questions provides multiple ways to approach perceived or direct concerns.

A person who discloses abuse needs time to talk about it with the health care provider. The clinician's approach should be nonjudgmental and supportive, while creating a relaxed environment in which to discuss difficult concerns. It is not uncommon for the person to understate or minimize the frequency and intensity of battering and the effects of it on self and family. Women tend to blame themselves or verbalize that the abuser could not help himself because of the effects of alcohol or other circumstances in his life. Always reassure the abused person, whether female or male, and emphasize that she or he is not responsible for the perpetrator's abusive behavior and does not deserve such treatment under any circumstances.

PEDIATRIC SETTINGS

Health care providers who care for children view issues facing the family as extremely important. Identifying and intervening on behalf of battered women may be one of the most effective means of preventing child abuse. Questions about family violence should become part of anticipatory guidance at each visit. Pediatricians incorporate routine screening and assessment for IPV among the parents of their patients because of the dangers that IPV poses for children in the home. In 1998, the American Academy of Pediatrics (AAP) Committee on Child Abuse and Neglect described the role of the pediatrician in recognizing and intervening on behalf of abused women and made specific statements regarding training and practice goals for uncovering child abuse. These guidelines are valid for all health care professionals:

— Intervention is crucial because children are also likely to be victims.

— Residency training programs and continuing medical education program leaders should incorporate education on family and intimate partner violence into curricula for pediatricians and pediatric emergency medicine department physicians.

— Pediatricians should attempt to recognize evidence of family or intimate partner violence in the office setting.

— Pediatricians should intervene in a sensitive and skillful manner that maximizes the safety of women and children victims.

— Pediatricians should support local and national multidisciplinary efforts to recognize, treat, and prevent family violence and IPV.

Adolescent health care providers caring for older adolescents, especially those entering dating relationships, must begin screening their patients for teenaged dating violence. For young people, both good and bad experiences learned in dating relationships serve as relationship "scripts" for the future. In situations in which a clinician may have concerns about the teenager's safety, the limits of confidentiality should be made clear at the outset. This precaution will hopefully prevent any feelings of betrayal from arising later should the clinician need to take action and involve others in keeping the teen safe. The health care provider should inquire about the safety of romantic or intimate relationships in which the teenage patient is involved. It is important to inquire in a nonjudgmental way into the nature of any sexual activity and exposure risks for unplanned pregnancy and sexually transmitted infections, as well as any concurrent drug and alcohol use. Areas to address with young persons include feelings of being pressured or coerced into having sex.

SCREENING TOOLS

Screening tools are a great help to the interview process. An effective tool helps clinicians to be consistent in the questions and approach to potentially abused persons. Easy-to-use, reliable screening methods, such as the Abuse Assessment Screen (**Table 8-7**) or the RADAR screening tool in **Figures 8-1** and **8-2**, can assist nurses and other health care professionals assess for IPV.

HELPING VICTIMS LEAVE AN ABUSIVE ENVIRONMENT

Clinics and offices should have intervention protocols in place and know what community resources are available in their region. It is essential that health care providers discuss safety plans with patients and offer appropriate information and referrals to legal and social service systems. If persons at risk cannot immediately leave the relationship or are unwilling to do so, it is especially important they have a plan that will facilitate personal safety in the event of further abuse or harm to self or family. Health care providers must assess the danger by determining the patterns of violence in a patient's relationship. If violence is escalating and victims fear returning home, then it may be necessary for them to contact a local women's shelter, IPV or domestic violence agency, or the police to ensure safety and protection. Professionals who work with IPV victims should be knowledgeable about state and regional laws that relate to protection and rights, especially professionals in health care, education, or childcare.

Table 8-7. Questions From the Abuse Assessment Screen
— Have you ever been emotionally or physically abused by your partner or someone important to you?
— Have you ever been pushed, shoved, slapped, kicked, or otherwise physically hurt by someone?
— Has anyone ever forced you to engage in sexual activities?
— Are you afraid of your partner or anyone you listed above?
Data from "The Abuse Assessment Screen: A clinical instrument to measure frequency, severity, and perpetrators of abuse against women" by Soeken et al.

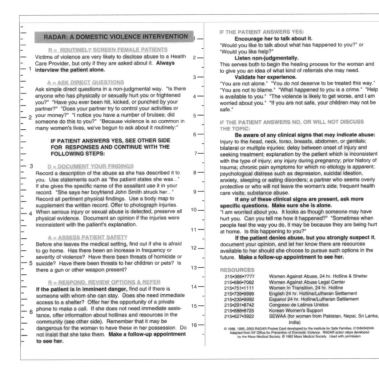

Figure 8-1. Screening tool used by health care providers. Reprinted with permission from the Institute for Safe Families.

Figure 8-2. *Screening tool used by pediatric health care providers. Reprinted with permission from the Institute for Safe Families.*

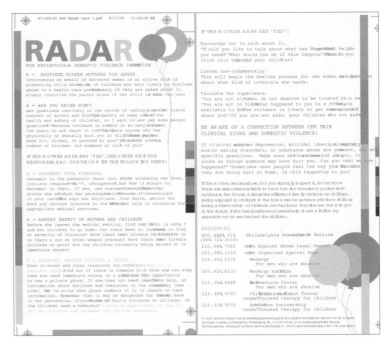

Developing a Plan

Abuse victims who plan to leave their relationships need to anticipate important decisions. Research shows that women who leave an abusive relationship still remain at a risk of violence. Questions that victims need to answer before leaving the abusive situation include the following: when they will leave, specific details of the exit plan, where they will go, and what resources they will have with them when they leave. Safety plans provide guidelines and specific actions that a person can take to ensure safety for self and family in the event of violence inside and outside of the home. A safety plan requires forethought of the actions that can be taken if a battering incident occurs. The American Bar Association (ABA) Domestic Violence Safety Plan recommends:

— Learn where to get help; *memorize emergency phone numbers.*

— *Keep a phone* in a room you can lock from the inside; if you can, get a cellular phone that you keep with you at all times.

— If the abuser has moved out, *change the locks on your door*; get locks on the window.

— *Plan an escape route* out of your home; teach it to your children.

— Think about where you would go if you need to escape.

— *Ask your neighbors* to call the police if they see the abuser at your house; make a signal for them to call the police, for example, if the phone rings twice, a shade is pulled down or a light is on.

— *Pack a bag* with important things you'd need if you had to leave quickly; put it in a safe place, or give it to a friend or relative you trust.

— Include *cash, car keys, and important information* such as: court papers, passport or birth certificates, medical records and medicines, immigration papers.

— *Get an unlisted phone number.*

— *Block caller ID* by dialing *67 on outgoing calls.

— *Use an answering machine*; screen the calls.

— *Take a good self-defense course.*

The ABA also has specific recommendations for action in the event that the parent and children are at home and are being threatened or attacked:

— *Stay away from the kitchen* (the abuser can find weapons, like knives, there).

— *Stay away from bathrooms*, closets, or small spaces where the abuser can trap you.

— *Get to a room with a door* or window to escape.

— *Get to a room with a phone* to call for help; lock the abuser outside if you can.

— *Call 911* (or your local emergency number) *right away for help*; get the dispatcher's name.

— Think about a neighbor or friend you can run to for help.

— If a police officer comes, tell him/her what happened; *get his/her name & badge number.*

— *Get medical help* if you are hurt.

— *Take pictures* of bruises or injuries.

— *Call a domestic violence program or shelter* (some are listed in this chapter); ask them to help you make a safety plan.

It is important to provide a list of referral contacts and agencies. The victim should know how to access community resources and find help with the coordination of services in the community so that resources are utilized optimally. Dealing with issues of IPV is a daunting undertaking for victims, communities, and professionals alike.

PROFESSIONAL STUDY AND CONTROVERSY

VALUE OF IPV SCREENING

Some professionals argue that universal screening tools that ask everyone whether they have been abused are not cost effective. Others say screening has no value because no "profile" exists that correctly identifies the high-risk group. What is clear, however, is that patients in health care settings consistently report that having the issue brought up by the health care provider makes it easier to disclose abuse. Also, patients voice support for the inclusion of IPV screening when it is appropriately introduced as part of a routine health care visit.

CONCLUSION

Health care professionals have a vital role in caring for adults and children who experience IPV. Ongoing screening to identify intimate partner violence is the standard of care for health maintenance and anticipatory guidance in health care interactions. The more professionals know about issues of violence, abuse, and family system dynamics, the better they can ask questions and focus on potential problems. Problem identification is the first step to a healthier lifestyle for the victimized children and adults. The next step is to help the family access support and resources to do something about the problem. Clinicians accomplish this by knowing their communities and the available services that deal with victimization and abuse in intimate relationships.

WHERE TO TURN FOR HELP

WEB SITES

American Bar Association

http://www.abanet.org

— Includes plans for increasing safety and protection at work and outside of the home.

National Coalition Against Domestic Violence

http://www.ncadv.org

— Lists all state coalitions; adult victims who decide to relocate can access contact information for coalitions in other states.

National Sexual Violence Resource Center

877-739-3895 (toll free)

http://www.nsvrc.org

— Offers 24-hour access to information, resources, and research regarding sexual assault.

Violence Against Women Online Resources

http://www.vaw.umn.edu

CENTERS, HOTLINES, AND PROGRAMS

ChildHelp USA

800-4-A-CHILD (800-422-4453)

http://www.childhelpusa.org

— Operates a multilingual, 24-hour hotline that offers crisis counseling, publications, and referrals to local organizations and child abuse–reporting hotlines.

The Battered Women's Justice Project

800-903-0111, ext. 1

http://www.bwjp.org

— Offers training, technical assistance, and resources on legal issues related to domestic violence.

Child Welfare Information Gateway

800-394-3366

http://www.childwelfare.gov

— Collects, maintains, and disseminates information on all aspects of child welfare and provides referrals to local organizations and child abuse reporting hotlines.

The Health Resource Center on Domestic Violence, Family Violence Prevention Fund

800-595-4889 (TTY)

http://endabuse.org

— Provides information, technical assistance, and library services to strengthen the health care response to domestic violence.

Institute on Domestic Violence in the African American Community

877-643-8222 (toll free)

http://www.dvinstitute.org

— Provides information on research, services, and responses to prevent and reduce family violence in the African American community.

National Domestic Violence Hotline

800-799-SAFE or 800-787-3224 (TDD)

http://ndvh.org

— Provides contact information for domestic violence programs in counties and states across the country, as well as interpreters that speak a variety of languages.

National Clearinghouse for the Defense of Battered Women

215-351-0010

— Offers assistance, resources, and support to battered women charged with crimes and to their attorneys, advocates, and expert witnesses.

National Resource Center on Domestic Violence

800-537-2238

http://www.nrcdv.org

— Provides information, resources, policy development, and technical assistance designed to enhance community response to and prevention of domestic violence.

Sacred Circle National Resource Center to Stop Violence Against Native Women

877-733-7623 (toll free)

http://www.sacred-circle.com

— Offers specialized training institutes, on-site technical assistance, and culturally specific materials addressing domestic violence in tribal communities.

Chapter 9

RISKS OF THE INTERNET

Maria D. McColgan, MD, MEd
Angelo P. Giardino, MD, PhD, MPH

Microchips, computers, access to the Internet, high-speed cable connections, and e-mail have revolutionized the manner in which we communicate with each other in what is now a global community. In this information age, the typical American has been described as having a full-time job just watching TV, playing video games, listening to music, and surfing the Internet. This technology has had a tremendous effect on children's lives. A survey of a nationally representative sample of 3000 children aged 2 to 18 years, called *Kids & Media @ the New Millennium: A Comprehensive National Analysis of Children's Media Use*, found that the typical American child spends 38 hours per week—nearly 5½ hours a day—using the various forms of electronic media. The most commonly used form of electronic media, according to both this survey and a UCLA Internet Report, remains the television, which, on average, children spend 2¾ hours of each day watching. The computer and the Internet, however, are gaining ground. A US Department of Commerce report states that computers are in 71% of US households that include children aged 8 to 17 years. An Internet connection is available in at least 67% of these families. For families without a personal computer, access is relatively available. Schools, in which the computer may be both part of the curriculum and a teaching aid, are providing critical Internet access for children who might have none. Both school and public libraries increasingly have personal computers.

For today's children, lacking computer skills is nearly equivalent to being illiterate. Perhaps most telling of how well children understand the growing value of computers is their response to the *Kids & Media* survey question of which form of electronic media they would they choose to bring to a desert island if forced to pick: 33% selected a computer with Internet access and 13% selected the television.

Today, anyone can access the Internet provided they have a modem, software (known as a Web browser), and a connection point such as an online service. The previously mentioned US Department of Commerce report also found that Americans' use of the Internet is growing substantially (**Table 9-1**). The Internet is very flexible and has appeal for almost every age group. For very young children, the Internet offers learning games, clubs, and publications. For teenagers, there are chat groups, online magazines, games, and teenaged clubs. Students can access organization and government sites, academic resources, virtual exploration sites, and commercial education sites. Children and teenagers benefit greatly from the self-directed learning experiences the Internet provides and especially from the boost of confidence that comes when they have successfully navigated it to find information. Today the Internet is widely considered a critical component of a child's education, but such potential benefits are not without risks, which parents should be aware of.

EFFECTS OF THE INTERNET

As the breadth of information available on the Internet is virtually limitless, so are the potential risks to children who use the Internet. Americans are deeply worried about

---

Table 9-1. US Internet Use

— The rate of growth of Internet use in the United States is at least 2 million new Internet users per month.

— As of September 2001, 143 million Americans, or approximately 54% of the population, were using the Internet (an increase of 26 million people in 13 months).

— As of September 2001, 174 million Americans, approximately 66% of the population, used computers.

— 97% of children aged 5 to 17 years, or 48 million children, used computers.

— 75% of 14- to 17-year-old youths use the Internet.

— Households with children younger than 18 years are more likely to access the Internet (62% compared with 53% of households without children).

— Computer availability at schools narrows the gap in computer usage between children from high-income families and those from low-income families.

Data from A Nation Online: How Americans are Expanding Their Use of the Internet *by the US Dept of Commerce.*

---

criminal activity on the Internet—in a Pew Internet and American Life Project report on online privacy, 92% of Americans said that they are concerned about child pornography on the Internet, and a federally sponsored report found that 68% of parents are more concerned about their children's exposure to material on the Internet than to material on television. According to the National School Boards Foundation, the 3 top concerns for parents around children using the Internet were that the children would encounter pornography, undesirable adults, and violent or hate content. This chapter will introduce some of the risks associated with children's use of the Internet and teach parents, caregivers, and educators methods to identify and prevent risky online behaviors. See **Appendix 9-1** for a glossary of Internet-related terms and **Table 9-2** for answers to parents' most common questions.

UNSOLICITED CONTACT

Some of the more than 77 million people accessing the Internet will do so for inappropriate or illegal reasons. Some will disguise themselves and use chat rooms, bulletin boards, or instant messaging services to communicate with children and inappropriately gain their confidence. Using this type of manipulation, the perpetrator will ask for, and many times receive, personal information. Unfortunately, some of these people then use the information to arrange a face-to-face meeting with a child for the purposes of sexual exploitation.

An area of major concern with regard to protecting children on the Internet is the chat room. Chat rooms are one of the most popular features of the Internet but pose significant risk to children. They allow Internet users to converse in real time with total strangers anywhere in the world by simply typing messages on the keyboard. Unlike instant messenger services, which also allow communication in real time, chat rooms provide nearly total anonymity.

Some of the most frequently used chat rooms are easy for children and adolescents familiar with the Internet to access. A 2001 Pew Foundation report on teens online found that 55% of online children aged 12 through 17 years visit chat rooms. These

---

Table 9-2. Frequently Asked Questions

What are some of the dangers my child may encounter on the Internet?

The major risks facing children on the Internet fall into the following 5 categories:

— Exposure to material that is inappropriate or encourages dangerous or illegal activities

— Exposure to harassment through e-mail chat or messages that harass, demean, or threaten the child

— Revealing financial information (eg, credit card numbers), producing negative consequences

— Engaging in activity that has legal ramifications, possibly violating the rights of others (eg, knowingly posting inaccurate information that causes others to act)

— Safety issues, including physical molestation or other injury resulting from sharing personal information and a child being lured into meeting a stranger in person

Who do I contact when my child has encountered an aggressive contact or dangerous Web site?

For exposure to unwanted material or aggressive behavior, contact the National Center for Missing & Exploited Children at 1-800-843-5678 (1-800-The-Lost) or via the Web at http://www.cyber tipline.com. In addition, contact your Internet service provider. You could also contact the Federal Bureau of Investigation. However, for immediate concerns such as a perpetrator planning a meeting with your child, contact your local police.

What measures can I take to prepare my child for what they may encounter on the Internet?

Although blocking software and other parental protective software may help limit your child's exposure to unwanted or harmful material on the Internet, no software program can be 100% effective. Additional measures must be taken, such as educating your child of the potential dangers of the Internet. Consider a contract with your child regarding the rules of Internet usage and an agreement for consequences when the rules are broken. Be sure the child understands that the rules are in place for their safety. Keep the computer in a public place in the house where you can supervise the activities. Computers with Internet access should never be kept in a child's bedroom. Discuss daily which sites your children have visited and ask what they saw and read. Consider checking the history list in your computer to review the sites your children have visited.

What can I do to prevent the sites from being available?

You can contact your Internet service provider to ask that the site be removed from their service. You can also contact your local, state, and federal elected officials or the Federal Bureau of Investigation.

---

chat rooms are listed on Internet directories by their names, which usually give an idea of the topic the room is discussing. To participate, a person selects a screen name by which he or she will be known while chatting. There is no verification that the name reflects the user; a 35-year-old man could choose a name that would suggest to other users that he is a 12-year-old girl. After the person selects a room, the screen name appears in the room. Most chat formats allow for a brief description or profile of the users. In this area, basic information about a user is stored for viewing by other users. Once a person enters the room, others can check this profile. A pedophile can easily learn the age and sex of a child and perhaps also a child's address and school.

Case Study 9-1*

Donny14 has been on the net for over 2 hours now. The regulars are on today as well as a few newcomers. He recognizes Rory16 from California, Hot4U from England, and Jafo from Toronto. Suddenly a new person enters the room, Billy14, with whom he immediately initiates chat (**Figure 9-1-a**).

After little more than 5 minutes images of child pornography are sent over the Internet. At the same time Donny14 starts to experience some sexual arousal and fantasies. He tries to imagine what Billy14 must look like, especially naked. Some would describe Donny14 as in a dissociate state as he pictures himself in sexual contact with this imaginary character. His thoughts and fantasies race as the conversation continues.

Donny14 spends the next 30 minutes talking to Billy14 about sexual acts. This includes a detailed account of his first acts of masturbation through his complete sexual history. At the same time he is constantly collecting information from Billy14. Periodically he remarks how sexually aroused he is and asks if Billy14 is also experiencing the same sexual arousal. Donny14 now has his pants down to his knees and is masturbating as he carries on this conversation. More pornographic pictures are sent. E-mail addresses are exchanged. Donny14 feels the opportunity and time is right and asks Billy14 what he thinks of guys in their 30s who like guys "their age." Billy14 responds favorably and feels this is perfectly normal. Donny14 then reveals that he is really 35 years old. Billy14 continues the conversation. This causes Donny14 to think of other possibilities. Donny14 now feels comfortable enough to send a real picture of him. He is on edge as he waits for Billy14's reaction. When Billy14 reacts favorably to the picture new thoughts and fantasies are generated and the conversation continues.

Donny14 has already ejaculated once during this conversation and his arousal again returns. He thinks of the possibilities of meeting Billy14 in real life. He brings up the idea and Billy14 is

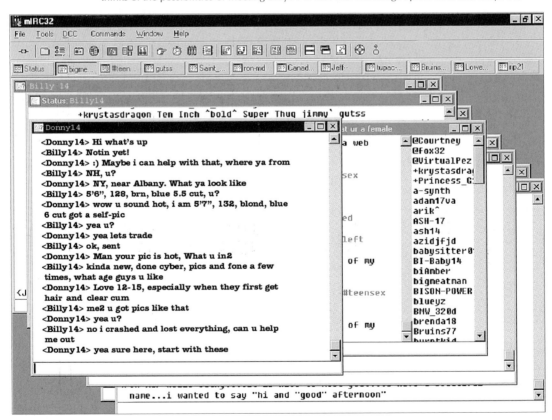

Figure 9-1-a. *Screen capture of Donny14's chat with Billy14. Adapted and reprinted with permission McLaughlin JF, Technophilia: A Modern Day Paraphilia.*

Adapted and reprinted with permission from McLaughlin JF. Technophilia: A Modern Day Paraphilia.

agreeable to the idea as long as it is kept secret and no one finds out, a condition that Donny14 quickly agrees to (**Figure 9-1-b**).

Child sexual offenders, according to most law enforcement agencies, are experts at "grooming" children—befriending them, talking to them, discovering their interests and weaknesses—and then exploiting them. Internet chats allow the child sexual offender private access to intended victims easily and often. The predator can talk with children at great length with little risk of being discovered and electronically send pornography to potential victims in order to gauge their responses and break down their inhibitions. This pattern of first engaging a child in relatively innocuous and nonsexual content matter and then, once he or she is comfortable, introducing sexual material, is analogous to the 1982 description by Dr. Suzanne Sgroi and colleagues of a child's gradual initiation into a sexually abusive situation. This initiation was explained several decades ago, before the Internet's widespread use. However, the Internet provides predators an advantage in this grooming process by allowing them to obtain information from children anonymously. If rebuffed, the predator can move on with little fear of being traced and apprehended. If a child expresses interest, the predator can then use the Internet to lure the child to a meeting place. The sexual assaults, which occur after grooming, are the end result of a seduction process in which the child sexual offender uses the intended victims' vulnerability, naiveté, and interest in exploration against them.

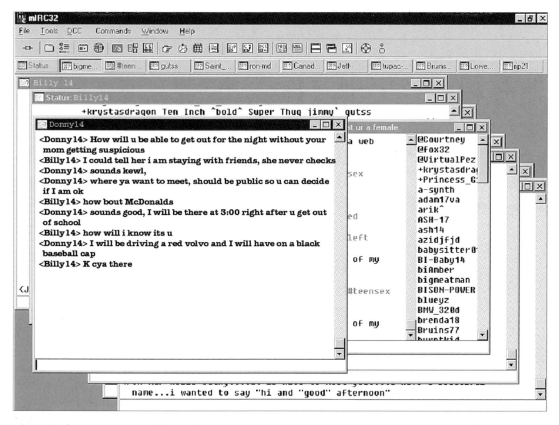

Figure 9-1-b. *Screen capture of the end of the chat. Adapted and reprinted with permission McLaughlin JF,* Technophilia: A Modern Day Paraphilia.

EXPOSURE TO INAPPROPRIATE CONTENT

An intended search on an innocent topic can result in a list of Web sites with material that is inappropriate for children. The *Kids & Media* survey found that 75% of teenagers aged 15 to 17 years have accidentally stumbled across pornography online. In a well-known study by Dr. David Finkelhor and colleagues, 25% of the 1501 children and teenagers (aged 10 to 17 years) who used the Internet regularly reported at least 1 unwanted exposure to sexual material in the previous year. Ninety-four percent of the exposures were nude images, 38% showed people engaging in sex, and 8% depicted violence in addition to sexual content. The route to the unwanted material came as a result of searches 47% of the time, misspelled addresses 17% of the time, and via links within a Web site in another 17%. The statements in **Table 9-3** concerning unwanted exposures to sexual material are from youth interviewed during the study.

Table 9-3. Details of Study on Online Victimization

— An 11-year-old boy and his friend were typing names in searching for game sites and typed in "fun.com" and found a pornography site.

— A 15-year-old teenager was searching for information about the family car, typed in "escort," and 1 result was a site dealing with an escort service.

— A 15-year-old teenager came across a bestiality site while he was writing a paper on wolves; the site contained a picture of a woman having sex with a wolf.

— A 16-year-old mistyped "teen.com" as "teeen.com" and came upon a pornography site.

— A 13-year-old boy interested in wrestling got an e-mail message with a subject line related to wrestling, and when he opened it, it contained pornography.

— A 12-year-old girl received an e-mail with a subject line "Free Beanie Babies," and when it opened, she saw a picture of naked people.

— 39% percent of the children and teenagers told their parents of the incidents, but 44% told no one.

— 23% of the children and teenagers reported that the exposure was very or extremely upsetting, and 20% were very or extremely embarrassed.

Data from Online Victimization: A Report on the Nation's Youth *by Finkelhor et al.*

INFORMATION ACCESS

Another major risk found on the Internet is related to dangerous or erroneous content on particular Web sites. Many parents worry about what their children might see or read online. Parents can learn a lot about their children's interests, concerns, and dangerous behaviors by reviewing the Web sites children visit.

Health-Related Web Sites

According to a study of Internet health resources by the Pew Internet and American Life Project, over 70 000 Web sites disseminate health information, and when faced with a question about their health, more than 90 million people turn to the Internet for answers. Older teenagers are more likely to have looked up health information than children aged 12 to 14 years. A 2001 Kaiser survey of persons aged 15 to 24 years found that 75% had used the Internet at least once to research health-related topics, and 39% had changed their personal behavior in response to information they found online. Adolescents have most frequently explored the topics of sexually transmitted diseases, diet, fitness, exercise, and sexual behaviors. Adolescent girls are also interested in birth control, physical and sexual abuse, and violence.

Many health professionals are concerned with the appropriateness and validity of health-related information on the Internet. A study lead by University of Michigan doctoral student Derek Hansen observed 68 adolescent health-related searches and reported that only 69% of the searches successfully located correct and useful answers to the health-related question. Furthermore, the adolescents paid little to no attention to the source of the answers to health-related searches: In the vast majority of cases, once an answer was located, it was simply assumed to be correct. Children, especially teenagers, will look to the Internet for information on topics from acne and obesity to sexuality and drugs, and parents should be aware of the sites that children are visiting so that they can discuss these topics with children and research the validity of the information that the sites offer.

Illegal Drugs and Raves

The amount of information on illegal drugs available through the Internet is staggering. Although much of the information is intended for research purposes, a child can easily find information on virtually any drug. Web sites offer information on the effect of amphetamines, cannabis, cocaine, ecstasy, heroin, ketamine, LSD, and mushrooms. The sites may offer information on addiction, mixing with other drugs, and detection times for drug tests, and they typically provide links to other sites that give various tips of dubious value such as how to "avoid a bad trip." Other sites offer information on how to make illegal drugs at home. Recipes for methamphetamines and ecstasy (MDMA) and other drugs are readily available on the Internet, and children can even arrange to purchase drugs illegally via the Internet. Many of the most available drugs are considered club drugs, which are widely used at teenaged dance parties called raves. Various Web sites provide lists of rave times and locations, along with other details such as the bands that will be playing at each location.

Sexuality, Puberty, and Sexually Transmitted Diseases

According to the Pew Foundation report *Teenage Life Online*, 18% of online youth admit to having looked online for sensitive sexual information, and more than one quarter of all online teenagers consider the Internet to be a useful source of such information. In another survey used in Dr. Dina Borzekowski and Dr. Vaughn Rickert's study of health-related cybersurfing, students reported that they most frequently use the Internet to find information on sexual activities, birth control, pregnancy, and sexually transmitted diseases:

"You may have noticed that I often note the website virtualkid.com," wrote one 16-year-old boy from the Greenfield Online group discussion. "It was a website for teens complete with forums and information and just help in general for teenagers.... Besides dating, the site had information on puberty and all the awkward teenage moments. It was a really nice, helpful site." Said another 17-year-old girl in the Greenfield group, "Yeah, I've done it before. It's less weird and cheaper than going to a doctor to ask."

Even with parental controls, children can access a variety of health-related and sexual content. Teenagers can also share information easily in chat rooms and unknowingly spread erroneous information and myths.

Dangerous or Illegal Activity

For almost any illegal activity one can imagine, Web sites exist with instructions on how to commit the crime. Sites are available on everything from how to become a computer hacker to how to commit murder. A search on "how to make a gun" provided sites on how to make a tattoo gun, how to make a stun gun, how to make any gun silent, and how to make gunpowder, fireworks, and other explosives. Children can even make arrangements to purchase weapons illegally via the Internet. A simple search on "how to" provided links to sites with instructions on how to become a computer hacker. Children can also learn how to send computer viruses via the Internet. A search for "how to kill someone" provides numerous sites with detailed information on who to kill, the weaknesses of the human body, and how to carry out the act. The more creative and dedicated an Internet surfer is, the more he or she can uncover.

Hate Crimes

The federal government defines a hate crime as "a crime in which the defendant selects a victim, or in the case of a property crime, the property that is the object of the crime, because of the actual or perceived race, color, religion, national origin, ethnicity, gender, disability, or sexual orientation of any person." According to Partners Against Hate, 33% of all known hate crime offenders are younger than 18 years and 29% are aged 18 to 24 years. Thirty-one percent of all violent crime offenders and 46% of the property offenders are younger than 18 years of age, as are 30% of aggravated assault victims and 34% of assault victims. Children can and do commit and suffer from crimes of hate.

The Internet provides a means for individuals to openly or anonymously perpetuate hate via mass e-mailings or Web sites. For example, the Partners Against Hate publication "Investigating Hate Crimes on the Internet" states that in September 1996, a 21-year-old expelled college student sent a threatening e-mail to 60 Asian students at the University of California–Irvine. In the e-mail, the student expressed hatred for Asians, threatening to hunt down and kill all Asians on campus if they did not leave the university, and signed the message "Asian Hater." Eventually, the student admitted that he sent the threatening message, and he was charged with violating federal civil rights laws. Unfortunately, many Web sites with similar racial divides and messages of hate exist today and are protected under First Amendment rights of free speech.

WHAT PARENTS AND CAREGIVERS CAN DO

SUPERVISION

The ability to supervise children using the computer and the Internet is a vital component of keeping our children safe. However, supervision requires skill, and in a survey of parents regarding their use of filtering software, only 31% percent of parents believe themselves to be advanced users or experts of the Internet, 44% report an intermediate ability level, and 25% classify themselves as beginners. Parental supervision of children using other, less complex forms of electronic media has been limited, especially of television. Specifically, the report *Kids & Media* states that among children aged 8 years and older, parents watch television with their children just 5% of the time, and 1 out of every 4 of these children watch more than 5 hours per day. In addition, approximately 65% of the children aged 8 years or older have a television in their bedroom, and 61% of these say that their parents have not set rules about what or how much to watch. Younger children are more supervised: 19% of parents watch television with children aged 2 to 7 years old. Children in this younger age group watch, on average, 3½ hours per day, and 1 of 3 has a television in the bedroom. Given these statistics, it is not unreasonable to be concerned that the majority of children are constantly vulnerable.

When a asked whether parents should serve as watchdogs or content guides for their children's Internet use at home, 67% of parents agreed that being a "guide to good content" was the most important parental role, and 24% agreed that being a "watchdog" was the most important role (see **Figure 9-2**). However, 78% of teenagers between the ages of 13 and 17 years reported in the same survey that they use the Internet alone, despite the fact that 67% of parents stated that someone else was in the room when their children were accessing the Internet. Also, according to *Kids & Media*, of the children older than 8 years who were surveyed, 21% reported that they had a computer in their bedroom. **Table 9-4** provides a list of guidelines for parents to use when deciding how to monitor their children's internet use.

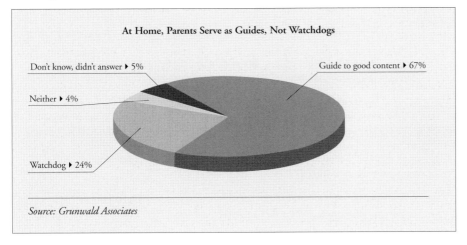

At Home, Parents Serve as Guides, Not Watchdogs

Don't know, didn't answer ▶ 5%

Neither ▶ 4%

Guide to good content ▶ 67%

Watchdog ▶ 24%

Source: Grunwald Associates

Figure 9-2. Percent of respondents to the question, "Which statement do you agree with more: 'In regards to the Internet, the most important role of a parent is as a guide to the good content' or 'In regards to the Internet, the most important role of a parent is as a watchdog?'" Reprinted with permission from "Safe and Smart: Research and Guidelines for Children's Use of the Internet." © 2000, National School Boards Foundation. All rights reserved.

Table 9-4. Dos and Don'ts of Monitoring Internet Usage
— Do talk to your children about potential online dangers and sexual victimization.
— Do spend time with your children online and have them show you their favorite online destinations.
— Don't keep the computer in a child's bedroom, but rather in a common area of the house where the screen can be visible by others in the home.
— Do use parental controls and monitor chat room usage by your child.
— Do maintain access to your child's online account; be upfront about your access and why you periodically check the history of Web sites visited.
— Do stay aware of other areas where your child uses the computer such as schools, libraries, and friends' houses and ask questions about safeguards in those locations.

The online safety of children and teenagers relies on communication between parents or caregivers and children. However, family conversations concerning privacy on the Web are lacking. Children and their parents do not necessarily hold the same attitudes about the topic or even recall having the same discussions. Dr. Joseph Turow and Dr. Lilach

Nir's research revealed that parent/child conversations about Web privacy issues were limited to "don't give out your name" or "don't talk to strangers," leaving the child unprepared to deal with strategies such as bartering information for free gifts or extending trust to a person without any factual data as to who that person really was. Further examples of discrepancies between parent and child perceptions of rules are listed in **Table 9-5**. Parents may consider signing a contract with their children that outlines the rules of Internet use and the consequences of breaking the rules. **Table 9-6** illustrates a sample contract.

Table 9-5. Child and Parent Perceptions of Internet Privacy

— 61% of parents said they have rules about Internet use, while only 37% of teenagers reported being subject to any Internet time-use strictures.

— 61% of parents reported checking to see what Web sites their teenagers had visited after the child was online, while only 27% of teenagers believe they have been checked.

— 68% of parents said they had sat with their children when they were online, whereas 48% of children recall such episodes.

— 45% of parents were concerned that the Internet leads young people to engage in dangerous or harmful activities, whereas 34% of children reported the same.

Data from Teenage Life Online: The Rise of the Instant-Message Generation and the Internet's Impact on Friendships and Family Relationships *by Lenhart et al.*

BLOCKING SOFTWARE

Internet service providers and software manufacturers provide software that blocks children from accessing certain sites or to document what sites the computer's user has visited on the Internet. To *Consumer Reports*, parents expressed general confidence in their ability to always know what their children are doing online. Over one fourth of parents reported using some form of parental-control software, often the controls built into their Web browser or offered through their Internet service provider. Only 4% chose to use software that they bought, installed, and maintained on their own. Parents should consider using blocking software when deciding how to best monitor their children's activities on the Internet.

In essence, 3 types of blocking are possible to filter out sites inappropriate for children: human analysis, software analysis, and site labeling. Human analysis creates a customized list of sites that are permitted and prohibited. This approach, however, requires a constant human review of new sites and is ultimately impractical. No matter how frequently these tools are updated, the number of Web sites published each day far exceeds the ability of software companies to review them and categorize them as acceptable or bad.

Software analysis screens a site's content and filters out those pages with objectionable phrases or images. However, applying rules around phrases and images contained within a site is not without its problems either. The primary criticism of site analysis has been that it blocks out many legitimate sites because at times the context of the content may be obscured.

Table 9-6. Parent/Child Contract for Internet Use

Contract for Internet Use

I, _____, and my parent(s), _____, have agreed to this contract for rules and regulations for Internet use for my safety and well-being.

— The computer will be kept in an area of the house where supervision can occur.

— I will never give out my actual name, address, phone number, school name, social security number, passwords, or other personal information.

— I will never post pictures of myself on the Internet or send pictures of myself to others.

— I will never download pictures from an unknown source because they may contain sexually explicit or other offending material.

— I will never accept offers of free merchandise or give out financial information such as credit card numbers or bank account information.

— I will never arrange a face-to-face meeting with someone I meet online. If I would like to meet someone I have met online, I will discuss this with my parents so that they can accompany me to a public place for the meeting.

— I will never respond to e-mail, chat comments, instant messages, or news-group messages that are hostile, belligerent, inappropriate, or make me feel uncomfortable.

— I understand that information I read on the Internet may not be true, and I will talk with my parents or teachers about any material that I encounter online that makes me uncomfortable, confused, or curious.

— If I break any of the above rules I will be banned from Internet use for a period of no less than _____ weeks/months, depending on the nature of the violation.

Signed: _____   _____

       Child's Signature   Parent's Signature

Finally, site labeling relies on screening based on the voluntary labeling of Web sites by their owners based on the Internet Content Rating System (ICRA). Its major drawback is that many sites have not chosen label content and, as a result, are not blocked even though their content is objectionable. If the filter is set to block all unlabeled sites, then an inordinate number of legitimate sites end up being blocked, which makes searching difficult. Blocking software is fallible and must be used in conjunction with, not in place of, parental supervision. Interested parties can also refer to computer magazine reviews to assist them in choosing the software that best suits their needs.

REPORTING VICTIMIZATION

If a caregiver determines that a child has been a victim of an online sexual offender, the offense should be reported immediately to law enforcement authorities via the Cyber-Tipline. Additional steps that local law enforcement might want to take include collecting forensic evidence from the computer. First, the child's computer needs to be immediately secured (that is, turned off and disconnected from Internet access) and provided to the law enforcement authorities. A computer forensics specialist must be able to examine the computer as soon as possible when the report of sexual assault is made. The simple acts of turning a computer on and off or opening files can change the date and time indicators on those files, potentially corrupting evidence. Second, the child should be questioned carefully about all contacts with the offender, including those over the Internet. The child needs to be handled in a sensitive manner because he or she may feel guilty about the actions and behaviors surrounding the victimization and need to be assured that he or she is not being blamed for what occurred. Third, the child will have to work with police to identify all communications with the offender that may remain on the victim's computer. The computer may be the best source of evidence to determine the identity of the child sexual offender and may contain valuable evidence to assist the prosecution of the offender, if caught.

PROFESSIONAL STUDY AND CONTROVERSY

ONLINE SOLICITATION

Finkelhor and colleagues found that 19% of the youths aged 10 to 17 years in their study group were the targets of unwanted solicitation during a 1-year period of time. Girls, older teenagers, those having problems of one type or another (troubled youth), those who used the Internet more frequently, those who participated in chat room discus-sions, and those who communicated with strangers online were most at risk. Not sur-prisingly, 25% of the children and teenagers who were solicited reported high levels of stress following the solicitation incident. The highest risk for distress was seen in children aged 10 to 13 years, those who were solicited while using a computer away from their home, and those who received aggressive solicitations defined as the solicitor attempting to make offline contact. Only 10% of the solicitations were reported to the police, Internet service provider, or other official; over two thirds of parents and three quarters of children and teenagers did not know where they could report the incidents. Some details from the full report of this study are in **Table 9-7.**

Table 9-7. Details of Study on the Effects of Online Sexual Solicitation

— On the basis of interviews, many of the sexual solicitations were propositions for cybersex, a form of fantasy sex via an interactive chat room session in which participants describe sexual activity and sometimes disrobe and masturbate.

— In 70% of solicitations the youth were at home, and in 22% they were at someone else's house.

— 65% of solicitations involved chat rooms, and 24% involved instant messages.

— In 10% of solicitations, defined as "aggressive," the perpetrator asked to meet somewhere; in 6% contact was made via regular mail, in 2% contact was made via telephone, and in 1% money and gifts were given.

— The following descriptions were received from youth interviewed:

    — A 13-year-old teenager stated that someone asked her about her bra size.

    — A 17-year-old teenager described someone asking him to "cyber" (have cybersex); the first time this happened, he reported not knowing what this meant and the second time he "just said, no."

    — A 14-year-old teenager reported that males claiming to be 18 to 20 years old sent her instant messages asking what her measurements were and other questions about her appearance; she was 13 years old when this happened, and the men were aware of her age.

    — A 12-year-old girl said that people had told her sexual things that they were doing to each other and asked her "to play with herself."

    — A 15-year-old girl said that an older man kept bothering her; he asked if she was a virgin and wanted to meet her.

(continued)

Table 9-7. *(continued)*

— A 16-year-old girl reported that a man would tell her sexual things that he wanted to do to her and suggested places he would like to meet her.

— A 13-year-old teenager said that a girl asked him how big his "privates" were and wanted him to "jack off."

— A 13-year-old teenager said that a man sent him a drawing of the man having sex with a dog.

— In terms of reaction to these solicitations, 75% of the children and teenagers had no or only minor reactions saying that they were not very upset or afraid after the solicitation; in 17% of the incidents, the youths were very or extremely embarrassed. In the aggressive solicitations, 36% of the children and teenagers were very or extremely upset, 32% were very or extremely embarrassed, and 25% were very or extremely afraid.

Data from "Risk factors for and impact of online sexual solicitation of youth" by Mitchell et al.

PARENTAL AWARENESS AND SUPERVISION

The study by Turow and Nir also revealed that almost half of US parents are not aware that Web sites gather information on users without users' knowledge. Most of the time, the personal information gathered is harmless and used for marketing or statistical analysis. However, when opportunity arises, criminal activity may take place. This study explored the level of parental supervision of children's Internet activities among the 1033 participating households that had home Internet access. Ninety-seven percent of the parents responded that they looked at the screen to see what the child or teenager was doing, 85% talked to the youth about being careful about chatting with strangers on the Internet, and 80% reported having rules about what to do or not do while using the Internet. Sixty-three percent of the parents checked the history function of the computer to see what sites the youth had visited, 48% checked files and diskettes, 44% made the youth ask for permission to go on the Internet, and 39% reported rules about the number of hours the youth could spend on the Internet. Also, 69% of parents did not know of a place to report troublesome Internet episodes, and only 10% could name a specific name or authority. To minimize the risks faced by children, general guidelines should be followed. Rules that have been recommended by law enforcement agencies and other professionals are listed in **Table 9-8**.

Table 9-8. Tips to Give Kids for Safe Internet Usage

— Never reveal passwords to anyone online, not even to online service staff members.

— Never reveal identifying information, real name (first or last); family members' names, home addresses, school or team names; details of parents' work; telephone numbers; social security numbers; or credit card numbers in a chat room or in a bulletin board message. Never give this information via e-mail to someone you don't know; remember, no matter how friendly someone seems on the Internet, that person is a stranger and may not be whoever he or she appears to be.

— Never accept offers of merchandise or information or give out your home street address for deliveries without getting permission from a parent or caregiver.

(continued)

Table 9-8. *(continued)*

— Never send a photo of yourself or offer a physical description of yourself or family members over the Internet.

— Never post or upload pictures of yourself onto the Internet or send them to people you do not know personally.

— Never download pictures from an unknown source because they may contain sexually explicit or other inappropriate images.

— Never continue a conversation that makes you feel uncomfortable or becomes personal. Just end the conversation by going to another area of the Internet, and tell an adult what happened.

— Never respond to e-mail, bulletin board system, or instant messenger items that are suggestive, obscene, rude, or make you feel uncomfortable in any way; tell an adult if you come across such messages so that they can be forwarded to the Internet service provider for investigation.

— Never arrange to meet someone in person whom you have met online, and if a meeting is arranged, it is of paramount importance that a parent or guardian is present and the meeting takes place in a public spot.

— Be careful when responding to e-mail: return addresses can be falsified to make the message look innocent. If you cannot verify from whom it came, do not answer it.

— Understand that what you are told or what you read online may or may not be true.

— Talk with your parents about their expectations and ground rules for Internet usage.

Conclusion

The major risks facing children on the Internet fall into the following categories: exposure to inappropriate or dangerous material, potential involvement in illegal activities, giving or receiving harassment, victimization by sexual predators, and the revelation of financial information. Although blocking software and other parental protective software may help limit children's exposure to unwanted or harmful material on the Internet, no software program can be 100% effective. Additional measures, such as educating children on the potential dangers of the Internet and setting rules or agreements to promote responsible online behavior, must be taken.

Where to Turn for Help

Family Guide Book: What You Always Wanted to Know About Filtering Software but Were Afraid to Ask. . .

http://www.familyguidebook.com/filtering.html

Henry J. Kaiser Family Foundation

GenerationRX.com: How Young People Use the Internet for Health Information

http://www.kff.org/entmedia/upload/Toplines.pdf

National Association of Anorexia Nervosa and Associated Disorders

http://www.anad.org/site/anadweb

National Center for Missing and Exploited Children CyberTipline

800-843-5678 (800-THE-LOST)

http://www.cybertipline.com

— Receives reports related to unwanted sexual solicitations and exposure to inappropriate material, wants to be alerted of the online presence of any child pornography, threatening messages, or evidence of criminal action.

NetSmartz Workshop

http://www.netsmartz.org

Parent's Guide to Internet Safety

http://www.fbi.gov/publications/pguide/pguidee.htm

— Provides parents with definitions of Internet terms, brief but useful information on
signs that a child might be at risk while online, steps to take if parents suspect that
children are communicating with a sexual predator, and what to do to minimize the
risk of online victimization.

Partners Against Hate

http://www.partnersagainsthate.org

Teen Safety on the Information Highway

http://www.safeteens.com/safeteens.htm

— Produced by Lawrence J. Magrid, the NCMEC, and a professional educator's
organization called The MASTER, Teen Safety on the Information Highway is
oriented toward adolescent users of the Internet and speaks to teenagers about the
general risk of the internet; specific risks related to chat rooms, instant messaging,
e-mail, peer-to-peer (P2P) systems, newsgroups, forums, and bulletin boards;
making parents aware of the values and risks of the Internet; and basic rules of
online safety.

APPENDIX 9-1. GLOSSARY OF INTERNET TERMS*

Bit: The smallest unit of data in a computer. A bit has a single binary value, either 0 or 1.
1000 bits equals 1 kilobit (Kb); 1 000 000 bits equals 1 megabit (Mb).

Bits per second (BPS): A unit of measure used to express the rate at which data is
transmitted, also referred to as baud rate. A 56K modem transmits data at 56 000 bits
per second.

Browser: Software used to look at various kinds of Internet resources; allows connection to the World Wide Web. Two of the most popular browsers are Microsoft
Internet Explorer and Netscape Navigator.

Bulletin board system (BBS): Computerized meeting and announcement system that
allows users to carry on discussion, upload and download files, and make announcements without being connected to the computer at the same time. There are many
BBSs around the world, though their number has dwindled as a result of the pro-
liferation of the World Wide Web; some are very small, running on a single PC with 1
or 2 phone lines, and others are very large endeavors.

---

* *Data from* Internet Safety Guide: Safe Surfing for Kids *by the Children's Partnership and the National
Criminal Justice Reference Service.*

Cable modem: A technology used to connect to the Internet at speeds significantly greater than a standard phone modem. Cable modems use the same coaxial cable used for cable television to transmit data at speeds up to 1544 megabits per second.

Chat: System that allows for real-time communication between computer users who are connected to the Internet.

Cookie: A small data file that can track such things as passwords and Web sites that have been visited, as well as the timing and frequency of those visits. Cookies are placed on a user's computer by a Web site, which uses that information for various purposes, such as customizing the advertising on the site for the individual user or obtaining the user's mouse movements to build marketing data.

Cybersex: A form of fantasy sex via an interactive chat room session in which participants describe sexual activity and sometimes disrobe and masturbate.

Cyberspace: Term originated by author William Gibson. Currently used to describe the whole range of information resources available through computer networks.

Digital Subscriber Line (DSL): A technology used to connect to the Internet at speeds significantly greater than a standard phone modem. DSL uses existing phone lines to transmit data at speeds up to 1544 megabits per second.

E-mail or electronic mail: Messages, usually text, sent from one person to another via computer. E-mail can also be sent automatically to a large number of addresses using mailing lists.

Emoticons: A combination of text characters to suggest an emotion when read sideways. Some examples are: :-) smiling face to express humor; :-(frowning face to convey sadness or displeasure; ;-) winking smiling face used to convey flirtation or humor. They are often used in instant messaging, chat rooms, and e-mail messages.

Ethernet: A technology used to transmit data. Ethernet cable resembles a phone line, but it can transmit data significantly faster, at up to 100 megabits per second. Ethernet is used to connect computers to a local network, DSL modems, cable modems, and other computer appliances that can communicate at high speeds.

File transfer protocol (FTP): Internet protocol used to transfer files between hosts, using a special program and sometimes a Web browser.

Frequently asked questions (FAQs): Documents that list and answer the most common questions on a particular subject. People who have tired of answering the same question repeatedly usually write FAQs.

Hit: As used in reference to the World Wide Web, a single request from a Web browser for a single item from the Web. Hits are often used as a rough measure of the popularity of a particular document or site (eg, "Our Web site has been getting 300 000 hits per month").

Home page: Most commonly a main Web page for a business, organization, or person; the first screen a user sees when entering a Web site.

Hyperlink: An object, text, or graphic containing a link to a Web page. Clicking on a hyperlink object automatically connects to another Web page, either on the same site or on another Web site.

HyperText Markup Language (HTML): The programming language used to create hypertext documents on the World Wide Web, allowing them to be read by the browser software. This is the most common programming language used to create Web pages.

HyperText Transport Protocol (HTTP): An information retrieval mechanism for HTML documents.

Instant messaging: A form of text-based communication using a program that allows users to find people online and exchange messages with them instantaneously. The instant messaging system alerts users whenever somebody on their "buddy list" is online or trying to contact them via computer. Users can then initiate a chat session with that person and send text messages back and forth. Instant messaging is considered more spontaneous than e-mail or chat rooms, allowing users to surf the Web together while having a text conversation at the same time.

Internet: The vast collection of interconnected computer networks, allowing them to function as a single, large virtual network.

Intranet: A private network on the Internet reserved for sole usage by a specific organization and not accessible to the general public.

Internet relay chat (IRC): A large, multiuser, live chat facility. A number of major IRC servers are found around the world and are linked to each other. Anyone can create a channel, and all others in the channel see anything that anyone types in a given channel. Private channels can be created for multiperson conference calls. A user can log on to the IRC anonymously and "chat" with other users without any identifying personal information being obvious. IRC chat rooms are one place where pedophiles meet to trade stories, and they are also a place where children may be at risk of being lured.

Internet service provider (ISP): An organization that provides access to the Internet in some form, usually for a fee. ISPs sometimes provide their own content, including chat rooms, newsgroups, and other material that is accessible only to other subscribers of their service.

Joint Photographic Expert Group (JPEG): A visual image file format, often used to share photographic images on the Internet.

Listserv: The most common kind of mail list; a convenient way for groups of e-mail users to share information on a group basis. Some listservs are moderated, where a participant reviews the e-mails before they are sent out to all participants, whereas others are not moderated and each member decides whether the content is useful and appropriate to be shared.

Login: (noun) Account name used to gain access to a computer system, most commonly a variant of a user's name; also referred to as "User ID." (verb) The act of accessing a computer system, usually with a User ID and password.

Mail list or mailing list: An automated system that allows people to send e-mail to one address, whereupon the message is copied and sent to all the other subscribers on the mail list. In this way, people who have many different kinds of e-mail access can participate in discussions together.

Modem: A device that connects a computer to a phone line, allowing the computer to talk to other computers through the phone system. Basically, modems do for computers what a telephone does for humans. The word "modem" is a contraction of the words modulate and demodulate, referring to the transformation of data to facilitate transmission via phone lines.

Moving Picture Experts Group (MPEG): A file format used for storing digital video.

Multiple Internet Mail Extensions (MIME): Items that may be included with e-mails such as audio, visual, and text messages.

Online: To be connected to the Internet or a network.

Password: A code used to gain access to a locked system. Strong passwords contain letters and numbers and are not simple combinations such as "virtue7." A good password might be "jyxk47pi."

Search engine: A program, or group of programs, that searches documents for specified keywords and then creates a listing of the documents in which the keywords are found. Search engines common to the Internet include Yahoo, Google, and AltaVista.

Shareware: Software that can be used for free for a trial period, after which a small payment is typically expected.

Site: See Web site.

Spam: A slang term used to describe unsolicited e-mail sent to multiple e-mail addresses. It also describes the act of sending such e-mail.

Uniform Resource Locator (URL): Indicates the Web address for a specific source of information; a string of characters that are typed into browsers to reach specific Web sites.

Web site: A page or set of pages containing text and graphics that can be accessed by anyone with an Internet connection.

World Wide Web (WWW): The universe of hypertext servers (HTTP servers) that allow text, graphics, sound files, and others to be mixed together.

Chapter 10

INJURY PREVENTION

Cynthia DeLago, MD, MPH
Nancy D. Spector, MD

There is nothing more agonizing for parents than to see their child suffer unnecessarily. Unfortunately, thousands of children die or suffer permanent disability from injuries sustained from accidents. Experts in the field of injury prevention no longer use the term *accident* because this implies unpredictable and unavoidable events. In reality, most injuries can be anticipated and avoided. A better term is ***unintentional injuries***.

Children learn through exploration of their environment. When parents are aware of their children's physical abilities and learn about the potential dangers of their environment, unintentional injuries can be prevented. Injury prevention is not about putting children in protective bubbles and severely restricting normal childhood curiosity. Rather, it is about creating a safer environment for children to explore without undue restrictions. This chapter will help parents and caregivers anticipate potentially dangerous situations and assist them in creating a safe environment for their children to explore and learn.

EFFECTS OF INJURY

National statistics are astounding: Unintentional injuries are the leading cause of death in children younger than 19 years. Statistics from the National Center for Injury Control and Prevention (NCICP) Web-based Injury Statistics Query and Reporting System (WISQARS) database reveal that 12 035 children younger than 19 years died from unintentional injuries in the United States in 2003. Most unintentional injury deaths occurred in children between 15 and 19 years of age, with boys outnumbering girls 2.3 to 1. The overwhelming cause of death in all age groups was injuries sustained in motor vehicle crashes. One study led by Susan Gallagher found that for every childhood death caused by an injury, approximately 45 children are hospitalized and 1300 receive treatment in emergency medical departments. Countless children receive medical care for injuries from their primary health care provider and from school nurses.

WHAT PARENTS AND CAREGIVERS CAN DO

Learning which injuries are most likely to occur in each age group allows parents and caregivers to anticipate the most likely ways a child will get injured and take the precautions necessary to protect that child. For example, toddlers are learning to walk and tend explore the world with their mouths. They also have a very limited sense of danger. Because they are very mobile, toddlers can get into dangerous situations that may result in drowning, suffocation, and burns. Falls, choking, and poisoning are also typical injuries for this age group. Also, if not properly restrained in a car seat, they can suffer serious injury or death during a collision. According to NCICP data, motor vehicle occupant injuries are the leading cause of unintentional injury death in this age group. Knowing this information, caregivers can keep objects that can cause choking out of reach, block off stairs or tall furniture down which or from which a toddler might fall, and always restrain their children properly in a car.

Children between the ages of 5 and 14 years face hazards similar to, but greater in range than, those of toddlers. Motor vehicle crashes are the most common cause of death for children this age. Drowning is the second most common, and fires and burns are third. Also, children in this age group are more independent and involved in sports activities in neighborhoods and at schools. As a consequence, many may seek medical care for injuries sustained from falls and collisions. Dog bites are another primary cause of injury. Sources of potential injury vary more for school-aged children because of their greater mobility and independence compared to younger children.

Adolescents are nearly as independent as adults, but their lack of experience and decision-making skills increases their risk for unintentional injuries. NCICP statistics show that teenagers are most often injured from or killed in motor vehicle crashes. The risk of teenagers causing a collision increases with inexperience or using poor judgment, such as driving after using alcohol or drugs. They are also likely to engage in risk-taking behavior around water and with watercrafts, so it is no surprise that poisoning and drowning are the second and third leading causes of injury and death in this age group. Adolescents have the additional distinction of being at increased risk for injuries from fighting. Teenagers injured from fighting without guns usually survive their injuries; those injured with guns often do not survive the trip to the nearest emergency room. Finally, many teenagers work. Approximately 80% of adolescents are employed at some time during their high school years. Unfortunately, data from the Centers for Disease Control and Prevention (CDC) reveal that approximately 200 000 adolescents are injured on the job every year. The next few pages describe ways to ensure that a home is safe and anticipate unsafe situations in the community where children play, go to school, or work. Questions parents and caregivers frequently have about childhood injuries are addressed in **Table 10-1**.

PREVENTING CHILDHOOD INJURIES

If a 2-year-old child is left at the curb of a 2-lane road, he or she will almost certainly venture into the path of a car and get injured. This extreme example illustrates how lack of supervision causes childhood injuries. However, as with this situation, most childhood injuries can be prevented. The first step is to anticipate unsafe situations, and the next is to either avoid these situations or turn them into safe ones with proper planning and supervision. Unsafe circumstances can occur in or out of the home or during transit.

IN-HOME INJURIES

Infants and toddlers will spend a significant amount of time being cared for at home. Although taking the time to "childproof" homes is extremely important, children's curiosity and drive to explore the environment will make it impossible to anticipate their every move. The most critical action parents and caregivers can take is to provide appropriate supervision at all times. All babysitters should be at least 13 years old and capable of responding to emergency situations. Infants and toddlers should never be left unattended unless in a crib or a playpen. Even when parents are watching children, they need to make certain their home is safe. Always expect the unexpected.

Falls

Infants are at risk of falls as soon as they are able to wiggle and push against objects with their feet. In fact, they are at risk from the very first time they move. Unfortunately, it is impossible to predict in advance when this may occur. Infants may begin to crawl as early as 6 months of age and may pull themselves into a standing position soon after that. Parents and caregivers can take certain steps to help keep infants safe from falls (**Table 10-2**). As toddlers begin to walk and climb, be aware of potential ways that they

---

Table 10-1. Frequently Asked Questions

How are children usually injured?

Most minor injuries occur when children fall or collide with something during play. Most fatal injuries occur during motor vehicle crashes because children are not wearing seatbelts or are not appropriately restrained in a child safety seat.

What should I do if my child is burned?

Put cold water on the burned area immediately and loosely cover the burn with a bandage or clean cloth. Always call a health care provider for further instructions.

What should I do if my child swallows a substance that is not food?

Call your primary health care provider or a Poison Control Center immediately. The national toll-free number for Poison Control Centers is 1-800-222-1222.

What should I do if my child is bitten by a dog?

Take your child to a safe place. Call your health care provider for advice on how to treat the wound because dogs can inflict deep puncture or crush wounds. Try to identify whether the attack was provoked; though rabies in dogs is rare, the risk is higher in an unprovoked attack. The health care provider may be required to report your child's dog bite to the Department of Public Health.

What should I do if our house catches on fire?

You should have a fire escape route mapped out before disaster strikes. All household members, especially the children, should know 2 escape routes from the house. Young children have a tendency to hide in closets when fire strikes. Teach your child not to do this. Other fire safety precautions you should teach your child include feeling the door for heat before opening it, since a warm door may mean there is fire behind it, covering his or her mouth and nose with a cloth and staying low to the ground if the room is smokey, and to stop-drop-and-roll if his or her clothes catch on fire.

Instruct everyone to get outside right away to a safe meeting place and call the fire department from a neighbor's house. Do not stop to get dressed—most fire-related deaths occur because victims suffocate from fumes, not because they are burned.

---

may climb to high places such as by using a stool or chair to climb on a bookshelf. Parents should also ensure that the surface under play equipment is soft enough to absorb a fall.

Burns

There are several ways that infants and children can be burned. Infants and toddlers are most often injured from scald burns because many adults do not realize that a full-thickness, or third-degree, burn can occur in only 6 seconds with a water temperature of 140°F (60°C). Toddlers and older children are at risk of burns from contact with hot appliances such as irons, playing with matches, biting electric cords, and sticking fingers or other objects into electrical sockets. **Table 10-3** highlights ways to protect children from burns.

Poisoning

In 1999, Poison Control Centers in the United States reported approximately 2.2 million poison exposures, 873 of which resulted in death. More than half of these poison

---

Table 10-2. Dos and Don'ts of Preventing Falls

— Do put infants in a safe place such as a crib or a playpen when you cannot hold them.

— Don't leave infants alone on an elevated surface such as a couch, changing table, or bed.

— Do use gates on stairways and close doors to keep your infant out of rooms with potential dangers and install window guards on all windows above the first floor.

— Don't use a baby walker. Infants can tip walkers over or fall down the stairs.

— Do remove hard or sharp-edged furniture from the room where your child plays.

— Don't leave crib sides down when the infant is in the crib.

— Do remove bumper pads from around the entire crib when infants begin to stand and lower the crib mattress when they can sit without assistance.

— Do stop using the crib when toddlers are taller than 35 inches (88.9 cm).

Table 10-3. Dos and Don'ts of Protecting Children From Burns

— Don't carry your infant and hot liquids, food, or other objects at the same time.

— Don't leave containers with hot liquid on tables or counter edges.

— Do set the water heater temperature to a maximum of 120°F (49°C).

— Do check electrical cords for breaks or frayed areas.

— Do use commercially available outlet covers on all outlets your infant or toddler can reach.

— Do turn off appliances that have hot surfaces such as irons, curling irons, ovens, wall heaters, and grills when you are finished using them.

— Do put infants in a safe environment, such as a playpen or high chair, while you are cooking.

— Do keep matches and lighters out of the reach of children and teach your child not to play with them.

— Do teach children to run for help if a fire breaks out in the house.

---

exposures occurred in children younger than 6 years. Children younger than 3 years are at the greatest risk of ingesting poisons because they will put anything in their mouths. Parents and caregivers can take various precautions to keep children safe from poisons (**Table 10-4**). If an infant or child does swallow a substance that is not food, call a pediatrician or a poison control center immediately.

It is important to note that the American Academy of Pediatrics (AAP) no longer recommends that parents keep syrup of ipecac, a medicine that induces vomiting, in households. Recent studies have shown that household access to syrup of ipecac increases the risk it will be used inappropriately, resulting in harm to the child. The AAP believes that these potential risks outweigh the potential benefits of having the ipecac in the home.

Table 10-4. Dos and Don'ts of Keeping Children Safe From Poisoning

— Do teach children not to eat or drink anything unless an adult they know gives it to them.

— Don't put cleaning or other inedible products in a food or drink container because a child may attempt to eat or drink from a container that usually contains a food or drink.

— Don't take medicine in front of a small child; children like to imitate adult behaviors.

— Do buy medicines and household products with childproof packaging and immediately replace the safety caps after use.

— Do keep all medicines and household cleaning products locked and out of reach of your child.

— Do frequently check your home for expired medications and discard them by flushing them down the toilet.

— Do have your heating system checked at least once a year to help prevent against carbon monoxide poisoning and install a carbon monoxide detector in all sleeping areas.

Choking and Suffocation

Infants and young children explore their environment by putting everything into their mouths. This is part of normal development, and certain precautions can be taken to protect the children from choking hazards and suffocation (**Table 10-5**). It is important to learn the methods to treat a choking child. Contact local American Red Cross offices at http://www.redcross.org/services/hss/ or the American Heart Association at http://www.americanheart.org for information about basic first aid and CPR classes. These classes teach parents and other caregivers what to do with a choking child. It is also helpful to keep a first aid poster in the house as a reminder. Talk to children's primary health care provider for clarification and further resources.

Dog Bites

According to the CDC, 368 245 persons were treated for dog bite–related injuries in emergency departments in the United States during the year 2001. This number represents less than half of all dog bites that occurred during that year. About 42% of those bitten were children younger than 14 years; boys were bitten more frequently than girls. At least 25 breeds of dogs have been involved in fatal attacks. In cases in

---

Table 10-5. Dos and Don'ts of Preventing Choking and Suffocation

— Don't leave small objects within your infant's reach, even for a moment.

— Don't allow your infant or toddler to play with stuffed animals, dolls, or toys that have potentially removable parts.

— Don't feed your infant hard pieces of food, such as carrots, apples, hot dogs, grapes, peanuts, and popcorn.

— Do cut all foods for an infant or young toddler into small pieces.

— Do keep plastic wrappers and bags away from infants and young children. These items can form a tight seal over a child's mouth and nose.

---

which the breed of the dog was known, rottweilers or pit-bull terriers were responsible for more than half of all fatal attacks. More importantly, the American Veterinary Medical Association Task Force on Canine Aggression found that intact (unneutered) male dogs were involved in almost three fourths of all dog bite incidents. Many children do not know how to behave safely around dogs. They should be taught never to disturb a dog while it is eating or sleeping, never to touch a strange dog or break up fighting dogs, and never to run from a strange dog. Children younger than 4 years should always be supervised around dogs, and infants younger than 1 year should never be left alone with a dog because the dog might be jealous of the attention the infant receives. Families who decide to adopt a dog should choose a dog that is friendly and tolerates children well. The American Veterinary Medical Association and the Humane Society avoid recommending one breed over another. The Humane Society does recommend waiting until all children in the house are 6 years old or older, or until they exhibit self-control, and adopting older dogs that are calm and friendly. The American Veterinary Medical Association urges pet sterilization, especially because intact males tend to be more aggressive. Family dogs must be protected against rabies with a yearly rabies vaccine; the first vaccination is normally given when the dog is 3 or 4 months old. Teaching a dog the commands "down" and "sit" and teaching children to use these commands is another important step in controlling the dog and preventing injury.

If a child is bitten by a dog, take the child to a safe place and examine the wound. Call a primary health care provider for advice on treatment because dogs can inflict deep puncture wounds and crush injuries that require professional attention. Try to identify whether the attack was provoked, whether the dog is a stray or known by someone in the home or neighborhood, and whether the dog has had its shots. Although rabies in dogs is rare, the CDC states that the risk a dog is infected is higher if the attack is unprovoked, if the dog exhibited unusual behavior before the attack, or if the dog is a stranger with an unknown immunization record. The health care provider may be required to report the dog bite to the Department of Public Health.

GENERAL HOUSEHOLD SAFETY

Furniture

When assessing a home for the potential dangers that it may present to an infant or child, it is essential to consider the safety of the furniture (**Table 10-6**). Furniture, particularly bookcases, chairs, and couches, offers opportunities for children to climb and fall. Tall and unsteady pieces of furniture may fall onto a child and cause significant injuries. Children who are learning to walk may fall against sharp-edged furniture, resulting in an abrasion or laceration.

Fire Safety

Children younger than 5 years are among those most at risk for injuries from residential fires. To lower the risk of injury, parents should install smoke detectors in the home, including in furnace and sleeping areas, test the batteries every month, and change them every year on a memorable date like daylight savings time. Heating systems should be checked and cleaned yearly. To avoid electrical fires, electrical cords should be monitored for breaks or frays, and electrical sockets never overloaded. Dryer lint traps clogged with lint are also a common cause of avoidable house fires. Smoking should not be allowed in the home, especially in bed, and matches and lighters must be kept out of the reach of children.

It is important for families to have an escape plan that includes several escape routes from the house and a place to meet after leaving the house, in case of fire. Conducting fire drills and practicing this escape plan can prevent confusion and panic if a fire does occur.

Table 10-6. Dos and Don'ts of Making Furniture Safe

— Do store toys on low, open shelves for easy access by your child.

— Do make sure toy chests have no tops because hinged lids can fall onto children as they search for toys or trap them if they have climbed or fallen in.

— Do teach children not to climb on furniture.

— Do make sure that tall pieces of furniture such as bookcases and armoires are secured to the wall with brackets, which can be purchased at hardware stores.

— Don't keep unnecessary furniture or furniture made of glass in play areas.

— Do cover sharp edges and corners of furniture and fireplace hearths with padding, which can be purchased at large, commercial toy stores, baby furniture stores, or via online baby product Web sites.

Firearms

A National Institute of Justice survey called "Guns in America" revealed that more than 44 million Americans owned firearms in 1994. Of those 192 million firearms, 65 million were handguns, and more than half of these were stored unlocked. Medical literature has demonstrated that guns in the home result in serious risk to children. More than 5000 children and adolescents are killed by gunfire each year, and injuries are almost always self-inflicted or inflicted by a sibling or friend. Research conducted for the Brady Campaign to Prevent Gun Violence showed that a gun kept in the home is 43 times more likely to kill someone known to the family than to kill a stranger in self-defense. Having a gun in the home triples the risk of a homicide occurring and makes the chances that someone who lives in the home will commit suicide 5 times greater. To eliminate this danger, guns, especially handguns, should not be kept in the home. **Table 10-7** discusses ways to minimize the risk of injury from firearms.

Table 10-7. Dos and Don'ts of Firearm Safety

— Do talk to children about the dangers of guns and tell them to stay away from guns.

— Don't allow your child to play with toy guns.

— Do ask if there are guns in the homes of children's friends before they go to play dates at friends' houses.

— If you choose to have a gun in your home, do keep the gun unloaded and locked in a chest or closet.

— Do lock and store the bullets in a place separate from the gun.

— Do hide the keys to the gun chest or closet in a locked box.

OUT-OF-HOME INJURIES

As children grow older, they spend more and more time away from home. Toddlers and preschool-aged children first venture outside at supervised play in parks, playgrounds, or swimming pools. School-aged children spend at least one third of their day at school. Teenagers spend most of their time at school and work. The major causes of injury-related deaths—motor vehicle crashes, drowning, and falling—occur outside of the home.

Transportation

Our society relies heavily on motor vehicles. Today, there is roughly 1 car per licensed driver, and, according to research published in *The American Journal of Public Health*, the paved landmass in the United States today is equal to the landmass of the entire state of Georgia. It is no wonder that the leading cause of death in the United States is motor vehicle occupant injuries. Motor vehicles also cause many pedestrian and bicyclist deaths. Data released from the National Highway Traffic Safety Administration (NHTSA) reveals that in 2004, motor vehicle crashes killed 42 636 people. Of these, 4641 were pedestrians and 725 were cyclists. Over the years, injury prevention efforts have focused on how individuals operate their cars, bicycles, and other modes of transportation. This focus has led to a greater understanding of how injuries are caused and what can be done to prevent them.

Two key determinants in preventing serious injury and death from motor vehicles are how both the motor vehicle operator and others on the road behave. Because the behavior of others is uncontrollable, it is all the more vital that parents and caregivers operate their cars responsibly. Do not drive when intoxicated, overtired, or distracted, and ensure that all occupants are properly restrained.

Child safety seats decrease the risk of death in infants by 71% and in children aged 1 to 4 years by 54%, according to the NHTSA. Children 9 years old or older who use seat belts have a 50% decreased chance of being injured in a car crash. Dr. Durbin and colleagues also found that belt-positioning booster seats decrease the risk of injury to children between 4 and 7 years old by 59%. All children 12 years or younger should ride in the back seat of a car because they are less likely to be fatally injured during a collision if seated there.

Infants riding in cars are safest if properly restrained in regulation infant safety seats in the backseat of cars, facing toward the back. Once they reach their first birthday and weigh 20 lbs (9 kg), children can be restrained in front-facing child safety seats in the back seat of the car. Child safety seats should be properly installed and used for toddlers until they weigh 40 lbs (18 kg) or reach their fourth birthday. Once they outgrow their car seat, children should immediately graduate to belt-positioning booster seats. These seats are designed for 4- to 8-year-old children or children less than 4 feet, 9 inches (1.66 m) tall. For further details regarding child safety seats, see the American Academy of Pediatrics' Web site and the National Traffic Highway Safety Administration Web site referenced in the section called "Where to Turn for Help."

Another concern with motor vehicle safety is leaving infants or children alone in a car. This should never be done, especially when the weather is hot. The temperature inside a car can increase very quickly, even when the windows are rolled down. Leaving a child alone in a car, even for a few minutes, is extremely dangerous or even deadly.

Motor vehicles are involved in about 90% of bicycle-related deaths. A study Dr. Baker and colleagues published with the Johns Hopkins Injury Prevention Center found that head injuries are the cause of death in 62% of these cases. Bicycle helmets reduce the risk of serious head injury by 85%. They also decrease the risk for serious upper face injuries by 65%, as the CDC states, but helmets do not reduce the risk of injury to other parts of the body. For these reasons, it is important that children and caregivers wear bike helmets when riding and for children to learn about basic road safety before being allowed to ride near roadways.

Check all family members' bike helmets to see if they are Snell B-95, ASTM, or Consumer Products Safety Commission (CPSC) approved. If not, buy new helmets. All bike helmets made since March 1999 must meet CPSC standards. In addition to wearing approved helmets, children need to understand basic safety recommendations and traffic laws, including:

— Wear bright colors and proper footwear and, when biking, avoid wearing loose clothing.

— Ride with traffic and not against it.

— Cross at crosswalks.

— Look both ways before crossing.

— Cross with the green traffic light.

These same traffic safety principles apply to pedestrians. Because young children do not have the vision, timing, or experience necessary to judge when it is safe to cross a street, teaching children these rules and properly supervising them while walking near traffic will keep them safe. For more information about pedestrian and bicycle safety, including helpful diagrams, refer to the Web sites listed in "Where to Turn for Help."

Teenaged bicyclists and pedestrians have different safety issues than younger children. In 1999, the CDC estimated that one third of pedestrians aged 14 years and older who were killed by a motor vehicle were intoxicated at the time. Baker and colleagues report that in the accidents they studied, about 14% of fatally injured bicyclists between the ages of 15 and 19 years were drinking alcohol before the accident, and 8% were legally intoxicated at the time of the accident. Unfortunately, the NCIPC has found that teenagers almost never wear bike helmets, another factor that increases their chances of sustaining serious injury.

Water

NCIPC data reveal that drowning is the second most common cause of death in children between the ages of 1 and 14 years. In general, younger children drown closest to home—the very young drown *in* the home. Children younger than 1 year drown in bathtubs, toilets, and buckets of water. Children between the ages of 1 and 4 years drown in residential swimming pools. Older children drown in rivers, lakes, and creeks. Drowning deaths in teens and young adults are associated with alcohol use 25% to 50% of the time.

Anticipating dangerous situations is the best way to prevent children from drowning. Supervising a young child can be very difficult, especially if the child is very active. Participation in infant and toddler swimming programs does not protect children from drowning, and parents should not allow the fact that their child has swimming skills give them a false sense of security. The AAP reports that in drowning cases involving 1- to 4-year-old children, many times the children were seen in their own homes by one or both parent minutes before the event.

Constant supervision is necessary whenever children aged 1 year or younger are near water in containers such as buckets, toilets, and bathtubs. Parents or caregivers whose families live near swimming pools need to be sure that the areas around them are completely surrounded by a non-climbable 5-foot fence and that the gates are self-closing and self-latching. If the house forms one side of the pool barrier, then doors with direct pool access should have an alarm. The door latch and door alarm controls should be out of reach of small children—usually at 54 inches (1.34 m) from the ground. Pool owners have the responsibility of ensuring the safety of others. Insist that anyone using the pool adhere to pool safety rules such as no diving in shallow areas. Anyone in the house who is older than 14 years should be certified in infant and child cardiopulmonary resuscitation (CPR).

Natural bodies of water pose more drowning risks to older children than do swimming pools. For any families that live near natural bodies of water and have small children, door alarms are essential. Children who live near water ought to know how to swim, but parents should not rely on swimming skills to prevent drowning. Children should never swim alone; swimming in areas guarded by lifeguards greatly reduces the chance of drowning. Encourage children to use lifejackets when boating and discourage the use of alcohol. Parents teach children responsible behaviors by example.

Playgrounds

The job of a young child is to play. Playing teaches children about social interactions and rules. It stokes the fire of imagination and helps develop physical dexterity. Toddlers and preschool children spend many hours playing outside at playgrounds. Likewise, school-aged children spend outdoor playtime at their school-based playgrounds. Playgrounds are wonderful places for children—if they are safe. Unfortunately, in 2002 more than 200 000 children 14 years old or younger were injured on playgrounds, according to CPSC and National SAFEKIDS Campaign studies on playground equipment. Almost half of these injuries required treatment in emergency departments. One third were serious injuries such as fractures, concussions, internal injuries, dislocations, and amputations. Swings, slides, and climbing equipment were involved in most of these cases. During this same time period, approximately one third of playground equipment–related deaths and 70% of injuries occurred on public playgrounds. The few children who died from playground equipment–related injuries died from strangulation or from falling from a height onto a hard surface.

What situations are unsafe and what can be done to make them safe? The first unsafe situation begins with the type of clothing worn on a playground. Clothing with drawstrings around the neck area, such as hooded jackets, can get caught and strangle the child. Likewise, children wearing bike helmets while playing on playground equipment risk strangulation from head straps that get caught.

Climbing equipment and slides are potentially hazardous, especially if they are not age appropriate. If the equipment seems too big for your child, it probably is not age appropriate. Playgrounds should have energy-absorbing surfaces to decrease the chance of serious injury from falls. Shredded rubber has the best energy-absorbing capability, but sand, wood fibers, and wood chips all perform well. The CPSC recommends a 12-inch (30.5 cm)-thick layer. This surface should extend 6 feet (1.83 m) beyond the edge of the equipment and should extend in the front and back of the swing at a distance twice the height of the suspension bar supporting it. The playing surface should be free of tripping hazards and poisonous plants. Climbing equipment more than 2.5 feet (76 cm) high should be spaced 9 feet (2.74 m) apart so that, in case of a fall, children do not hit other structures. Unsafe situations exist if the equipment is not correctly installed, anchored, or well maintained. Check for sharp points or edges and loose or dangerous hardware, such as S-shaped hooks. Check for openings or spaces that measure more than 3.5 inches but less than 9 inches, as these can entrap small children.

A final caution about the materials used in building many playgrounds: Wood that is pressure treated with chromated copper arsenate is often used to build playgrounds and decks. This wood leaches arsenic. Arsenic exposure increases a person's lifetime risk for bladder and lung cancer. Children transfer the arsenic on the wood to their bodies by putting their hands in their mouths after playing on the equipment. The CPSC is considering a petition to ban the use of pressure-treated wood products. In the meantime, minimize children's exposure to arsenic by thoroughly washing their hands after playing on playgrounds and decks.

School and Sports

Children spend almost as much time at school as they do at home. Many of the safety issues discussed in this chapter should be applied to the school environment, especially the information about playgrounds, because most school injuries occur outdoors during playtime. Many children, adolescents, and young adults are involved in either community-sponsored sports programs or school sports. The National Center for Health Statistics reports that sports-related injuries account for 33.9 emergency visits per 1000 persons between the ages of 5 and 24 years. There are some simple measures parents and caregivers can take to avoid some sports injuries.

First, parents and coaches should be mindful of the young athlete's developmental stage. Young children have very short attention spans and learn better if the coach instructs by demonstration. They also may not be developmentally capable of performing some maneuvers intrinsic to the sport, such as dribbling a basketball. Just as some children go through puberty earlier than others, some children have more advanced motor development than others. Organized sports participation should be fun for all children participating. If it is not fun for the child, then participation should be reconsidered.

Second, children should receive sports physicals at least once a year. Older athletes should be reexamined within 1 to 2 months before a new sport is started. This is especially important for athletes who suffered previous injuries because these injuries can predispose them to new injuries if muscle weakness or limitation in range of motion is still present. Sports physicals are designed to detect these problems and allow for proper rehabilitation before active participation resumes.

Third, take the time to observe how sports practices are conducted. Most community sports programs rely on volunteer coaches who may or may not know much about child development or injuries and injury prevention. There are some very basic principles that all coaches should know and follow:

— All athletes should have access to water, especially on hot days; fluid restriction in any sport is an unsafe practice.

— The equipment being used to protect athletes should be in good repair, including the playing surface; some equipment such as helmets, mouth guards, and eye protection should be certified.

— Athletes should go through warm-up and cool-down exercises at the beginning and end of practice to prevent muscle strains and sprains.

— Finally, coaches need to listen to their athletes: Athletes, especially older athletes, often do not complain to their coaches unless they are having real problems. Any complaints should be taken seriously, and the athlete should receive prompt attention. Sometimes athletes do not complain even if they are having real difficulty. Coaches need to be observant and remove these athletes from practice or the game so they can be properly evaluated and treated.

Parents and caregivers who observe any unsafe practices should speak to the coach or the sports commissioner about your concerns. Sports offer tremendous benefits to children but can be dangerous if they are improperly supervised or if the equipment is faulty.

Last, the goals of involving young children in sports are for them to develop the proper techniques and skills necessary to perform the sport, to build self-esteem and self-discipline, and to learn to cooperate with each other for the good of the whole team. Unfortunately, many parents and coaches lose sight of these goals, and once this happens, the precautions needed to prevent injuries are often ignored. The American Academy of Pediatrics Committee on Sports Medicine advises against intensive training and sports specialization in young athletes because the strong emphasis on competition and long hours of training places inordinate physical and psychological stress on children that predisposes them to overuse injuries.

Jobs

Many teenagers work part-time, often about 20 hours per week. Employment is a rite of passage into adulthood and provides extra spending money. Teenagers can learn job skills, manage responsibility, and become more independent, but they can also be injured. Despite working less dangerous jobs than adults, the US Department of Health and Human Services publication *Promoting Safe Work for Young Workers* reports that young workers are injured at higher rates. There are several reasons for this. First, teenagers are often tired from going to school all day before going to work. Also, they enjoy the responsibility and challenge of a job and are often willing to do whatever is asked of them, even if they are unprepared or physically incapable of doing the task. Because of their inexperience, teenagers are not able to anticipate hazards and avoid injury, and because of their youthfulness, they are less willing to know their rights and ask questions. Last, some teenagers believe they are invincible. They may be exposed to unhealthy conditions such as unsafe levels of noise, extreme temperatures, hazardous chemicals, poor air quality, infectious agents, and tasks requiring repetitive motions. These exposures may pose long-term health risks, yet many teenagers still choose to work under these conditions.

Child labor laws restrict the number of hours and types of jobs teenagers can work. Nevertheless, teenagers are injured at legal jobs as well as illegal jobs; they are just more at risk for injury on illegal jobs. Seventy teenagers die from work-related injuries each year, and approximately 100 000 youths between 15 and 17 years old visit emergency rooms every year. More than 200 000 youths are injured each year. Typical injuries include cuts, scrapes, bruises, burns, sprains, strains, dislocations, and fractures. Most teenagers are injured working at the types of jobs that most often employ teenagers—retail stores, restaurants, and grocery stores.

To be safe on the job, teenagers need to understand their rights as workers and adhere to the child labor laws. They need to become aware of potential hazards and be encouraged to ask questions. The National Institute of Occupational Health and Safety created an easy-to-read document for teenagers entitled "Are you a working teen? What you should know about safety and health on the job." This document is available on the Internet at http://www.cdc.gov/niosh/adoldoc.html. Parents and caregivers need to use their judgment. Ask questions about supervision and working conditions. Although they need to respect their adolescents' decisions, parents should not forget that their role is to help guide their children in making correct decisions.

Summer Camps

Choosing a summer camp for children is often difficult. During this process, an extremely important factor to consider is the safety of the camp environment. According to the American Camp Association, the organization that accredits camps on the basis of nationally recognized standards, only 2200 of the 8500 US day and resident camps are accredited. The American Camp Association Web site provides valuable information on the accreditation process (see "Where to Turn for Help"). Whether the camp is accredited, obtain answers to the questions in **Table 10-8** before enrolling children in camps. Also, if a child has specific medical problems, discuss camp with his or her pediatrician, who may require activity restrictions, alter medication prescriptions, or suggest requesting special accommodations for the child at camp.

PROFESSIONAL STUDY AND CONTROVERSY

Although no one can argue that injury prevention is important, some might argue over the current approach taken to tackling the problem of unintentional injuries in children. As more information is available on how to prevent injuries, an increasing number of rules and regulations are being instituted that dictate personal behavior in cars, homes, places of work, and recreation. These laws save lives and prevent serious disability. Yet, how far should lawmakers go in this direction? How much can be regulated and legalized before personal rights are infringed?

Injury-prevention research principles are based on the Haddon Matrix, developed by Dr. William Haddon in 1972. Haddon contended that injuries are not caused by accidents. Rather, he argued, they are often predictable and preventable events that can be studied in the context of 2 perspectives. The first is from the perspective of the person injured: What instrument or mechanism injured the person; what were the envi-

---

Table 10-8. Questions to Ask Before Enrolling Children in a Summer Camp

— Are the children well supervised? What is the ratio of staff to campers? What are the experience and qualification requirements of the staff? What special training do staff members receive?

— What precautionary measures does the camp take to prevent injuries on the playgrounds, sports fields, and water, or during transportation?

— How are minor medical situations handled? Is there a nurse available on a full-time, part-time, or on-call basis?

— If my child requires medication routinely, who will be responsible for the administration of the medication?

— If my child suffers from food allergies, what precautions are taken to prevent exposure of my child to certain foods?

— What happens in the case of serious injury or trauma? Do local Emergency Medical Services, physicians, and hospitals know the camp's location and operating dates?

— Are infection control measures in place?

ronmental conditions at the time the injury occurred; and what happened to the person injured? The second is from the perspective of time: What events occurred just before the injury; what was going on at the time of the injury; and what happened to the person after the injury occurred? Subsequently, injury-prevention researchers began using this matrix to examine injuries primarily from the perspective of individuals. For example, what type of injury is the most lethal to a bicyclist, and what can be done about it? Data collected from many bicycle injuries and an examination of common themes show that bicyclists are more apt to die from head injuries. The solution is to alter something about the individual before the event, such as wearing a bike helmet. The Haddon Matrix approach has greatly expanded our knowledge of and ability to predict and prevent injuries, but it can be used in a more expansive sense by focusing more on pre-event environments that predispose whole groups of people to certain types of injury.

Several authors featured in the September 2003 issue of *The American Journal of Public Health* espouse an increased focus on pre-event environments. They propose that readers look at the "built environment," or the environment created when communities are built. One such movement underway is called "Smart Growth America," a national coalition that challenges the way communities are planned and built. Proponents decry suburban sprawl because it increases dependency on cars, increases air pollution, destroys the environment, promotes sedentary lifestyles, and increases the risk for traffic-related injuries. Drs. Risa Lavizzo-Mourey and J. Michael McGinnis define the term *sprawl* as "any environment characterized by low-density residential development; rigid separation of homes, shops and workplaces; a lack of distinct, thriving activity centers, such as strong downtowns or suburban town centers; and a network of roads marked by very large block size and poor access from one place to another." Lavizzo-Mourey and McGinnis found that urban sprawl is directly related to traffic and pedestrian fatalities: More fatalities occur where sprawl is greater.

Another movement called "Active Living" challenges community planners to incorporate bicycle- and pedestrian-safe designs, safe routes to schools, traffic-calming measures, public gardens, and other plans that promote increased physical activity and safe recreation by changing community designs and improving transportation. The Active Living Network includes designers, community planners, engineers, transportation experts, recreation officials and public health officials. These professionals collaborate to discuss, research and implement creative community designs to make home and work environments more conducive to safe walking, playing, and bicycling for people of all ages.

Other aspects of improving the built environment have to do with how cities are revitalized and open spaces preserved. Many schools in the United States are close to 50 years old, and the infrastructures of many municipal systems need repair. This repair will provide opportunities to replan and rebuild, keeping in mind that there are different and better ways to structure communities to promote healthier and safer living. Restructuring communities and improving the environment can increase safety without necessarily passing more laws or infringing on individual rights.

All citizens, especially parents, teachers, and health care workers, should become actively involved in community planning issues. Look at different models and ideas and take these to planning boards. A simple place to start is to look at the "bikeability" of a community, using the checklist provided on the National Highway Transportation Safety Administration Web site listed in "Where to Turn for Help," which helps assess a community's friendliness to bicycle riders. This checklist can evaluate the condition of municipal playgrounds, including how safe it is to get to them by walking and riding bikes. This may give concerned adults the information necessary to get people in their communities interested.

CONCLUSION

The world can be a dangerous place, and the possibility of a child getting injured in some way is frightening. Fortunately, many unintentional childhood injuries are preventable if parents and caregivers remember to ask the right questions and monitor their children's surroundings.

WHERE TO TURN FOR HELP

GENERAL INJURY PREVENTION
American Academy of Pediatrics Parenting Corner

http://www.aap.org/parents.html

— Allows parents to search by injury prevention topic.

SafeUSA

http://www.safeusa.org

POISONING PREVENTION
American Association of Poison Control Centers

http://www.aapcc.org

FIRE PROTECTION
National Fire Protection Association

http://www.nfpa.org

TRANSPORTATION
National Center for Injury Prevention and Control: National Child Passenger Safety Week

http://www.nhtsa.dot.gov/people/injury/childps/CPSWeekPlanner2005/pages/index.htm

National Highway Transportation Safety Administration: Traffic Safety: Bicycles

http://www.nhtsa.dot.gov/

— Contains information on traffic safety, including diagrams for properly using safety seats, pedestrian safety, including school bus safety, and bicycle safety information.

National Highway Transportation Safety Administration: Bikeability Checklist

http://www.nhtsa.dot.gov/people/injury/pedbimot/bike/Bikeability/index.htm

— Helps assess community "bikeability" and offers tips for improving safety.

National Highway Transportation Safety Administration: Traffic Safety: Child Passenger Safety

http://www.nhtsa.dot.gov/

— Features a great resource for child passenger restraints, including a chart for proper usage.

National Highway Transportation Safety Administration: Vince and Larry's Safety City

http://www.nhtsa.dot.gov/kids

— Designed to teach young bicyclists and pedestrians about road safety.

PLAYGROUND SAFETY
US Consumer Product Safety Commission

http://www.cpsc.gov/cpscpub/pubs/playpubs.html

— Has numerous publications on playground safety.

SPORTS SAFETY
National Institute of Arthritis and Musculoskeletal and Skin Diseases and the National Institutes of Health: Childhood Sports Injuries and Their Prevention

http://www.niams.nih.gov/hi/topics/childsports/child_sports.htm

National Youth Sports Safety Foundation: National Campaign for Safety Equipment

http://www.nyssf.org/safetyequipment.html

— Lists protective sports equipment and certifying agencies.

TEENAGER EMPLOYMENT
National Institute of Occupational Health and Safety: "Are you a working teen? What you should know about safety and health on the job."

http://www.cdc.gov/niosh/adoldoc.html

SUMMER CAMPS
American Camp Association

http://www.acacamps.org

— Accredits camps based on nationally recognized safety standards; the Web site provides information about camp accreditation, as well as information on how to choose a camp.

Chapter 11

ENVIRONMENTAL HEALTH

Hans B. Kersten, MD

Environmental health concerns the protection of children and the larger community from toxic hazards in the environment as well as from other hazards such as exposure to ultraviolet radiation in sunlight. Children are at particular risk for exposure to environmental hazards because their small size and developmental abilities keep them in close contact with objects and elements of their environment. The fact that children's brains and other organs are still developing makes them more susceptible to the effects of these hazards. The developmental disability that can result from this damage may be irreversible and permanent.

According to current medical references on environmental toxins, more than 80 000 chemicals are allowed in the United States alone. Chemicals pervade the environment, and children are continuously exposed to toxins in air, food, and water. Traces of man-made toxins are believed to exist in all humans and mammals. Research on a few known neurodevelopmental toxins, such as alcohol and nicotine, has demonstrated multiple mechanisms by which these compounds disrupt normal brain development. Complex interactions among genetic, chemical, and social factors influence the extent of the resulting developmental disability. The purpose of this chapter is to discuss the unique ways in which children are susceptible to environmental toxins, explain some of the many toxins to which children are frequently exposed, and explore the ways that parents, teachers, nurses, and childcare and health care workers can help decrease the exposure of children to environmental hazards.

EFFECTS OF ENVIRONMENTAL EXPOSURES

REASONS CHILDREN ARE AT SPECIAL RISK

From life in the womb to adolescence, children are particularly susceptible to the effects of environmental toxins. They are biologically immature and grow rapidly; in no way are they little adults. A developing brain is particularly susceptible to environmental toxins, and so exposure to toxins can have serious consequences for children.

A fetus experiences very rapid cell growth. Each time a cell divides, the fetus is at risk for a mutation or damage that can have lifelong implications. A fetus is primarily exposed to environmental toxins through the placenta. This fact was first illustrated by a well-known study that noted the development of a form of cervical cancer called adenocarcinoma in children whose mothers took diethylstilbestrol, a synthetic estrogen used to prevent miscarriages. Although the placenta protects fetuses from many substances, it is unable to protect them from toxins such as cigarette smoke, mercury, and lead.

After birth, a newborn is exposed to environmental toxins through the blood and those organs and tissues that continue to have rapid growth, namely the lungs, skin, and nervous system (which includes the brain). The exposure route and effect depends on the age of the child. Infants are most susceptible to damage resulting from an immature, "leaky," or more technically, "permeable," gastrointestinal tract (GI) and skin. Infants are most likely to be exposed to lead or other toxins through their skin.

Infants and toddlers are at high risk of exposure to air pollutants and ingested toxins. They have a higher respiratory (breathing) rate and a more active metabolism, or in other words a higher basal metabolic rate measurement, than adults. Toddlers also engage in a lot of hand-to-mouth activity, are close to and often crawl or play on the ground, frequently play outside, and constantly touch objects in their environment. All of these behaviors place them at risk for exposure to toxins. A higher respiratory rate and vigorous outdoor play exposes them to air pollutants such as secondhand smoke and smog. The hand-to-mouth and exploratory behaviors expose them to such things as lead paint chips or pesticides in the house, garage, or yard. In addition, according to research by Dr. Benjamin Gitterman, the Codirector of the Mid-Atlantic Center for Children's Health and the Environment, the fact that toddlers' diets are less varied and contain more fruits and vegetables than adults makes them more vulnerable to pesticides, lead, and nitrates. Finally, the more rapid metabolism or higher basal metabolic rate of children makes them much more susceptible to damage caused by a dose of a toxin than adults because they would absorb it faster.

When children start school, they are out of the home for extended periods of time and not as closely supervised. They explore other environments and may be exposed to various toxins at school, such as automobile pollutants from roadways, poor drinking water, toxic arts and crafts supplies, playground equipment, and chemicals dumped in empty lots or present in mud puddles. School-aged children are susceptible to toxins that affect cognitive development, asthma, and chronic cough.

During adolescence, children often venture into new environments and are likely to ignore or misjudge the risks of environmental hazards. They are still susceptible to effects on cognitive development, asthma, and chronic cough, and they may also directly expose themselves to environmental toxins if they start smoking, use or abuse drugs, or display dangerous behaviors such as inhaling chemicals in commercially available glue or other substances. Inhaling products similar to glue is commonly referred to as *huffing*.

Lead, mercury, tobacco smoke, and UV radiation are other examples of common environmental toxins to which children are exposed. **Table 11-1** answers questions parents and caregivers frequently have about environmental exposures and children.

LEAD
Lead poisoning was first described over 2000 years ago when the Greek physician Dioscorides noted that lead "made the mind give way." The detrimental effects of lead exposure on the brain were also described during the Roman Empire and by Benjamin Franklin. Some researchers feel that lead poisoning may have even led to the premature death of Ludwig van Beethoven. Lead poisonings as severe as these occurred when there were very high levels of lead in the body; patients were noted to have seizures, coma, or serious brain dysfunction (encephalopathy). Low levels of lead poisoning were not recognized at the time; patients generally did not have any symptoms, and there was no way to measure blood lead levels (BLLs). Pediatrician Randolf Byers and psychologist Elizabeth Lord first recognized the effect of low levels of lead on intelligence quotient (IQ) and behavior in the 1940s. Since that time, many research studies have shown profound effects of these low BLLs on IQ and behavior, in spite of the lack of symptoms in the children studied. The American Academy of Pediatrics (AAP) reports that millions of children had elevated lead levels as a result of exposure to leaded gaso-

Table 11-1. Frequently Asked Questions

Our home was built in the early 1900s, and we have been told that it probably contains a lot of lead paint. I am worried that my young children may be exposed to lead. What should I do?

Since your home was built before 1960, it probably does contain lead-based paint, probably on windows, windowsills, doorways, and porches. Lead paint becomes a problem when the paint peels or chips off. When peeling or chipping occurs, lead paint and dust are spread in the house, and children can be exposed to lead and become poisoned. Lead paint dust can also be created when homes are renovated and scraping, sanding, or burning removes paint. If your house contains peeling paint, then it is likely that your children are being exposed to lead and should be tested for lead poisoning. If their lead level is above 20 mcg/dL, the Department of Public Health may want to inspect your home. Blood lead levels less than 45 mcg/dL are generally not treated with medicines. You can also test your home for lead-based paint yourself with home lead testing kits available from your local hardware store. Any lead-based paint you find needs to be covered up or removed; the removal process can be very expensive and difficult. Contact your local Department of Public Health for recommendations on how to remove lead-based paint, or remediate the home to cover up the paint and prevent lead poisoning.

I recently heard that fish have high levels of mercury in them. I thought fish was supposed to be good for you. Can I still feed my children fish?

Your family still can and should eat fish, but you need to be careful. Eating fish can be an important part of a healthy diet for children and adults because of the high-quality proteins and unsaturated fats in fish. However, small children, pregnant women, nursing mothers, and women who become pregnant are at highest risk for the toxic effects of methylmercury. This group needs to be careful about the quantity and type of fish they consume and should follow the EPA and Food and Drug Administration joint recommendations. Children should follow these same rules, except the serving sizes should be smaller. However, childhood staples like fish sticks and chunk-light tuna are regarded as safe, as long as children do not consume more than 6 ounces (about 2 meals) of this type of fish each week.

My children all have been diagnosed with asthma. My husband and I smoke, but we always go outside. My neighbor told me this was not enough. Is that true?

Although it is a good idea not to smoke around your children, smoking outside probably does not protect them from the harmful effects of cigarette smoke on their asthma. The smoke gets in your clothes and the indoor air (indoor pollutant) in spite of your best efforts and may make your children's asthmatic symptoms worse. The best thing for your children's health, and your own, is for you and your husband to stop smoking altogether. This is the only way to be sure you are not putting your children at risk of the harmful effects of secondhand smoke.

The news has reported about the increased incidence of skin cancer in America. My children and I love to spend time outside, especially in the summer. What should we do to protect ourselves from the sun?

Protecting you children and yourself from the effects of sunlight, or ultraviolet radiation (UVR), is very important. The American Academy of Pediatrics, the American Cancer Society, and the Centers for Disease Control and Prevention all recommend the practice of sun-safe behaviors. Sun-safe behaviors include the use of sunscreen while exhibiting other behaviors to reduce the exposure to the harmful effects of UVR (eg, wearing tight-weave cotton clothing to cover up).

(continued)

> **Table 11-1.** *(continued)*
>
> Infants younger than 6 months should be dressed in long, lightweight pants, a shirt, and a brimmed hat. A minimal amount of sunscreen may be used on infants' faces or the back of their necks. Young children should apply a sunscreen with an SPF (sun protection factor) of 15 at least 30 minutes before going outside. Older children should be encouraged to cover up with a hat with a 3-inch brim, cotton clothing with a tight weave, and sunglasses that block 99% to 100% of UVR. Keep children in the shade whenever possible, avoid sun exposure during peak hours (10 AM to 4 PM), and reapply sunscreen every 2 hours or after swimming or sweating.

line and paint, and the collective research finally led to efforts toward the removal of lead from gasoline and paint in the mid to late 1970s. Although there has been a dramatic decrease in the prevalence of lead poisoning in children since that time, a National Health and Nutrition survey found that over 250 000 children in the United States have elevated lead levels, though most do not have any symptoms.

Removing lead from paint and gasoline may have decreased the prevalence of lead poisoning, but it did not eliminate exposure. Young children continue to be exposed to lead primarily through paint chips and dust in older homes. There are many other less common sources of lead, including some imported eye cosmetics (kohl, or surma) traditionally used in Middle Eastern and North African cultures, home remedies used to treat illness in Hispanic cultures (the medicines azarcon or greta), and painted pottery from South American and other countries. Lead levels in these preparations may be very high. Children can also be exposed to lead when parents bring home lead from their occupation or hobby (auto repair, battery recycling, painting). Recent cases of lead poisoning have even resulted from school-aged children swallowing or sucking on metal jewelry from department stores or trinkets from gumball machines, which can be as much as 40% lead. All of these sources are summarized in **Table 11-2**. The main risk factors for exposure to lead are listed in **Table 11-3**.

Lead enters the body when children eat or ingest lead-containing material, such as paint chips, and through inhalation of lead dust. Lead dust is created when window or door surfaces that contain lead are opened and closed. The frequent hand-to-mouth activity of children until reaching 2 to 3 years of age, and children's higher respiratory and metabolic rate, accounts for their lead exposure being almost 20 times higher than adults'. Once inhaled or ingested, lead is absorbed and stored in bones, where it may remain for several years. Then the lead begins to exert its effects, most profoundly on the brain and IQ development. Research studies have shown that low levels of lead decrease the IQ of young children by 3 to 7 points over time for every level above 10 mcg/dL. Children are at the highest risk for lead poisoning until 2 or 3 years of age because of their developmental abilities and rapidly growing brains. A *Pediatrics* review article on environmental neurotoxins reports that more recent studies show the most profound effects of lead may occur at blood levels lower than the standard set by the Centers for Disease Control and Prevention.

MERCURY

Mercury is an element that has been used in many different man-made products. Use of these products has resulted in exposure throughout the environment. Mercury has been in products as diverse as latex paint, fluorescent light bulbs, vaccines (as a preservative), folk remedies, and liquid in thermometers. Mercury was actually used as a medicine to

---

Table 11-2. Sources of Lead

— Lead-based paint

— Soil

— Household dust

— Parental occupation or hobby (auto repair, battery plants, pottery making, refinishing furniture)

— Food imported from outside the United States

— Traditional folk medicines and cosmetics

— Imported or antique dishes and ceramic ware

Table 11-3. Risk Factors for Exposure to Lead

— Living in or regularly visiting a house with peeling or chipping paint, built before 1960

— Living in or regularly visiting a house with recent or ongoing renovation, built before 1960

— Having a sibling or housemate who was treated for lead poisoning

— Living with an adult whose job or hobby involves exposure to lead

— Living near an industry likely to release lead (ie, battery recycling or auto repair shop)

— Being developmentally delayed

— Low income or minority status

---

treat sexually transmitted diseases in colonial times, and research by historian Stephen Ambrose reveals that during Lewis and Clark's expedition at the turn of the 18th century, many of the men on the expedition took oral mercury treatments, probably for syphilis. Although everyone is exposed to small amounts of mercury in the environment, it is now widely recognized by the medical community that serious neurological and systemic toxicities can occur from this exposure.

Sources of mercury in the environment include fossil fuels, such as coal and petroleum, and mercury's natural form, cinnabar (mercury ore). Environmental contamination occurs from mining, processing or smelting, industrial waste of fossil fuels, coal-burning power plants, municipal waste combustors, and medical waste incinerators. Inappropriate disposal or incineration of solid or liquid mercury can be dangerous. After mercury is discharged into the air, it is deposited into water. Bacteria in lakes, streams, and oceans then convert elemental mercury into organic mercury (primarily methylmercury), in which form it accumulates in fish and is transferred up the food chain as fish and their predators are consumed. This process occurred in Minamata Bay, Japan, during the 1950s after a factory dumped large quantities of waste containing mercury. More than 40 deaths resulted from consumption of contaminated fish, and there were numerous cases of profound brain injury in infants born to mothers who had consumed contaminated fish during their pregnancies. Another large-scale mercury exposure occurred in Iran in the 1970s, when grains were accidentally treated with a fungicide containing mercury. Hundreds of people suffered mercury poisoning when they ate the grain during a famine. Because of these and other cases of mercury poisoning that occurred secondary to environmental exposure, the AAP subsequently developed recommendations to remove mercury from the environment and decrease exposure to its sources.

Methylmercury, ethylmercury, and phenylmercury are all organic mercury compounds found in pesticides, antiseptics, fungicides, and preservative agents. All of these compounds are fat or lipid soluble, so they are easily absorbed through the GI tract. Methylmercury is particularly ubiquitous in the environment because bacteria easily convert elemental mercury into methylmercury, which quickly accumulates in the aquatic food chain. The highest concentrations are found in sea mammals and larger predator fish such as sharks, swordfish, and mackerel. After a person consumes methylmercury, the GI tract absorbs more than 95% of it, but once in the bloodstream, mercury readily crosses the blood-brain barrier, where it can cause neurological effects in adults and children. Methylmercury can cause neurotoxic effects such as emotional instability, speech disturbance, and ataxia in those who consume it in significant quantities.

Methylmercury also passes through the placenta or into breast milk, causing birth defects in a developing fetus or developmental problems in an infant. An unborn fetus, however, is much more profoundly affected. The fetus may develop a small head (become microcephalic), seizures, mental retardation, or cerebral palsy. The fetus may demonstrate these symptoms even if the mother does not show clinical symptoms. The study in Minamata Bay, Japan, demonstrated the significant neurological impairments in children and birth defects in the fetuses even though the mothers did not necessarily demonstrate any symptoms of mercury poisoning. Studies of the long-term effects of mercury in fish-eating populations such as the Republic of the Seychelles and the Faroe Islands are ongoing but have been inconclusive to date. Some studies show an effect on attention and memory related to maternal mercury levels, though other studies show no effect. Researchers have speculated that the effects may be cumulative and that the differences in the studies may be related to larger amounts of mercury consumption in one population. The particular health implications of mercury exposure through fish consumption are yet to be completely described. Hopefully, more will be learned through further studies.

The toxic effects of the other 2 forms of organic mercury are not as well known. Ethylmercury was made into thimerosal and used as a preservative in childhood immunizations before 1999. This created a potential risk of mercury exposure in children receiving routine vaccines. Some studies have shown that children receiving multiple thimerosal-containing vaccines may have higher than normal levels of mercury in their blood and stool. However, the levels are considered safe by the AAP, and it is thought that mercury may be eliminated in the stool. No long-term effects of vaccine-related mercury exposure have been demonstrated in any study. However, as a result of this potential exposure, the AAP and the US Public Health Service recommended the replacement of thimerosal in all vaccines, and now all routine childhood vaccines in the United States are thimerosal-free. Phenylmercury was previously used as a fungicide in latex paints. Although it is generally considered less toxic than methylmercury and ethylmercury, it was removed from paint in 1991 because of the possible risk of mercury vapor inhalation.

TOBACCO SMOKE

Tobacco smoke is one of the environmental toxins that children most frequently encounter, and it is perhaps the one that is most likely to affect them. Numerous medical problems have been related to environmental tobacco smoke exposure. According to estimates from the World Health Organization, which the AAP reported in an article titled "Tobacco's Toll: Implications for Pediatricians," in 1998 there were 1.1 billion smokers worldwide and 10 000 tobacco-related deaths every day. Forty-eight million people in the United States smoked in 1992, and recent surveys have demonstrated that 43% of children aged 2 months to 11 years live in homes with at least 1 smoker. Children spend much of their time indoors, so it is no wonder that there have been so many medical problems related to exposure to environmental tobacco smoke.

Indoor air contains high amounts of suspended particles and chemical vapors. Pediatricians and other health care professionals consider cigarette smoke the most important determinant of particulate matter in indoor air. Children are exposed to the particles from indoor smoke when they breathe air into their lungs. After the particles enter the lungs, they primarily affect the many different parts of the respiratory tree. The health effects that have been reported are often greater with higher levels of cigarette smoke and may continue even after children are no longer exposed to cigarette smoke.

Many acute and chronic health effects have been attributed to children's passive exposure to cigarette smoke (**Table 11-4**). This represents a tremendous incidence of disease for the children and their parents to face. The most common effect is lower respiratory tract infection—for example, bronchitis and pneumonia. Almost 40 years ago, a correlation was noted between having a smoker in the home and having a perceived increase incidence of disease. Subsequent studies have looked at this relationship very closely and repeatedly confirmed these concerns. Research reported in *Pediatrics* demonstrates that as few as 5 cigarettes a day may result in 2.5 to 3.5 more incidents of lower respiratory tract illness for every 100 children exposed to tobacco smoke. One study showed an increased likelihood of not only bronchitis and pneumonia, but also sinusitis and acute nasopharyngitis. A recent AAP study on tobacco smoke exposure also found that children 5 years of age or younger who are exposed to passive smoke are 4 times more likely to have a serious infectious illness that will require hospitalization. Clearly, children exposed to tobacco smoke are sick more often and more seriously than children who are not.

Table 11-4. Health Effects of Environmental Tobacco Smoke on Children

— Increased incidence of respiratory tract disease, especially bronchitis and pneumonia, and middle ear effusion

— May cause increased incidence of asthma in children

— Causes higher levels of total cholesterol, and lower levels of the protective (high-density lipoprotein) cholesterol

— Smoking in the home is associated with sudden infant death syndrome

— Earlier exposure of children and infants to passive smoke is associated with later lung carcinoma in adults

Data from the AAP Committees on Environmental Health and Substance Abuse and "Environmental Toxicants and Children" in UpToDate.

The incidence of asthma has risen over the past few decades, and clinical experience and statistics reveal that more children die from asthma now than in the past. Exposure to environmental tobacco smoke may be partly to blame. Data reported by the AAP show that asthmatics exposed to tobacco smoke have more frequent and severe asthma symptoms than asthmatics who are not exposed to tobacco smoke. More important, it has been demonstrated that when parents of asthmatics reduce the children's exposure to tobacco smoke, the asthma symptoms become less severe.

Children exposed to environmental tobacco smoke may also develop effusion, which is a collection of fluid in the ear. If the fluid persists, it may impair the child's ability to hear and affect his or her language development. Children with persistent effusion often need to have tubes placed in their eardrum (myringotomy tubes) to help the fluid drain. A study of Danish children demonstrated that children were 60% more likely to have middle ear effusions if their parents smoked. Another study in Seattle looked at the risk factors for middle ear effusions. It showed that children who lived in a home in which more than 3 packs of cigarettes were smoked per day were more likely to need myringotomy tube placement. These studies have demonstrated that not only is middle ear fluid more common in children whose parents smoke, but the fluid persists in the ear much longer than in children not exposed to tobacco smoke.

Although lower respiratory infections and middle ear effusions are the most studied effects of tobacco smoke exposure, a number of other serious health effects are also associated with it. Sudden infant death syndrome (SIDS) is a disorder in which infants die suddenly and unexpectedly. Much research has been conducted to try and determine the cause of this disorder, and evidence increasingly indicates a relationship between tobacco smoke and SIDS. The AAP has noted that infants whose parents smoke are more likely to die from SIDS than infants whose parents do not. This risk appears to be independent of other risk factors such as birth weight and gestational age.

Exposure to environmental tobacco smoke has also been associated in professional studies with higher levels of total cholesterol and lower levels of the protective or high-density lipoprotein cholesterol in persons who were exposed to it as children. This may be part of the reason that coronary artery disease has been more often observed in passive smokers. The link between lung cancer and passive smoking has also been studied. Studies have demonstrated that exposure to passive tobacco smoke during childhood and adulthood increases the overall risk of cancer. Some research has linked environmental smoke exposure before 10 years of age to leukemia and lymphoma in adulthood. The US Environmental Protection Agency (EPA) has concluded that environmental tobacco smoke is a serious carcinogen because of the causal association between exposure and cancer.

Ultraviolet Radiation

Skin becomes red and then tanned as a protective response to sun exposure or sunlight. The amount of tanning that occurs is dependent on the type of skin, the thickness of the skin, the amount of skin pigments (melanin) and their effectiveness, and the intensity of sun exposure. Sunlight is divided into 3 different types: visible, longer infrared, and shorter ultraviolet radiation (UVR). Ultraviolet radiation is the type of sunlight that causes acute and chronic damage to the skin, and it can be further divided into types UVA and UVB. UVB rays have been shown to cause skin damage and has been associated with nonmelanoma skin cancers (NMSCs) and cutaneous malignant melanoma (shortened to melanoma). UVB radiation is most intense during the summer months, during the middle of the day, at places that are close to the equator, and at high altitudes.

Exposure to sunlight over a prolonged period of time is an important component in the development of NMSCs. Periodic exposure to large amounts of sunlight has also been shown to be significant in the development of melanoma. Almost 1 million cases of NMSCs occur annually in the United States alone, and the incidence of melanoma has steadily been increasing. An article from the AAP states that it has now been estimated that as many as 1 in 75 people in the United States will develop it at some point in their lifetime. According to the same article, studies have shown that melanoma is more likely to occur in people with less skin pigmentation—it occurs about 10 times more frequently in white persons than in black persons. Melanoma also occurs more commonly in white persons who live closer to the equator and in persons with rare medical conditions whose cells lack the ability to repair DNA damage done by the sun.

Over the last 100 years, sun tanning and possessing a tanned complexion have been associated with good health. In the early 1900s, UVR was shown to be helpful for some medical conditions, and in the 1930s physicians promoted sunbathing as beneficial for children. As a result of these and other associations, sunbathing became very popular, spawning a surge in the popularity of sunlamps and sun tanning salons dating from the 1940s. The first commercial sun tanning facility was opened in the United States in 1978, and according to research published in *Mayo Clinic Proceedings*, now more than 2 million people use these types of facilities every day. Unfortunately, exposure to sun beds or sunlamps has also been associated with an increased risk of melanoma, particularly in young children. Using of sun beds more than 10 times a year has been associated with melanoma in all who use them, in spite of the fact that sun beds were initially believed to cause less UVR exposure and, ultimately, less skin damage to the skin than the sun.

As a result of the strong association between sun tanning and sun bed use with melanoma and NMSCs, a public health campaign by the Centers for Disease Control and Prevention, American Cancer Society, American Academy of Dermatology, and the Environmental Protection Agency to educate the public about sun exposure began in the 1970s. Although other risk factors like family history and skin type are important in the development of skin cancers, sun exposure is the only one that can be prevented. Eighty percent of a person's exposure to sunlight is believed to occur before he or she is 18 years old, and episodic sunburns in childhood and adolescence are also thought to increase the risk of melanoma. Children are estimated to receive about 3 times more annual UVB light exposure than adults, primarily because they spend more time outside in the summer months. Some researchers have estimated that sun avoidance in childhood and adolescence could reduce NMSCs by almost 80%.

In the initial awareness campaign, and in another campaign in the 1990s, people were taught about the sun, sun tanning, sunscreen use, and the proper clothes, glasses, or hats to wear to protect them from the development of melanomas. These sun-safe behaviors were supposed to help reverse the trend of tanning or sun seeking behavior. However, over the last 15 or 20 years, people have learned about the risks of exposure to sunlight with varying success. Recent surveys for research led by Boston University professor Alan Geller show that 94% of people are concerned about exposure to the sun, and 88% are more careful than they were 10 years ago. However, 68% of people "felt better" with a tan, and 55% still sought a tan. As many as 83% of children had a least 1 sunburn and about one third had 3 or more sunburns. Only one third of youths used sunscreen overall, and 10% said they used a tanning bed. Education campaigns have taught people about the risks and concerns of UVR exposure but have not dramatically changed their behavior.

WHAT PARENTS AND CAREGIVERS CAN DO

LEAD

Prevention and Recommendations

Parents and caregivers must recognize and pay attention to children's environments. Classrooms or other rooms in buildings built before 1979 that have peeling paint or are in disrepair are more likely to have lead-based paint that could affect children. Older plumbing pipes contain lead, and lead solder was used to connect theses pipes. Both sources can contaminate the drinking water of children in school or childcare. Parents can ask whether an environmental assessment, including risk of lead exposure, has been done; they can also ask to see it or request that one is done. Although the amount of lead in dirt from leaded gasoline has drastically reduced, dirt may still be contaminated from auto repair or battery recycling shops. Parents must be aware of the surrounding environments in which children are playing, as inexpensive department store jewelry and toy trinkets can contain lead.

Older homes are likely to have lead paint in them, though lead paint is a problem only when children are exposed to it. There are lots of ways to clean a home or children's toys and to prevent lead dust from accumulating, such as mopping the floors and wiping the windows and doorways at least once a week, washing toys and pacifiers frequently, and cleaning children's hands and faces before all meals and snacks. The behaviors that may help decrease the exposure to lead are outlined in **Table 11-5** and should be done in any home or school with old paint that has young children who may be exposed to the lead. Children should also receive regular meals that are high in calcium and iron, which may help prevent lead from being absorbed from the GI tract.

Recognition and Treatment

The severe symptoms of lead poisoning that were classically described do not occur often because public health efforts have dramatically reduced the burden of lead in the environment. Most children with lead poisoning do not have any symptoms. However, lower levels of lead poisoning may cause children to have new behavior problems or outbursts; problems in school; seizures, inattention, or hyperactivity; or somatic complaints such as stomachache or a headache that cannot be otherwise explained.

Children younger than 3 years are at the highest risk of becoming lead poisoned in old homes. Parents who believe that their child has a high lead level should notify a primary health care provider of concerns and any unusual behaviors immediately. Children with low levels of lead poisoning will not need medical treatment, but the Department of Public Health may want to inspect the homes of those with levels above 20 mcg/dL. Treatment guidelines from the AAP are to give children whose lead levels are moderately high (greater than 45 mcg/dL) oral medicines such as succimer; children with very high lead levels (greater than 70 mcg/dL) require treatment with intravenous medicines such as BAL (British Anti-Lewisite) and calcium-EDTA. Once a child has been poisoned, lead levels may be decreased, but the deleterious effects cannot be reversed. The most important action for parents, teachers, nurses, and child and health care workers to take is to check the environment and report any unusual concerns to the school or the Department of Public Health. This department will be the most qualified to deal with a problem that may affect an entire home, classroom, school, or neighborhood.

MERCURY

Prevention and Recommendations

As previously stated, children are most likely to be exposed to methylmercury, primarily from fish consumption. In March 2004, the Food and Drug Administration and the

Table 11-5. Dos and Don'ts of Preventing Lead Poisoning

— Do make sure that children do not have access to peeling paint or chewable surfaces painted with lead based paint. Pay particular attention to windows, windowsills, and window wells.

— If a house or school was built before 1960 and has hard surface floors, do wet mop at least once each week with a high-phosphate solution (such as Acme brand dishwashing liquid or powder, or Spic and Span cleaner). Other surfaces, such as windowsills and baseboards, should be wiped with a similar solution. Do not vacuum these hard surfaces, as this will disperse lead dust.

— Do let the faucets run for 3 to 4 minutes every morning before using the water if the home has old pipes with lead pipes or lead solder. Use only cold water for cooking and drinking. Do not use hot water from the sink, as this may cause lead to leak from the pipes.

— Do wash children's hands and face before they eat a meal or a snack, and also wash toys and pacifiers frequently.

— Do plant grass, other ground cover, or bushes in the soil surrounding your house if it is likely to be lead contaminated so that your child cannot play in the soil or near the outside walls of the house. The outside walls of the house often have the highest amount of lead.

— Don't store food in open cans, especially if the cans are made outside the United States.

— Do make sure your child eats breakfast, lunch, and dinner regularly. More lead is absorbed on an empty stomach.

— Don't use pottery or ceramic ware for eating, serving, or storing food.

— Do ensure that your child's diet contains plenty of iron and calcium. Examples of sources of iron and calcium:

Iron	Calcium
Liver, beef, pork	Milk
Cereals (some)	Yogurt
Cooked legumes (lentils)	Cheese
Spinach	Cooked greens
Prunes	Legumes (navy beans)

— Do call the closest public health official to find out whether someone can come out to your house and identify sources of lead in your house.

EPA released combined recommendations aimed at the populations (pregnant women, women who may become pregnant, nursing mothers, young children) most at risk of mercury poisoning (**Table 11-6**). Various reports on environmental mercury state that in studies of women and their children, some women of childbearing age were thought to have high enough levels to affect the developing fetus, though the children were found to have normal levels of mercury. Other studies have found that the most likely exposure to mercury is from the environment. Concern for mercury exposure from fish and shellfish must be balanced with the knowledge of the health benefits of eating fish. It is important to remember that the high-quality proteins and unsaturated fats obtained from fish are part of a nutritious diet.

Recognition and Treatment

Symptoms caused by exposure to mercury in the environment cause a variety of neurological problems that could be attributed to a variety of causes. To make the

Table 11-6. Advisory on the Consumption of Mercury in Fish

— Do not eat shark, swordfish, king mackerel, or tilefish because they contain high levels of mercury.

— Do not eat more than 4 to 6 ounces of tuna each week. This includes white meat tuna fish in cans. Pregnant women, nursing mothers, women who may become pregnant, and small children can consume more "chunk light" tuna once a week, as this product contains less mercury.

— Eat up to 12 ounces (about 2 meals) a week of a variety of fish and shellfish that are lower in mercury (eg, shrimp, canned light tuna, salmon, pollack, and catfish).

— Check local advisories about the safety of fish caught by family and friends in local lakes, rivers, and costal areas.

— Children follow the same guidelines as adults, except that the serving sizes should be smaller. Fish sticks and chunk-light tuna are safe, and children may consume up to 6 ounces (about 2 meals) of this type of fish each week.

Data from the FDA and EPA revised consumer advisory on methymercury in fish.

diagnosis of mercury poisoning, one must have a high index of suspicion based on the history and physical exam. When a child is examined for these kinds of symptoms, ask questions about the potential risk of exposure in the environment in which the child lives, including at home and school, possible parental occupation or hobbies, sources in the child's diet, and nearby industrial exposure. The only way to effectively treat mercury exposure is to remove the source from contact with the child.

If mercury exposure is suspected on the basis of a child's history or physical examination, a physician can measure the child's mercury levels. Organic mercury can be measured in blood or hair samples. Inorganic mercury can be measured with a 24-hour urine collection sample; it remains in the bloodstream for a short amount of time, so blood levels do not accurately reflect the potential poisoning. After mercury accumulates in the blood, central nervous system, and kidneys, it is slowly eliminated. There is some evidence that elemental or inorganic mercury may be removed using treatments that draw the chemical out of the blood (chelation therapy), but the effects on toxicity or symptom recovery are not clear. Organic mercury, however, has no effective chelating agent, and it is more resistant to removal. There is some evidence that chelation therapy may be useful for higher levels of poisoning, but the treatment may also be harmful. Any level of mercury poisoning should be treated in consultation with an experienced physician and chelation should be considered with high levels of mercury, especially acute toxicity.

TOBACCO SMOKE
Prevention and Recommendations
A tobacco-free environment is essential for preventing the deleterious health effects of tobacco smoke, and adults are role models and sources of information for smaller children. Parents and other family members can begin by setting a good example for children and refraining from smoking. Parents should also educate family members about the ill effects of tobacco smoke and encourage those who smoke to quit. There are a number of organizations that can help people stop smoking (see "Where to Turn

for Help"). Teachers and health care providers should also inform parents about the health hazards of passive smoking, particularly if it affects their child, and make available information and guidance on avoiding environmental tobacco smoke or smoking cessation. Evidence from AAP tobacco research indicates that children older than 5 years should be educated about the dangers of tobacco smoke. If children do not start smoking, their environment will be healthier and they will be more likely to escape adverse health effects. Working with children to inform them of the hazard or cooperating with the child or with the family's physician could be another way to help family members stop smoking.

Parents, caregivers, and professionals who work with children can also advocate at the community, state, or national level to promote policies that ban tobacco products from restaurants, hospitals, day cares, and schools. Politicians can be urged to make areas that children frequent smoke free. Only when parents and caregivers begin to affect all of these levels of prevention will they see a significant effect on the acute and chronic health effects in children.

Recognition and Treatment
There is no specific treatment for exposure to environmental tobacco smoke other than to take steps to decrease exposure. The numerous acute and chronic health effects that have been associated with environmental tobacco smoke must be treated individually.

ULTRAVIOLET RADIATION
To reduce exposure to sunlight in children in the United States, the AAP has recommended teaching children to practice sun-safe behaviors; these behaviors are summarized in **Table 11-7**. It is important to remember that sunscreen alone does not provide enough protection from the sun and UVR. Avoidance of the sun during childhood, using these measures, may actually decrease the risk of nonmelanomatous skin cancer over a lifetime by as much as 80%, according to research by Dr. Geller and by the AAP Committee on Environmental Health. Caregivers and health care providers are in a perfect position to promote sun-safe behaviors among children and families. The AAP recommends that in addition to practicing these behaviors, caregivers and health care professionals consult the UV index when it is available, schools educate the students about the dangers of sun exposure, and governments mount campaigns to educate the public about the dangers of sun exposure.

PROFESSIONAL STUDY AND CONTROVERSY
MERCURY
The EPA made recommendations in late 2003 to try to improve air quality by reducing emissions of sulfur dioxide and nitrogen oxides from coal-burning power plants. The Interstate Air Quality Rule states that companies will have to either install currently available pollution controls or trade emissions with other companies if they cannot install the controls. These pollution controls may reduce toxic emissions by about 30%. Regardless of which method companies choose, the goal is to reduce mercury emissions by 70% by 2018.

Physicians and hospitals have been encouraged by the American Hospital Association to phase out all mercury-containing thermometers and other medical equipment in order to decrease mercury exposure from the incineration of medical waste. Although there is thought to be little danger from the exposure to mercury in any one thermometer, there have been case reports of mercury poisoning of children who played on carpets or floors contaminated by a broken thermometer. Parents should contact local or state health agencies for assistance if there is a significant spill. Caregivers and health care pro-

Table 11-7. Summer Safety Tips for Fun in the Sun

INFANTS YOUNGER THAN 6 MONTHS

— Avoid sun exposure and dress infants in lightweight long pants, long-sleeved shirts, and brimmed hats.

— If adequate clothing and shade are not available, then parents can apply a minimal amount of sunscreen to small areas, such as the infant's face and the back of the neck.

YOUNG CHILDREN

— Apply sunscreen at least 30 minutes before going outside.

— Use a sunscreen with an SPF of 15 or greater.

OLDER CHILDREN

— Always cover up:

— Wear a hat with a 3-inch brim or a bill facing forward.

— Wear cotton clothing with a tight weave.

— Wear sunglasses that block 99% to 100% of ultraviolet rays.

— Stay in the shade whenever possible.

— Avoid sun exposure during peak intensity hours (between 10 am and 4 pm); children should play outside only when their shadows are longer than they are.

— Use a sunscreen with an SPF of 15 or greater and be sure to use enough sunscreen (about 1 ounce).

— Reapply sunscreen every 2 hours, or after swimming or sweating.

Data from the AAP press release "Keeping Skin Safe and Healthy."

fessionals need to pay attention to children's health and behavior and take or refer children to a physician when they develop unusual symptoms. Physicians may be able to make the connections between the symptoms and how they relate to known toxic agents and the illnesses they cause.

Many regulations have developed as a result of the toxic effects of mercury that affect consumers—regulations of which consumers may be unaware. The EPA determined that the acceptable level of mercury in drinking water and bottled water is 2 mcg/L. Federal agencies have also been trying to develop guidelines for the consumption of mercury in food. More information may be forthcoming as the agencies complete their reports (see "Where to Turn for Help").

ULTRAVIOLET RADIATION

Programs sponsored by the AAP, Centers for Disease Control and Prevention, American Cancer Society, and EPA have been modestly successful at changing sun-seeking behavior in the past few years. Australia, which once had the highest incidence of melanoma in the world, is a positive example. The country mounted a long-term, nationwide campaign over the last 25 years to combat UVR exposure. The incidence of melanoma peaked in 1985 and has not risen since as a result of the extensive and coordinated efforts to educate the public. The United States should also develop a coordinated campaign to educate a new generation of children and adolescents and to help prevent them from developing skin cancer.

CONCLUSION

The ways children are exposed to, absorb, and metabolize environmental toxins make them uniquely susceptible from the time when they are a fetus to adolescence. Environmental toxins can significantly affect the growth of children's organs, especially of the brain, and overall development. The effects of exposure to lead, mercury, tobacco smoke, and UVR serve as examples of the variety of problems that can occur as a result of environmental toxins. Parents, teachers, nurses, childcare, and health care professionals are uniquely situated to observe children and be able to dramatically impact children's lives if they recognize the signs and symptoms of a potential exposure to an environmental toxin. With the combined effort of children's families, caregivers, and physicians, environmental toxin exposure can be treated and prevented.

WHERE TO TURN FOR HELP

ENVIRONMENTAL HEALTH
Agency for Toxic Substances and Disease Registry

http://www.atsdr.cdc.gov/toxprofiles

American Academy of Pediatrics Committee on Environmental Health

http://www.aap.org/visit/cmte16.htm

Children's Environmental Health Network

http://www.cehn.org

Environmental Protection Agency: Children's Health Protection

http://yosemite.epa.gov/ochp/ochpweb.nsf/content/homepage.htm

LEAD
Centers for Disease Control and Prevention: Childhood Lead Poisoning Prevention Program

http://www.cdc.gov/nceh/lead/links/links_2.htm

Environmental Protection Agency

http://www.epa.gov/opptintr/lead

MERCURY
Environmental Protection Agency: Fish advisories

http://www.epa.gov/ost/fish

Environmental Protection Agency: Mercury

http://www.epa.gov/mercury

Food and Drug Administration Center for Food Safety and Applied Nutrition

http://www.cfsan.fda.gov

TOBACCO SMOKE
Centers for Disease Control and Prevention: Facts about secondhand smoke

http://www.cdc.gov/tobacco/research_data/environmental/ets-fact.htm

Environmental Protection Agency: Smoke-free homes program

http://www.epa.gov/smokefree/index.html

Foundation for a Smokefree America

http://www.anti-smoking.org

ULTRAVIOLET RADIATION

American Cancer Society: Sun safety

http://www.cancer.org/docroot/PED/PED_7.asp?sitearea=PED

EPA: SunWise Program

http://www.epa.gov/sunwise/index.html

National Council on Skin Cancer Prevention

http://www.skincancerprevention.org

Chapter 12

EMERGENCY MEDICAL SITUATIONS

Paul S. Matz, MD

In 2002, children visited emergency rooms more than 24 million times. Many parents will have the experience of rushing a child to an emergency department for an illness or injury, and nearly all parents or caregivers will, at some point, face a situation in which a child under their care becomes ill or injured. Many of these situations can be managed without a trip to an emergency department. However, most parents have difficulty accurately assessing the level of intervention and care their child requires.

For the purposes of this chapter, *emergency medical situations* are defined as any medical situation *perceived by a caregiver* as an emergency. These can include life-threatening emergencies, such as severe allergic reactions, or more routine illnesses and injuries, such as fevers or lacerations. *Illness* refers to a medical condition, such as asthma, bacterial or viral infection, or other chronic or acute diseases a child may have. *Injury* refers to physical trauma. Many doctors prefer to use the term *injury* in place of *accident*, as the latter word implies an event that could not be prevented. As noted in Chapter 10, Injury Prevention, many childhood injuries can be avoided. This chapter will review several common medical situations and discuss how to determine whether a child should be seen in an emergency department or treated at home.

The most important thing parents and caregivers should remember is to remain calm in any situation. A sick or injured child will be frightened and look to them for comfort and cues on how to react. It is caregivers' job to control their anxiety so that they can keep children as calm as possible. Keeping personal fears under control will also help caregivers think clearly so that they can make rational and safe decisions.

Basic preparation is also important. Anyone who cares for children should consider taking courses in first aid and cardiopulmonary resuscitation (CPR). These courses teach caregivers what to do when children choke, stop breathing, or become injured. While these courses cannot prepare parents for every possible situation, they do cover many of the most common problems and are useful in building overall confidence in dealing with emergencies. Analogous to self-defense courses, first aid and CPR courses can simply help parents and caregivers feel more calm and confident in dealing with an emergency medical situation. The American Red Cross offers a Babysitter's Training Course that includes basic first aid for older teenagers (see "Where to Turn for Help").

As part of preparation, teachers and child care providers should know how to reach every child's parent or guardian. Important phone numbers (relatives, physicians, poison control, fire, police, ambulance) should be placed near phones in children or caregivers' homes in case of emergencies. Refer to **Table 12-1** for frequently asked questions about emergency medical situations.

Table 12-1. Frequently Asked Questions

My 6 month old is about to start daycare. He has had episodes of wheezing in the past, and I am nervous about sending him to daycare. What should I do?

First, talk with the owner or director of the daycare to discuss the training of the staff. Make sure the staff has training in CPR and first aid. Then, talk with your health care provider for help in organizing a plan of care while he is at daycare. If your child needs daily medicine, make sure the daycare is able to administer it. Finally, leave them clear instructions on what to do if he becomes ill. Instructions can include administering medications, calling you or the health care provider, or going to an emergency department. As always, it is better to prepare for an emergency before it happens.

My 2 year old has been vomiting for 5 days and has not improved. I spoke to her doctor when it started, who said it was "a stomach flu." Should I be worried if it hasn't gotten better?

Although episodes of vomiting can be due to viral infections, a physician should evaluate prolonged or recurrent vomiting. Vomiting that lasts longer than 2 days or is accompanied by severe abdominal pain or fever can be serious.

My 8 year old was recently diagnosed with a peanut allergy. Nothing serious has happened yet, but I am concerned about him having a severe reaction at school. What should I do?

Allergies to foods, especially peanuts, can be serious. Talk to your son's school to find out how it can help keep him safe. Many schools have "peanut-free zones" to help allergic children avoid exposure to peanuts. Speak to the principal or school nurse to organize a plan in case of an allergic reaction. Talk to your child's primary health care provider about prescribing an epinephrine auto-injector (EpiPen, EpiPen Jr.) for school.

My 13 year old just experienced his second head injury playing soccer. He was not knocked out but did have a headache for 1 week afterwards. Is it OK for him to play soccer again this season?

Head injuries in children can be dangerous, not just because of the immediate effects, but also because of long-term effects. Repeated head injuries can cause significant brain damage, leading to cognitive and developmental problems, even if the child is not knocked unconscious by the injuries. These long-term effects multiply quickly after repeated injuries. Talk to your child's physician about when he can return to play. A child should NEVER be allowed to play while suffering from effects of a recent concussion (headache, dizziness, difficulty concentrating, poor memory). In addition, many physicians will request a consultation with a neurologist to help decide on returning to play. Many times there is pressure for the child to return to play and decisions are made that are not in the best interest of a child. This decision should *not* be left to the child or the child's coach, but rather to a health care professional.

My 3 year old suffered burns on her leg after spilling a cup of coffee onto herself. Will these burns leave scars?

Superficial burns like sunburns never scar. The skin may peel as it heals, but will heal without scarring. Some partial-thickness, or second-degree, burns will scar, but most small ones will heal without incident. To heal partial-thickness burns or lacerations, suntan lotion can be applied once the wound has healed and dried. The lotion can reduce the severity of the scarring.

TYPES OF EMERGENCY MEDICAL SITUATIONS

ASTHMA ATTACKS

Asthma is the most common chronic childhood disease. It is responsible for nearly 2 million emergency department visits and more than 10 million missed school days per year. *Asthma* is a chronic lung disease in which narrowing of the airways and increased mucus production lead to wheezing, coughing, and difficulty breathing. Children may have chronic symptoms as well as acute exacerbations, or asthma "attacks." The most common trigger for an exacerbation is an upper respiratory infection—in other words, a cold. Other triggers include allergies (eg, to dust, animal dander, pollen), cigarette smoke, cold air, or exercise. These attacks can develop and worsen over the course of several days, or they can occur suddenly. Many mild asthma attacks can be managed at home with the advice of a physician, but more serious attacks require a visit to a primary health care provider or emergency department.

Asthma medicines are generally divided into 2 categories: controller medicines and rescue medicines. Controller medicines are used daily to help *prevent* asthma symptoms and are not helpful during an acute asthma attack. The decision to use daily controller medications should be made in consultation with a child's pediatrician. Rescue medicines, primarily albuterol, help to *immediately relieve* symptoms during an attack. Albuterol is administered either through a nebulizer or a metered-dose inhaler (MDI).

NOSEBLEEDS

Nosebleeds (epistaxis) are another very common childhood problem. Bleeding from the nose can result from several factors, including breathing dry air, upper respiratory infections (or colds), allergies (like hay fever), nasal injury, or nose picking. Many children, from toddlers to teenagers, occasionally pick their nose, sometimes using materials other than their fingers. In addition, trauma to the nose from falling and being punched or kicked can cause nosebleeds. Children with bleeding disorders such as hemophilia or von Willebrand disease can also be prone to nosebleeds.

LACERATIONS

Small cuts—or *lacerations*—are almost a rite of passage for children. Toddlers' poor balance makes them prone to falling and potentially receiving small cuts. In addition, as mentioned in the section on head injury, toddlers' heads are relatively large when compared to their body size, increasing the chance of them hitting their heads when they fall. For this reason, head lacerations on the scalp or face are very common in this age group. Older children begin to take greater risks and play more aggressive sports, increasing their risk for injuries of all types, including lacerations. Animal bites may also cause lacerations.

In most cases, bleeding will be relatively easy to control by applying direct pressure on the wound and, if possible, elevating it above the level of the heart. If bleeding lasts for more than 30 minutes or if the cut is very deep, children should be seen in an emergency department. Children with bleeding disorders, such as hemophilia or von Willebrand disease, may need to be seen by a physician or take appropriate medicines before 30 minutes have passed. In addition, if a wound is bleeding heavily and cannot be controlled quickly, the child should be taken to a hospital immediately, unless the laceration is on the scalp or face. These wounds can bleed profusely but are often easily controlled with direct pressure.

For most small lacerations, the risk of infection is fairly low. These can be cleaned with soap and water and covered with an antibiotic ointment and a bandage. However, if a wound is dirty or the result of an animal bite, the child should be evaluated by a physician. Tetanus can also be a concern; if children have not received a tetanus immunization in the last 5 years, they may need a booster shot. Wounds that are deep, jagged, or have gaping edges will probably require sutures (stitches) to be closed, both to aid in healing and to reduce the formation of scars.

HEAD INJURIES

Like lacerations, minor head injuries are very common in children, especially toddlers. Older children suffer head injuries because they tend to engage in more forceful play and take more physical risks. Motor vehicle accidents are an additional cause of head injury for all people, especially when seatbelts are not used. Sometimes, children can exhibit symptoms of head injury when in a car that is hit or stops suddenly, even if they did not strike their head, though the situation is uncommon. In this chapter, the term *head injury* refers to any physical trauma to the head that may cause concussions or bleeding in the brain. It will not include simple scalp abrasions or lacerations, which should be treated as cuts on any other part of the body.

After a less severe head injury, it is normal for children to become very tired. It is acceptable to let them sleep, but they must be checked frequently (as discussed in "What Parents and Caregivers Can Do"). In addition, they may become nauseous and vomit. However, vomiting that occurs or continues for more than 3 hours after the head injury is not normal, and in this case children should be immediately taken to an emergency department for evaluation.

VOMITING AND DIARRHEA

In children, vomiting and diarrhea are usually caused by a viral infection called *gastroenteritis*. These infections can cause fevers and rashes, and they are often referred to as the stomach flu. If vomiting and diarrhea persist for more than a few hours, it may cause children to lose water and become dehydrated. Although most children with vomiting and diarrhea can be treated safely at home, parents should learn how to assess their child for signs of severe dehydration, which does require professional medical treatment.

The easiest way to monitor children's hydration is to be aware of their urine output. A sufficiently hydrated child will urinate at least 3 times per day (1 time every 8 hours). Other signs of dehydration include lack of tears when a child cries, dry mouth and tongue, and sunken eyes. Severely dehydrated children may be lethargic or irritable and feel cool to the touch.

FEVER

Nearly all children will experience an illness with a fever during their first few years. Most of these illnesses are colds or upper respiratory infections that can be safely managed at home. Many parents believe that the fever itself can be dangerous for the child, but this is very rarely the case. A fever is not dangerous if it is less than 106°F (41.1°C), but it is an indication that something is wrong.

For children older than 2 months, doctors generally consider a fever to be a temperature above 101°F (38.3°C). Temperatures should be measured either orally (older children) or rectally (for infants and young children). Forehead strips and ear thermometers are not as reliable as oral and rectal thermometers.

For infants younger than 2 months, a temperature of 100.4°F (38.0°C) is considered a fever. Very young infants have a lower fever marker because their immature immune systems are less able to produce high fevers and because they are more likely to develop severe infections.

Fever itself is not a disease, but rather the immune system's natural reaction to an infection. However, fevers can make children feel tired or lethargic and decrease their appetites, leading to dehydration. The goal of caring for a child with a fever is not to treat the *fever*, but rather the underlying problem. Medicine that reduces fevers merely makes a sick child feel better; it does not treat the infection that causes the fever.

Children between 6 months and 5 years of age can develop a fever complication known as febrile seizures. These seizures, or convulsions, can happen when a child has a fever, regardless of the underlying source of the fever, and are frightening to watch. However, these seizures are usually short-lived, end spontaneously, and are only rarely associated with more serious complications. The vast majority of children who experience a febrile seizure recover completely. Although these seizures are not dangerous, a physician should examine any child who experiences a febrile seizure for the first time in order to ensure that no other serious diseases triggered the seizure.

ALLERGIC REACTIONS AND INSECT BITES

Allergic reactions are an exaggeration of the body's normal immune response to foreign proteins, which are called **allergens** or **antigens**. Unfortunately, this exaggerated response can lead to symptoms ranging from mild (eg, hives) to life threatening (wheezing, swelling of the lips or tongue, swelling of the airway, lowered blood pressure). The most severe of these allergic reactions is anaphylactic shock, which results from hypersensitivity, and it can be accompanied by all of the other symptoms.

Children can have allergies to foods (peanuts, shellfish, milk), plants (poison ivy, oak or sumac; latex rubber), medicines (such as antibiotics, especially penicillin), and insect venom (bees, wasps, hornets). Simple insect bites, such as those from a mosquito, non-poisonous spider, or flea, are simply a form of local allergic reaction.

Food allergies, particularly to peanuts, are an increasingly common source of serious allergic reactions. Some individuals are extraordinarily sensitive to peanuts and can even react when exposed to very minute doses. This can include non–peanut-containing foods processed on equipment previously exposed to peanuts or airborne peanut allergens from nearby peanut products (eg, elsewhere in a school cafeteria). Shellfish, tree nuts, eggs, and dairy products are other foods that can trigger serious reactions.

SPRAINS AND FRACTURES

Sprains are injuries to the ligaments, while *fractures* are injuries to bones (broken bones). *Ligaments* are the elastic bands that connect bones to each other and help hold our joints together. Common sprains occur in ankles, knees, wrists and elbows and range from mild (requiring minimal attention) to severe (requiring prolonged rest or even surgery). There are many different types of fractures and some may not be obvious immediately after an injury. *Compound*, or *open*, fractures occur when a broken bone tears through the skin above it. Sprains and fractures commonly result from sports, other physical activities, or automobile or bicycle accidents. The impulsivity common in younger children can increase their risks of receiving these injuries.

Sprains and fractures are not the same as muscle or tendon strains. *Strains* result from the overuse of certain muscles or tendons. Classic examples are little league pitcher's elbow, tennis elbow, and shin splints. These usually cause chronic pain and are rarely emergencies.

BURNS

Hot water, fires, chemicals, electricity, and exposure to hot objects can cause burns. Burns are divided into 3 main categories, depending on the depth of the injury.

Superficial burns, formerly called first-degree burns, involve just the topmost layer of skin and have redness and pain, but no blisters. Sunburn is an example of a superficial burn. *Partial-thickness burns*, formerly second-degree burns, involve deeper layers of skin but do not go through to the underlying tissue. These burns are red, painful, and have blisters. Deeper burns will have areas of white. *Full-thickness burns*, formerly third-degree burns, are the most serious; they are often white or black and fairly painless because the nerves in the skin have been destroyed.

WHAT PARENTS AND CAREGIVERS CAN DO

ASTHMA ATTACKS

Asthma attacks usually begin with coughing and wheezing. For children with a history of asthma, any new coughing or wheezing, no matter how mild, may indicate the early stages of an attack. Helping children remain calm is the first step in managing attacks because anxiety or stress can make an attack worse.

Table 12-2. When to Go to the ER: Asthma Attacks
— Rapid breathing
— Blue lips or fingers
— Difficulty speaking
— "Sucking in" of the neck, chest, or abdomen when breathing
— Inability to eat or drink
— Inability to lie down
— Rescue medicines (albuterol) provide no relief
— Relief from rescue medicines lasts less than 4 hours

Physicians will have prescribed albuterol as a rescue medicine for most children with a history of asthma. When children begin to show symptoms of an attack, parents should begin to administer the albuterol as often as every four hours. If a child's symptoms do not improve with albuterol, or if the improvement lasts for less than 4 hours after a treatment, a physician should be consulted as soon as possible. Many attacks can be managed successfully at home, with the advice and support of children's pediatricians. However, the need for rescue medications more than every 4 hours is an indication that a child's asthma is worsening, and caregivers who cannot reach a pediatrician should take children to an emergency department for evaluation (**Table 12-2**).

Parents should be aware of warning signs that indicate severe respiratory distress and the need for immediate medical care. These include rapid breathing, difficulty speaking, blue fingers or lips, increased sleepiness, or a child's chest appearing to "suck in" when he or she inhales. An inability to eat or drink because of breathing difficulty is also a warning sign.

Because asthma attacks are frequently triggered by a cold, parents often treat a cough with over-the-counter cough or cold medicine, failing to realize that the cough is a sign of asthma exacerbation and not merely a cold symptom. Before giving a child with asthma regular cough or cold medication, consult his or her pediatrician.

NOSEBLEEDS

Nosebleeds rarely last long or lead to significant blood loss. A few simples measures will nearly always stop the bleeding.

First, keep the child calm and have him or her sit next to you. A young child may sit on your lap. Pinch the bottom part of the nose with a tissue, closing off both nostrils. Do not try pinching the bridge of the nose to stop the bleeding; this part of the nose is bone, and pinching here will have little effect. Pinching the nostrils closed places direct pressure on the nose, allowing clotting to begin. Once the blood clots, bleeding will stop.

While holding the nostrils closed, have the child tilt his or her head *forward*. In the past, it was commonly thought best to tilt the head backward. However, this allows the blood to drip into the throat and be swallowed, potentially making children nauseous and causing vomiting. Have the child sit, holding the nose closed, leaning forward for at least 5 minutes. Time can seem to go very slowly while this is occurring, so using a watch may be helpful. Parents usually check often to see if the nose has stopped bleeding, but letting go of the nostrils too soon interferes with development of a clot. After 5 minutes have passed, gently release pressure and see if there is still bleeding. If the bleeding continues, pinch the nostrils and repeat the above steps for another 5 minutes.

Once the bleeding has stopped, clean the outside of the child's nose. Do not try to clean inside, and do not have the child blow his or her nose to clean out the blood. Doing so may move the clot that has formed and restart the bleeding. Most nosebleeds last for less than 10 minutes. If a nosebleed continues for longer than 30 minutes, the child should be seen by his or her primary health care provider or in the emergency department (**Table 12-3**). If a child has repeated episodes of nosebleeds, consult a physician.

Table 12-3. When to Go to the ER: Nosebleeds
— Prolonged bleeding lasting more than 30 minutes
— Rapid, profuse bleeding cannot be controlled
— Child has a bleeding disorder

LACERATIONS

For any laceration, the primary concern is to control the bleeding. This can usually be accomplished by simply holding gauze or towels directly over the wound, applying steady pressure, and elevating it above the level of the child's heart. If the wound is on an arm or leg, have the child sit or lie down and lift the limb above the level of his or her heart. Just as for nosebleeds, hold the pressure for 5 minutes before checking the wound. Then, slowly release pressure to see if the bleeding continues. Checking more frequently can interfere with blood clotting. If the wound is still bleeding after 5 minutes, resume holding pressure and check after another 5 minutes. Repeat this, as needed, for up to 30 minutes. If a wound is still bleeding at this time, take the child to see a physician. If the gauze or towel becomes soaked with blood, do not remove it. Instead, apply a new layer of dressing on top. If a wound bleeds pro-fusely even with the application of direct pressure, the child should be taken to an emergency department immediately (**Table 12-4**).

Table 12-4. When to Go to the ER: Lacerations
— Prolonged bleeding lasting more than 30 minutes
— Rapid, profuse bleeding cannot be controlled
— Child has a bleeding disorder
— Wounds are deep, jagged, or gaping
— Lacerations are due to an animal bite
— Face or genitals are involved

Once the bleeding has stopped, inspect the wound. If it is clean, straight, shallow, and small, it can be treated at home. Wash it with soap and water and apply an antibiotic ointment and a bandage. The wound may begin bleeding again when it is washed, but this bleeding can be easily controlled after the wound is clean. The single greatest protection against infection is to clean the wound as soon as possible, so do not stop washing the wound because of a small amount of rebleeding. Lacerations should heal within 7 to 10 days and form a scar. Wounds that are large or deep, dirty, jagged, or the result of animal bites should be examined by an emergency department physician. Any wound that becomes red, swollen, or releases purulent drainage (pus) must also be examined by a physician.

HEAD INJURIES

Children may become unconscious after a head injury. They will look asleep but will not respond when parents try to wake them. Caregivers trained in CPR should check to see if children are breathing and if their heart is beating. If not, begin CPR and have someone dial 9-1-1. Caregivers who have not been trained in CPR should dial 9-1-1 immediately. Any child who becomes unconscious after a head injury must be taken to an emergency department immediately (**Table 12-5**). Head injuries can be particularly frightening for both parents and children. As long as children do not require immediate emergency treatment, the most important thing parents and caregivers can do is to stay in control of the situation and to help calm and comfort their child.

If a child is awake, but tired, after hitting his or her head, it is fine to let the child go to sleep. However, check on and wake the child every 2 hours for the first 12 hours following the injury. If a child will not wake up completely; is disoriented, dizzy, or unable to walk; or extremely irritable, he or she must be taken to an emergency department. If a child wakes easily and acts normally, he or she can be left to sleep until the next check.

It is normal for children to have headaches after hitting their head. However, a physician should evaluate any pain that lasts longer than one day or seems particularly severe. The day after a mild head injury, most children will be acting normally. However, children who are not acting "like themselves" or who are vomiting the next day should see their primary health care provider. A minor head injury can cause an actual brain injury, though this occurrence is uncommon. In these cases, children often display new behavioral thinking, such as unusual disorganization or inattention, or learning problems. In these situations, take children to their physician.

Table 12-5. When to Go to the ER: Head Injuries
— Any loss of consciousness (or change in consciousness)
— Seizures associated with head trauma
— Child will not wake up when prompted
— Vomiting lasts longer than 3 hours after the injury
— Child has a bleeding disorder
— Irritability
— Dizziness or inability to walk
— Severe or prolonged headaches
— Personality or behavioral changes are apparent

VOMITING AND DIARRHEA

When a child has vomiting or diarrhea that lasts for more than a few hours, caregivers should begin to look for signs of dehydration. Children who show signs of dehydration should be evaluated by a physician or taken to an emergency department. Parents can take steps to prevent dehydration from happening—namely, make sure that children consume liquids in order to replace the water that they have lost. Children younger than 1 year can be given breast milk, formula, or an electrolyte solution. Older children can be given water, diluted juices, or popsicles. Parents should not give children tea, soda, or other caffeinated beverages because caffeine can worsen dehydration. Avoid sports drinks as well because ingredients may vary and contain supplements that are unsuitable for sick children.

Children who are vomiting or have diarrhea will not be able to tolerate normal amounts of liquid in a single serving, so they should be given smaller amounts more frequently. Instead of 8 ounces every 4 hours, for example, they should drink 1 ounce every 15 minutes. Sometimes a child will require even smaller amounts at a time in order to prevent vomiting. If the child continues to vomit these small amounts, the child's pediatrician should be consulted. Also, if a child begins to show the signs of dehydration mentioned above, call a pediatrician or go to the emergency department (**Table 12-6**). A child who has vomited blood (which looks red or brown, like coffee grounds) or bile (green vomit), passed blood with the diarrhea, or has severe abdominal pain should receive urgent medical care. Consult a pediatrician when symptoms last longer than 3 days, even if the child is not dehydrated.

In general, pediatricians do not recommend giving children medicines that stop vomiting or diarrhea. Antidiarrheal medications can lengthen the time it takes for the infection to pass through the body. The best treatment is to keep children from becoming dehydrated with small frequent sips of appropriate liquids as discussed above.

FEVER

When caring for a child with a fever, remember that the fever itself is not dangerous. Generally, the key factors are how a child feels and acts, not the height of the fever. A 3 year old with a temperature of 103°F (39.4°C) who is playing normally, eating and drinking well, breathing comfortably, and exhibiting few other symptoms can be treated safely at home with over-the-counter medicines, such as acetaminophen or ibuprofen for comfort. However, a 3 year old with a lower fever of 101°F (38.3°C) who is listless, lethargic, irritable, refusing to drink, not urinating normally, or having difficulty breathing should visit a physician.

Children younger than 2 months with any fever should be taken to an emergency department (**Table 12-7**). Again, this is not because the fever is dangerous, but because the fever could be an indication of a serious infection that requires antibiotics.

If a child experiences a febrile seizure, remember that these seizures are rarely dangerous, despite how scary they can be to watch. Make sure the child cannot injure himself or herself while convulsing. If the child vomits, turn his or her head to the side to help keep the airway clear. It is unnecessary to be concerned that children will swallow their tongues while having a seizure, as it does not actually happen. However, do *NOT* put anything into the mouth of a child who is having a seizure—the child might choke. If the seizure lasts longer than 5 minutes, dial 9-1-1 for assistance. If the seizure is brief, take the child to the hospital for evaluation after it has stopped.

Other circumstances that warrant evaluation by a physician include prolonged or very high fevers. Fevers that persist for more than 3 days may represent an infection that should be treated by a health care professional. A physician should also see any child with a fever greater than 106°F (41.1°C).

Table 12-6. When to Go to the ER: Vomiting and Diarrhea

— Signs of severe dehydration:
  — Dry mouth and tongue
  — Lack of tears
  — Decreased urination
  — Sunken eyes
  — Skin feeling cool and clammy
— Persistent vomiting of even small amounts of fluid
— Vomiting blood or bile
— Blood in the diarrhea
— Severe abdominal pain

Table 12-7. When to Go to the ER: Fever

— Fever of 106° F (41.1° C) or higher
— Seizures
— Irritability
— Lethargy
— Difficulty breathing
— Severe dehydration
— Refusal to eat or drink
— Child is younger than 2 months

Fever medications include acetaminophen (Tylenol) or ibuprofen (Motrin or Advil). The dose of acetaminophen should be 15 mg per kilogram of a child's weight. (One kilogram equals 2.2 pounds; see **Table 12-8** for general conversions.) For ibuprofen, the dose is 10 mg per kilogram. For example, a child weighing 22 pounds (10 kg) could receive 150 mg of acetaminophen or 100 mg of ibuprofen. Although these medicines can be taken together, this should only be done under direction of a physician. Generally, 1 medicine is adequate. Do not mix medicines except under the direct supervision of a child's primary health care provider. Even though baby aspirin is still available over the counter, *NEVER* give aspirin to a child with a fever unless a pediatrician orders it.

ALLERGIES AND INSECT BITES

Insect bites are local allergic reactions and require little care. An over-the-counter antihistamine such as diphenhydramine (Benadryl) can help with the itching. If a child has injured his or her skin from excessive scratching, an over-the-counter antibiotic ointment can also be used to reduce the risk of infection. Diphenhydramine is available as an oral medication as well as a topical lotion, but they should not be used together because too much of the medication can cause side effects.

Insect repellents containing less than 10% DEET can be used to help prevent insect bites. Children may absorb DEET through their skin and experience side effects if repellents contain higher concentrations. If children seem to be acquiring insect bites inside the home, washing their clothes and sheets in hot water might eradicate the insects.

Antihistamines can be used to treat itching from other allergic rashes, such as hives, which are not dangerous but can be extremely itchy, or poison ivy–like reactions. Loratadine (Claritin) is another antihistamine available over the counter. It tends to cause less drowsiness and fewer behavior problems than diphenhydramine, and it only needs to be taken once per day. However, loratadine is not usually as effective as diphenhydramine in reducing itching. New hives may develop for several days after an allergic reaction. Rarely do hives continue for several weeks after the reaction. If they have not cleared up after 4 to 5 days, discuss the situation with the child's primary health care provider.

Serious allergic reactions involve body systems other than the skin. Any allergic reaction that causes wheezing, mouth swelling (including the lips or tongue), difficulty breathing or swallowing or loss of consciousness requires emergency treatment (**Table 12-9**). If a child shows any of these symptoms after taking a medicine, eating certain foods, or being stung by an insect, dial 9-1-1 as soon as possible.

Any child who has a serious allergic reaction should visit a pediatric allergy specialist so that the offending allergen can be identified and, hopefully, avoided. Additionally, children who have previously had a serious allergic reaction should always have access to an emergency epinephrine (adrenalin)

Table 12-8. Weight Conversion

Weight (pounds)	Weight (kilograms)
11	5
22	10
33	15
44	20
55	25
66	30
77	35
88	40
99	45
110	50

Table 12-9. When to Go to the ER: Allergic Reactions and Insect Bites

— Difficulty breathing

— Wheezing

— Difficulty swallowing

— Swelling of lips or tongue

— Loss of consciousness

— Known exposure to an agent that has caused anaphylaxis in the past auto-injector (EpiPen or EpiPen Jr). These medicines can be prescribed by a physician for any person with a history of life-threatening allergies and should be used when such a child shows any allergic symptoms after an exposure. Always seek emergency care after an auto-injector is used, even if the child appears much improved. In many cases, the epinephrine does not completely stop the allergic reaction, but rather slows it down enough to allow access to emergency medical care. These auto-injectors should be with the child at all times—at home, school, camp, sporting events, and relatives' houses. Caregivers of children with severe allergies, especially to foods, should notify schools or childcare facilities so appropriate measures can be taken.

SPRAINS AND FRACTURES

Immediately after an injury, children should be made to rest so that parents or caregivers can assess the situation. Initially, it may be very difficult to determine if an injury is a sprain or a fracture. If there is any evidence of a compound fracture or an obvious deformity in the bone, take children to the nearest emergency department (**Table 12-10**). For other injuries, ice or cold packs can be applied for 15 to 20 minutes to reduce the swelling. After this, reassess the injury. If a child experiences a large amount of swelling or skin discoloration, take the child to an emergency department. If not, a careful attempt should be made to use the injured extremity (moving an arm or wrist, or attempting to walk). Arm injuries that are significantly painful or limit movement should receive urgent medical care. If children have leg injuries and cannot walk or put weight on a leg, they should be taken to an emergency department. Do not instruct children to "walk it off," as this may exacerbate the underlying injury.

Table 12-10. When to Go to the ER: Sprains and Fractures
— Compound or open fractures
— Obvious deformity of an arm or leg
— Severe swelling or skin discoloration
— Severe pain
— Inability to use the injured extremity
— Injured leg cannot bear weight
— Swelling and pain that does not improve after 48 to 72 hours

If swelling and pain are not severe, children may remain at home and follow the **RICE** guidelines: **R**est, **I**ce, **C**ompression, and **E**levation. The affected extremity should be rested and placed above the level of the heart. Ice or cold packs should be placed on the injury for 20 minutes at a time and then removed for 20 minutes. This can be continued for several hours. Bags of frozen vegetables make an excellent, moldable cold pack. It is important not to leave the ice or cold pack in place for more than 20 minutes, or frostbite can occur. A compression bandage, such as an ACE bandage, can be applied to help reduce swelling.

Swelling will often worsen for the first 24 to 48 hours after an injury. At any time, if pain becomes severe (ie, a child describes the pain as being significantly worse or the child is noticeably more irritable and uncomfortable), or if a child cannot bear weight on an injured leg, the child should be taken to an emergency department. Most mild sprains will be significantly better 48 to 72 hours after the injury. More severe sprains and fractures will not improve so quickly, so persistent pain and swelling beyond 48 to 72 hours signifies the need to for medical evaluation.

Young children's bones are not as strong as those of adults, so they are more prone to fractures. It is important to know that fractures in children's bones do not always show up on initial X-rays, and children may need to be evaluated repeatedly.

Table 12-11. When to Go to the ER: Burns
— Signs of full thickness burns: white skin, black or charred skin, large blisters
— Blisters involving face, hands, feet, genitals, or joints
— Blisters with cloudy fluid or other signs of infection
— Fever, swelling, pus
— Any electrical or chemical burn

Burns

First, remove the child from the heat source to prevent further damage. Then, assess the burn. If signs of third degree, or full-thickness, burns are obvious (white areas of skin, black or charred skin), the child must be taken to an emergency department (**Table 12-11**). For other burns, run cool water over the injury to reduce further damage to the skin. Common misunderstandings of burn treatments involve putting ice, oil, or butter on the skin. These can be dangerous and increase the risk of infection. After applying cool water for several minutes, reassess the burn. A physician should examine burns with large blisters, or blisters on the face, hands, feet, genitals, or joints.

Electrical and chemical burns are extremely serious. Electrical burns can be merely the most visible sign of injury after electrocution. More significant damage can be difficult to detect. Chemical burns can also be deeper than they appear. For this reason, an emergency medical physician should always evaluate these 2 types of burns.

Superficial burns or partial-thickness burns with small blisters can be treated at home. Running cool water over the burn will reduce pain and swelling. Superficial burns and burns with blisters can be treated with an antibiotic ointment or topical anesthetic and bandaged. Blisters should not be drained, or "popped," at home because this may increase the risk of infection. If the fluid in the blister appears cloudy or yellow, the child should be examined by a physician for signs of an infection. In general, physicians should examine burns with blisters within 24 to 48 hours, or sooner if the blisters are large or show signs of infection—such as swelling, pain, or purulent drainage (pus).

Conclusion

Many of the medical situations mentioned in this chapter can be managed with a small amount of preparation and by calmly following simple treatment steps with your child. First aid, CPR, and babysitting classes are available through local Red Cross chapters and through local community centers and schools. Learning some basic first aid techniques and stocking some basic supplies and medications can go a long way to getting you and your child through these situations. Lastly, because this chapter addresses only the most common emergency medical situations, consult a physician for any particular concerns.

Where to Turn for Help

Books
Zand J, Walton R, Rountree B. *A Parent's Guide to Medical Emergencies*. Garden City Park, NY: Avery Publishing Group; 1997.

Web Sites
American Red Cross

http://www.redcross.org/services/hss/courses/community.html

— Offers courses in emergency medical care.

KidsHealth for Parents: First Aid and Safety

http://kidshealth.org/parent/firstaid_safe

National Poison Control Hotline

American Association of Poison Control Centers

800-222-1222

http://www.aapcc.org

Peanut Allergy: What You Need to Know

Allergy, Asthma and Immunology Society of Ontario

http://www.allergyasthma.on.ca/peanut1.htm

Chapter 13

TERRORISM: DEALING WITH THREATS

Paul S. Matz, MD

The attacks on New York City, Washington, DC, and Pennsylvania on September 11, 2001, reminded Americans that we are not immune to the terrorism that plagues much of the world. The attacks were followed by the distribution of anthrax as a biological weapon via the US postal system. All of these events brought the fear of terrorism to the minds of many Americans. Terrorist attacks can involve the use of bombs and explosions, as well as biological, chemical, or radioactive weapons.

BIOTERRORISM

Biological weapons, also known as bioweapons, are natural living organisms—primarily bacteria and viruses—that have been adapted for use as weapons. Toxins naturally produced by bacteria or viruses are also considered bioweapons. Some bioweapons are designed to kill, and some are intended to sicken and incapacitate enemies. Biological terrorism, or bioterrorism, is the use of biological weapons to attack civilians and incite fear in a population.

The history of biological weapons is surprisingly long. Ancient armies tried to infect their enemies using the bodies of bubonic plague victims. In the French and Indian War, British troops gave blankets used by smallpox victims to the Native American tribes they were fighting. The United States, USSR, Iraq, North Korea, Nazi Germany, Japan, and many other countries have each developed bioweapons at some point in their history. The commonly studied infections include anthrax, smallpox, bubonic plague, and botulism. (For more information on these agents, see **Appendix 13-1**.) Governments and terrorist groups have also experimented with ricin, a naturally occurring poison that can be extracted from the beans of the castor plant.

Programs developing bioweapons were generally kept secret, even when deaths occurred. The American military conducted tests of simulated bioweapons against civilian populations in the United States during the 1950s and 1960s. These tests, along with a handful of illnesses and 1 possibly related death, were not public knowledge until the 1970s. An accidental release of anthrax from a Soviet bioweapons plant killed 66 people in Russia in 1979, but the Soviet government initially claimed it was a natural outbreak.

Terrorist attacks using bioweapons have been rare. In the early 1990s, the Japanese terrorist group Aum Shinrikyo released anthrax and other biological weapons in Japan, but no illnesses were reported. In the United States in the 1990s, antigovernment terrorist groups obtained ricin but were arrested before using the poison.

The first incident of bioterrorism against the United States occurred in 1984 in Oregon and received little media attention. A religious cult purposely sprayed *Salmonella* bacteria onto restaurant salad bars, leading to the hospitalization of 45 people. The second event—the anthrax attacks of 2001—sickened 22 people and killed 5. This

189

attack received a comparatively great deal of media attention, and the source of the attack remains unknown to this day.

CHEMICAL TERRORISM

Chemical weapons are generally synthetic chemicals used to kill or injure enemies, and chemical terrorism is the intentional use of these agents by nongovernment groups to kill or terrorize civilian populations. These weapons were first used effectively on a large scale in World War I. The first chemical weapons developed were blistering or suffocating agents, such as mustard gas, phosgene, and chlorine gas. Thousands of soldiers on both sides of the war were killed or injured by these chemicals. Later agents developed are related to insecticides called organophosphates. These newer chemicals are called "nerve agents" and include Sarin and VX. These agents are extremely toxic.

Many governments developed chemical weapons during the 20th century. Even though the international community has banned these weapons, they have nevertheless been used on civilian populations several times. The Iraqi government of Saddam Hussein used them to kill Kurdish civilians in 1987 and 1988. In addition, Aum Shinrikyo released Sarin gas into the Tokyo subway system in 1995, killing 12 people and injuring thousands more.

RADIATION TERRORISM

Radiation terrorism is the use of radioactive materials as a terrorist device. This method of terrorism can involve the production of a nuclear (atomic) bomb or a "dirty" bomb, which consists of a conventional explosive device with radioactive materials designed to spread radiation over a large area. Nuclear weapons are dangerous not only because of their destructive explosions, but also for the radiation that is released. Fortunately, making an atomic bomb requires a significant degree of expertise, and assembling a device that will actually work is difficult. Several countries currently have nuclear weapons; terrorist groups have consistently sought them, but fortunately they have not yet been successful. The only use of a nuclear bomb in war was in 1945 in Japan during World War II. Terrorist groups have not yet utilized nuclear weapons.

An attack using a dirty bomb is more likely than an attack using a nuclear bomb. This type of bomb consists of conventional explosives packaged with radioactive elements. The radioactive element can be highly radioactive material, such as uranium or plutonium, or less radioactive materials, such as radioactive waste from hospitals or research laboratories. The initial explosion from these bombs may be no more destructive than other conventional weapons, but it can spread radioactive materials over a large radius. In addition to causing radiation injuries and deaths, this contamination could leave a large part of a city uninhabitable for many years. Terrorists may also attack nuclear power plants directly, leading to a local release of radiation. One of the materials that would be released during an attack or dirty bomb explosion is radioactive iodine, which can cause thyroid cancer. Although it is believed that terrorist groups have sought dirty bombs, as of 2005 none has yet been used in a terrorist attack.

EFFECTS OF TERRORISM

Although it is frightening to read about these forms of terrorism, keep in mind that such events are very uncommon. As of 2005, only 2 episodes of bioterrorism, and no episodes of chemical or radiation terrorism, have occurred in the United States. Often, the main risk to a child's health and well-being is not the a terrorist attack itself, but the fear associated with the possibility of such an event. See **Table 13-1** for frequently asked questions about terrorism and its effect on children.

Table 13-1. Frequently Asked Questions

It seems unlikely that my family will actually be involved in a terrorist attack. Do we really need to prepare?

Although terrorist attacks have been rare in the United States, families should be aware of the risks in their community. Many of the steps needed to prepare for an event are fairly simple (storing food, water, medical supplies) and inexpensive. These preparations are also useful in the event of natural disasters, which are far more common.

I feel compelled to watch television stories about possible terrorist attacks. My 3 year old plays in the room but doesn't seem to be watching. Is this okay?

Television's addictive nature can compel young children to watch it, even if the program doesn't really interest them. Even if children are not watching, they are still hearing news stories and absorbing this information. Parents should try to avoid watching potentially frightening news programs while young children are in the room. If older children watch these programs, parents should supervise so that children can ask questions and discuss their feelings.

After the September 11 attacks, my teenager seemed obsessed with the events and talked about the people who died for several months. This got better, but he gets this way every year around the anniversary of the attacks. Is this normal?

Children may become overly obsessed with terrorist events and may experience "anniversary reactions" for years after an event. Some of these symptoms may be normal, but if they are extreme or children seem obsessed, consult the child's pediatrician or a mental health care professional.

Our home is about 10 miles from a nuclear power plant. I have seen ads on the Internet selling potassium iodide. Do I need to buy it?

The American Academy of Pediatrics does recommend that families living within 10 miles of a nuclear power plant store potassium iodide (KI) in their homes. KI tablets are available without a prescription, but you should discuss this with your pediatrician before purchasing it. Always wait for instructions from authorities before taking potassium iodide or giving it to children.

My child requires a ventilator to breathe and our family can't afford a backup generator. What should we do to prepare?

Special needs and technology-dependent children face unique issues during terrorist attacks or natural disasters. It is vital that caregivers notify local law-enforcement, fire, and emergency personnel of their child's health status, so that they may receive higher priority during a disaster. Also, speak to your child's physician about obtaining equipment that allows you to feed or manually breathe for your child during an electrical outage.

PHYSICAL EFFECTS

Children are particularly vulnerable to many of the agents used in biological, chemical, and radiation terrorism. Children breathe faster than adults and can inhale more airborne toxins; also, because of their higher metabolic rate, they absorb more of the noxious substances. They are smaller than adults, and so the same amount of a toxin will have a greater effect on them. Finally, many terrorist agents are heavier than air, and so higher concentrations are found closer to the ground, exposing children to larger amounts of the agents than adults. Children are also more susceptible to developing cancer after a radiation exposure than adults.

EMOTIONAL EFFECTS

Children are highly sensitive and easily pick up on parents' and other adults' emotions. One of the primary ways that children are exposed to these events is through the media. Sensationalized news programs often make terrorist events seem much more likely to occur than is actually the case. Even if children are not allowed to watch such programs at home, they are likely, due to the pervasive nature of the media in our culture, to run into the information somewhere.

Television can often be so addictive that children will pay attention to whatever is on, even if it is something that adults would not expect to catch their interest. Children may need parental assistance in understanding what they see and hear on the news. For example, young children who still tend to think in very concrete terms may misunderstand rebroadcasted news events as separate occurrences. Media excitement about potential events can make a terrorist attack seem imminent to children.

Although parents and caregivers cannot always protect children from knowledge of scary events, they can help mediate these fears by having discussions that allow children to ask questions and process their feelings. As always, the most important thing to do is encourage children to talk about their feelings. Often, they will not initiate these discussions, and it is up to parents to start the conversation.

Very young or less mature children are not able to express themselves well in words. They may incorporate frightening world events into their games (for example, a police-versus-terrorists car chase) or drawings. Parents can ask to play with their children and allow them to control the game so that their ideas, feelings, and concerns can be expressed. Such play, drawing, or coloring may lead to opportunities to raise issues for discussion as well.

WHAT PARENTS AND CAREGIVERS CAN DO

PREPARATION FOR A TERRORIST ATTACK

Parents and schools can take steps to prepare for the possibility of a terrorist attack. Most of these guidelines also apply to natural disasters (hurricanes, tornadoes, earthquakes, floods). Unlike some natural disasters, for which some level of prediction is possible, terrorist events are intended to generate chaos and mass tragedy and thus generally occur with little or no warning. Living in constant fear is certainly unnecessary, but families should prepare in advance for any emergency. The first step is to create a family disaster plan detailing evacuation plans, meeting places, and methods for reaching shelter. Second, parents and caregivers should assemble a disaster supply kit. This kit should consist of anything a family will need if confined to the home for a prolonged period time. **Tables 13-2** and **13-3** list some of these items.

Foods included in the disaster kit should be nonperishable canned or dry food items. Families often store candles to use in case of power loss, but candles are a fire hazard. Flashlights and extra batteries are safer. A cellular phone may be useful for contacting family members or emergency services if landline phone service is lost.

In addition to basic over-the-counter medicines like pain relievers and antibiotic ointments, kits should include a 1-week supply of any prescription medicines family members use. Remember to replace these medications every few months so that the stocked medicine does not expire. Some medicines, like insulin, are absolutely necessary for an individual's survival and need to be refrigerated. If a family member requires this type of medication, consider purchasing a small backup electric generator in case electric power is lost. Families with infants should stock additional diapers, wipes, bottles, formula, and other necessary infant supplies.

Table 13-2. Family Disaster Supplies

— Water: one gallon per person per day for 3 to 7 days

— Food: enough for each family member for 3 to 7 days

— Sleeping bags or warm blankets

— Clothing and shoes: one complete change of clothes for each family member (include warm clothing and boots in cold climates)

— First aid kit

— Toiletries

— Flashlight and radio, along with several sets of batteries for each

— Keys

— Basic tools: wrench, utility knife, eating utensils, can opener

— Fire extinguisher

— First aid book

— Important family documents, such as identification, bank and insurance records

— Cellular phone

Table 13-3. Items for a First Aid Kit

— Adhesive bandages

— Antibiotic ointments

— Eye wash solution

— Medicines, prescription

— Medicines, over-the-counter:

  Acetaminophen

  Ibuprofen

  Antidiarrheal medicine

  Antacids

  Antihistamines

— Scissors

— Soap

— Sterile dressings or gauze

— Tape

— Thermometer

Children with special needs will need additional assistance during a terrorist event. When creating a family disaster plan, assign particular family members to assist these children. For special needs children in school or childcare, consider including their primary health care provider's phone number along with family contact numbers in case the family cannot be reached in an emergency. Medical alert tags can be useful if a special needs child is at school or childcare during an emergency. Parents should make sure that their child's school has a supply of medication and any other important supplies (feeding tubes and formula, suction catheters, or oxygen).

Parents should discuss disaster planning with their children's childcare providers, teachers, or principals. These facilities should have disaster plans that include a disaster supply kit and emergency evacuation plans. Families should identify a predefined meeting point for their children. Schools should have contact information for all family members of children in their care. Teachers and childcare providers should take an active role and address these concerns with principals and supervisors. Parents should ask school officials about the school's disaster plan and offer to assist in disaster preparation at their child's school.

193

Finally, all family members should have phone numbers for the entire family (home, work, mobile, neighbors). In addition, it is often helpful to pick 1 out-of-town relative or friend whom everyone will contact if local phone lines are busy or disabled. Meeting points close to home should be identified in case family members are unable to contact each other.

The American Academy of Pediatrics (AAP) has a Web site with information on preparing for a terrorist attack or natural disaster. The US Department of Homeland Security's preparedness Web site has information for businesses, families, and children regarding disaster preparedness (see "Where to Turn for Help"). Families should utilize both of these resources when preparing for disasters. Also see **Table 13-4** for tips on preparing for and responding to a terrorist event.

IN EVENT OF AN ATTACK

Just as in any other emergency situation, a caregiver's first responsibility during a terrorist attack is to remain calm. Children look to parents, teachers, and other caregivers for cues on how to react to the event. Remaining calm will help everyone stay focused on taking the steps necessary to protect themselves.

Table 13-4. Dos and Don'ts of Preparing for and Reacting to a Terrorist Event

— Do organize a family disaster plan.

— Do prepare an emergency disaster kit.

— Do know which local authorities to contact for questions.

— Do talk to your children often about their fears (and yours).

— Do answer your children's questions honestly.

— Do watch television with older children, but limit the amount of coverage to which any child is exposed.

— Do watch for signs and symptoms of depression or other mental health problems after an event.

— Don't allow yourself to become overly frightened about these events.

— Don't ignore your child's questions and fears.

— Don't ignore instructions from authorities after an event.

Paying attention to television and radio news for emergency instructions from authorities is important. If an attack happens nearby, consider activating the family emergency plan and seeking shelter or evacuating. Use contact numbers or emergency meeting places to locate children and other family members, remembering to provide extra help for any children with special needs. Once federal or local authorities have ordered evacuation or shelter, listen to the radio for updates and further instructions.

These instructions also apply to teachers and childcare providers during an emergency. Their job may be more difficult as the ratio of children to caregivers will be higher. As always, remaining calm will help the children in your care to do the same. In addition to activating an emergency plan, schools and childcare providers have the added responsibility of contacting parents and other family members of children in their care.

The effects of a terrorist attack that uses biological or chemical agents may not be realized until people become sick, and this may take several days. In these situations, caregivers may have more time to obtain information and instructions from authorities before deciding to implement their family's emergency plan.

In general, parents and caregivers are more likely to be aware of a terrorist event elsewhere in the country or world that does not threaten the health or life of their family members. Although there is no immediate safety threat in this situation, the greater concern for most children will be the fear that such an event could happen again closer to home.

TALKING TO CHILDREN AFTER AN ATTACK

When terrorist attacks or disasters do occur, raw footage is broadcast on television almost immediately. This footage can include images of buildings collapsing, bombs exploding, or even people dying. Many people in the United States experienced this on September 11, and they may have experienced some of the same feelings when watching footage of the Indian Ocean tsunami on December 26, 2004. Again, children and adults were exposed to horrifying images and tales of death and destruction. Adults often feel drawn to the television after a major event as they attempt to process what has happened. In addition, television is a source of important instructions from authorities, as well as information about an event. However, these types of images are even more difficult for children to process, when they realize that what they are seeing is occurring live and not as a part of an "after the fact" news story.

If an event has not occurred nearby, there is less need to obtain instructions and information. In this instance, parents should minimize their own television viewing in order to minimize that of their children. Repeated exposure to horrific images will merely raise children's anxiety. Older children may be allowed to watch some of these events on television, but caregivers should be with them, both to answer questions and gently ask them to discuss how this event makes them feel.

Children will naturally have questions after a terrorist event, and questions should be encouraged. Having their concerns ignored can worsen children's anxieties. Caregivers should give truthful answers tailored to the child's level of understanding. Younger children need fewer details and often simply need to be reassured that caregivers will keep them safe. Older children may require more details.

Focus on how the event might make a child feel. Adolescents will not be as easily reassured that their parents will protect them. They are more aware of the randomness of terrorist attacks and understand that their parents cannot always protect them. In these instances, ask children to discuss their concerns. Parents who share their own reactions and feelings let their teenagers know that their concerns are not unique and model how to cope with fears. Children may not be ready to discuss events immediately after an attack and should not be forced to do so. Periodically, offer to discuss the events so they know that someone is ready to help them when they are more comfortable.

Finally, be aware of behavior changes in your child after an event. Note symptoms of depression, such as sadness, irritability, or others mentioned in Chapter 15, Depression and Suicide. Also, children may have nightmares or act out the terrorist events during play. Parents should use these events to prompt children to discuss fears. During stressful situations, children's development may regress. For example, children who were recently toilet-trained may begin having accidents. Young children may also become clingier with parents and caregivers. Some of these symptoms are to be expected and should improve over time. If a child becomes overly obsessed with a terrorist event or symptoms of depression or nightmares are prolonged or seem extreme, parents or caregivers should consult their child's primary health care provider or a mental health professional.

Posttraumatic stress disorder (PTSD) can occur in some children who are actually exposed to a terrorist event or lose a loved one in a terrorist attack. Effects of PTSD may include reliving the event (often through dreams and nightmares), being easily upset by common stimuli (loud noises, television images), and avoiding events that remind them of the terrorist attack. A pediatrician or mental health professional should evaluate children with these symptoms. Even children exposed to an event from a distance, such as through television, may develop some of these symptoms, though the symptoms will usually be less severe.

PROFESSIONAL STUDY AND CONTROVERSY

Families who live near nuclear power plants have one additional issue to consider. As previously mentioned, radioactive iodine can be released after an incident at a nuclear plant. The thyroid gland, which is located in the neck, can absorb this radioactive iodine, leading a person to the develop thyroid cancer. *Potassium iodide*, also known by its elemental symbol, "KI," is a form of salt that can, if taken early, enter the thyroid gland and block absorption of the radioactive iodine. The AAP recommends that all children and families living within 10 miles of a nuclear power plant store potassium iodide for use in case of emergency. The potassium iodide should be used as soon as possible after a confirmed radiation release. Families may need to mix the salt with food to disguise the taste. KI is available over the counter, but families should discuss their concerns with their pediatrician before buying it and wait for notice from authorities before using the potassium iodide.

After a large radiation exposure, the adult dose of potassium iodide is 130 mg. This should be given to anyone over 70 kg (154 lbs), including pregnant or nursing women. Children aged 4 years and older can receive half this dose, or 65 mg. Children aged 1 month to 3 years should receive 32 mg and newborns (up to 1 month) should receive 16 mg. Potassium iodide can be purchased as either 65-mg or 130-mg tablets. Each dose lasts 24 hours, and if it is not possible to evacuate a contaminated area, the dose should be repeated each day for 1 week.

For the smaller doses required by children, parents can make their own solution of potassium iodide. Crushing a 130-mg tablet and mixing it in 40 ml (8 tsp) of water makes a solution that has 16.25 mg of potassium iodide per teaspoon. Newborns should receive 1 teaspoon, children younger than 3 years should receive 2 teaspoons, and children older than 4 years should receive 4 teaspoons. If a 65-mg tablet is used to prepare this solution, then all the doses should be doubled (2 tsp, 4 tsp, or 8 tsp). As potassium iodide tastes very salty, soda, juice, or flavored syrup can be substituted for half the water in the recipe above. These solutions will last 1 week in the refrigerator.

Schools and childcare providers located within 10 miles of a nuclear power plant should also consider stockpiling potassium iodide in their disaster kits. Families should discuss this with their childcare providers. Schools and childcare facilities should notify families if they are considering keeping this medicine at their facility. These facilities should await instructions from authorities before administering potassium iodide to students and children in their care.

In the year following the September 11 attacks, the US government recommended stocking duct tape and plastic sheeting (or heavy plastic garbage bags) in order to seal off a room against biological or chemical agents. While considered controversial by many, the US Department of Homeland Security and the American Red Cross continue to recommend these measures in case of a chemical or biological attack. These are fairly inexpensive preparations to take, and families should consider storing these items. Families should await word from authorities before retreating to a sealed room.

Conclusion

The possibility of terrorist attacks has unfortunately become a reality. Parents and caregivers should to take steps to prepare for the unlikely event of an attack, both at home and at school. More importantly, caregivers should spend the time to talk to their children about their fears, before and after an event takes place.

Where to Turn for Help

American Academy of Pediatrics (AAP): Children, Terrorism, and Disasters

http://www.aap.org/terrorism/index.html

AAP: Family Readiness Kit—Preparing to Handle Disasters

http://www.aap.org/family/frk/frkit.htm

AAP: Responding to Children's Emotional Needs During Times of Crisis—An Important Role for Pediatricians

http://www.aap.org/terrorism/topics/parents.pdf

American Red Cross: Terrorism—Preparing for the Unexpected

http://www.redcross.org/services/disaster/0,1082,0_589_,00.html

American Red Cross/Federal Emergency Management Agency: Food and Water in an Emergency

http://www.redcross.org/disaster/safety/Foodwtr.pdf

US Department of Homeland Security: Ready.gov

http://www.ready.gov

Appendix 13-1: Biological Agents Used for Terrorism*

The Centers for Disease Control and Prevention (CDC) recommends that health care providers and public health officials monitor their patients for any unusual diseases or increased numbers of illnesses that might be associated with a terrorist attack, especially because of post–September 11 intentional anthrax exposures in Florida, Washington, DC, and New Jersey. The biological agents that the CDC defines as agents with the potential to be used as bioweapons include *Bacillus anthracis* (anthrax), smallpox variola major, *Yersinia pestis* (plague), and *Clostridium botulinum* toxin (botulism). This appendix provides a brief overview of the CDC information available on these biological agents, and on members of the species *salmonellosis*, which have also been used in at least 1 act of terrorism against the United States (see "Bioterrorism").

Anthrax

Anthrax is caused by *Bacillus anthracis*, a bacterium that forms spores (**Appendix Figure 13-1**). The 3 types of anthrax are cutaneous (skin) (**Appendix Figures 13-2-a** and **b**), inhalation (lung) (**Appendix Figure 13-3**), and gastrointestinal (digestive) (**Appendix Figure 13-4**). Anthrax is not spread from person to person, but humans can become

---

*Appendix 13-1 adapted from CDC.

infected with anthrax by handling products from infected animals or inhaling anthrax spores. People also can become infected with gastrointestinal anthrax by eating undercooked meat from infected animals. Antibiotics are used to treat all 3 types of anthrax.

Symptoms vary depending upon the type of anthrax. The first symptom of cutaneous anthrax is a small sore that develops into a blister, which becomes a skin ulcer with a black area in the center. The sore, blister, and ulcer do not hurt. Gastrointestinal anthrax begins with nausea, loss of appetite, bloody diarrhea, and fever, followed by bad stomach pain. Inhalation anthrax's initial signs are like cold or flu symptoms and can include a sore throat, mild fever, and muscle aches. Cough, chest discomfort, shortness of breath, tiredness, and muscle aches develop with inhalation-acquired anthrax.

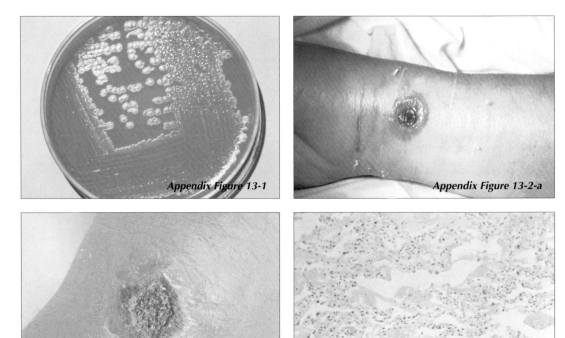

Appendix Figure 13-1

Appendix Figure 13-2-a

Appendix Figure 13-2-b

Appendix Figure 13-3

Appendix Figure 13-1. *Agar culture plate growing Baccillus anthracis colonies. Reprinted from CDC Public Health Image Library.*

Appendix Figure 13-2-a. *Cutaneous anthrax lesion on the arm of a 50-year-old woman, who had been a carder in a wool factory for 6 years. This lesion is on the eighth day of the illness. Cutaneous anthrax usually occurs after skin contact with contaminated meat, wool, hides, or leather from infected animals. Reprinted from CDC Public Health Image Library.*

Appendix Figure 13-2-b. *Anthrax lesion on the skin of the forearm caused by the bacterium Bacillus anthracis. The disease has manifested as a cutaneous ulceration, which has begun to turn black. Reprinted from CDC Public Health Image Library.*

Appendix Figure 13-3. *Photomicrograph of lung tissue infected with Bacillus anthracis bacteria. Bacillus anthracis spores can live in the soil for many years, and humans can become infected with anthrax by handling products from infected animals or by inhaling anthrax spores from contaminated animal products. Reprinted from CDC Public Health Image Library.*

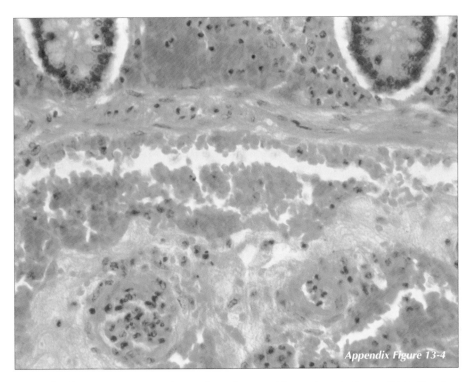

Appendix Figure 13-4. *Micrograph revealing submucosal hemorrhage in the small intestine, in a case of fatal human anthrax. Reprinted from CDC Public Health Image Library.*

SMALLPOX

Smallpox is caused by the variola virus that emerged in human populations thousands of years ago. Except for laboratory stockpiles, the variola virus has been eliminated. There are 2 clinical forms of smallpox. Variola major is severe and the most common form of smallpox, featuring a more extensive rash and higher fever. There are 4 types of variola major smallpox: ordinary, which is the most frequent type and accounts for 90% or more of cases; modified, which is mild and occurs in previously vaccinated persons; and flat and hemorrhagic, which are rare and very severe.

Variola major has an overall fatality rate of about 30%; however, flat and hemorrhagic smallpox usually are fatal. Variola minor is a less common presentation of smallpox, and a much less severe disease, with death rates of 1% or less.

Direct face-to-face contact and direct contact with infected bodily fluids or contaminated objects such as bedding or clothing spreads smallpox from one person to another. A person with smallpox is sometimes contagious with onset of fever, but is the most contagious with the onset of rash. Rarely, smallpox has been spread by virus carried in the air in enclosed settings such as buildings, buses, and trains. Humans are the only natural hosts for smallpox; insects and other animals do not transmit this disease.

Exposure to the virus is followed by an incubation period, which averages about 12 to 14 days but can range from 7 to 17 days. During the incubation period, people are not contagious, may feel healthy, and may not show any symptoms.

Initial symptoms of smallpox include fever (usually in the range of 101°F to 104°F), malaise, head and body aches, and sometimes vomiting. At this time, people are usually too sick to carry on their normal activities. This ***prodrome phase*** may last 2 to 4 days.

A rash emerges first as small red spots on the tongue and in the mouth. These spots develop into sores that break open, spreading large amounts of the virus into the mouth and throat. The person is the most contagious during this stage. Around when the sores in the mouth break down, a rash appears on the skin, starting on the face and spreading to the arms and legs and then to the hands and feet (**Appendix Figures 13-5-a** and **b**). Usually the rash spreads to all parts of the body within 24 hours. As the rash appears, the fever usually falls, and the person may start to feel better. By the third day of rash development, it turns into raised bumps. By the fourth day, the bumps fill with a thick, opaque fluid and will often have a depression in the center that resembles a bellybutton. This depression is a major distinguishing characteristic of smallpox. Fever often will rise again and remain high until scabs form over the bumps.

There is no specific treatment for smallpox disease, and the only prevention is vaccination. Supportive therapy (eg, intravenous fluids, medicine to control fever or pain) and antibiotics for any secondary bacterial infections can help patients.

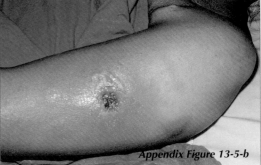

Appendix Figure 13-5-b

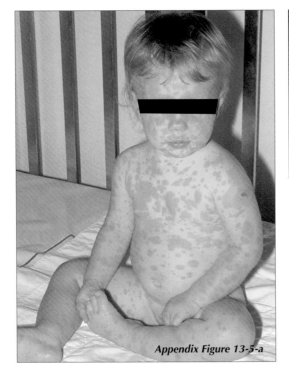

Appendix Figure 13-5-a

Appendix Figure 13-5-a. *After receiving a smallpox vaccination, this 1-year-old child developed erythema multiforme. Erythema mutliforme major, also referred to as Stevens-Johnson syndrome, is a toxic or allergic rash in response to the smallpox vaccine that can take various forms, and range from moderate to severe. Reprinted from CDC Public Health Image Library.*

Appendix Figure 13-5-b. *This female patient with chronic myelogenous leukemia manifested symptoms of vaccinia gangrenosum 1 month after a smallpox vaccination. Reprinted from CDC Public Health Image Library.*

PLAGUE

Plague is caused by *Yersinia pestis*, a species of bacteria found in rodents and their fleas. ***Pneumonic plague*** affects the lungs and is transmitted when a person inhales *Yersinia pestis* particles from the air. ***Bubonic plague*** is transmitted through the bite of an infected flea or exposure to infected material through a lesion. Symptoms include swollen, tender lymph glands called ***buboes*** (**Appendix Figure 13-6**). Buboes are not present in pneumonic plague. If bubonic plague is not treated, the bacteria may spread through the bloodstream and infect the lungs, causing a secondary case of pneumonic plague.

Yersinia pestis used in an aerosol attack could cause cases of pneumonic plague. One to 6 days after becoming infected with the bacteria, people would develop pneumonic plague, and, once they have the disease, they can spread bacteria to others with whom they are in close contact. Control of the disease becomes more difficult because of the delay between being exposed to the bacteria and becoming sick; infected persons might travel over a large area before becoming contagious and possibly infecting others. Using *Yersinia pestis* in a bioweapon is feasible because the bacterium occurs in nature and could be isolated and grown in quantity in a laboratory.

The signs and symptoms of pneumonic plague are usually fever, weakness, and rapidly developing pneumonia with shortness of breath, chest pain, cough, and sometimes bloody or watery mucus. Nausea, vomiting, and abdominal pain may also occur. Without early treatment with antibiotics, pneumonic plague usually leads to respiratory failure, shock, and rapid death. Currently, no plague vaccine is available in the United States.

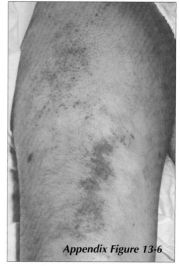

Appendix Figure 13-6

BOTULISM

There are 3 main kinds of botulism. *Foodborne botulism* (**Appendix Figures 13-7-a** and **b**) occurs when a person ingests a preformed toxin that leads to illness within a few hours to a few days. Foodborne botulism is a public health emergency because the contaminated food may still be available to people other than the patient. It can occur in all age groups. *Infant botulism* occurs in a small number of susceptible infants who harbor *Clostridium botulinum* in their intestinal tract. *Wound botulism* occurs when wounds are infected with *C botulinum* that secretes the toxin (**Appendix Figure 13-7-c**). Botulism is not spread from person to person.

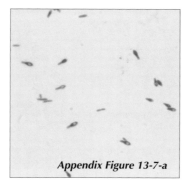

Appendix Figure 13-7-a

Appendix Figure 13-7-b

Foodborne botulism symptoms begin within 6 hours to 2 weeks (most commonly between 12 and 36 hours) after eating contaminated food. Symptoms include double vision, blurred vision, drooping eyelids, slurred speech, difficulty swallowing, dry mouth, and muscle weakness that descends through the body—first the shoulders are affected, then the upper arms, lower arms, thighs, calves, and so on. Botulism may also cause paralysis of the breathing muscles, which can lead to death if not treated and managed appropriately with life support.

Antitoxin against botulism, effective in reducing the severity of symptoms if given early in the disease course, is maintained by the CDC. Most patients recover after weeks or months of care.

SALMONELLA

There are many different kinds of *Salmonella* bacteria (**Appendix Figures 13-8-a** and **b**) that can cause diarrhea in humans. It usually infects humans who eat foods contaminated with animal feces, but infected food handlers who do not adequately wash their hands with soap after using the bathroom can also infect food.

Appendix Figure 13-6. This patient acquired a plague infection through abrasions on his upper right leg. Bubonic plague is transmitted through the bite of an infected flea, or as in this case, exposure to inoculated material through a break in the skin. Symptoms include swollen, tender lymph glands known as buboes. Reprinted from *CDC Public Health Image Library.*

Appendix Figure 13-7-a. Gram-stained micrograph of Clostridium botulinum type A in thioglycollate broth, incubated for 48 hr at 35° C. Reprinted from *CDC Public Health Image Library.*

Appendix Figure 13-7-b. Clostridium botulinum type E colonies displaying an opaque zone grown on a 48-hour egg yolk agar plate. C botulinum type E is an indigenous organism in the aquatic environment, and is the type mainly associated with botulism from seafood products. Reprinted from *CDC Public Health Image Library.*

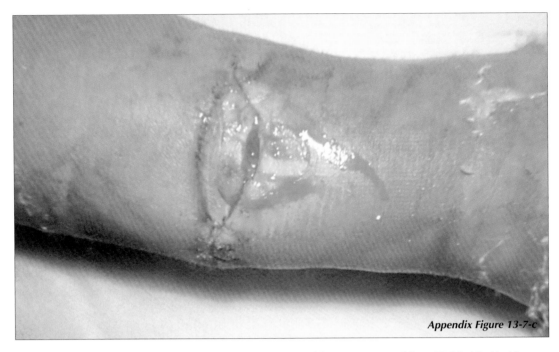

Appendix Figure 13-7-c

Appendix Figure 13-7-c. *Wound botulism on a boy who fractured his arm. Reprinted from CDC Public Health Image Library.*

Appendix Figure 13-8-a. *Colocinal growth pattern displayed by* Salmonella choleraisuis *subsp.* arizonae *bacteria grown on a blood agar culture plate. Reprinted from CDC Public Health Image Library.*

Appendix Figure 13-8-b. *Histopathology of a lymph node in a case of Typhoid fever. After initially being ingested in contaminated food such as shellfish, or water, the* Salmonella typhi *bacteria migrate through the intestinal mucosa of the terminal ileum into the submucosal lymph nodes. Reprinted from CDC Public Health Image Library.*

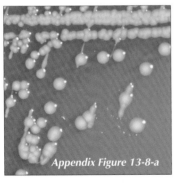

Appendix Figure 13-8-a

Diarrhea, fever, and abdominal cramps usually occur 12 to 72 hours after infection, and the illness lasts 4 to 7 days. Most patients recover without treatment, but diarrhea can be severe enough to warrant hospitalization and intravenous hydration. *Salmonella* infections typically do not require antibiotics unless the patient becomes dehydrated or the infection spreads from the intestines to the bloodstream. The infection can then move to other body sites and cause death if antibiotic treatment is not administered. Some *Salmonella* bacteria have developed a resistance to antibiotics, but it can usually be treated with a number of different antibiotics. Severe illness is more likely in the elderly, infants, and those with impaired immune systems.

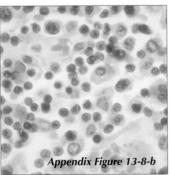

Appendix Figure 13-8-b

Chapter 14

TATTOOING, PIERCING, AND BRANDING

Hans B. Kersten, MD

Children in each generation have found different ways of expressing themselves, and children today are no different. Although tattoos, body piercing, and branding were often associated with bikers, convicts, gang members, and hippies in the 1960s, they have become more popular with adolescents since the 1990s as a form of self-expression or community identification. According to one self-report study conducted by professor Myrna Armstrong, who specializes in body art research, as many as 8% to 13% of adolescents have tattoos, and an additional 30% to 50% have reported considering one. Additionally, 27% of adolescents surveyed had body piercings, and 12% had multiple piercings. According to Armstrong, adolescents who have tattoos have reported that they "just wanted one," or got one to be "part of a group." As many as 30% just liked feeling defiant at the time they got the tattoo. Less than one third of the parents of these adolescents knew about the tattoo at that time. There is some concern among health-care professionals about these trends, as a number of behavioral risk factors and medical problems are thought to be associated with having a tattoo, body piercing, or branding. Many efforts have been made to lessen the risks of receiving a tattoo or body piercing, and much research has been aimed at determining the risk factors associated with obtaining various types of body art. This chapter will focus on the risks associated with obtaining body art so that parents, teachers, and childcare providers can be better prepared to understand these issues and to intervene when necessary.

In spite of the recent resurgence in the prevalence of body art, the practice has been around for thousands of years. Tattoos appeared in Egyptian culture in 4000 BCE and were believed to ensure good luck and health in some societies. Body piercings were a sign of courage and virility in Egyptian culture, and navel piercings were considered a rite of passage for pharaohs. Branding does not have such an extensive history. King Henry VIII of England used it in the 15th century as a way of marking outcasts and criminals. Criminals had an "S" for slave branded on their cheeks. Fortunately, the practice was abolished in the 18th century, though some fraternities in the United States reportedly use branding as an initiation rite. Sun tanning, like tattooing, is an ancient practice. Many cultures considered the sun to be the source of all life and sun gods the source of all goodness. Due to this thinking, Aesculapian health clinics used sunbathing as a way to help restore good health 2000 years ago. Even in the last 100 years, sun tanning has been associated with good health, until its connection to melanoma and nonmelanoma skin cancers was discovered in the 1970s. In spite of this impressive history, the resurgence of body art and certain associated behaviors has generated concern among some parents and other adults in modern society.

EFFECTS OF BODY ART

ASSOCIATED RISKS

Many health care providers and parents associate body art with low academic achievement, criminal activity or psychiatric disturbances due to its association in the 1960s with members of motorcycle gangs, criminals, and sailors. However, the notion that tattoos and body piercings are associated with gang members, criminals and military personnel is outdated. Many professionals, clergy, and other respected members of society have body art. Dr. Armstrong's recent studies have also shown that the majority of tattooed adolescents surveyed had A or B grades in school, refuting the notion that tattoos are associated with low intelligence or underachievement. Still, many adolescents who have tattoos report that they consider themselves "risk-takers," and, in a recent study of adolescents published in the journal *Pediatrics*, having a tattoo was associated with high-risk behaviors such as sexual intercourse, binge drinking, smoking, marijuana use, fighting, gang membership, truancy, and school failure. Tattoos were also more highly associated with eating disorders, drug use, and suicide. An increase in the number of body piercings was associated with an increase in abuse of drugs such as cocaine and ecstasy. All of these findings, along with data from college students, showed no difference in high-risk behaviors between youth who did and did not have tattoos. Research by Forbes and Armstrong has indicated that students who have tattoos are just as likely to have strong family relationships, parents with college degrees, daily prayer habits, and strong religious faith as those without. No studies have yet assessed the association between tanning and school performance. Parents and caregivers need to be aware of all of these trends and pay attention to children who choose to use body art as a form of self-expression. Parents and caregivers must also be careful not to react negatively or distance themselves from children who express themselves this way. Doing so will damage their chances of maintaining a working relationship with children and recognizing any problems or complications that may arise or be associated with the body art.

TATTOOING, PIERCING, AND BRANDING PROCESSES

A *tattoo* is the painting or tapping of dyes into the skin surface, and the word means "to strike or mark" in Tahitian. Common tattoo designs include names, crosses, animals, cartoon characters, hearts, and freehand designs. Although tattoos have been prevalent for thousands of years, Japan and Polynesia are credited with introducing the tattoo to Western cultures via European and American sailors on command or naval visits. Today, most tattoos are applied in commercial studios, though some are self-applied or done by friends. The artist applies the tattoo to the skin using a hand-held electrically powered machine that uses a varying number of needles to insert the pigment into the skin, repeatedly puncturing it and wiping away the blood and fluid that seep out. After the tattoo has been applied, it is generally bandaged and kept clean for a few days to weeks. Homemade tattoos are usually done by amateurs who are too young to legally obtain a tattoo or cannot afford a professional tattoo. Mascara or charcoal is often used as a pigment in these tattoos, which are made with sharp objects like a pen or pencil. Designs can have very specific meanings: Tattoos of dots, crosses, or webs placed between the thumb and forefinger may signal gang membership, and a teardrop or spider web may mean many different things, including the death of a loved one, a year served in jail, or that the wearer has murdered someone.

Table 14-1. Common Piercing Sites
— Ear lobe
— Eyebrow
— Tragus of the ear
— Navel
— Tongue
— Nose
— Lip
— Nipple

Body piercing involves piercing parts of the body with metal or other objects (**Figure 14-1-a** through **d**). Body piercing is often performed in tattoo studios, but it may also be done in jewelry stores or at home. The ear is the most commonly pierced body part, though other sites have become more common (**Table 14-1**). The piercer cleans the skin with alcohol or iodine before piercing it. A spring-loaded gun containing the

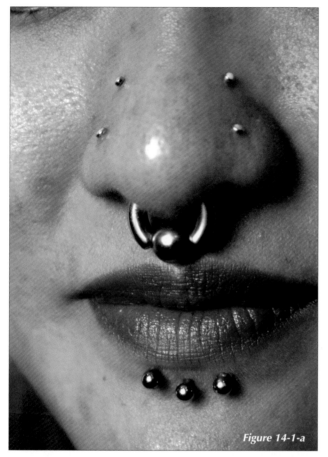

Figure 14-1-a

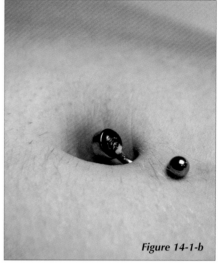

Figure 14-1-b

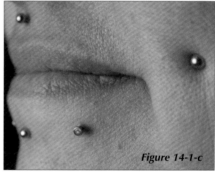

Figure 14-1-c

Figure 14-1-d

Figure 14-1-a. *Multiple facial piercings involving stainless steel jewelry; areas pierced include skin below lower lip, and nose with nose ring and 4 stud-type jewelry along each side of the nose. Photo courtesy of the Association of Professional Piercers.*

Figure 14-1-b. *Piercing involving the umbilicus (belly button) with stainless steel jewelry. Photo courtesy of the Association of Professional Piercers.*

Figure 14-1-c. *Multiple facial piercings involving skin below the lower lip, above the upper lip, and on side of the face below the cheek bone area. Photo courtesy of the Association of Professional Piercers.*

Figure 14-1-d. *Stainless steel jewelry piercing involving skin over the bridge of the nose. Photo courtesy of the Association of Professional Piercers.*

earring stud is usually used to pierce ears; sterile, hollow bore needles are often used to pierce nontraditional sites such as the lip, tongue, navel, or even genitalia. The piercer uses forceps to force the needle through the tissue and place the jewelry. However the piercing is done, the jewelry must be left in place for weeks, and the site must be cleaned at least twice a day for a week or more. Piercings, like tattoos, will have a small amount of bleeding.

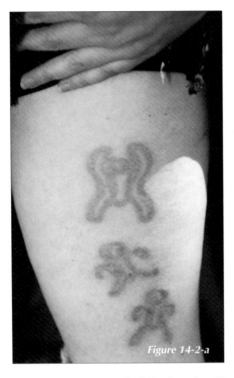
Figure 14-2-a

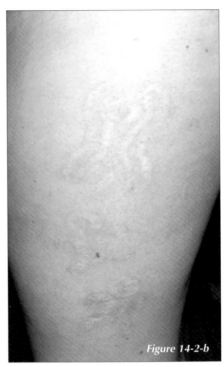
Figure 14-2-b

Figure 14-2-a. *A 6-month-old leg branding. The characters were done from bottom to top; the bottom 2 brandings were struck, and the top was done using the electrocautery technique. Photo courtesy of Rae Schwarz, Body Art Editor of bellaonline.com.*

Figure 14-2-b. *Same branding as in **14-2-a**, 5 years later. The brands have turned almost completely white. Most brandings lose their color when they heal. Photo courtesy of Rae Schwarz, Body Art Editor of bellaonline.com.*

Branding is the process of pressing an extremely hot piece of metal onto the skin (**Figure 14-2-a** and **b**). It is generally done on flat surfaces of skin, such as the shoulders, upper back, arm, or thighs. Several strikes of the hot metal tool are often necessary to complete the design. Although there is usually not much bleeding with branding, this process is extremely painful and may involve deeper layers beneath the skin. It is considered the most dangerous form of body art because of the involvement of the deeper layers of the skin that contain blood vessels and nerves. As a result, brandings are more likely to have complications than tattoos or piercings.

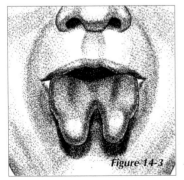
Figure 14-3

Figure 14-3. *A split tongue.*

The newest and most controversial form of body modification is tongue splitting. Although it is not yet commonplace, it is becoming increasingly popular as tattoos and body piercings become more common. *Tongue splitting* involves actually splitting the tongue down the middle (**Figure 14-3**). The procedure has been done surgically, but many surgeons and body piercers refuse to perform it. Some consider this form of body modification so severe that they lobby state governments to ban it, and it has recently been banned in the state of Illinois. Tongue splitting is also prohibited in some branches of the armed forces. Although advocates consider it beautiful, spiritual, or say that it enhances kissing, opponents cite the higher likelihood of bacterial infection or affected speech as reasons to prohibit it. In blogs and online body art communities, some people have described having to relearn how to speak once their tongue was split.

Although tanning is not traditionally considered body art, it is a common behavior that youths practice for cosmetic purposes, and it has potential health risks. Sun exposure, in the form of ultraviolet radiation (UVR), is recognized to cause melanoma skin cancer worldwide. Studies on sun exposure have suggested that limiting sun exposure during childhood and adolescence could reduce the lifetime risk of developing nonmelanoma skin cancers. In Boston University professor Alan Geller's study of US children and adolescents, as many as 83% reported experiencing at least 1 sunburn during the previous summer, and more than one third had 3 or more sunburns. Sunscreen use was reported only about one third of the time, and almost 10% reported the using a tanning bed during the previous year. Some studies show that adults and children continue to expose themselves to ultraviolet light even when they are aware of the associated risks. See Chapter 11, Environmental Health, for more information on the risks of UVR.

COMPLICATIONS

The most common complications associated with body art are bleeding and infection (**Table 14-2**). Information is hard to obtain because of infrequent reporting of complications. However, a review of ear piercing complications published in the *Journal of General Internal Medicine* found that 30% involved redness and swelling, 24% had infection, 11% had bleeding, 26% had drainage, and 3% resulted in large scars. As many as 68% of adolescents receiving tattoos recalled having bled after the procedure in 1 study, and in another, 4% recalled experiencing skin irritation and 3% photosensitivity. Sources of infection are numerous and include the ink well, dye containers, needles, tattoo bar, or piercing gun, lack of precautions, and improper skin preparation. Children who receive amateur tattoos are more likely to have compli-

Table 14-2. Summary Statistics of Self-Reported Piercing Complications

Complication	%
Bleeding	11
Redness and swelling	30
Infection	24
Drainage	26
Large scars	3

Data from "Body piercing: medical concerns with cutting edge fashion" *by Koenig & Carnes.*

cations because the tattoos are usually applied with sharp objects in unsterile environments with crude materials (eg, mascara or charcoal). Because of these concerns, the American Red Cross does not allow people to donate blood for 1 year after obtaining a tattoo or piercing.

Localized bacterial skin infections are the most common body art complication. These infections are most likely in people with newly acquired piercings, especially of the ear and navel. Skin flora (*Staphylococcus aureus* bacteria) is the most likely cause, though *Pseudomonas aeruginosa* has also been a reported cause of infection. These infections may even result in bacteremia, osteomyelitis, meningitis, and toxic shock syndrome. However, septic arthritis, skin, heart, and kidney infections caused by group A *Streptococcus* have occasionally been reported.

Viral infections are also a complication of body art. Herpes simplex virus; human papillomavirus; and hepatitis B, C, and D have all been reported as a result of body art as through the process of tattooing or body piercing, or from reused or inadequately sterilized instruments. No cases of HIV have been reported in connection with body art, but the virus's long incubation period makes it difficult to correlate. The transmission of hepatitis B is cause for concern because it is considered very contagious, and there are no standard state or federal regulations requiring artists to be immunized. The actual risk of acquiring these infections is unknown, but using new needles for each new tattoo or piercing and selecting a studio with an educated artist are likely to reduce these risks significantly.

With the increasing popularity of tongue and lip piercings, oral complications are becoming more common. Piercings may cause gingival trauma or infection and teeth may become chipped, fractured, or cracked. They have also been known to cause speech problems, swallowing and chewing difficulties, and even airway obstruction.

Tattoo pigments or metal used for jewelry can cause generalized skin reactions. Many of the pigments used in the dyes, many of which are not FDA-approved, can cause a hypersensitivity reaction after the tattoo is applied. Contact hypersensitivity to the metal can be avoided by using 14-karat gold, surgical stainless steel or niobium, or titanium. Keloid (large scar) formation is also a known complication in susceptible individuals (**Figure 14-4**).

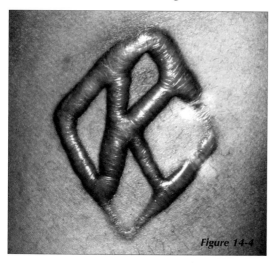

Figure 14-4

Figure 14-4. *A hypopigmented (darker) area is from an intralesional steroid injection attempting to flatten the keloid. Photo courtesy of Ella Toombs, MD.*

Finally, there are some reports on the addictive potential of tattoos or piercings. The pain triggers the body to release endorphins, which are chemicals in the brain that suppress pain and are associated with pleasure, and may make the procedure enjoyable to some people. Further research is needed in this area.

The most frightening complication of tanning or tanning bed use is the development of melanoma and nonmelanoma skin cancers. The risk of skin cancer is directly related to the amount of UVR exposure people receive from tanning and tanning bed use. An increased prevalence of melanoma associated with tanning or sunbathing was recognized in the 1970s. The more that children and adolescents are exposed to ultraviolet light and the more often they sunburn, the more likely they are to develop melanoma later in life.

CARING FOR BODY ART

Tattoos, piercings, and branding are relatively permanent forms of self-expression, and this fact, combined with possible complications and the risk behaviors associated with children who receive body art, make it imperative that parents and caregivers understand body art and know how to help care for it.

Although local infection is the most common complication of tattooing or piercing, there are a lot of actions children and patients can take to minimize the complications. Individuals who choose to obtain a tattoo or piercing should understand the procedure and the complications that might occur afterward. **Table 14-3** highlights advice parents

---

Table 14-3. Advice to Give Adolescents Considering a Tattoo

— Parental consent is necessary; most studios will not tattoo minors without it.

— Take time to make the decision: Tattoos are permanent and expensive to remove.

— Talk to others who have tattoos.

— Carefully choose the design and placement. Remember that people will react to a tattoo.

— No decision should be made while intoxicated or under peer pressure.

— Shop around: Go look at shops before tattooing, and make sure tattooing is done under sterile conditions.

— Never use a topical anesthetic.

— Learn about what it costs to obtain and/or remove a tattoo.

— Be aware of the risks of local and general infections.

— Refer to brochures and Web sites for important facts and tips.

---

can give adolescents who are considering getting a tattoo. If adolescents do decide to obtain a tattoo or piercing, they should go to a studio that uses proper sterilization techniques and carefully follow the after-care instructions for cleaning and main-tenance. In general, jewelry should not be removed after it is placed and the site should be gently washed twice a day for a few weeks. In the event of infection, jewelry should still be kept in place to provide an outlet for drainage. Most piercings will heal within a couple of weeks, but some genital piercings may take up to 6 weeks to heal and some navel piercings up to 1 year.

Tattoos also require careful attention after their application. They should be kept band-aged for 1 to 2 days and then washed with warm soap and water. All blood and soap need to be removed before a topical antibiotic is applied. The tattoo should not be exposed to direct sunlight or be allowed to dry. Prolonged bathing, hot tubs, and swimming should be avoided.

Due to the extreme nature of branding and tongue splitting, there are no standardized care instructions for these types of body art. Brandings should be treated like a partial-thickness burn, and tongue splitting should be treated like an open wound. See "What Parents and Caregivers Can Do: Burns" and "What Parents and Caregivers Can Do: Lacerations" in Chapter 12, Emergency Medical Situations, for instructions.

The most important part of caring for children with a tan or sunburn is to avoid either of them by practicing sun safe behaviors. If a child has a tan or sunburn, it can be treated with a moisturizer and a topical or oral analgesic. However, the damage is already done to the skin once the tan or burn occurs. Taking care of the skin at this point does not negate the previous exposure to UVR and the future risk of skin cancer.

What Parents and Caregivers Can Do
Although body art is becoming a more common form of self-expression in today's youth, the presence of body art does not mean that individuals are engaging in high-risk

behaviors. It is important to remember that body art is becoming more common in adults respected in the community, such as physicians, lawyers, politicians, and even clergy, and that many of the adolescents who have received tattoos are good students. Parents do not need to panic if they discover that their child has a form of body art, but they should consider it a warning that they need to observe whether the child is displaying high-risk behaviors such as having sexual intercourse, binge drinking, smoking tobacco or marijuana, or using other drugs. **Table 14-4** addresses questions parents and children frequently ask about body art, and **Table 14-5** lists points for parents to remember when responding to a child who wants or has obtained a form of body art.

One of the most important things parents and caregivers must try to remember when they discover that an individual has received body art is not to be judgmental, as difficult as this may be. Adolescents are very perceptive of verbal and nonverbal clues, and may tune out if parents yell or scream at them. When parents react this way, they miss an important opportunity to connect with and influence their children. Parents must be able to talk to their children about alcohol, drugs, and sexual behavior and know where to turn when they do not have the answers.

Table 14-4. Frequently Asked Questions

Can my child acquire hepatitis B from a tattoo?

Yes, but it is unlikely. When a tattoo or piercing is done, it can cause bleeding that places the individual at risk for hepatitis B or C infection. HIV is also a risk, though no reported cases of HIV have been the result of a tattoo or piercing. How often individuals actually acquire hepatitis B or C from tattooing or piercing is unknown. Although these infections have occurred before, there are many measures that tattoo and piercing studios have done to significantly reduce the risk of transmission of these diseases. It is important for adolescents to check out studios before obtaining a tattoo or piercing to be sure that the artist uses gloves during the procedure, uses sterile needles, cleans the area before the procedure and that the paints are not reused for tattoos. By assuring that these precautions are made during the procedures, the risk of contracting hepatitis B or C and HIV will decrease dramatically.

I have recently discovered that my teenaged son has a tattoo. I have heard of the link between drug and alcohol use and tattoos and it scares me. Is it true?

The notion that individuals who have tattoos and piercings are bikers, criminals, or in the armed forces is outdated. Recent studies have shown that most of the adolescents who have tattoos are A or B students. Just because your son has a tattoo does not mean that he is engaged in high-risk behaviors. However, there have been other recent studies that have looked at the behavior of adolescents who have tattoos and found that tattoos are associated with high-risk behaviors such sexual activity, binge drinking, smoking, marijuana, drug use, and dropping out of school. This is the more alarming statistic and the one that you can do something about. It is important to communicate with children about alcohol, drugs, cigarettes, and sexual activity. There are many things you can do to influence your child's behaviors if you are careful not to alienate him by overreacting or being judgmental.

(continued)

Table 14-4. *(continued)*

Can my body piercing set off metal detectors in airports?

Possibly. Most body piercings are too small to be detected by metal detectors, which screen for large pieces of metal. However, the more piercings a person has, the more likely they are to be detected. In addition, with the heightened airport security in place since September 11, security screeners may pay more attention to small pieces of metal. Removing the metal may be the best way to avoid potential embarrassment for unusual piercings. However, if the piercing was recently applied, then you must be careful of removing it because the hole may close. It may be important to consult a professional to replace the jewelry after it has been removed.

What can I do to prevent a local infection after a tattoo or piercing?

Proper hygiene is the best way to prevent local infection after a tattoo or piercing. The risk of infection is most likely to occur just after they are applied. Therefore, be sure the artist uses precautions to prevent infection—such as cleaning the area before applying the tattoo or piercing and taking care of the tattoo or piercing after obtaining it. Wash the tattoo with warm water and soap, and keep it covered and moist for the first week or so after it is applied. To care for a piercing, keep the jewelry in place and wash the area with warm water and soap as well. Areas such as the navel may take up to 6 months to properly heal. Consult your primary health care provider if there is persistent drainage from the areas or if you experience a lot of redness and pain.

Table 14-5. Dos and Don'ts of Responding to Children Who Want or Have Body Art

— Don't panic or overreact if your child wants or gets a tattoo, piercing, or branding. You will alienate your child and lose an opportunity to learn about the good or bad motivation behind the body art.

— Don't believe in the stereotypes of people who have body art. Today, it is a popular form of expression among people of all social and professional levels.

— Do encourage children considering body art to seek professional artists who work in sterile environments and use healthy techniques to apply the art.

— Do encourage children to think carefully about the type of body art they are considering, where they will have it placed, how people will react to it now and in the future, and the cost of obtaining and removing it.

— Do ensure that children take proper care of new tattoos, piercings, brandings, or other art. Watch for signs of complications, and seek medical care when necessary.

When parents and caregivers take the opportunity to educate children about body art they must also be aware that many adolescents who get tattoos later regret doing so. In a tattooing study reported in *The Journal of Adolescent Health*, many individuals (22%) regretted the quality of a tattoo, and even more (44%) regretted having a tattoo. Tattoos have been shown to contribute to a sense of lowered body image, even though individuals may initially be pleased with the results of the tattoo. Many adolescents may come to regret their decision so much that they want the tattoo or piercing removed. Removing a tattoo can cost thousands of dollars. The process involves using specialized lasers that disrupt the dyes used in tattoos, and it generally causes residual scars and pigmentation changes. **Figures 14-5** and **14-6** show tattoos before, during, and after the laser removal process. In some rare cases, adolescents have been so upset by their tattoos that they have tried to remove them with a potato peeler or razor blade. Piercings may be removed more easily, though some residual scaring may occur.

Figure 14-5-a

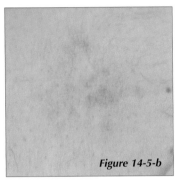

Figure 14-5-b

Understanding the alternatives to tattoos and body piercings may be helpful to individuals who are interested in body art. Temporary or fake tattoos are readily available; they are cheap, easy to apply, and last a few days or weeks. Many of the designs are quite elaborate. Henna tattoos are one example and may last for a few days or weeks. Non-piercing jewelry made with magnetic backings is also available at many accessory stores in shopping malls. These alternatives forms of body art allow the adolescent to experiment without the risks of permanence or infection.

There are no known high-risk behaviors associated with tanning and tanning bed use. The medical risk for melanoma is real, and the efforts of parents and caregivers should aim to provide guidance about sun exposure and prevention. The American Academy of Pediatrics (AAP) recommends decreasing exposure to sunlight and UVR, using a sunscreen with an SPF of 15 or higher, and limiting the amount of time children and adolescents spend in the sunlight or tanning bed, especially if a child has pale skin (see **Table 11-7** in Chapter 11, Environmental Health).

Figure 14-6-a

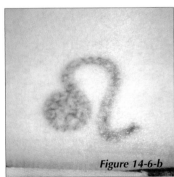

Figure 14-6-b

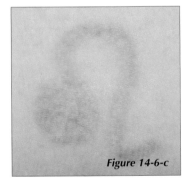

Figure 14-6-c

Figure 14-5-a and *b*. Tattoo before and after 12 laser removal treatments. Photos courtesy of Adrienne Glaich, MD.

Figure 14-6-a, b, and c. Tattoo before laser removal had begun (*a*), after 3 treatments (*b*), and after 6 treatments (*c*). Photo courtesy of Adrienne Glaich, MD.

WHAT HEALTH CARE PROFESSIONALS CAN DO

The role of a nurse or physician is to provide factual information to patients so that they can make informed decisions about body art. The regulation of tattoo and piercing studios varies from state to state, but most legitimate studios require individuals to be 18 years old before an artist will apply a tattoo or piercing without parental consent. Children should be encouraged to take their time to make a decision about obtaining body art, especially because negative judgments are often made about individuals with piercings and tattoo designs. They should be careful of the type of art and design they choose and where they have the tattoo or body art applied. Placing art in an obscure area allows individuals to express themselves and yet retain some control over others' perceptions of them. Children should never make the decision to obtain a body piercing when they are intoxicated, under peer pressure, or hurried. Encourage them to shop around for studios to be sure that the artists are using disposable gloves, sterilized needles, and are cleaning before the procedure. A topical anesthetic should never be used to obtain body art. All individuals should be aware of the risks of local or systemic (hepatitis B or C) infection when obtaining body art, the costs involved, and the permanence of their body art. Lastly, try to find brochures, videotapes, and Web sites to help educate patients about obtaining and maintaining body art (see "Where to Turn for Help").

Conclusion

Body art, especially tattoos and piercings, is becoming a common way for adolescents to express themselves. Parents, caregivers, and health care professionals must be aware of this trend and pay attention to youth. Parents must make sure that children who suddenly obtain a tattoo, piercing, or brand are not also engaging in high-risk behaviors. Parents must remember not to be judgmental because they may lose the opportunity to influence their children in the future. Screaming or yelling will not change the fact that a child has body art. Talking to children about their body art and discussing the behaviors that have been associated with it are the most important actions that caring adults can take.

Where to Turn for Help
Body Art
About.com

http://tattoo.about.com

Tattoos
Cool Nurse

http://www.coolnurse.com/tattoo.htm

Chapter 15

DEPRESSION AND SUICIDE

Paul S. Matz, MD

Depression is a common problem for children, particularly adolescents. The most serious complication of depression is suicide, or intentionally taking one's own life. The American Psychiatric Association's *Diagnostic and Statistical Manual of Mental Disorders* (DSM-IV) currently defines symptoms of depression as sadness, fatigue, changes in sleep patterns, changes in activity patterns, inability to concentrate, and feelings of guilt or worthlessness. A clinical diagnosis of depression requires such symptoms to persist for at least 2 weeks.

Several disorders other than depression can cause similar symptoms. Children sometimes develop adjustment disorders after experiences such as moving, losing a loved one, or in response to other severe family stress. Generally, children with adjustment disorders have symptoms similar to but less severe than depression, and the symptoms usually improve within several months. Another disorder related to depression is bipolar disorder, sometimes referred to as manic-depression. Bipolar children experience depressive symptoms alternating with symptoms of mania, which can include euphoria, increased energy, decreased need for sleep, hypersexuality, temper tantrums, or irritability. Depression and mania may alternate over several days or weeks. It is unusual for children or adolescents to experience mania, but some children experiencing depression may later develop bipolar disorder. Many children with the manic symptoms of bipolar disorder are initially misdiagnosed with attention deficit hyperactivity disorder (ADHD). Conditions such as mononucleosis or hypothyroidism may also mimic some of the symptoms of depression. Finally, children with chronic illnesses may be more prone to developing depression. It is important to be aware of this possibility because depressive symptoms can interfere with the identification and treatment of a chronic disease.

RISK FACTORS

Data from research by Drs. Michael Jellinek and James Snyder and from national mental health institutes provide much insight into the rates and patterns of depression in children and adolescents. The rate of depression in preschool-aged children is estimated to be 0.9% and increases to 2.5% in elementary school. In these young children, boys and girls are at similar risk for developing depression. The situation is much different in adolescents. Rates of adolescent depression can be as high as 5% to 6%, mirroring the adult rate of approximately 5%. In addition, after puberty, girls' risks are twice that of boys. As might be expected, this rise in the rate of depression in teenagers is associated with a rise in the rate of suicide.

Suicide is rare among young children but becomes more common among adolescents. In children aged 5 to 14 years, the suicide rate is approximately 0.7 per 100 000. The prevalence rate increases substantially in older teenagers and young adults to about 10 per 100 000, accounting for approximately 4000 deaths per year. In 2000, suicide was the third most common cause of death in teenagers and adults 15 to 24 years old, after accidents and homicide.

Many more children, both with and without depression, attempt suicide than actually complete it. As many as 2 million teenagers attempt suicide each year. Statistics for suicide are similar to those for depression: Girls are 1.5 times more likely to attempt suicide than boys, but boys are up to 5 times more likely to actually die. Girls are more likely than boys to engage in dramatic gestures, such as superficial cutting or overdosing on pills and then informing a friend or caregiver. Boys are more likely to use a weapon, jump from a height, or attempt suicide using other more lethal means.

Children who attempt suicide have an increased risk for both attempting and completing suicide in the future, even if their first gesture was dramatic or nonlethal. No matter how dramatic, nonlethal, or even laughable a child's suicide attempt may seem at the time, parents and caregivers must be on watch for future attempts. **Any suicide attempt or suicidal gesture is a psychiatric emergency and should be treated with utmost seriousness. Any child who threatens suicide must be taken seriously because he or she is at high risk for committing suicide.**

Although depression is a major risk factor for suicide, other psychiatric disorders and/or a history of substance abuse increase the likelihood of an attempt. Factors that may provoke a suicide attempt include child abuse, issues of sexual orientation (among gay, lesbian, or bisexual adolescents), or other severe psychosocial stressors, such as family disturbances or academic failure.

Just as it is more common to attempt suicide than complete it, so it is also more common to think about suicide than to attempt it. Many normal, healthy children, especially adolescents, have suicidal thoughts, or "ideations." School-aged children and younger adolescents may still not fully understand that death is final. Even though it is not uncommon for teenagers to think about how their death might affect friends, family, and other caregivers, it is serious when teenagers actually plan their suicide or begin to collect pills, acquire a weapon, or write a suicide note.

EFFECTS OF DEPRESSION

The tragedy of adolescent suicide is certainly the most devastating complication of depression, but there are other effects. Children may experience feelings of guilt for family events that are beyond their control, such as divorce or the death of a loved one. The fatigue and impaired concentration depression causes may lead to problems at school and a difficulty maintaining friendships. These children may feel that they are worthless and have no hope of changing. In rare cases, children with severe depression may experience psychotic symptoms, such as hearing berating voices (auditory hallucinations). All these symptoms can lead to further complications, including the exacerbation of other medical conditions, worsening of family and other social situations, and problems in school.

Although most episodes of depression resolve in 6 to 18 months without treatment, untreated depression can last as long as several years. Although it may sound encouraging that depression usually gets better, even if untreated, living with these symptoms for several months can be devastating for a child. For example, an episode of depression lasting 18 months would constitute 10% of a 15-year-old teenager's life. Imagine a child who is unable to function properly in school, with friends, or at home for this long, and the potential toll of depression on his or her future is clear. Furthermore, even if a child's episode of depression resolves spontaneously, he or she has a very high likelihood of experiencing another episode. Research by Jellineck and Snyder indicates that three fourths of depressed children will experience another episode in the next 5 years. As might be expected, suicide risk increases with increasing length of an individual depressive episode, as well as with the number of recurrent episodes. It is important to keep in mind that depression can be a fatal illness. It is imperative that children suffering from depression are appropriately identified and treated.

WHAT PARENTS AND CAREGIVERS CAN DO

It is crucial to identify children at risk, begin treatment, and help monitor their symptoms as they wax and wane. As it can be very difficult for depressed children or teenagers to have insight into their own symptoms, this role often falls to caregivers, especially parents, guardians, and teachers. These caregivers should be aware of the outward signs of depression and be able to recognize them in children for which they care (**Table 15-1**). Like many other features of children's cognitive and emotional development, the signs of depression change with age. **Table 15-2** addresses questions parents frequently have about childhood depression and suicide.

Depression is less common in young children and is often harder to diagnose. Young children may experience episodes of sadness or crying, apathy, irritability, sleep problems, decreased appetite, anxiety when separating from a caregiver, or they may withdraw from a caregiver. In very young children, failure to thrive (poor weight gain) and developmental delays are often observed. Obviously, nearly all toddlers occasionally display crying, sadness, and separation anxiety, but these episodes are usually short-lived. Episodes that are prolonged or represent an abrupt change from a child's normal behavior may be due to depression. For example, it is normal for young toddlers to experience both separation anxiety and anxiety when faced with strangers, but these behaviors

Table 15-1. Signs of Depression
— Prolonged sadness or crying episodes
— Fatigue
— Sleep disturbances (needing significantly more or less)
— Withdrawing from social activities
— Low self-esteem
— Feeling guilty
— Irritability and hostility
— Poor performance in school or missing school
— Exaggerated reactions to normal events
— Chronic physical complaints such as headache or stomachache, especially when these clearly happen before a stressful situation
— Preoccupation with death and dying
— Comments about leaving home or school
— Any comment, no matter how minor, about committing suicide

would be unusual if they developed suddenly in a 5 year old. Many toddlers, even those who are quite verbal, can have difficulty expressing their feelings in words. Caregivers play the primary role in identifying symptoms of depression in young children.

Children in elementary school may experience many of the same symptoms of depression, but their reactions can be more complex. They may begin to internalize events beyond their control, such as blaming themselves for their parent's divorce. Children at this age are also eager for praise from parents or teachers, praise that is often tied to academic performance. As schoolwork becomes more complex, a depressed child's fatigue, inability to concentrate, and other symptoms may lead to school problems and eventually failure. These failures can worsen a child's self-image and increase symptoms of worthlessness and sadness. Some children may be able to express these feelings of sadness, but others may only verbalize their negative self-image—eg, "I'm just stupid." Elementary school-aged children may develop very nonspecific complaints when depressed, such as headaches and stomachaches, often before or during school or as an attempt to escape other situations that cause anxiety or fear. As a

---

Table 15-2. Frequently Asked Questions

All children go through sad phases; shouldn't you just let them work themselves out?

Although it is true that all children will have occasional episodes of sadness or crying, it is not normal for these episodes to last several weeks. Parents should be aware of their child's usual behavior patterns and note any changes.

Don't children sometimes threaten to commit suicide just to get a reaction from caregivers?

Some children may make idle threats about suicide, but all threats should be taken seriously. Children who threaten suicide do often commit suicide. Any threat must be taken very seriously. Talk to your child and to a health care professional to assess your child's risk of suicide.

My 11 year old started asking questions about death after his grandfather died. I feel uncomfortable discussing this and don't want to encourage him. Should I ignore his concerns?

It is very normal for children to have questions about death and dying, especially after the death of a relative or family pet. Encourage your child to talk about his feelings and reassure him that it is normal to feel sad after losing a loved one. If his concerns last for a prolonged period of time or he becomes preoccupied with death and dying, consider having him assessed for depression.

My 13 year old just told me that her classmate is thinking of committing suicide, but my daughter asked me not to tell anybody. What should I do?

While maintaining your daughter's confidentiality is important, there are occasions when it is inappropriate to do so. If a child's life or health is in danger (from abuse, homicidal threats, or suicidal threats), confidentiality must be breached to protect the child at risk. If possible, call the child's parent or guardian to discuss her threat. If that is not possible, speak to a teacher, nurse, or school principal. Just as you would not ignore these threats from your own child, do not ignore them from someone else's child.

My 15-year-old son was just released from the hospital after a suicide attempt. I have no idea what to say or do around him and am nervous about sending him back to school.

A child's suicide attempt can be difficult for the child, his family, and his friends. First, do not ignore the subject or avoid it if he brings it up. Although constantly interrogating your son about his thoughts and feelings is not useful, maintain open communication and allow him to talk about it. You may also consider meeting with his therapist to discuss these specific issues. Talk to your child's teachers, principal, and mental health provider about his return to school. Many children need to return part-time initially in order to acclimate to the stress in the new environment. Additional therapy groups or meetings with a school counselor may give your son extra support.

---

result, some withdraw from social activities. Other children display the opposite behavior and attempt to garner praise from parents or teachers by excelling at school, sports, or merely by improving their behavior. Depression often goes undetected because children are not obviously sad and do not cause problems in school or at home. Again, the key to recognizing depression in any child is to know their normal behavior patterns and be able to identify changes. Any self-demeaning comment a child makes should be taken seriously, and caregivers need to explore these feelings with the child.

Adolescents with depression present unique challenges. Although the symptoms of depression in an adolescent are more similar to the classic symptoms seen in adults, the normal process of forging their own personalities and identities can make detecting depression more difficult. It is normal for a teenager's behavior patterns to change, often somewhat abruptly. As any caregiver with an adolescent knows, "normal" teenagers may experience wild mood swings, exaggerated reactions to beginning and ending relationships, apathy, and disdain for authority—often in a single day! Their sleep patterns change, as does their appetite. It is vital for caregivers to be aware of their teenager's behaviors as they transition from elementary to middle school. Teenagers need some freedom to begin the process of differentiating themselves from their families, but adults must stay involved in their teenagers' lives. The balance is clearly very difficult to maintain.

Parents should pay special attention to particularly abrupt changes in their teenagers' behaviors, routines, or social habits. These changes can include withdrawal from previously enjoyed social activities, decreasing academic performance, obvious sadness, feelings of hopelessness or worthlessness, or changes in weight or sleep patterns. Like younger children, adolescents may develop stress-related physical symptoms, such as headaches and abdominal pain. They may also blame themselves for outside events or express exaggerated self-loathing in response to poor grades. Any of these should be cause for concern. However, children who abuse drugs or alcohol or are victims of physical or sexual abuse may manifest similar symptoms, so do not rule out other reasons for sudden changes in a child's habits or behavior.

Any teenager can begin thinking about death and the concept of suicide, but depressed teenagers may spend an excessive amount of time thinking, talking, or writing about death or suicide. They may romanticize them or see death as an escape from sadness or stress. Although depression clearly increases a child's risk of becoming suicidal, it is not a prerequisite. Even a teenager who has no history of depression may become suicidal when faced with a particularly stressful life event such as ending a relationship, loss of a loved one, or difficulty in school. Involved parents and caregivers will be aware of these new stressors and can help adolescents cope with them.

Any individual involved in a teenager's life can play a role in identifying children at risk. Parents or guardians are often most aware of a potential problem, but they may not know what steps to take or feel helpless, overwhelmed, or guilty for contributing to their child's symptoms (through divorce, for example). The most important step parents can take is simply to talk to their child. Ask how the child is feeling. Be aware of changes in schoolwork and outside activities and be careful to recognize any sign that symptoms go beyond the normal, occasional sadness. Some children will hint at not being around much longer, give away prized possessions, or seem suddenly happy because they have decided to commit suicide. **These behaviors need to be taken very seriously**, as they may be a significant manifestation of hopelessness and desperation on the part of the child or adolescent. When in doubt, consult the child's primary care physician or a mental health care worker (psychiatrist, psychologist, or social worker). Any health care professional would be happier to hear from parents or caregivers regarding their concerns, no matter how mild, than realize later that an opportunity to intervene in a depressed child's life had been missed.

Other individuals who come in contact with children also have the opportunity to help identify depression. For children between the ages of 5 and 18 years, school is the equivalent of work. They spend 6 to 8 hours every weekday in contact with teachers, guidance counselors, and athletic coaches. Teachers may be aware of changes in school performance and peer relationships months before parents are. Particularly during adolescence, when there is a normal process of distancing from parents, teachers and coaches may be the adults teenagers confide in when something is wrong. School workers often have more training than parents in identifying these problems, and they may need to take an active role and approach the child and family. Any concerned adult should communicate with a parent, guardian, or health professional when they are aware of a child exhibiting uncharacteristic or distressing behavior. Even though it may feel wrong to betray a teenager's trust, personal discomfort must be weighed against the potential consequences of untreated depression.

When parents and teachers talk with a child they think may be depressed, they are often concerned that the child is contemplating suicide. Adults are often afraid to face this concern and raise the topic because they fear introducing the very idea of suicide to the teenager. It is vital for caregivers to realize that bringing up the idea of suicide does not suggest to the teenager that it is a viable option. Depressed adolescents are even more likely to have suicidal thoughts than healthy adolescents, and, for this reason, it is extremely important to address this topic directly. **Failing to try and assess whether a depressed child is at risk to commit suicide is dangerous**. In fact, depressed teenagers often desperately want to talk with someone about these issues and may feel relieved that there is someone with whom no topic is off limits.

Caregivers should ease into the discussion of suicide in a nonconfrontational way. Questions such as, "I know that when some kids are sad, they think about hurting themselves or killing themselves. Have you ever thought about that?" can help to reassure the adolescent that it is common to think about death and that it is ok to talk about it. For caregivers without health care training, hearing a child talk about taking his or her own life can be extremely frightening. It is hard for parents to realize that their sweet, young, innocent child can possess such thoughts, and they may be tempted to dismiss what they have heard as childish thinking or pretend it never happened. It is crucial not to make this mistake. If a child has expressed suicidal thoughts, caregivers must be open to the discussion. Remain nonjudgmental and ensure the child knows that it is better to talk about the issue than remain silent.

Once a child has revealed depressed or suicidal thoughts to a caregiver, follow-up actions must be considered. At the very least, the caregiver should discuss the situation with a health care professional as soon as possible. If a child says that he or she is actively considering suicide, a primary physician, mental health worker, or emergency room physician must evaluate him or her **immediately**. Knowledge of whether the child has worked on a plan to commit suicide, obtained pills or a weapon, written a suicide note, or decided when to act can be used by professionals to assess the risk level of the child or adolescent. Adults who recognize that someone else's child is suicidal should inform the child's parents. Parents then need to discuss the child's situation with a health care professional.

Parents and guardians are often confused about where to turn for help for their depressed or suicidal child. For an actively suicidal child, an emergency room is often the best, and most readily available, first resource. In the case of a child who is not in imminent danger, caregivers should call the child's physician. At the very least, the physician should be able to help the family access the mental health system. In most cases, depression is a very treatable disease, and it is important so seek help. For parents and caregivers who do not know where to turn, calling national suicide hotline numbers can be an appropriate first step. See "Where to Turn for Help" for these numbers and helpful Internet resources on depression and suicide. The American Academy of Pediatrics' *Caring for Your Teenager* can be a useful written resource. Any adult who cares for children should take an active role if he or she thinks a child may be depressed or suicidal. Again, treatment is available for depression and suicide can be prevented. Refer to **Table 15-3** for a list of dos and don'ts on communicating with children about these important subjects.

Table 15-3. Dos and Don'ts of Preventing and Confronting Childhood Depression

— Do stay involved in your child's life.

— Do stay aware of any abrupt or extreme changes in children's activities or behavior.

— Do foster an environment that allows your child to come to you with problems.

— Do talk to a child that you suspect is depressed.

— Do seek help immediately if you have ANY concerns about depression or suicide.

— Don't let your child shut you out.

— Don't ignore symptoms of depression hoping they will just go away.

— Don't ignore comments about death or suicide from any child.

TREATING DEPRESSION

Treatment for depression has become more complicated as new evidence suggests that some of the common medications for depression may not be as safe as previously thought. The treatment options for depression include therapy (also called "talk therapy" or psychotherapy) and medication. With the advent of new antidepressants over the last 20 years, focus has moved away from therapy. However, therapy can be just as effective at treating depression as medication and has no risk of medication-related side effects. In fact, some studies show that after finishing treatment, the benefits of therapy last longer than those of medication. Therapy can include individual therapy, family therapy, or group therapy.

THERAPY

Finding or choosing a therapist can be difficult. The first step is to speak with a child's primary physician and ask for recommendations. In addition, many cities and counties have mental health or behavioral health offices. Due to the dominance of health maintenance organizations (HMOs), insurance may limit choice of providers. Parents can call their insurance company and ask for help in finding a provider.

There are numerous types of therapists who may perform therapy with children. Psychiatrists are medical doctors who have had 4 years of medical school after college, and 4 or more years of specialized training in psychiatry or child and adolescent psychiatry. Many psychiatrists perform psychotherapy, but constraints from HMOs have limited payment to these providers. For this reason, many patients will see a psychiatrist for medications but see others for psychotherapy.

Licensed psychologists can have a PhD or PsyD degree and have completed a 4- to 5-year doctoral program after college. Licensed psychologists are doctors who provide therapy but cannot prescribe medication. Masters-level psychologists, masters-level social workers, and licensed clinical social workers are providers who have completed several years of training after college. The level of training a provider has is not as important as a parent's and child's level of comfort with the provider. Many times, families need to meet with several providers to find the best fit. The best provider is the one that can work well with a child and his or her parents. Parents of children with chronic disorders or special needs may find it beneficial to seek a provider who has experience dealing with these conditions.

MEDICATION

Antidepressant medications have been available for several decades. One of the earliest classes of antidepressants is the tricyclic antidepressants, which have been used for many years but have side effects that must be monitored. Over the last 20 years, a new class of antidepressants called selective serotonin reuptake inhibitors, or SSRIs, has become available. These drugs have fewer side effects and are generally much safer than tricyclic antidepressants. Their safeness encouraged many physicians, such as pediatricians and family physicians who had little psychological training or experience with these medications, to prescribe them. Medications then began to replace therapy, and managed care health insurance contributed to this change by decreasing payments and the number of visits allowed to psychiatrists and therapists. Primary care physicians were pressured to prescribe these medicines instead of referring patients for more expensive psychotherapy.

Then, in late 2004, new data revealed that many antidepressants increased suicidal thoughts and suicidal behaviors in children. Medications from both classes of anti-depressants were implicated. At congressional hearings, some families described the pain of losing a child on antidepressants to suicide, while other families spoke of the dramatic improvements in their child's depression and their belief that the medications saved their child's life. Other data showed that pharmaceutical companies were aware of these risks and had not informed the public. Finally, in October 2004, the US Food and Drug Administration (FDA) announced that many of these medicines would require a warning on their label about the risk of suicidal thoughts and behaviors. **Table 15-4** has a list of these medications.

Parents and caregivers may be confused by these stories. It is important to note that the worrisome side effects seem to be uncommon. The new warnings specify that children treated with these medicines must be monitored closely. The prescription of these medicines should be restricted to psychiatrists or other physicians with experience in using them and in monitoring children who take them. In addition, use of any medication must be based on an accurate diagnosis, so it is vital for children with depression to be evaluated by an experienced mental health professional. Although they can play an important role in recovery from depression, antidepressant medicines should *NOT* be used for children in place of therapy, but rather as a complement or addition to therapy with a qualified mental health professional. Antidepressants are not a quick, easy cure, as many once thought, but instead should be used in conjunction with therapy and close monitoring. Parents of children taking 1 or more of these medications or of children who are going to start one of these medications need to be alert for any signs of sudden behavior changes or suicidal comments. Do not allow a child to stop taking medication without first discussing it with his or her mental health care provider. Remember that untreated depression can be a fatal illness, and the benefits and risks of medication should be weighed against the risk of untreated depression. The decision to use these medicines must be made in concert with a child's mental health provider. Report any concerns about a child's behavior while on antidepressants to the provider immediately.

PROFESSIONAL STUDY AND CONTROVERSY

DEPRESSION AND CHRONIC ILLNESS

Chronic medical illnesses and depression frequently coexist in children. Living with a chronic illness such as diabetes, cancer, or asthma is stressful and may place a strain on the whole family. The limitations placed on a child's life by a chronic illness can increase feelings of sadness and social withdrawal. Children may begin to feel guilty, either that

Table 15-4. Commonly Used Antidepressants	
Older Antidepressants (Tricyclics and Monoamine Oxidase Inhibitors)	**Newer Antidepressants (SSRIs and Related Medicines)**
Anafranil (clomipramine)	Celexa (citalopram)
Aventyl (nortriptyline)	Cymbalta (duloxetine)
Desyrel (trazodone)	Effexor (venlafaxine)
Elavil (amitriptyline)	Lexapro (escitalopram)
Limbitrol (chlordiazepoxide/ amitriptyline)	Luvox (fluvoxamine)
Ludiomil (maprotiline)	Paxil (paroxetine)
Marplan (isocarboxazid)	Pexeva (paroxetine)
Nardil (phenelzine)	Prozac (fluoxetine)
Norpramin (desipramine)	Remeron (mirtazapine)
Pamelor (nortriptyline)	Sarafem (fluoxetine)
Parnate (tranylcypromine)	Serzone (nefazodone)
Sinequan (doxepin)	Symbyax (olanzapine/fluoxetine)
Surmontil (trimipramine)	Wellbutrin (bupropion)
Tofranil (imipramine)	Zoloft (sertraline)
Triavil (perphenazine/amitriptyline)	Zyban (bupropion)
Vivactil (protriptyline)	

Data from FDA Public Health Advisory: Suicidality in Children and Adolescents Being Treated With Antidepressant Medications.

they somehow brought the illness on themselves or that the illness has increased stress in the family. Fears about their ability to function in the future or about death may be difficult for a child to contemplate, let alone discuss with a parent.

The fatigue, impaired concentration, and apathy associated with depression may make it difficult for a child to properly care for their illness. It is important for caregivers and health care professionals to be even more vigilant for signs of depression in these children. Treatment for depression may have a secondary effect of improving children's motivation and perceived energy level and increasing their ability to participate and cooperation in managing their chronic illness.

Family History of Depression
Family history of mental illness must also be considered when caring for a depressed child. Children of depressed parents are more likely to become depressed, and affected parents may not notice signs of depression in their children. Alternate caregivers such as teachers, social workers, and others should have a heightened awareness of depressive symptoms in these children.

Cutting

The practice of cutting, or voluntary self-mutilation, has been discussed in the press in recent years, and many parents have questions about that behavior. First, cutting is *NEVER* a normal behavior. Children who routinely cut their skin are rarely trying to kill themselves but may still be suffering from a mental illness. Cutting can be associated with depression, but it is also associated with borderline personality disorder. Voluntary mutilations like cutting should be taken seriously and discussed with a health care provider. Cutting is usually a habitual behavior and should be differentiated from piercings or tattoos, which are not associated with depression or suicide (see Chapter 14, Tattooing, Piercing, and Branding).

Conclusion

Depression is a problem affecting many children and adolescents. Untreated depression can have numerous consequences including problems maintaining social relationships with friends and family, school failure, and, most severely, suicide. When symptoms and warning signs are recognized, it is nearly always possible to treat depression and prevent suicide.

Where to Turn for Help

Hotlines
National Suicide Hotlines

800-SUICIDE (1-800-784-2433)

800-273-TALK

http://www.suicidehotlines.com

Books and Articles
Graydanus DE, ed. *Caring for your Teenager*. New York, NY: Bantam; 2003.

Jellinek MS, Snyder JB. Depression and Suicide in Children and Adolescents. *Pediatrics in Review*. 1998:19(8);255-264.

Son SE, Kirchner JT. Depression in Children and Adolescents. *Am Fam Physician*. 2000;62:2297-2308, 2311-2312.

Web Sites
American Academy of Child and Adolescent Psychiatry Facts for Families

http://www.aacap.org/publications/factsfam/index.htm

American Association of Suicidology

http://www.suicidology.org

American Psychological Association Help Center

http://helping.apa.org

Befrienders Worldwide

http://www.befrienders.org

International Foundation for Research and Education on Depression (iFred)

http://www.ifred.com

National Institutes of Mental Health: Depression

http://www.nimh.nih.gov/healthinformation/depressionmenu.cfm

National Mental Health Association: Helping Depressed Teens

http://www.nmha.org/infoctr/factsheets/24.cfm

National Mental Health Association: Young People and Suicide

http://www.nmha.org/suicide/youngPeople.cfm

Suicide Awareness Voices of Education (SAVE)

http://www.save.org

Chapter 16

AGGRESSIVE, DEFIANT, AND DELINQUENT BEHAVIOR

Hans B. Kersten, MD

Juvenile delinquency is defined as an illegal act committed by youth younger than 18 years, and it is considered to be a major public health concern with tremendous law enforcement and judicial implications. According to recent aggression research published in the *American Journal of Health Behavior*, the United States has the highest rate of violence of any developed country. Other data reported in *Pediatrics in Review* indicate that as many as one third of adolescents are arrested for delinquent behavior by the age of 18, and over 80% of this age group self-report that they have committed some type of delinquent act. There is a predictable pattern of delinquent behavior in late childhood and adolescence that begins after 10 years of age, peaks around 16 years of age, and then tends to wane. This pattern is found in many different cultures, and studies have shown it to be remarkably consistent over time.

The delinquent behavior seen in adolescence may actually have as its root aggressive and defiant behavior in earlier childhood. Children become delinquent as a result of complex interactions between their environment, parenting, and personality. For example, children who commit delinquent acts are more likely to belong to a gang and to have a history of school problems, substance abuse, and mental health problems. Research shows that boys thought to be noncompliant in multiple settings in earlier childhood are also more likely to become delinquent. Family, school, community, peers, and the media are all significant influences. However, children with positive influences or factors such as a strong family or a positive attitude toward school may be able to counteract the effect of the negative influences. Fortunately, parents, teachers, and nurses are in frequent contact with children at home or at school, and if they recognize the warning behaviors early, there are many opportunities to intervene and influence children to lead productive lives.

DEFINITIONS

The terms *antisocial behavior, noncompliance, oppositional defiant disorder* (ODD), and *conduct disorder* (CD) are sometimes used when discussing juvenile delinquency. *Antisocial behavior* is a descriptive term that defines acts that are inappropriate because they may harm others or the society—like lighting fires. Some experts feel antisocial behavior may be quite common in children, since only 3% to 34% of adolescents denied it in some studies. Because antisocial behavior is so common, it is reasonable for parents to view these behaviors from a developmental perspective and to expect some oppositional behavior from their children at times. For example, a 2 year old may say "no, no, no" to anything a parent says, and a 14 or 15 year old may resist curfew as he or she begins to feel more independent. Most children do, in fact, sometimes demonstrate behavior that could be considered antisocial or noncompliant.

Noncompliance describes an instance in which a child actively or passively fails to perform a behavior that an adult authority figure (parent, caregiver, or teacher) has requested from him or her. An example of this type of behavior is a 5-year-old child who refuses to clear his or her dinner plate from the table after a parent requests that he or she do so. As children grow, some experts feel there is a maturity gap that encourages antisocial behavior as a part of their normal process of development. This behavior is brief and does not usually persist beyond adolescence.

Children may be noncompliant in particular settings as a result of internal and external factors. First, noncompliance may be considered normal behavior, depending on the setting. In fact, University of Pittsburgh researchers Larry Kalb and Rolf Loeber have reviewed studies on childhood disobedience and reported that 25% to 65% of parents feel that their child is somewhat noncompliant. Although parents need to explore when and why these situations occur and make a plan to deal with them, the episodes should not be of major concern. However, when noncompliance becomes persistent in frequency, intensity, or duration, it indicates *persistent noncompliance*, also called *oppositional behavior*. These terms have been used interchangeably with defiance, though Kalb and Loeber suggest that these terms be used separately. *Defiance* describes behaviors that occur in response to parental requests (eg, temper tantrums and whining). Noncompliance has much broader implications than defiance and can include instances in which a child might intentionally ignore a parental request.

Oppositional defiance disorder and *conduct disorder* are more serious diagnostic terms. *Oppositional defiance disorder* defines the persistent appearance of angry, defiant, irritating, and oppositional behaviors at an age that is developmentally inappropriate. Psychiatrist Robert Vermeiren has found that as many as 16% of children may display signs of ODD during adolescence, though it may be difficult to diagnose because they often have other unrelated conditions such as depression or attention deficit hyperactivity disorder (ADHD). *Conduct disorder* defines a repetitive and persistent pattern of behavior in which the basic rights of others or major age-appropriate societal norms or rules are violated. Children who commit repeated and/or serious acts of delinquency often are diagnosed with antisocial behavior, ODD, and CD. Conduct disorder, according to Dr. Vermeiran, may be diagnosed in as much as 9% of girls and 16% of boys at some point during adolescence, though a more typical prevalence is between 2% and 9% in the United States.

The focus of this chapter will be delinquent behavior and the formative behaviors and risks factors that appear before children become delinquent. The more serious mental health disorders, such as ODD and CD, will not be discussed further. Parents who need more information on ODD and CD should contact their child's physician or visit the Web sites of the American Academy of Child and Adolescent Psychiatry or Mental Health Matters to find out more information (see "Where to Turn for Help").

EFFECTS OF AGGRESSIVE, DEFIANT, AND DELINQUENT BEHAVIOR
MODELS OF DELINQUENCY AND VIOLENCE
Research has demonstrated that the children who are most likely to become delinquent adolescents show signs of oppositional, defiant, or noncompliant behavior during early childhood. Many factors can profoundly influence whether children develop these attributes. Models of delinquency and violence best demonstrate how peers, family, school, and living environment can influence children's behaviors.

Carolyn Webster-Stratton and Ted Taylor have developed a model using their research that is useful for understanding how the interactions of children, parents, family, peers, and environment can reinforce noncompliant behavior that develops in early childhood (**Figure 16-1**). Toddlers who are more impulsive, hyperactive, or quick to anger parents may overwhelm parents' ability to effectively deal with problematic behavior. As a result, parents may cope by severely punishing children or by giving in to all of a child's demands. These harsh or inconsistent responses do not effectively address children's behavior. Harsh parenting with excessive punishment presents a negative model of parenting that fails to promote good social behavior. Conversely, an inconsistent or relaxed response involving little discipline or correction may promote early onset conduct problems because negative behaviors are not stopped or defined as unacceptable. The opportunity to deter these behaviors is lost. Environmental stress—eg, job loss, financial strain, and significant health problems—may worsen these forms of ineffective parenting. Both parenting styles can adversely affect the development of necessary adaptive skills and cognitive abilities or inadequately promote academic and social development.

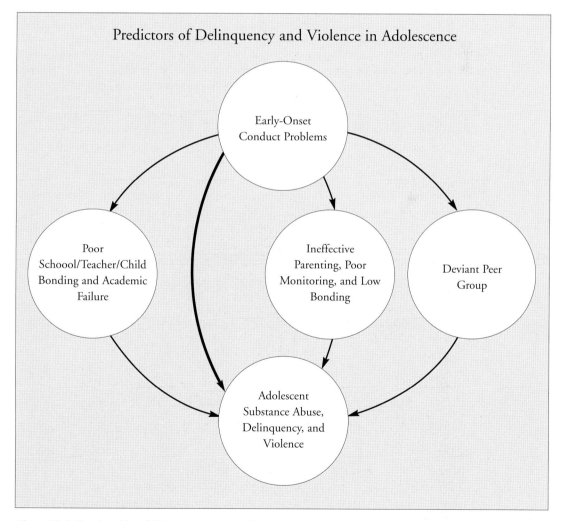

Figure 16-1. *Reprinted from Webster-Stratton & Taylor. Nipping early risk factors in the bud: preventing substance abuse, delinquency, and violence in adolescence through interventions targeted at young children (0-8 years).* Prevention Science. *2001;2(3):165-192, with permission from Springer Science and Business Media.*

Kalb and Loeber have devised a second model to describe delinquent behavior, and it begins when children enter school (**Figure 16-2**). This model of delinquency is more complex because it incorporates the school and teachers' responses to children's behavior. From this model's perspective, a hyperactive or impulsive school-aged child may receive frequent criticism from a teacher, especially if the teacher feels unable to effectively deal with the behaviors, and feel that he or she receives less instruction and support than the other children in the classroom. Teachers with ineffective classroom management skills, who may not be able to effectively deal with problems that arise between children in the classroom, compound the scenario. The child's behavior might worsen in response, further decreasing his or her learning opportunities and increasing the likelihood that peers and teachers will reject him or her. Parents who are not actively involved in their children's education only increase these feelings of rejection. These children end up seeing themselves as academically incompetent and outside the norm of their peers. As a result, they are apt to form groups with other "rejected" children who reinforce their antisocial behavior and complicate the difficulty the teacher has dealing with the behaviors. The more risk factors children have, the more likely they are to enter a cycle of academic and familial problems that can lead to delinquency.

RELATIONSHIP OF NONCOMPLIANCE, OPPOSITIONAL BEHAVIOR, AND DEFIANCE

Age, physical ability, and environment affect how children manifest noncompliance. For example, a 2 year old may repeatedly draw on the wall even after being told to stop,

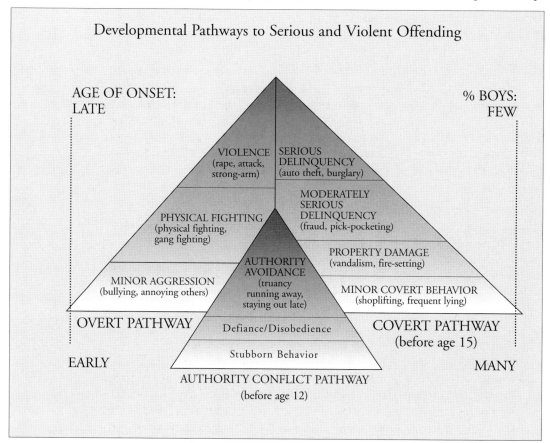

Figure 16-2. *Reproduced with permission from* Pediatrics, *111:641-652, © 2003 by the AAP.*

while a teenager might repeatedly miss curfew. A 4 year old may behave wonderfully in a health care provider's office but become noncompliant later when he or she sees ice cream in the supermarket. Some children are noncompliant in school, in medical settings, or toward peers or older children. Different situations affect each child uniquely, and a child's behavior may vary depending on the situation. Noncompliant behavior may be a sign of a willingness to break set rules, whether the rules originate from a parent, teacher, or society as a whole. Kalb and Loeber have proposed that noncompliance by an individual remains relatively stable over time, even though it may be expressed differently at varying ages. However, when a child becomes persistently noncompliant in multiple situations, there is reason for concern.

Kalb and Loeber found that persistent noncompliance is a problem among 65% to 95% of children referred to psychologists or psychiatrists. There is also evidence that it is associated with aggression and antisocial behavior throughout childhood. Not surprisingly, children who are rebellious or considered "problem" peers are more likely to become delinquent. There is considerable concern among heath care professionals that children who are recognized as persistently noncompliant by the age of 7 years are more likely to continue to be noncompliant and develop disruptive and delinquent behavior as they age. These children are at risk of becoming truant, running away, and developing even more serious behavioral problems such as ODD and CD. Other studies have demonstrated that children who display aggressive behaviors (eg, break rules repeatedly, are unable to follow directions, or cannot participate in structured activities with other children) at an early age are more likely to become chronic offenders. Boys are more likely to become violent than girls, and a child who has a medical problem such as ADHD or impulsivity in addition to persistent noncompliance is more likely to be aggressive. Research signals that these problems have the potential to be severe and last throughout childhood.

Children's attitudes toward their problem behavior also affects their risk of future delinquency, and their attitudes are closely related to their family's attitude and perception of the behavior. Those who refuse to acknowledge their behavior are more likely to become delinquent, as are children who are not taught alternatives to aggression. Parents, teachers, nurses, childcare, and health care professionals spend a lot of time with children and have a unique opportunity to observe problem behaviors and intervene when necessary.

ASSOCIATED RISK FACTORS

There are 5 factors other than an individual child's disposition that may relate to his or her likelihood of future delinquency: family, school, community, peers, and media. Many of these factors fit into multiple categories, but it is helpful to think of how these categories may influence a child's future behavior. The factors are synergistic as well as cumulative and are represented in the models of delinquency mentioned earlier.

Children spend a significant portion of their time at home or with their family, and so it is no surprise that family is one of the most significant influences. Families who cannot manage conflict or discipline are more likely to have delinquent children, as are families who experience constant discord. Parental attitudes have a remarkable effect on children; those children who do not have a warm or friendly relationship with their parents, or those whose parents use severe forms of punishment, are more likely to exhibit misconduct. Also, research reveals that children growing up in single-parent households are more likely to be exposed to violence, which can promote delinquency. The strongest predictor of later delinquency, however, is poverty. Regardless of how effective parents are, children who live in poverty have the highest likelihood of becoming delinquent because poverty creates frustration, anger, feelings of deprivation, and hopelessness, all of which fuel antisocial behavior. All of these familial factors profoundly influence the development of children's social skills and cognitive development.

Children who do not develop good social skills or do not live in an enriching environment may not develop the other skills needed to succeed at school. Children who experience academic problems or failure are more likely to become aggressive or violent over a period of time after failure. Also, a lack of commitment to school is associated with becoming a chronic offender later in life, and antisocial behavior at school has been associated with delinquency. Some professionals have suggested that if children cannot adapt at school and develop a sense of belonging, they are more likely to associate with delinquent groups and perform delinquent acts. However, teachers who demonstrate effective behavior management skills, spend more time teaching, and are enthusiastic can dramatically affect classroom performance. These teachers may even be able to disrupt the perpetuation of noncompliance if they identify children with persistent problems early enough.

Community and environment also influence delinquency. Environments in which crime and firearms are common, drugs are easily available, and delinquent or violent behavior are considered normal encourage delinquency. In addition, children who have friends with behavioral problems or travel in peer groups that demonstrate problem behaviors are more likely to exhibit the same behaviors. Children in gangs are also more likely to display violent behavior as a direct result of their involvement with other members because membership places tremendous pressure on individuals to conform.

Television and video games can be considered extensions of the environment in which children live. Researchers in various fields are increasingly recognizing and studying this connection. Violence is increasingly portrayed on television and in movies, and children spend much of their free time viewing these types of media. The amount of time that children spend watching television is associated with the amount of violent behavior they display. Also, the content of shows exerts a strong influence on their behavior. The American Academy of Pediatrics (AAP) has reported that children who watch violent shows are more likely to develop offensive behaviors, and the more violent the content, the more violent the behaviors are. That study also showed that delinquent children watched more hours of television than children who were not delinquent. Further studies on the effect of television and media on children's behavior will provide concerned adults with a better idea of how strong the media influence is.

The effect of any risk factor on a child's delinquency depends on the child's developmental age, and certain factors may be more influential at some ages than at others. These risk factors appear to have similar effects in any cultural or ethnic group and may be predictors of substance abuse, teenaged pregnancy, and school dropout in addition to delinquency and violence.

FACTORS THAT PROTECT AGAINST DELINQUENCY

Various research on nondelinquent children exposed to the same risk factors as delinquent children reveals that a number of protective factors and processes exist (**Table 16-1**). Interventions providing enhanced exposure to protective factors may be successful in promoting positive outcomes for children at risk. For example, children who excel at school are less likely to be considered outcasts or have low self-esteem. Children need to be exposed to and encouraged by adults and caregivers who value educational success or have other healthy beliefs, as evidenced by involvement in the community, church or school. If caregivers can help them form positive social orientations or resilient tem-

---

Table 16-1. Factors That Protect Against Future Delinquency

The following factors act in any of the following ways: to decrease the influence of risk factors on children, modify how individual children will respond to risk factors, promote activities that will substitute for or are incompatible with the risk behaviors, or strengthen orientation toward positive social institutions (eg, family, school, or church).

— High intelligence

— Academic success

— Positive attitude toward school

— Aspirations or intentions to attend college

— Active involvement in prosocial activities within the family or community

— Strong family bonds

— Resilient temperament

— Strong social bonds: warm, supportive, affectionate relationships

— Healthy beliefs

— Clear standards of behavior from family or community

— Positive reinforcement for good behavior or consistent punishment for bad behavior

— Opportunity for involvement in family, school, or community socializing institution

---

peraments, children will be less likely to become delinquent. Caregivers need to assist those with tempers in managing their anger in a positive or socially acceptable manner and help them develop outlets for their anger and frustration early in life. Children who have had positive reinforcement for good behavior and are consistently disciplined in a balanced manner for negative behavior are less likely to develop delinquent behaviors. Also, those who are involved in social activities and have affectionate, supportive, or warm relationships are less likely to become delinquent. Parents and caregivers should encourage children to develop strong interactions and social skills that lead to healthy peer interactions in school.

WHAT PARENTS AND CAREGIVERS CAN DO

RECOGNIZING THE RISK FACTORS

Many of the children who become delinquent or violent in adolescence begin displaying persistently noncompliant behavior at a young age, usually by 7 years. Webster-Stratton and Taylor have found that the earlier these children are identified, the more likely parents and caregivers will be able to positively affect their development (**Table 16-2**). Older children with established learning and behavioral problems do not seem as responsive to treatment as younger children. Parents, teachers, nurses, and other health care and childcare professionals are in a unique position to recognize these behaviors as early as possible and can appropriately intervene and help prevent later delinquency.

As mentioned previously, children often break rules or ignore parental requests. This behavior is normal. However, when children repeatedly break rules in multiple settings for multiple adults (parents, grandparents, teachers), there may be cause for concern, especially if they are also unable to participate with other children in structured activities (games, sports, or outings), have poor academic progress, or cannot follow directions or classroom procedures. These children may find interactions with 'compliant' children stressful and become involved with other peers who are failing school. They are often aggressive at home and in school, break rules, fail to follow directions, and abuse alcohol or drugs. Parents and caregivers need to watch older children (aged 10 to 12 years) for aggressive behavior, associations with antisocial peers, and a low commitment to academic achievement.

Table 16-2. Age-Specific Behaviors That May Be Early Warning Signs of Delinquency

TODDLERS AND PRESCHOOL-AGED CHILDREN

— Quick to anger, often overwhelming parents

— Frequent temper tantrums, or tantrums that last longer than 15 minutes or that cannot be calmed down by the parents

— Frequent aggressive outbursts

— Recurrent impulsive or hyperactive behaviors

— Refusal to follow directions from adults

— Repeatedly breaking rules

— Detachment from parents

— Unable to participate in structured play with other children

— Engagement in play with violent themes

— Frequently watching violent programs on television

SCHOOL-AGED CHILDREN

— Constantly disrupting class

— Early school failure or poor performance

— Difficulty concentrating or paying attention in class

— Repeatedly breaking rules in the classroom

— Often fighting with other children in school

— Inappropriate response (rage, blame) to criticism or disappointments at school

— Few friends at school

— Friends who are aggressive or poor students

— Insensitive or cruel to classmates

— Playing violent video games or watching violence on television

— Refusing to follow directions from teachers

(continued)

Table 16-2. *continued*

TEENAGERS

— Poor school performance

— Ignoring the feelings or rights of other students

— Frequently ignoring authority figures

— Skipping school without permission

— Reacting violently to disappointments or confrontations with peers

— Frequent school suspensions or dropping out

— Feeling life has treated him or her unfairly

— Belonging to a gang or associating with gang members

— Involvement in fighting, stealing, or destroying

— A criminal record

PROGRAMS TO MANAGE PROBLEMATIC BEHAVIORS

Once problematic behaviors are recognized, parents and other caregivers need to intervene. Programs that involve children, parents, family, and teachers or the school have demonstrated the most success and can help children achieve positive relationships with peers, parents, and teachers. The goal of any program should be to manage children's aggression in a way that promotes more socially acceptable behavior.

Classroom-focused interventions have been effective at increasing academic and social competence and reducing aggression. School failure is associated with later school dropout, substance abuse, and delinquency, and supporting a child's academic needs may prevent the escalation of behavioral problems. Children who are taught social and behavioral skills and whose academic competence is promoted tend to be successful. Programs that train teachers, such as the Perry Preschool Project or Contingencies for Learning Academic and Social Skills (CLASS) have been shown to be most effective.

However, the most successful programs are multifaceted and combine parent training with classroom-focused programs. Researchers are beginning to recognize the need to target multiple risk factors, and school programs are a natural link between these risk factors. Several studies have shown that interventions that target parents, teachers, and children together lower rates of later delinquency, substance abuse, and school adjustment problems. Examples of this type of program are First Step, which was developed at the Oregon Social Learning Center, and the Incredible Years Parent Teacher Series. In Webster-Stratton and Taylor's study, prevention programs consistently demonstrated short-term improvement in classroom behavior in 78% of disruptive students when teacher training was included. See "Where to Turn for Help" for information on the programs mentioned in this section.

Parents and caregivers need to be able to help delinquent children when school programs are not available or not effective enough. One alternative is a program called Functional Family Therapy, as described by Blueprints for Violence Prevention (see "Where to Turn for Help"). The program is designed to engage and motivate the family after problems and risk factors are assessed, and it involves health care professionals who sometimes visit the home. Participating families have reported successful behavioral changes in adolescents with juvenile delinquency, violence, substance abuse, CD, and other behavioral problems.

For adolescents who are serious or repeat offenders, a more coordinated approach is necessary, such as the Blueprints Model Programs Multisystemic Therapy. Without addressing the many different areas that are likely to contribute to the problem, programs are unlikely to be successful. Successful programs address substance abuse, school problems, and family issues in addition to delinquent behavior. The juvenile justice system may very well become involved depending on the rules that the child or adolescent has broken.

PARENTING AN ADOLESCENT

Adolescence can be a very challenging time for children and their caregivers, and parents, teachers, nurses, and other health care and childcare professionals need to be aware that children experience many personal, social, emotional, physical, and cognitive changes. As children go through puberty, they struggle with autonomy, relationships with friends, identity, and cognitive development. Teenagers may demonstrate more independence, want to spend more time with their peers, and demand more privacy or space. This period of transition to adulthood can be as stressful for parents as it is for children, especially if children are persistently noncompliant and/or oppositional. Awareness of the changes that are going on during adolescence and being prepared to deal with the behavior changes in a productive manner can make this challenging time easier for both parents and adolescents. For example, parents may interpret adolescents' independence or objections to rules as challenges to parental authority. One simple solution may be for parents and adolescents to negotiate the rules together or for parents to allow adolescents more privileges as they show more responsibility. A summary of these developmental needs of adolescents and possible solutions to these needs are outlined in **Table 16-3**.

The American Medical Association (AMA) and the AAP have published guidelines like the *Adolescent Health Update* to help parents manage adolescent children successfully. Effective parenting is the first step. Parents need to anticipate changes in their children and understand, or at least acknowledge, what children are going through. Although there are many different ways to parent, more extreme parenting styles are not usually as effective. Strict, rigid, parents who "lay down the law, no questions asked" are authoritarian. Although they may have high expectations with clear limits, they also often have little warmth, affection, and patience. These parents may reject the inevitable changes in their adolescent or family and may not be available for their child when needed. At the other extreme, permissive parents may be nurturing and loving but have few expectations. They do not want to restrict their adolescent's personal choices. Although permissive parents may always be available for their children, they do not provide enough structure or expectations. The most effective type of parenting is authoritative. Authoritative parents provide love, warmth, and acceptance, while providing reasonable expectations, rules, and structure. **Table 16-4** provides guidelines on how parents can be more authoritative in their interactions with their children.

The AMA and the AAP also stress that it is very important for parents to set clear standards for children's behavior. Parents must monitor adolescents' activity at all times and provide consistent, but not severe, consequences for noncompliance and misconduct. Parents must be firm and fair, supporting their children and being flexible at times. Both organizations encourage parents to pick their battles and be willing to reconsider or reevaluate rules. Parents should only assert their authority when necessary and reward children with more privileges or independence as they demonstrate increased responsibility. Parents should know their children's interests and be available for them, and they need to communicate an understanding of children's individuality. This may seem like a lot to ask of parents of an adolescent. However, this approach is felt to promote social competence, good peer relations and self-esteem, appropriate moral standards, and compliance with rules in adolescents. It also provides many

Table 16-3. Developmental Needs and Expected Behaviors

DEVELOPMENTAL NEEDS	HOW TEENS MAY SEE IT	HOW PARENTS MAY SEE IT	SOLUTION
Independence autonomy, and individuation	Parents are too controlling, not giving enough freedom	Teen constantly challenging the "order of command"	Negotiate rules together
	Teen doesn't have enough input into rules, household responsibilities	Teen wants to be able to "call the shots"	Link increased independence to increased responsibilities
		Teen doesn't want to follow rules, or meet responsibilities	Provide safe opportunities for exploration/ freedom
		Teen wants more freedom, challenges any restriction	Maintain high expectations, allow some rebellion, but set limits and enforce rules consistently
Peer affiliation	Wants to spend more time with friends, less time with family	Teen rejects family to be with friends	Allow teen time to develop important friendships
		Embarrassed to be seen with family	Establish family rituals and make it clear that teen is expected to participate
			Allow teen freedom to choose friends
Identity formation	Needs to "try on" and experiment with a lot of different identities	Egocentric, narcissistic and inconsistent	Be patient
			Keep sense of humor
			Choose your battles
	Needs privacy and space	Secretive	Respect need for privacy, but be aware that too much seclusion may a sign of problems

(continued)

Table 16-3. *continued*

DEVELOPMENTAL NEEDS	HOW TEENS MAY SEE IT	HOW PARENTS MAY SEE IT	SOLUTION
Cognitive development	Teen can think for himself	Argumentative	Provide rationale for decisions
	Can reason abstractly	Challenging	Appreciate intellectual development as positive change
		Teen "knows it all"	Remember that judgment and insight are limited
		Opinionated	

Used with permission of the American Academy of Pediatrics. In: Ryan SA. Helping parents communicate with their teens part 1: assessment and general strategies. Adolescent Health Update, *11:1-8. © 1999 by the AAP.*

opportunities to influence children's well-being. In order to have a positive relationship with mutual trust and respect, parents and children need to be able to balance adolescents' developmental needs with parental expectations. When open communication exists, parents and caregivers can identify risky behaviors more easily.

There are times when it may be difficult to be an authoritative parent, or when negative adolescent behaviors are recognized after they have progressed to delinquency. Such cases may call for a more intensive approach. Some parenting programs have been shown to successfully reduce adolescent alcohol use and delinquent behavior by promoting the effective parenting skills discussed above and teaching parents to be aware of the developmental changes going on in their adolescent. Without parental understanding and involvement adolescence can be even more difficult. Contact doctors, social service offices, or community centers to find out what programs are available locally. **Table 16-5** lists answers to questions that parents and caregivers commonly have about aggressive, defiant, and delinquent behavior.

RUNNING AWAY

Running away may occur at the time in adolescence when parents seem to have the most difficulty communicating with their children, and it can be a very frightening event for any parent. Multiple studies have reported that as many as 1 of 7 children will run away before the age of 18 years and that as many as 1.3 million runaways live on the street at any time in the United States. The AAP has found that running away happens most commonly between the ages of 13 and 15 years and usually occurs as a way for the adolescent to manage a stressful situation or conflict in their family. Adolescents may also run away because of poor self-esteem, mental or emotional health issues, problems at school, or family issues such as substance abuse, separation or divorce, or finances. These adolescents may be as frightened as their parents, and about 50% of runaways stay within 10 miles of home. Adolescents who have run away often suffer inadequate nutrition and sleep, physical abuse or assault, or even substance abuse while away from home.

If a child runs away, it is very important for parents to remain calm and do whatever they can to locate the child as quickly as possible. As stressful as it may be, getting angry will only make the stressful situation more trying or make remembering the important

Table 16-4. How To Be an Authoritative Parent

START WITH LOVE AND TRUST

— Let your teenager know that you you will be there for him or her, no matter what happens.

SET CLEAR AND REASONABLE LIMITS

— Set achievable standards for behavior.

— Establish rules and expectations for this behavior.

SEE THAT BOTH PARENTS ENFORCE RULES CONSISTENTLY

— Be firm but fair.

— Be supportive. Remember that your teenager does not have your sense of experience or proportion.

— Pick your battles. Learn when to draw the line and when to be flexible.

— Be willing to reconsider a rule when it does not seem to apply.

— Be willing to reevaluate rules over time.

RETAIN YOUR RIGHT TO ASSERT PARENTAL AUTHORITY

— Balance control with independence.

— Know how much control is too much.

— Grant freedom in stages. Avoid giving too much too soon.

— Tie increased privileges to responsible behavior.

— Teenagers need to experience the natural consequences of their behavior. Within reasonable limits, stand back and let that happen. (For example, while drinking and driving would not be tolerated, the teenager who oversleeps should perhaps face the consequences at school.)

WORK AT STAYING CLOSE AND CONNECTED WITH YOUR ADOLESCENT

— Be available.

— Spend uninterrupted time alone together.

— Get to know your teenager's interests, passions, and concerns.

— Share your own concerns, interests, passions, and feelings.

— Use humor wisely.

RESPECT YOUR ADOLESCENT

— Acknowledge your teenager's individuality by accepting his or her choices with respect to clothing, activities, and friends.

— Do not ridicule your teenager's choices. Model and insist upon civil discourse.

Data from pages 12-26 [adapted into table] from You and Your Adolescent *by Laurence Steinburg and Ann Levine. © 1990 by Laurence Steinburg and Ann Levine. Reprinted by permission of HarperCollins Publishers.*

Table 16-5. Frequently Asked Questions

My 12-year-old daughter has threatened to run away. This thought frightens me, and I am not sure what to do.

Having a child run away, or even just threaten to run away, can be a frightening experience. As children enter adolescence they go through developmental stages in which they may challenge parental authority and resist efforts to spend time with their family. Talk of running away can be part of normal development, but it may also be a response to more serious conflict or stress. It is extremely important to talk to your daughter about any conflicts or stressors that may have triggered her threat. Do not get angry or upset because it may make your child feel worse and more inclined to leave home. When parents can control their emotions, conflicts can be discussed and resolved. Simple things like letting your child know that you love her no matter what, setting clear and reasonable limits, being consistent, firm and fair with the rules, and respecting her can go a long way toward helping you understand her and develop a good relationship with her. Then, hopefully, she will feel comfortable enough to choose to talk to you about problems rather than run away.

My 13-year-old son is very smart and has done well in school. Since his father died a few years ago, he has started hanging out with the wrong crowd, getting into trouble at school, and seems angry. It is becoming difficult for me to manage his behavior at home. What can I do before he gets into real trouble?

You have every right to be concerned, and it is very important that you have recognized behaviors that may be warning signs of potential delinquency or violence. However, the fact that your son has been academically successful, is intelligent, and seems to have a caring and concerned parent are positive factors that may protect him from becoming delinquent. Adolescence can be a difficult time for a child, especially one who has lost his father. Children often start to get into trouble if they hang around with the "wrong crowd." The most important thing that you can do is to get actively involved in his life. Parents who are authoritative and express love, concern, and work to set firm, but flexible limits should be able to handle many of the issues that arise in adolescence.

Your son also needs to see a therapist who can help him deal with the loss of his father. His behavior may be his way of acting out his anger at his father's death, and it needs to be addressed so that it does not get worse. He may benefit from individual therapy, or it may be helpful to go as a family. His peers are also affecting his behavior. Efforts should be made to prevent him from hanging out with peers that you consider bad influences. Involvement in sports, community events, or church or school activities may be helpful ways to keep him occupied outside of the home. Convincing him to go to counseling or to avoid the company of his current friends will not be easy, but it may prevent him from developing more concerning delinquent behaviors and/or getting into trouble with the law.

If your son has already been in trouble with the law or if the above measures are ineffective, he may need a more intensive intervention. The most successful programs involve the family and school. Information about these other types of programs can also be obtained by contacting your local school, visiting the Blueprints for Violence Prevention Web site at http://www.colorado.edu/cspv/blueprints, or calling the National Youth Violence Prevention Resource Center toll free at 866-SAFEYOUTH.

(continued)

Table 16-5. *continued*

My 2-year-old boy is bad. Is he likely to become delinquent?

No, he is not. Most 2 year olds display "bad" or noncompliant behavior from time to time. Temper tantrums are a normal response from children who do not get their way at this developmental stage. He should eventually grow out of this if you learn how to correctly manage the behaviors— overreacting, for example, can make the behavior worse. If your son's behavior becomes severe or very persistent, talk to your pediatrician or family physician for advice. You can also visit http://www.incredibleyears.com for information on some innovative programs that they offer. Only when noncompliant behavior becomes persistent or severe and does not vary with multiple caregivers can it be associated with delinquency.

details of a child's appearance or behavior before they disappeared more difficult. As soon as a child is discovered missing, check the child's room for notes or missing toys, contact any friends with whom he or she may be staying, and call the local police to file a missing persons report. Runaways often keep in contact with their close friends. Parents should also call the National Runaway Hotline at 800-621-0000 or visit the Web site. This organization may be able to help locate missing children or communicate with them as a middleman. Team H.O.P.E. is a support network for families with missing children and can be reached at their toll free number 866-305-HOPE (4673). See also "Where to Turn for Help."

Once a runaway returns home, it is vital for parents and caregivers to express relief and happiness. Often, runaway children fear the initial encounter, and responses of anger, disgust, or a desire to punish may only make them more angry or frustrated. After the child understands how much he or she is loved and was missed, parents need to focus on communicating with him or her. The police, school, and friends may need to be contacted to let them know the child has returned safely, and the child may need rest or medical attention. Also, concerted efforts must be made to discover why the child left home—ie, what stresses existed or what caused the anger or unhappiness—and to develop a plan to work on those problems. A counseling service should also be contacted for the whole family, and the family should work together to address the stressors and make sure that the child does not run away again.

WHAT SCHOOLS, TEACHERS, AND HEALTH CARE PROFESSIONALS CAN DO

IDENTIFYING CHILDREN AT RISK FOR BEHAVIORAL PROBLEMS

Teachers, nurses, and other health care and childcare professionals need to watch for problem behaviors or signs of physical injury or trauma that signal a child might be difficult for parents to manage. Teachers and nurses should also be concerned with parents who are inconsistent disciplinarians or not involved with their child's problems at school. Children and adolescents who are chronic and serious offenders often showed poor school performance or persistent behavioral problems or aggression by 7 years of age. Children from disadvantaged backgrounds are at particular risk if their parents are antisocial or live in a neighborhood that has drugs. When children live in poverty, it significantly increases their risk factors.

PREVENTING DELINQUENCY

Although parents remain the most important factor in preventing delinquency and violence in adolescence, schools are also very important. Children spend much of their day in school, where peers, teachers, and academic achievement may influence their behavior. Programs that focus on nonviolent strategies for dealing with violence and address conflicts that occur in school are felt to be effective in preventing violence in schools. Violence prevention specialists and peer mediators can address conflicts that arise, reinforce skills that they have taught, and serve as role models for nonviolent resolution. Because school-aged children have many different developmental levels, the programs must recognize this and teach accordingly.

Increased collaboration between home and school will result in decreased levels of conduct problems and school violence, and increased academic success. Parents, teachers, and nurses should routinely screen children to see which might benefit from extra support. Schools are encouraged to train school counselors, teachers, and nurses to provide parenting programs and maintain a resource room for parents with informative pamphlets and videotapes on parenting, social skills, and problem-solving skills. Researchers have stressed the need for schools to use resources and partner with parents to promote social competence in an effort to prevent violence and delinquency.

PROFESSIONAL STUDY AND CONTROVERSY
EARLY BEHAVIORAL MANAGEMENT PROGRAMS

The earlier a behavioral program starts, the more effective it may be. Some parent-focused programs for at-risk children begin during pregnancy. These types of programs provide parental education during pregnancy and infancy about important topics such as nutrition, avoidance of smoking, alcohol and drugs during pregnancy, infant care, and appropriate expectations for child development, behavior, and discipline. The programs often have nurses who go into the homes of high-risk mothers to provide education and guidance. Results have demonstrated a lower likelihood of child abuse, neglect, and fewer parental arrests. Children who were followed through adolescence were also less likely to have been arrested, run away, or consume alcohol than their peers.

There are also more specific behavioral parent training programs for children older than 2 years who are beginning to have temper tantrums, or become disobedient or defiant. Programs for groups of parents and for individual parents have been shown to improve parenting practices and reduce conduct problems in children. Studies demonstrate that as many as two thirds of the children in these programs developed more appropriate behaviors at home and at school at the end of the study. The results were less consistent if the child's teacher was not involved in the behavior modification, however. Programs that had training available in individual, group, and self-administered formats were most effective. Examples of these parent-focused programs include home visiting, The Future of Children, The Natural Child Project, The Incredible Years Parenting Program, DARE To Be You, Focus on Families, and those in the books *Living With Children* and *Helping the Noncompliant Child*.

Some child-focused programs teach children social, emotional, and cognitive competence by addressing the child's social skills, problem solving abilities, anger management abilities, and language emotions. Examples include Peer Coping Skills Training and The Incredible Years Dinosaur Program. The results are not consistently effective, though they are considered promising. Overall, these programs are less effective than parent or family interventions. See "Where to Turn for Help" for books and Web sites providing information on all of the programs mentioned above.

PROGRAMS FOR DELINQUENT CHILDREN

A number of programs focused on children with histories of delinquency have not yet proven successful. Juvenile boot camps, wilderness/challenge programs, deterrence programs and individual therapy have not been shown to be as successful as the programs previously discussed. These programs may challenge children but do not, in general, address the many factors that initially place the child at risk. Programs that are not comprehensive are less likely to change problem behaviors.

CONCLUSION

Juvenile violence and delinquency are major public health concerns. Early recognition of problem behaviors in children by parents, teachers, nurses, and other health care and childcare professionals is extremely important. If these behaviors are recognized early, successful intervention with the child, family, and/or school to change the behaviors and prevent later delinquency is possible.

WHERE TO TURN FOR HELP

BOOKS

Hops H, Walker HM. *CLASS: Contingencies for Learning Academic and Social Skills Manual*. Seattle, Wa: Educational Achievement Systems; 1988.

McMahon R, Forhand R. *Helping the Noncompliant Child: Family-Based Treatment for Oppositional Behavior*. 2nd Ed. New York, NY: The Guildford Press; 2003.

Patterson GR. *Living With Children: New Methods for Parents and Teachers*. Champaign, Ill: Research Press; 1977.

WEB SITES

American Academy of Child and Adolescent Psychiatry

http://www.aacap.org

Blueprints for Violence Prevention

http://www.colorado.edu/cspv/blueprints/model/overview.html

DARE To Be You

Colorado State University

http://www.coopext.colostate.edu/DTBY/

Edutopia: The George Lucas Educational Foundation

http://www.edutopia.org

Functional Family Therapy

http://www.fftinc.com

The Future of Children

http://www.futureofchildren.org

The Incredible Years

http://www.incredibleyears.com

Mental Health Matters

http://www.mental-health-matters.com/disorders

The Natural Child Project

http://www.naturalchild.com

Perry Preschool Project

http://www.highscope.org/Research/PerryProject/perrymain.htm

ESPECIALLY FOR RUNAWAYS
Child Inc.

http://www.childinc.com/runaway.htm

Focus Adolescent Services: An Internet Clearinghouse of Information, Resources, and Support

http://www.focusas.com/Runaways.html

National Runaway Switchboard

800-621-0000 (800-621-0394 for hearing-impaired families)

http://www.nrscrisisline.org

National Youth Violence Prevention Resource Center

866-SAFEYOUTH or 800-243-7012 (TTY)

http://www.safeyouth.org

Team H.O.P.E.

866-305-HOPE

http://www.teamhope.org

Chapter 17

DISCIPLINE AND CORPORAL PUNISHMENT

Laura E. Smals, MD

The art of disciplining children is one of the biggest challenges parents face. Their feelings of success or failure as parents are often closely linked to the outward behaviors of their children. Because no one is a perfect, the disciplining process may work beautifully sometimes and at other times fall short in managing the child's behavior. Every parent commits disciplinary errors at one point or another. Nevertheless, there are some basic, helpful principles parents can follow when trying to correct their children's behaviors.

EFFECTS OF DISCIPLINE

DISCIPLINE VERSUS PUNISHMENT

One of the primary fears new parents have is that they will be unable to discipline their child and still maintain a loving relationship with him or her. Yet one key to obtaining a good relationship is for parents to be effective disciplinarians. The terms *discipline* and *punishment* are frequently used interchangeably, but they are, in reality, distinctly different. **Discipline** comes from the root *disciplinare*, which means "to teach" or "instruct," while **punishment** comes from the root *punio*, which means "to avenge" or "give a penalty." Discipline, therefore, refers to guiding and teaching children behavior instead of merely admonishing unwanted behavior. The difference may seem merely semantic, but the distinction is very important. A good disciplinary system does not simply punish; it teaches.

In order for any disciplinary system to work, it must be implemented in a loving, nurturing environment. Excessive control, absence of affection, or child maltreatment will impair the effectiveness of any system. A loving bond between child and caregiver is an essential element of its success. The aims of the system should be to instruct children to avoid harmful behaviors, encourage desirable behaviors, and teach children to make good decisions as they grow and mature. The American Academy of Pediatrics (AAP) recommends a comprehensive approach to parenting and discipline that considers the unique aspects to each parent-child relationship, the social and individual value of using reinforcement to promote desired behaviors, and the delivery of consistent consequences for negative behaviors. The AAP views corporal punishment as having limited effectiveness that is outweighed by potentially negative and unwanted side effects.

WHAT PARENTS AND CAREGIVERS CAN DO

PREVENTION

As is true for many problems, it is always better to prevent bad behavior before it ever begins than to correct it later. No child is perfect, and all will occasionally disobey or misbehave. Because preventing disobedience and promoting good behavior is the true goal of discipline, creating an environment where children *want* to behave appropriately is the key to success. No one likes obeying rules, and children are no exception. The challenge, then, is to allow the children, to the extent their developmental stage makes possible, to see the advantage of behaving properly.

REINFORCEMENT

Most techniques for modifying human behavior are based on theories of reinforcement. *Reinforcement* is the phenomenon by which a consequence occurs immediately after, or in association with, a behavior and affects the likelihood of that behavior reoccurring. If the consequence increases the likelihood that the behavior will reoccur, it is called *positive reinforcement.* An example of positive reinforcement is placing a sticker on a chart every time children make their beds—if they see the sticker as a reward or recognition of the action, they are more likely to make their beds again. If, however, the consequence causes a behavior to change in an effort to *avoid* that consequence, the consequence is called *negative reinforcement.* When a child has to go into time-out every time he or she hits a sibling, the child will change his or her behavior to avoid the time-out. If, however, a misbehavior receives an *inconsistent* response each time it occurs, it is receiving *variable reinforcement.* Behaviors associated with variable reinforcement generally increase in frequency because children are unsure whether the positive or negative response will occur. They continue the behavior hoping to receive the positive response. Consequently, if parents occasionally use candy to bribe a whining child to stop, the child will probably whine more in order to try and get more candy. Similarly, when a parent only intermittently punishes a child for a negative behavior, the child will often continue that behavior in hopes that this time he or she will get away with it. Parents often do not realize that what they do to stop a behavior in the short term will actually increase the occurrence of the behavior in the future. The key to changing behavior is consistency: If parents are consistent, behavior changes, but if parents are inconsistent, behavior does not change and may even get worse.

FACTS ABOUT DISCIPLINE

There is no one way to discipline children. Specific techniques vary depending on the child and the situation. Key components of effective discipline can be summarized in the word **FACTS**. First, the disciplinary technique must be *fair.* In other words, the punishment should fit the crime: Caregivers must have reasonable, offense-driven consequences for children's misdeeds. A child should not, for example, be grounded for 6 months the first time he or she violates curfew. *Age-appropriate* discipline takes into account the developmental age of the child. A time-out will not deter a 12 year old, nor will taking away privileges impact a 1 to 2 year old. Thirdly, the discipline must be *consistent.* If a child knows that he or she is only sometimes punished for an action, he or she will continue that behavior, each time hoping to get away with it. Any disciplinary technique must also be *timely.* Children have short attention spans and will have difficulty understanding that a punishment they are receiving now is related to an act that they performed hours before. In order for children to learn from their behaviors, the action and consequence must be closely linked in time. Finally, parents and caregivers must always *say what they mean.* In other words, do not threaten a punishment and then fail to follow through with it. For example, if children are not cooperating as the family is preparing to go to grandmother's house at Christmas, parents should not say, "If you don't hurry up, we are not going." The family will go regardless of how well or how quickly the children prepare, and the children know this. Empty threats only confuse them and teach them that parents do not mean what they say.

AGE-APPROPRIATE DISCIPLINE

CHILDREN AGED 9 TO 18 MONTHS

The first time children need discipline is typically when they start to crawl or walk (**Table 17-1**). As curious infants reach for the electrical outlet or hot stove, parents' job is to prevent them from sustaining injury and teach them not to do it again. Very young children have not developed the ability to reason, and a "why" explanation will be wasted on them. Instead, give infants and toddlers a firm "no" and remove them from the tempting item. If these actions are repeated every time a child attempts a dangerous or improper behavior, the behavior will eventually stop because the child is not getting what he or she wants.

Table 17-1. Dos and Don'ts of Disciplining a 9- to 18-Month-Old Child

— Do say "no" and avoid long explanations.

— Don't give positive reinforcement to a dangerous or negative behavior by responding with excessive attention or cuddling.

— Do redirect or distract the child's attention to something else.

— Do remove the tempting item.

— Do practice consistency.

Caregivers often inadvertently give positive reinforcement to children in this age group —as when, for example, a mother sweeps her child up into her arms whenever he or she reaches for the stove, holds him or her closely, and tells the child, "Mommy loves you so much and doesn't want you to get hurt." A more appropriate response would be to take the curious child away from the stove and place him or her in another room with a firm "no, that's hot." Being taken away from an object of interest teaches children that the object is off limits and, if the object is dangerous, keeps them safe. Similarly, parents who whisk a child away to play every time he or she breaks a sibling's toy merely teach the child a method for gaining parental attention. Instead, parents should tell the child "no," take the sibling's toys away, and withhold the toys until the child is less destructive. The children in the 2 examples above will continue their negative behavior because their parents are giving them attention in order to stop the behavior. Even children this young can quickly learn which behaviors result in outcomes they like and which do not.

CHILDREN AGED 18 MONTHS TO 5 YEARS

As children become more verbal, the challenges of discipline change. Children in this age group tend to be more openly defiant than at earlier ages, and "no" becomes a common household word. They are trying to test out their environment and see what the rules and their parents' limits are. The way parents discipline children during these formative years is critical and sets the tone for future discipline.

Time-Out

Time-out is a very effective tool for disciplining children between 18 months and 5 years of age (**Table 17-2**). Time-out means that children are placed in a designated "time-out area" and made to remain there for a specific period of time. A time-out accomplishes several things; primarily, it serves as negative reinforcement for the activity in which a child was engaged. Children, in general, do not like to sit still or be bored. Requiring this of them, even for a short time, is often more disagreeable to them than other forms of punishment. In order to work, the time-out location must be separate from the stimulating environment of the house and devoid of any forms of entertainment—television, books, games, or other people. A stair step or a chair in the living room usually works well. Sending children to their bedrooms is not usually a good idea because the entertainment available there often makes bedrooms fun places to play.

Table 17-2. Keys to a Successful Time-Out
— They should last 1 minute for every year of a child's age.
— Don't start the time-out until the child is quiet.
— It must take place in an area with little stimulation (no TV, books, games, or music).
— Do not talk to the child during the time-out.
— Afterwards, do not continually remind the child of his or her misbehavior.

Time-outs also remove children from the tempting stimulus and allow them to calm down. A time-out should last about 1 minute for every year of a child's age (eg, 2 minutes for a 2 year old). Use a timer to track the minutes, and if a child screams, do not start the timer until he or she stops and sits still in the chair. Also, do not speak to children during these minutes—it is not a time for lectures or explanations as to why they are in time-out. When it is necessary to make sure a child knows why he or she is going into time-out, the explanation should be brief and clear. "Time-out: hitting" is all that should be necessary as long as the child knew the rule against hitting. One of the reasons for not speaking to children during time-out is to avoid providing positive reinforcement for their actions. Receiving a lot of attention for misbehavior, even negative attention, can increase children's disobedience. When the time-out is over, there should not be long discussions about it, nor should children be continually reminded of their bad behavior. If the behavior recurs, return children to time-out each time until it stops. This consistent action-reaction pattern will quickly teach children that parents truly mean what they say. When this type of discipline is first introduced, it may have to be implemented several times before children change their behavior, especially if prior discipline was inconsistent. Children will test to see if their parents will really follow through with the discipline they threaten. However, if parents are consistent, children will learn, the behavior will extinguish, and discipline will get easier with time.

Children who refuse to sit in the time-out chair can be held in the chair, provided that parents are careful not to use excess force or cuddle with children. Parents should be behind, not in, the chair, holding children by their shoulders or waist. Again, it is essential not to talk to children in order to avoid giving the behavior positive reinforcement.

The other key aspect of the time-out disciplinary technique is the "time-in." Children must desire to stay in "time-in" for time-out to work. Time-ins are special time parents spend with children or moments in which they praise their children for good behaviors. Parents need to make a point to comment on good behaviors to reinforce them. Children who get a lot of positive contact with their parents will not like the absence of this contact during time-out.

Temper Tantrums

The temper tantrum is one of the primary weapons that very young children have against their caregivers. These dramatic fits of rage and destruction, which are expressions of frustration and are usually responses to being told "no," terrify and embarrass parents, and most will do anything to extinguish them. Nearly every child will throw a temper tantrum at one time or another, and the only way to end tantrums is to not reinforce them. Begging children to stop, yelling at them, or trying to hold or comfort them all teach children that a temper tantrum is a good way to get attention, and they will take negative attention if they cannot get positive attention. If a child's fit was precipitated by the denial of something, parents *cannot* try to stop the tantrum by giving the child the desired item or privilege. When parents yield, children only learn to have another fit the next time they are told "no." The only way to respond to a temper tantrum is to ignore it. Remove any objects near the child that might harm him or her and simply walk away. If the child follows, return to the first room. Do not speak to the child except in simple phrases like "I am not going to answer you until you stop screaming." Parents should also do their best to not look directly at children while they are throwing a tantrum. Performances like these rarely continue for long without an audience.

It is every parent's fear that his or her adorable child will suddenly turn into a screaming tyrant in front of a room full of strangers, and sometimes this fear is fulfilled. However, parents who can manage tantrums thrown at home can competently manage those that occur in public, for they require very much the same response. Yielding to children's requests will only teach them to have more fits in the grocery store (or other public places) to get what they want. Instead, take the child out to the car, place him or her in the car seat, and wait until the fit stops. When children learn that parents would rather leave a cart full of groceries than give into their demands, they will eventually stop using tantrums to try and get their way. Children are smart, and if a behavior is not working to get them get what they want, they will stop doing it. **Table 17-3** lists tips for disciplining an 18-month- to 5-year-old child.

Table 17-3. Dos and Don'ts of Disciplining an 18-Month- to 5-Year-Old Child

— Do utilize time-outs.

— Do balance time-out with time-in.

— Don't give into children's demands when they throw temper tantrums.

— Do ignore children or give them as little attention as possible during tantrums in order to avoid encouraging the behavior.

— Don't interfere with safe opportunities for children to learn the natural consequences of their actions.

Natural Consequences
Another tool for disciplining children is merely to allow the natural consequences of their actions to occur. If a young child drops all of his or her cookies on the floor, then the cookies are lost and cannot be eaten. If a child plays too roughly with toys and a toy breaks, then it is simply no longer available. Parents can interfere with this natural learning process by giving a child more cookies or replacing the broken toy. Letting children learn the consequences of their actions can be a powerful tool for teaching children how to make decisions.

CHILDREN OLDER THAN 5 YEARS

Removing Privileges

As children get older, time-outs become less effective. After the age of 5, and sometimes earlier, removal of privileges becomes parents' primary disciplinary tool. Every person has possessions that he or she values or activities he or she enjoys doing, and children are no exception. When children are disobedient or disrespectful, these possessions or activities can be taken away temporarily. For example, parents may refuse to allow a 6 year old who did not put away toys as he or she was instructed to play with a friend that afternoon. A teenager who violates curfew might not be allowed to go out the following night. When taking away privileges, parents must take care that the punishment is appropriate. A minor violation should not be punished with an extreme deprivation of privileges. Also, the removed privilege must be relatively close in time to the misbehavior, or the action will lose its effect. Young minds have difficulty relating to distance in time and thus are unlikely to learn from it. A child cannot be banned from a party 1 month from now for an infraction committed today. Finally, the privilege lost cannot be something that the child truly needs, such as food, clothing, education, or a safe environment.

Earning Privileges

Another way to change older children's behavior is to let them *earn* their privileges. Creating a sticker chart or token economy can help children feel responsible for and take ownership of their decisions. An example of a token economy is one in which children can only get allowance by making their beds every day. There is no punishment for not making the bed, but there is no reward, either. This method can be used for many different circumstances and enables children to feel empowered in their decisions. However, be cautioned not to take this to the extreme. Bribing children into simple obedience is not the goal of this disciplinary technique. Also, if children already have all the privileges that they want or need and what a parent offers is extra, parents run the risk of prompting noncompliance. A child might simply decide, "I don't need any money right now, so I am not going to do my chores." Token systems are only successful when the token is something consistently desirable. Phone privileges, computer privileges, and basic—not extra—allowance can all make good tokens. When children know that they must do basic family duties in order to keep basic privileges, they are more likely to fulfill their responsibilities consistently. Sticker charts may work well for younger children because putting a star by their name can be exciting, and a week of stars might result in a special activity or treat. Finally, the token must be a reward for accomplishing a task that is within a child's control. Giving children money for school performance, for example, may be problematic if a child is really struggling with certain subject matter. Parents need to make sure children are motivated and able to perform in the economy that has been established, or the system will fail.

PARENTAL GUILT

One of the principal barriers to effective discipline is parental guilt. Parents frequently feel guilty that they are being "too mean" or worry that their child will resent them later in life. When parents start to feel that way, they need to stand back and consider the punishment objectively: Are they being too harsh? Is the punishment age-appropriate? Are they responding purely out of anger or frustration or is it truly a response to misbehavior? If parents can objectively view a punishment as fair and deserved, they need not feel guilty for administering it. Children need and crave discipline; they are looking for someone to teach them the right and wrong ways to behave. A home without consistent discipline leads to a much more chaotic and unhappy environment than one in which actions and consequences are clearly understood. **Table 17-4** explores questions parents frequently have about disciplining their children.

Table 17-4. Frequently Asked Questions

What is the most common mistake that parents make?

Being inconsistent. Parents unintentionally follow through with their punishment some of the time. Children quickly learn that their parent may let them get away with misdeeds, and so they test them out. If parents say that a child will receive a particular punishment for a behavior, they need to follow through with the punishment. Parents who struggle with inconsistency are frequently tired and worn down, and so they give in "this time." However, children only learn that they can get away with misbehavior more when parents are tired or stressed. The only way to win the battle is to make sure that you are consistent—each time a child misbehaves, he or she must get the promised punishment. The child will quickly learn to avoid the behavior.

What should I do if my child acts out in public?

Parents need to put aside their embarrassment and discipline their child, even in public. The rules of discipline are the same in public and in private. If a child is making a scene, remove the child—take him or her to the car or a quiet corner and discipline accordingly. Time-outs can take place in cars, privileges can be removed, and, in some cases, the parent and child may have to leave the public setting and go home. If children learn that parents are willing to leave a party or a shopping mall in order to make sure that they comply, they will give up testing their parents in public. Children who see that their parents are more likely to "give in" to public fits out of embarrassment will have more fits in public in order to get what they want.

What if my child won't stay in time-out?

Children who are first introduced to time-out after having problems with disobedience will be a challenge to keep in time-out. For the first few, parents may have to restrain their child in the time-out chair. This should be done gently but firmly, with the parent sitting or standing behind the chair and holding the child's waist. Do not begin the time-out until after the child stops fighting, crying, or screaming. If you can make it through the first few times, the child will learn that the time-out is shorter when he or she cooperates.

My child is out of control, and as soon as I started using some of these methods, things got worse. Does that mean the methods are not working?

If parents have not had a good disciplinary structure and then start to implement one, the first response children have is usually to increase their bad behavior. Children who are not used to being disciplined act out in response to the new structure and discipline in order to see if parents are really serious. Parents need to remain firm and continue the consistent discipline. After the initial testing period ends, children's behavior will improve.

I have tried taking away privileges, but my child doesn't seem to care. What am I doing wrong?

Every child values something—a toy, a TV show, an activity, or a privilege. The key is to figure out what that is and then use it to motivate the child to comply with house rules. If a child is very disrespectful or openly defies the rules, take away that toy or activity until the behavior changes. Just remember that essentials like basic food or clothing should not be used as disciplinary tools.

PROFESSIONAL STUDY AND CONTROVERSY

CORPORAL PUNISHMENT

Spanking is a controversial subject. Although the majority of Americans will report using spanking as a form of discipline at one time or another, the effectiveness of this method is still under much debate among primary care physicians. Proponents of spanking argue that it is an effective way to elicit immediate obedience from a child, and even the AAP recognizes that spanking can certainly elicit immediate compliance, especially from children 1 to 3 years of age. However, spanking raises multiple concerns among child health professionals. One is that spanking will alter the parent-child bond. Irwin Hyman, who was a family therapist and the director of the National Center for the Study of Corporal Punishment and Alternatives at the time of his death in 2005, argued that adults playing the role of caretaker, nurturer, and "pain-giver" may confuse children. Spanking also gives children the message that harming another person physically is okay, and this message will be especially confusing for a child who is being spanked for hitting someone. Another, greater concern is that spankings may get more forceful with each encounter, especially if parents are frustrated or upset and children fail to comply with rules. Spanking may get out of hand and may place children at risk for physical harm or abuse.

CONCLUSION

Discipline is paramount to effective and successful parenting, and it is one of parents' foremost challenges. Discipline that is administered effectively, consistently, and fairly will teach children to respect adults and their peers, strengthen the parent-child bond, and help children understand that their actions and decisions have consequences. Successful discipline can prepare children for success in life.

WHERE TO TURN FOR HELP

BOOKS AND ARTICLES

Hyman IA. *The Case Against Spanking: How to Discipline Your Child Without Hitting.* San Francisco, Calif: Jossey-Bass Publishers; 1997.

Stein MT, Perrin EL, for the American Academy of Pediatrics and the Committee on Pyschosocial Aspects of Child and Family Health. Guidance for effective discipline [published correction appears in *Pediatrics.* 1998;102:433]. *Pediatrics.* 1998;101:723-728.

WEB SITES

American Academy of Child and Adolescent Psychiatry: Discipline

http://www.aacap.org/publications/factsfam/discplin.htm

American Academy of Family Physicians: Child Behavior: What Parents Can Do to Change Their Child's Behavior

http://familydoctor.org/201.xml

Keep Kids Healthy: Discipline Guide

http://www.keepkidshealthy.com/parenting_tips/discipline

KidsHealth: Disciplining Your Child

http://kidshealth.org/parent/emotions/behavior/discipline.html

Chapter 18

SELECTING CHILDCARE PROVIDERS

Cynthia DeLago, MD, MPH

Almost 12 million children between birth and the age of 5 years, or 63% of children in this age group, regularly receive childcare, according to a US Census Bureau Population Report. More women are entering the work force than ever before, and they return to work sooner after giving birth than in the past. Census Bureau statistics reveal that in 1976, 31% of women returned to work before their child's first birthday, compared to 55% in 2000. As a result of the increasing number of families with 2 working parents, the childcare options available for today's families encompass a variety of settings, and parents and professionals are paying greater attention to the quality and effects of childcare on children.

EFFECTS OF CHILDCARE

One of the most stressful aspects of being a parent is worrying about the physical and emotional safety of their children while at work. Certainly, concerns about children's safety are warranted. The 1999 Children's Defense Fund publication *Key Facts: Essential Information on Child Care, Early Education, and School-Age Care* refers to 2 studies of childcare quality. The first, a 1995 study of childcare centers in 4 geographically and economically diverse states by University of Colorado researchers, found that 1 out of 8 centers did not meet the health and safety needs of the children or provide exposure to interactions or materials that enhance learning. More than half of the infant and toddler rooms had poor general health practices. Only 1 out of 7 centers received a good quality rating. The second study, in which Ellen Galinsky and colleagues evaluated family childcare homes, rated one third of the homes to have inadequate quality and only 9% as good quality. The US Consumer Products Safety Commission (CPSC) evaluated 220 licensed childcare settings looking specifically at 8 product areas including cribs, soft bedding, playground surfacing, playground maintenance, use of child safety gates, window blind cords, use of clothing with drawstrings, and presence of recalled nursery and child products. It reported that 2 out of 3 settings had at least 1 safety hazard. For example, 8% of childcare settings were using cribs that did not meet current safety standards, 19% had cribs that contained soft bedding, 24% did not have safe playground surfacing, 27% did not maintain playground surfacing well, 13% did not use child safety gates where necessary, 26% had loops on window blind cords, 38% had children wearing clothing with drawstrings, and 5% were using recalled infant and child products.

Before beginning the process of selecting a safe and nurturing childcare arrangement, parents need to know some basic facts about the different types of childcare available, how each is regulated, and how to assess the quality of a potential provider. **Table 18-1** contains questions that parents and caregivers frequently have about selecting an appropriate childcare provider.

Table 18-1. Frequently Asked Questions

When can children be left alone to care for themselves?

Formal childcare providers will usually care for children up to age 12 years. Many children are responsible and mature enough to care for themselves, but studies show that unsupervised children are at greater risk for physical injury as well as psychological and emotional harm, especially if their neighborhoods are not safe. Arrangements for older children are usually after-school programs or supervised care. However, research from the Urban Institute reveals that 5% of 6 to 9 year olds and 24% of 10 to 12 year olds care for themselves after school and that children are home alone for an average of 1½ hours a day for no more than 4 hours at a time. These statistics are probably under-estimated because some parents may feel social pressures not to admit that they leave their child home alone. Some early adolescents left alone will use this unsupervised time to experiment with what they perceive to be grown-up activities such as tobacco smoking, alcohol consumption, drug and sexual experimentation. So, even though some early adolescents are mature enough to care for themselves, it is risky leaving them alone for an extended length of time.

Why are children in childcare always sick? Are these children less healthy later in life?

Infants and young children have immature immune systems. The immune system "matures" with frequent exposures to the common viruses and bacteria that tend to make us all sick. When children first attend childcare, they are exposed to many children who may carry these viruses and bacteria but lack the antibodies to avoid becoming ill. Over time, children will develop these antibodies and be able to fight off common illnesses much more quickly. Eventually, they will be sick less frequently. Exposure to viruses and bacteria do not make children less healthy later in life.

How can I be sure my child is safe while I'm at work?

There are no guarantees that your child will not get hurt in childcare, just as there are no guarantees that your child will not get hurt when he or she is home with you. Your best protection is to choose your child's childcare setting wisely, after first assessing the safety of each facility and the responsibility level of each potential provider.

WHAT PARENTS AND CAREGIVERS CAN DO
CHILDCARE OPTIONS

Children and infants can be cared for in their own homes, at the home of a family-based or home-based childcare provider, or at a childcare center (**Table 18-2**). Nannies and au pairs provide professional in-home care. A *nanny* is any person hired to look after someone else's children. Nannies may be self-employed or work for nanny agencies. An *au pair* is a young person from another country who signs a contract to provide childcare and perform household duties for a specific period in exchange for food, lodging, and a nominal weekly salary. Au pairs are hired through services specialized in this type of childcare. Some parents choose in-home care because they have several children, work unconventional hours, or travel frequently and feel that their children are safer and more comfortable with this arrangement. Parents may also arrange for family members such as grandparents, aunts, uncles, or siblings to care for their children either in their home or out of their home. This type of arrangement is referred to as *relative care*. Parents choosing this option may do so for peace of mind, especially if their children are younger. *Home-based* or *family-based* childcare is offered in the provider's home. Parents may choose this option due to convenience, size, cost or preference for a homelike environment. *Center-based* care is offered in a nonresidential

---

Table 18-2. Comparison of Childcare Options

In-Home Care

Providers: Nannies, au pairs, relatives

Pros: Convenient; child has one-on-one care in a comfortable, familiar setting

Cons: Provider may not be educated in child development issues, may provide just custodial care, minimal regulatory oversight, little to no opportunity to interact with other children

Cost: Can be expensive or very expensive

Out-of-Home, Small (up to 6 children) Family Day Care

Providers: Friend, mutual acquaintance, home day-care operator

Pros: Homelike setting, small groups

Cons: Minimal oversight and regulation

Cost: Low to moderate

Out-of-Home, Large (7 to 12 children) Family Day Care

Providers: Home day-care operator

Pros: Home like setting, larger groups, regulated (provider is required to have preservice training)

Cons: Larger group of children

Cost: Low to moderate

Out-of-Home, Center-Based Care

Providers: Staff

Pros: Trained staff, usually has educational program, regulated

Cons: Larger groups, more children, may have high staff turnover

Cost: Moderate

---

setting such as a business, church, or school. This type of care is reliable and subject to oversight by government regulators, and parents may choose this option specifically for that reason. In fact, the US Census Bureau reports that center-based care is the type of arrangement chosen for about 23% of children in childcare. **Table 18-3** lists dos and don'ts for parents and caregivers to keep in mind as they select a childcare provider for their children.

Regulation

Regulation is the responsibility of individual states and may be in the form of licensing, meaning minimum health, safety, and sometimes programmatic standards are in place before childcare services can be offered to specific numbers of children, or registration, meaning childcare providers are either encouraged or required to self-identify to authorities to certify they are in compliance with state standards or requirements. In-home care, relative care, small family day-care home providers, and nanny and au pair agencies are often not regulated or licensed by the government. In 1993, only 8 states and

---

Table 18-3. Dos and Don'ts of Choosing Childcare

— Do visit the day care home or center and use your checklists to evaluate for quality.

— Do interview the provider.

— Do obtain references and contact these individuals.

— Do ask if the provider is licensed or accredited.

— Don't choose a provider because the individual or center costs the least or most. High cost doesn't always equate with high quality.

— Don't choose a provider solely because of convenience.

— Don't choose a provider without doing your homework. Use some of the Web sites and guides provided in this chapter.

---

the District of Columbia required all family day cares be registered. More recently some states have tried some minimal regulatory standards, such as criminal history checks and child abuse and neglect clearances, for all nonrelative providers who receive part or all of their payment from government childcare subsidies. Some states may regulate nanny placement agencies.

Regulation of small family childcare homes varies from state to state, depending on the number of children being cared for in the home. Some states require providers caring for as few as 2 children or as many as 7 children to register with state agencies. Registration is often voluntary for those caring for fewer children. State agencies set minimum health, safety and nutrition standards and may require preservice and/or ongoing training. They may also require criminal background checks and child abuse and neglect clearance. Some states exempt faith-based and part-time childcare providers.

All states require childcare centers to be licensed. Licensing ensures that these centers maintain certain minimum health, safety, and caregiver training standards. All sites are inspected at least once a year. Parents should keep in mind that licensing is only as good as the licensing standards, and though all centers are licensed, not all centers are of the same quality. Since regulation of childcare providers varies state by state, parents should check requirements with their state's childcare licensing agency. State-by-state regulation and licensing information can also be accessed from the National Resource Center for Health and Safety in Childcare's Web site at http://nrc.uchsc.edu/STATES/states.htm.

Cost

The cost of childcare is substantial, and it is one of the greatest child-related expenses that families incur. The Child Defense Fund surveyed 50 states and published the results in the brief "The High Cost of Childcare Puts Quality Care Out of Reach for Many Families," which states, "Child care can easily cost an average of $4000 to $6000 per year. In certain areas of the country, families may be spending more than $10 000 a year on child care." It also reports that center-based infant care is about $1100 more per year than the average price for the care of 4 year olds, which ranged from $4000 to $8000 per year in the urban areas the Children's Defense Fund surveyed. This figure is greater than the average annual cost of public college tuition. Generally, in-home nanny care is the most expensive childcare arrangement, followed by center-based care. Family childcare homes are usually moderately to low priced.

Quality

Regulation, licensing, and cost are not necessarily measures of quality. Some childcare providers offer low quality care, and, if the environment is unsafe or the provider is physically or emotionally abusive, pose a danger to children. Average childcare providers are neither harmful nor beneficial; they provide custodial care to the child by supplying basic needs. Good childcare providers offer more than custodial care. They provide a safe, nurturing, and stimulating environment that helps children grow socially, emotionally, and intellectually. Quality childcare providers are sensitive to the needs of their clients' children and are attentive to the children in their care. Studies have shown that children exposed to high-quality childcare, regardless of the type of arrangement and child socioeconomic factors, are safer, more secure, and more ready for school than children exposed to average or low-quality childcare. Accreditation is another indicator parents can use to assess quality. It is voluntary and indicates that a provider is committed to quality improvement by achieving standards that foster child development. The National Association for the Education of Young Children (NAEYC) provides accreditation for center-based care and the National Association for Family Childcare (NAFCC) provides accreditation for home-based programs.

Parents need to consider many factors when choosing childcare. These factors include parents' work hours, income, the type of childcare available in the community or at work, the number and ages of the children in the household, and the personality, physical health, and arrangement preference of each child. Parents of children with special health care needs should consider not only the size and setting of a childcare facility but also whether the childcare provider has the training necessary to provide the level of care the child needs. This chapter offers guidelines on how to select a quality provider (refer also to "Where to Turn for Help").

ASSESSMENT OF POTENTIAL PROVIDERS

When arranging for childcare, some decisions may already be made. For example, some parents may live in an area where options are limited, or certain programs may not be affordable. Even if the options are limited, parents still need to assess which one will provide the healthiest, safest, and most stimulating environment for their child. The next few sections discuss how to evaluate the health and safety practices of a program, along with its overall quality. Parents must keep in mind that many of the health, safety, and quality features that apply to programs can be applied to their home and nanny, if this is the arrangement they choose. **Appendix 18-1** contains a checklist that may be useful for assessing a potential childcare provider.

Transmission of Illness

Physicians, childcare providers, teachers, and parents of several children know that children become ill more frequently when they are around other children on a regular basis. Infants and toddlers are more susceptible to viruses and bacterial infections than older children because their immune systems are less mature. Young children in out-of-home childcare arrangements are more frequently exposed to these agents and more often sick. The National Institute of Child Health and Human Development Early Childcare Research Network studied more than 1200 children younger than 3 years in a variety of childcare settings and found that rates of ear infections, upper respiratory tract, and gastrointestinal tract infections were greater among children 2 years or younger who were in childcare than among those who were not. Those children in childcare settings with large numbers of children were sick more frequently with upper respiratory illnesses during their first 2 years of life than those receiving care in smaller settings. However, this study also found that by the age of 3 years, infection rates among children being cared for in their own homes were no different than those for children in other childcare arrangements.

Childcare providers can greatly decrease the spread of infections by adhering to policies and procedures designed to protect the health of all the children. These practices include policies requiring children and caregivers to have updated immunizations, periodically screening employees for tuberculosis, notifying parents when children are exposed to others with infectious diseases that require medicated treatment, and excluding sick children from attending childcare until they are healthy. Childcare providers and the children in their care can also wash their hands frequently with liquid soap and dry them on disposable paper towels. Bathrooms should be separate from food preparation areas, and diapers should be changed only in specified areas and on appropriate surfaces. Using disposable wipes and discarding diapers in containers with disposable linings and foot-pedal controlled lids can also greatly reduce the spread of infectious diseases. Infectious diseases commonly seen in children in out-of-home care include viral upper respiratory infections (colds), ear infections, conjunctivitis or pink eye, and viral and bacterial causes of gastrointestinal illnesses.

Environmental Health and Poisoning

Parents should also determine if a childcare facility has the potential to expose their child to environmental toxins such as lead, tobacco smoke, pesticides, and household poisons. Any childcare arrangement involving housing built before 1978 should be inspected for lead dust. Do not leave a child with a caregiver whose facility is not lead-free, especially if the child is an infant or toddler. The most common cause of lead poisoning is lead-based paint. Infants and toddlers put their hands and other objects in their mouths frequently, and if paint chips or lead dust are in the facility, children will ingest them and develop lead poisoning. This poisoning is most damaging to the brains of infants and young children and can impair a child's intellectual capabilities for life. See Chapter 11, Environmental Health, for more information on lead poisoning.

Tobacco smoke is another environmental toxin that can affect children's health. Children exposed to tobacco smoke have more frequent upper respiratory infections, including ear infections, and more problems with asthma than unexposed children. Caregivers who smoke should not smoke around children in their care. Smoking is prohibited in regulated and licensed family childcare programs and at childcare centers. Regulated or not, caregivers are not monitored and may smoke around children. Additionally, children learn behaviors by modeling their caregivers. Parents must decide if they want children to have a role model who smokes. For more information on environmental tobacco smoke, see Chapter 4, Tobacco and Smoking.

Pesticides are frequently used in homes and businesses to control insects, even in those that provide childcare. When pesticides are improperly applied or buildings are improperly ventilated, children may be exposed to high levels of these chemicals. Dr. Philip Landrigan, a well-known researcher of environmental toxins, has observed that children are particularly susceptible to overexposure because they play close to the floor, where many pesticides are applied and settle, and use more hand-to-mouth behaviors. The US Environmental Protection Agency considers integrated pest management (IPM) an environmentally safe approach to vermin control and preferable to pesticides. Inquiring about the use of pesticides or IPM techniques in or near a facility will help parents make an educated decision about where their child is safest.

Finally, children can be poisoned by accidentally ingesting household products, houseplants, or medications intended for others. Household cleaning products should be stored out of reach in a locked cabinet. Houseplants should be nonpoisonous or out of reach of children. Accidental poisonings occur when medications are easily accessible to curious children. In-home providers, babysitters, relatives, and home-based providers may carry personal medications in handbags or backpacks and inadvertently leave these lying around the house. Storing personal belongings out of reach of children can prevent tragedy. If a child swallows a poison, the most current American Academy of Pediatrics (AAP) recommendation, which was issued in 2003, is *not* to give syrup of ipecac. Syrup of ipecac induces vomiting and was previously considered primary treatment for poison ingestions. The AAP now recommends calling the Poison Control Center at 800-222-1222 for information and instructions when the child looks well or immediately dialing 9-1-1 if the child is not breathing, having seizures, or is unconscious. The AAP has noted that many states have not updated their regulations for childcare providers and may still require them to have syrup of ipecac in first aid kits. Childcare providers should comply with state regulations and follow the most recent medical recommendations. See Chapter 10, Injury Prevention, for more information on poisoning.

Potential for Injury

Injury is the most common cause of disability and death to *all* children in *all* settings. Preventing injuries in childcare settings should be a top priority of all caregivers. See also Chapter 10, Injury Prevention, for information on preventing injuries in and out of the home. Comparing the rates of injuries sustained in different settings is difficult because many family-based childcare homes are unlicensed. Dr. Frederick Rivara and colleagues compared the rates of injuries in childcare centers to the rates of injuries occurring in homes and found that injury rates were lower in childcare centers than in home care. In center-based programs, injuries occur most often among 2 year olds at a rate 2 to 3 times greater than is seen in infants. The more serious injuries occurred outdoors on playgrounds. Another study by Abbey Alkon, principal investigator for the Child Care Health Linkage Project in California, and colleagues found that injuries to girls occurred more frequently in low quality centers.

Infants in childcare face different safety issues than toddlers and preschool children. The primary concern for very young infants is sudden infant death syndrome (SIDS). Researcher and pediatrician Dr. Rachel Moon and colleagues found that a disproportionate number of SIDS deaths occur in childcare. SIDS deaths have decreased 44% since the public health education program "Back to Sleep" was launched in 1994, and studies attribute this decrease to parents placing their infants on their backs to sleep. Dr. De-Kun Lin and colleagues reported that infants who always sleep on their backs but are suddenly placed on their bellies to sleep are at greater risk for SIDS; this was the cause of many of the SIDS deaths Dr. Moon and colleagues studied. Discussing sleep positions with the provider, along with making sure that cribs are free of soft bedding and pillows, can protect infants. Check to see that the cribs have firm mattresses and meet CPSC safety standards for spacing between the bars (no more than 2⅜ inches wide). Also, note whether cribs are near windows with blinds because the cord loops can entangle and strangle older infants.

As infants mature, they become more mobile and curious. They crawl, start to walk, and explore the world with their mouths. Consequently, a 2002 Centers for Disease Control (CDC) bulletin listed injury from falls as the leading cause of nonfatal injury in toddlers and choking as the 4th leading cause. Look at the safety features of the home or center to see if there are toys containing small parts lying around. Find out if the facility serves foods like peanuts, popcorn, whole grapes, hard candy, raw carrot rounds, or hot dogs, or if the facility stores plastic bags and latex balloons out of reach of children. These items are common choking and suffocation hazards. Baby walkers should never be used because children who fall down stairs while using them can be seriously injured or killed.

Toddlers and older children have greater mobility and assertive personalities. According to the CDC, falling, hitting and/or stabbing with objects, biting, burning, poisonings, choking, and motor vehicle accidents are the most common ways toddlers and pre-school-aged children are injured. Even though many toddlers sustain minor injuries from tripping over their own feet, proper supervision and play equipment are key to preventing falls that result in serious injury. Most of these falls occur outside on playground equipment. Playground equipment should be age-appropriate, well main-tained, and well anchored. Certified playground safety installers and inspectors should install and approve it. The National SAFEKIDS Campaign states that the surface of a playground area, which includes the area under and extending 6 feet around the perimeter of all stationary play equipment, should consist of at least 12 inches of energy-absorbing material like sand, mulch, pea gravel, or wood chips. Children should not wear clothing that has drawstrings, especially on hoods, since these can get caught on the equipment. Other features that help prevent playground injuries include spacing equipment 9 feet apart; providing enough equipment so that children do not push, shove or bite each other to use it; maintaining enough open space for play; and having shaded play areas that are free from hazards that will trip children or otherwise endanger their health, like poisonous plants and animal feces.

Indoor injuries can be prevented if childcare equipment meets safety standards, hazards are eliminated, and children are properly supervised. Providers should use highchairs that meet safety standards according to their proper instructions, remove toys and equipment that are recalled by the CPSC, and install smoke detectors. Stairs should have gates at the bottom and top of the staircase, electrical sockets should be covered with safety plugs, and the hot water heater should be set at 120°F or lower to prevent scald burns. Children should not be allowed in the kitchen, and caregivers should not drink hot beverages around them. Spills should be cleaned up promptly. If food is served by the daycare provider, make sure sanitary food preparation techniques are followed (see specific guidelines in Chapter 4 of the book *Caring for our Children*, which is listed under "Where to Turn for Help") and that the foods that are served do not pose choking hazards for children, such as peanuts, popcorn, carrots and hotdogs sliced like coins, and whole grapes, to name a few. If your child has food allergies, be sure to provide written instruction about avoiding these foods and what procedure to follow if the child is inadvertently exposed to offending foods. Also provide medications to treat this reaction and emergency phone numbers. Maintaining adequate staff-child ratios, and keeping children in small groups with enough toys and materials for all, will help prevent children from fighting, biting, and inflicting cuts, abrasions, or bruises on each other. Staff-child ratios vary depending on the ages of the children. These standards are set to ensure proper supervision (**Table 18-4**).

Many children between 5 and 12 years of age attend after-school programs or have other childcare arrangements. The majority of the safety principles discussed previously apply to this age group—particularly offering age-appropriate activities, adequate and age-appropriate play equipment, and maintaining general safety features and proper supervision.

If a childcare provider transports children in motor vehicles, ensure that proper infant and child car seats are used. Older children who are too small to use seat belts should be

Table 18-4. General Guide for Group Size and Adult to Child Ratios for Childcare

Group With Same-Aged Children*	Adult to Child Ratio†	Maximum Recommended Number of Children per Group‡	Minimal Number of Adults for Group Size
Infants (1 to 12 months)	1:3	6	2
1 to 2½ years	1:4	8	2
2½ years to 3 yrs. 11 mos.	1:7	14	2
4 to 5 years	1:8	16	2
6 to 8 years	1:10	20	2
9 to 12 years	1:12	24	2

Data from Caring for Our Children *by the AAP and the National Association for the Education of Young Children.*
*In mixed age groups, the maximal number of children per group and adult to child ratio should be followed for the youngest child in the group.
†If a child within the group requires additional adult help or attention, the number of children per adult should decrease.
‡The number of children per group includes the childcare provider's own children.

secured in child booster seats, even though only some states mandate this by law. Transportation should be entrusted to qualified drivers who can handle emergency situations, especially when transporting children with special health care needs. Drivers should be trained to provide proper supervision, never leave a child alone in a vehicle, and follow safe drop-off and pick-up procedures. Parents and caregivers must know who is transporting their child and what procedures are followed.

Finally, childcare providers should have an emergency plan prepared. At least 1 staff member should be trained in CPR, a first aid kit should be available, and staff should have ready access to emergency contact information and a telephone.

Quality

Children in programs with high environmental safety standards may still experience unnecessary injuries. High-quality childcare programs that have safe environments have the best track record for lower injury rates, especially for girls. A quality program is one that provides a safe and *nurturing* environment. Some researchers refer to quality in terms of structural quality measures such as child-to-staff ratios, group size, and staff education and training. Childcare professionals, also include in their definition of quality the provider's ability to relate to children and refer to it in terms of caring, sensitivity, teaching, discipline, and stability. Certainly, individuals trained as childcare providers have a breadth and depth of knowledge about children that helps them nurture children emotionally, socially, and cognitively as well as keep them safe. Some providers may not have this type of training but may still be very nurturing. There are a few ways to assess a childcare provider's ability to relate to children.

First, take the time to talk to potential caregivers about their jobs. Quality providers are committed to their jobs and view their work as important and fulfilling. Do they seek out opportunities to learn about child development and childcare? What is their level of education and training? Quality providers may be highly educated and participate in family childcare training. They network with other childcare providers, participate in state regulatory processes, and may work to achieve voluntary accreditation. All of this raises the cost of childcare, so quality providers may charge higher rates and have a more professional attitude toward their business and safety practices. They also often care for larger groups of children and may have slightly higher adult to child ratios.

Second, take the time to observe the children's interactions with each other and the provider. Quality providers plan activities and experiences for the children and anticipate their needs. Does the provider have an educational program in place? Are the children busy doing activities or are they bored? If children are fighting over toys, it may be a sign that there are not enough age-appropriate toys available. Quality caregivers are also sensitive and responsive to children's needs. Observe interactions between providers and children. How are children with behavioral difficulties handled? Does the caregiver speak to children at their eye level? Do they seem to like their caregiver? Finally, find out if the facility has a high staff turnover rate. Stability helps young children develop a sense of security and is an important feature of any childcare arrangement.

CHILDREN WITH SPECIAL HEALTH CARE NEEDS
Children with special health care needs (CSHCN) should have equal access to childcare facilities since the Americans with Disabilities Act does not allow discrimination on the basis of disability. If a child has special needs, parents may want to critically evaluate a childcare provider using the checklist for CSHCN (see **Appendix 18-1**) in addition to all of the information previously discussed. Once parents have narrowed a list of potential providers, they should make an appointment with the director to discuss their child's specific condition to determine how his or her needs can be met.

PROFESSIONAL STUDY AND CONTROVERSY
Most controversial discussions about childcare today are those centered on child development. The primary issues under debate are whether childcare is helpful or harmful to children's social and cognitive development, how childcare affects children who enter it as infants, and whether a certain arrangement is better than others.

IMPACT ON SOCIAL AND COGNITIVE DEVELOPMENT
Researchers studying children in childcare are beginning to answer some questions about how it affects them. Children who receive high quality childcare are more secure and ready for school than peers who attended average or low quality childcare facilities. Katherine Magnuson and Jane Waldfogel published a study in *The Future of Children* which found this observation to be true for children of all ethnicities and in all types of childcare arrangements. Researchers define quality childcare as that which provides a safe and healthy environment, and caregivers who are responsive to the children's physical, emotional and developmental needs.

Reviews of many research studies assessing the benefits of childcare revealed that quality childcare helped low-income children become more socially, emotionally, and academically prepared for school. One National Institute of Child Health and Human Development (NICHD) Early Child Care Research Network study demonstrated that children who spent more time in all types of childcare arrangements had slightly more problem behaviors such as conflicts with adults and externalizing behaviors when they were 4½ years old and on entry to kindergarten than children with lesser amounts of time spent in the care of people other than their mothers. The most well-designed studies of the effects of out-of-home childcare on child intellectual development conclude that children in high-quality childcare centers benefit from the experience. They have better intellectual development than their peers and enter kindergarten ready to learn.

INFANTS, EARLY MATERNAL EMPLOYMENT, AND CHILDCARE

The effect that childcare has on infants is still being debated. Because the need for childcare first arose when both mothers and fathers began entering the workforce, a way to study the issue is through analyzing the effect maternal work status has on infants. One thousand, three hundred sixty-four families participated in the NICHD study of this question. Researchers found that infants whose mothers were employed out of the home before they reached 9 months of age performed less well on cognitive testing at 36 months of age than infants whose mothers returned to work later. Infants of mothers rated more sensitive or who attended high-quality childcare showed fewer negative effects on cognitive tests at 36 months of age. The effect was more pronounced when the infant's childcare had a poor or average quality rating or if the mother was less responsive to her child's physical and emotional needs. Boys were affected more than girls, and infants of 2-parent households were affected more negatively than infants from single parent homes. The observations from this study need more long-term study and by no means imply that women should not go back to work. Unknown factors other than maternal sensitivity, childcare quality, and time of maternal employment may have influenced these findings. Besides identifying the need for further research on maternal employment on infants and childcare, the results of this study highlight 2 areas whose improvement could benefit infants of working parents: quality of infant care and extended family leave policy. Extending maternity and paternity leave from 3 to 9 months would allow parents to spend more time with infants and introduce them into childcare environments at a later age. This study clearly illustrates that having high quality childcare and placing children in that care at later ages results in better intellectual outcomes for children. The NICHD study is ongoing and more information is continually being generated about all aspects of the effects of childcare on children. Researchers involved in this study produced a list of publications accessible at http://secc.rti.org/publications.cfm.

BEST CHILDCARE ARRANGEMENT

Another area of question and controversy is whether a certain type of childcare is better than another. The answer is in the quality of care delivered. Information generated by the NICHD highlights the importance of considering maternal and family qualities when studying the effects of childcare on a child. Other important factors are child to caregiver ratios, caregiver education and training, and group sizes. Studies of this question will help inform policy for state lawmakers for improved regulations about child to staff ratios and caregiver qualifications.

CONCLUSION

Choosing a childcare provider is one of the most important decisions parents will make. A high quality provider offers more than just custodial care and can start a child out on strong social and intellectual footing. A low quality childcare provider can have the opposite effect, and some may even jeopardize children's health. Quality is judged by the provision of a safe, caring, nurturing, and stimulating environment for the child. Child Care Aware and the US Consumer Products and Safety Commission have created checklists to help parents and providers to assess the safety of the childcare site (see "Where to Turn for Help"). The safety of the facility and quality of care that a provider can give children is more important to overall child development than whether the arrangement is in-home, family-based, or center-based.

WHERE TO TURN FOR HELP

BOOKS

American Academy of Pediatrics, American Public Health Association, National Resource Center for Health and Safety in Childcare. *Caring for Our Children. The National Health and Safety Performance Standards. Guidelines for Out-of-Home Childcare Programs*. 2nd ed. Elk Grove Village, Ill: American Academy of Pediatrics/American Public Health Association; 2002.

Douglas A. *The Unofficial Guide to Childcare*. New York, NY: Simon & Schuster Macmillan. 1998.

WEB SITES

American Academy of Pediatrics: Healthy Childcare America

http://healthychildcare.org/materials.cfm

American Red Cross Health and Safety Services: Caregiving

http://www.redcross.org/services/hss/care

Baby Center

http://www.babycenter.com/childcare/

Babysitters.com

http://www.babysitters.com

Child Care Aware

http://www.childcareaware.org

Consumer Product Safety Commission: Childcare Safety Checklist for Parents and Childcare Providers

http://www.cpsc.gov/CPSCPUB/PUBS/childcare.pdf

National Association for the Education of Young Children

http://www.naeyc.org

National Resource Center for Health and Safety in Childcare: Licensure Regulations

http://nrc.uchsc.edu/STATES/states.htm

Penn State: Better Kid Care

http://www.betterkidcare.psu.edu

APPENDIX 18-1: CHILDCARE FACILITY EVALUATION CHECKLISTS

Abbreviated Safety Checklist: Indoors

❏ Working smoke detectors are on every level.

❏ Hot water heater temperature is set at 120°F or less.

❏ Safety plugs covering electric sockets.

❏ Electric cords are not accessible to children and out of traffic patterns.

❏ Gates are at the bottom and top of staircases.

❏ Cribs meet US CSPC safety standards. (Slats are no more than 2⅜ inches apart.)

❏ No soft bedding in cribs.

❏ No loops on window blinds or curtain cords.

❏ Home or center is free of smoke, lead, and pesticides.

❏ No choking/suffocation hazards—no balloons, plastic bags, toys with small parts, foods that pose choking hazards, like hot dogs cut like coins, peanuts, whole grapes, and popcorn.

❏ No baby walkers.

❏ Cleaning supplies and other potential poisons, including medications, are out of reach of children.

❏ The center or home has an emergency response plan.

❏ Exits are unobstructed.

❏ No unlocked firearms in home.

❏ All children are well supervised.

Abbreviated Safety Checklist: Outdoors

❏ Playground equipment is installed properly and well maintained.

❏ Playground equipment is age-appropriate.

❏ Building and grounds contain no spaces greater than 3½ inches but less than 9 inches. (Children can become trapped in spaces this size.)

❏ No dangling ropes or cords (these are strangulation hazards).

❏ Playground equipment pieces are spaced appropriately.

❏ Playground surface has 12 inches of energy-absorbent material under the equipment and extending 6 feet from the perimeter of stationary equipment.

❏ Play area is free of hazards (poisonous plants, tripping hazards, etc) and is shaded.

❏ Children are well supervised.

❏ Children are not permitted to play on equipment while wearing clothing with drawstrings, necklaces, helmets, purses, or scarves. (These items pose strangulation risks.)

Abbreviated Safety Checklist: Transportation

❏ Drivers are qualified.

❏ Age-appropriate car seats or booster seats are used.

Quality Check List

❏ Caregiving is the provider's preferred job.

❏ The provider has education or training that prepares him or her for this work.

❏ The provider networks with other childcare providers.

❏ The children seem to like the provider.

❏ The provider is sensitive to children's feelings.

❏ The provider anticipates the needs of the children.

— There are enough age-appropriate toys and equipment.

— There is an educational plan or program.

❏ The provider speaks to the children at their level.

❏ The adult to child ratio is adequate.

Checklist for Children With Special Health Care Needs (CSHCN)

❏ The facility is handicapped accessible.

❏ The facility's emergency evacuation plan accommodates safe evacuation of your child.

❏ The facility has the appropriate medical equipment needed for your child (eg, a nebulizer machine for children with asthma).

❏ Medical equipment is in good working condition.

❏ Staff is adequately trained to operate the medical equipment.

❏ The staff is trained to properly administer medications.

❏ The facility has a physician consultant to advise staff on policies and procedures for children with specific special needs.

❏ There is enough space for your child to move around and participate in activities.

❏ The facility has care plans that specifically outline procedures to follow when medical problems related to his or her disability arise. For example, if your child has epilepsy, does the facility have a written care plan for seizures?

❏ Caregivers are trained to implement these care plans. (Standard care plans for specific medical conditions can be found in the AAP book *Caring for Our Children*.)

❏ Playground equipment is handicapped accessible.

❏ In facilities caring for children with and without special needs, the staff sets children's limits appropriately and does not overprotect any of them.

❏ The staff encourages children to try new activities.

❏ Staff encourages the children to help each other.

❏ The facility has educational materials that promote acceptance of CSHCN—for example, children's books that feature children who use wheelchairs or other ambulation devices.

Chapter 19

DIVORCE AND CUSTODY ISSUES

Nancy D. Spector, MD

It is extremely common today for children to belong to a family that has experienced divorce. According to recent research by Dr. George Cohen and the American Academy of Pediatrics (AAP), 50% of first marriages and 60% of second marriages end in divorce, and each year more than 1 million children are affected. Data from the US Census Bureau reveals that divorce rates are highest among adults aged 25 to 29 years (**Table 19-1**), and the majority of divorces and remarriages involve 2 or more children (**Figures 19-1-a** and **b**). Some experts even estimate that by the year 2010, more than half of school-aged children will live in a single-parent home or with a stepfamily.

EFFECTS OF DIVORCE

Divorce is extremely difficult for the adults involved, but it can be even more devastating for their children. It signals the end of a child's family as he or she knows it and consequently represents a significant loss. Recent statistics from the AAP are astounding: In 1995, approximately 60% of US children were living with both biological parents, nearly a quarter of children were living with their mother only, about 4% were living with their father only, and the remainder were living in various situations including stepfamilies, adoptive families, kinship care, or unrelated foster families. Almost half of all children whose parents divorce never see their fathers again. Contact with extended family can change, and when children move into a different home and school, they have less contact with friends. In families that experience a change in financial status and significant financial pressures, the primary caretaker—usually the mother—may have to return to work, and new caretakers enter children's lives. Children might also have to adjust to a new standard of living. These changes have potentially serious short- and long-term psychological implications for them. Studies show that almost half of children whose parents divorce will experience psychological difficulties during the first year. Children of families experiencing ongoing parental conflict, poverty, parental depression, or other psychiatric problems face an increased risk of developing long-term psychological problems such as a fear of intimacy or commitment. **Table 19-2** features questions parents frequently have about divorce and children.

Multiple factors influence how children react to divorce. A child is more likely to experience emotional difficulties if, prior to the divorce, the parents' relationship was volatile and involved frequent verbal or physical fighting. A poor understanding of the changes divorce entails and feelings of guilt, vulnerability, rejection, or responsibility for the separation also contribute to emotional problems. Some children are at increased risk if they have a negative temperament. Other important factors are family members' attentiveness to children throughout the divorce process and the degree to which children and parents' temperaments complement one another. A final influential factor is age, as children of different ages can react very differently to divorce.

Table 19-1. Current Marital Status by Age and Sex for Those Ever Divorced: 2001

MEN

AGE	TOTAL NUMBER (IN THOUSANDS)	TOTAL	PERCENT DISTRIBUTION			
			NOW DIVORCED	NOW MARRIED	NOW SEPARATED	NOW WIDOWED
Total, 25 years and older	22 130	100.0	41.7	54.8	1.8	1.7
25 to 29 years	689	100.0	62.4	35.9	1.8	-
30 to 34 years	1552	100.0	45.5	52.0	2.5	-
35 to 39 years	2454	100.0	54.5	44.1	1.4	-
40 to 44 years	2824	100.0	42.6	55.3	1.9	0.2
45 to 49 years	3439	100.0	42.0	55.4	2.6	-
50 years and older	11 172	100.0	36.8	58.4	1.6	3.3

WOMEN

AGE	TOTAL NUMBER (IN THOUSANDS)	TOTAL	PERCENT DISTRIBUTION			
			NOW DIVORCED	NOW MARRIED	NOW SEPARATED	NOW WIDOWED
Total, 25 years and older	26 035	100.0	46.6	44.0	2.7	6.8
25 to 29 years	1095	100.0	62.1	35.5	2.4	-
30 to 34 years	1896	100.0	49.9	45.8	4.0	0.3
35 to 39 years	3119	100.0	48.7	47.1	3.3	0.9
40 to 44 years	3703	100.0	48.2	47.1	3.5	1.2
45 to 49 years	4108	100.0	46.7	49.0	2.8	1.5
50 years and older	12 114	100.0	43.5	41.0	2.1	13.3

- Represents or rounds to zero.
Data Source: US Census Bureau, Survey of Income and Program Participation (SIPP), 2001 Panel, Wave 2 Topical Module.
Reprinted from Current Population Reports *by the US Dept of Commerce.*

Knowing when young children are having trouble coping with a divorce can be difficult because their verbal abilities are limited. The reactions of infants and children younger than 3 years to divorce will usually reflect their parents' reactions. If parents are grieving, distracted, and distraught, infants and toddlers are likely to cry frequently and exhibit irritability, separation anxiety, and fearfulness. They often develop sleeping problems and become more aggressive, and some will regress in behavior and development. For instance, a toddler who was toilet trained may suddenly start having accidents or refuse to use the toilet. Children who are 4 to 5 years old often worry and blame themselves for their parents' problems. They frequently fear that because their parents are breaking up, they will be abandoned, and so they become clingy. Children in this age group

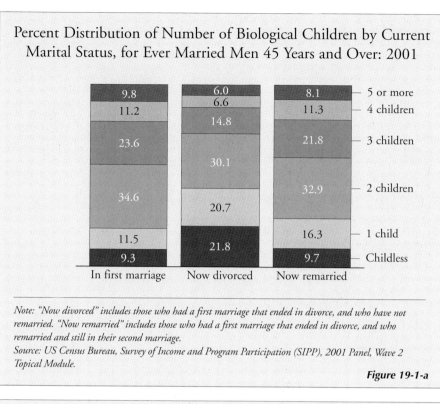

Percent Distribution of Number of Biological Children by Current Marital Status, for Ever Married Men 45 Years and Over: 2001

Note: "Now divorced" includes those who had a first marriage that ended in divorce, and who have not remarried. "Now remarried" includes those who had a first marriage that ended in divorce, and who remarried and still in their second marriage.
Source: US Census Bureau, Survey of Income and Program Participation (SIPP), 2001 Panel, Wave 2 Topical Module.

Figure 19-1-a

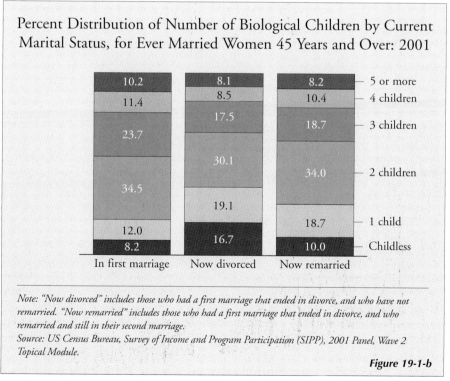

Percent Distribution of Number of Biological Children by Current Marital Status, for Ever Married Women 45 Years and Over: 2001

Note: "Now divorced" includes those who had a first marriage that ended in divorce, and who have not remarried. "Now remarried" includes those who had a first marriage that ended in divorce, and who remarried and still in their second marriage.
Source: US Census Bureau, Survey of Income and Program Participation (SIPP), 2001 Panel, Wave 2 Topical Module.

Figure 19-1-b

Figures 19-1-a *and* **b.** *Most divorces involve 2 or more children. Parents of 2 or more children are also more likely to remarry than parents with only 1 child. Reprinted from* Current Population Reports *by the US Dept of Commerce.*

Table 19-2. Frequently Asked Questions

When should I tell my child that we are getting a divorce?

It is best to tell a child about an impending divorce only when the decision is final. Children have a difficult time understanding and processing their parents' struggles over the divorce decision. Prior to the decision being made, parents should shield children from their conflict as much as possible. Once they have made the decision, they need to tell the child about the plan before the parent who is leaving moves out.

Who should tell my child about the divorce?

Ideally, both parents should sit down together to tell the child, answer his or her questions honestly, and reassure him or her that both parents love him or her very much.

How should I tell my child about the divorce?

It is best to limit the detail and use words and explanations that are appropriate for his or her developmental stage. It is also important to curb extreme emotion, especially anger.

How can I assure that my child will adjust to the divorce as positively as possible?

Children do best after divorce when parents accept all of their emotions and they are reassured that they are loved. Maintain consistent discipline and normal daily routines as much as possible.

How do I know if my child needs professional help?

You should seek the advice of a pediatrician if your child shows any of the following signs: excessive crying, fearfulness, or anxiousness; aggression; headaches, stomachaches, or other health complaints that cannot be explained; regression in developmental skills; nightmares or other sleeping problems; problems in academic performance; substance abuse; depression; or inappropriate sexual behavior.

usually have difficulty articulating their concerns, so their anxiety will manifest as behavioral changes. See **Table 19-3** for a summary of these and other behavioral changes.

Although school-aged children have a more sophisticated understanding of the issues involved with divorce, they too tend to develop behavioral problems. They may be moody, temperamental, or preoccupied, and, their academic performance may decline as a result. School-aged children may also become angry because they feel rejected or deceived by the parent who left the home. Alternatively, children may struggle to figure out how to be loyal to both parents at the same time. Overall, these children are likely to feel confused and ill at ease.

Adolescence is a time of emotional turmoil under the best of circumstances, and when divorce complicates those circumstances, adolescents can experience serious emotional reactions. Some may become angry and confused, and others develop adaptive behaviors to help deal with their feelings. For example, children might become emotionally independent from parents at an early age, rejecting parents' influence and advice in an effort to distance themselves from negative feelings about the divorce. Studies published in *Pediatrics* and *The Journal of Adolescent Medicine* have shown that adolescents whose parents get divorced are at significant risk for relationship problems, depression, substance abuse, delinquency, inappropriate sexual behavior, and other problems listed in **Table 19-3**. (See also Chapter 3, Alcohol, Drugs, and Illicit Substances, Chapter 15, Depression and Suicide, and Chapter 16, Aggressive, Defiant, and Delinquent Behavior, for related information.)

Table 19-3. Ways Children May React to Divorce

INFANTS AND CHILDREN YOUNGER THAN 3 YEARS

— Increased crying, irritability, fearfulness, separation anxiety

— Difficulty falling asleep or staying asleep

— Regression in developmental skills

4 TO 5 YEAR OLDS

— Frequent misbehavior or acting out

— Fear that they will be abandoned

— Nightmares

SCHOOL-AGED CHILDREN

— Moody, temperamental

— Acting out

— Academic problems

ADOLESCENTS

— Decreased self-esteem

— Relationship problems

— Academic problems

— Substance abuse

— Inappropriate sexual behavior

— Signs of depression, such as disinterest in friends or previously enjoyed activities, poor sleep, decreased appetite and weight loss

— Delinquent behavior

ALL CHILDREN

— Frequent headaches or stomachaches, which may indicate psychosomatic illness

— Increased anger or aggression

Data from "The pediatrician's role in helping children and families deal with divorce" by the AAP, "Children of divorce: recent findings regarding long-term effects and recent studies of joint and sole custody" by Wallerstein & Johnston, and "Helping children survive divorce" by Sammons & Lewis.

Some problems can occur in children of any age. Children can develop psychosomatic health complaints such as headaches or stomachaches in response to anger, loss, grief, or feeling unloved. For example, a child may develop headaches or stomachaches, and may consequently find comfort in the attention that results. Other children may test limits and rules or play 1 parent against another in an attempt to gain control in their life. However, Judith Wallerstein, a famous divorce researcher, has found that most children feel responsible for the separation and work extremely hard in an attempt to get their parents back together.

WHAT PARENTS AND CAREGIVERS CAN DO

Because divorce can have so many negative effects on children, it is important that the adults in their lives are sensitive, supportive, and attentive. First, parents, caregivers, teachers, and health care professionals should be aware of the factors that, when present, place children at an increased risk of experiencing difficulties. Also, as caring adults, they can try to reinforce certain factors associated with emotional stability and positive postdivorce behavioral outcomes. Children adjust better after a divorce if they have a positive temperament and an optimistic view of the future. They also tend to be better adjusted if their parents demonstrate love, affection, and acceptance and happier if they receive consistent discipline and continue to keep their normal routines. The importance of consistency in children's lives cannot be overstated. Children of divorced parents are comforted most when maximum stability in school routines, extracurricular activities, and relationships with family and friends is achieved.

When a family is going through a divorce, children's well-being is directly linked to that of their parents. Professional studies have demonstrated that mothers who are going through divorce are likely to react to daily stressors, become overwhelmed, and feel humiliated or insecure about their parenting skills. Fathers often feel excluded from their children's lives and may be less accepting of them. Both parents need to be aware of how their problems can affect their children and seek help if they need it.

Grandparents, too, can have difficulties in adjusting to divorce. They often perceive that their relationship with their grandchildren is compromised because their visits tend to be linked to 1 parent's visitation schedule, and they worry about the health and happiness of their grandchildren. Grandparents can be a vital source of stability and fun, and neither they nor the children should have their relationship severed or damaged as a result of divorce. If family relationships become damaged and 1 parent will not allow grandparents to see their grandchildren, grandparents can petition the courts for visitation rights. See "Where to Turn for Help" for resources that can help grandparents face the anger, frustration, sadness, confusion, or fear they may experience when their children are divorcing, as well as for contact information for the organization Grandparents Rights.

HOW TO PREPARE CHILDREN FOR DIVORCE

A common misconception is that because children may not understand all the reasons for their parents' divorce, they need not be told. However, it is important to prepare children for the divorce by explaining why and when one of the parents is leaving. Both parents should participate in this discussion, if possible, and they should answer children's questions as honestly as they can. It is best if neither parent displays extreme emotions. **Table 19-4** contains questions that children often ask after learning that their parents are divorcing along with the best ways for parents to respond to these questions.

Families who are experiencing divorce often find it helpful to seek the counsel and guidance of their pediatrician. Pediatricians can help assess the extent to which the divorce might negatively affect children. When both parents are involved in the relationship with the pediatrician, the physician can give a better assessment. If a child demonstrates any of the negative behavioral consequences described previously in this chapter, parents should seek advice from a pediatrician or a mental health professional.

Children's schools should be notified when parents decide to divorce. Guidance counselors, principals, and teachers may be able to help children cope, recommend resources that will help, or organize events to generate an open dialogue between children of divorced parents. Good communication with teachers is especially impor-

Table 19-4. Questions Children Ask Parents About Divorce

Who is going to move out of the house?

Explain which parent will move out and where he or she will go. Also, be clear about who will live with the child so that the child feels safe and will not worry about being abandoned.

Why is Mom/Dad leaving?

Be honest and straightforward. Consider a child's developmental level and his or her ability to understand the complexities of the situation when deciding what information to share. Do not overwhelm children with too much information. Also, do not be overly negative when speaking about the other parent; refrain from name-calling or making statements of blame.

Why will I be living with one parent and not the other?

Emphasize that the child's well-being and comfort motivated the decision. Do *not* state that you love the child more than the other parent or that you are a better parent, except when it has been obvious for some time that the other parent is abusive.

Where is Mom/Dad going to live when she/he leaves?

It is best to be as specific as possible without sharing too many details, particularly if that parent has decided to live with another partner or family.

What will happen to me?

All children, but especially school-aged children, are concerned about how their life will change. Examples include: What school will I go to? Can I take my toys? Can I still see Grandma? Can we take the cat? Tell the child that everything that can stay normal will, and that you will deal with whatever changes are necessary together.

Will Mom/Dad ever come back?

Not all separations lead to divorce. Be as honest as possible, but only suggest that the other spouse could return if reconciliation is a realistic possibility.

---

tant because teachers are instrumental in identifying any divorce-related academic or behavioral problems. Request that, when possible, notices from the school are sent to both parents so that they feel equally included in children's lives.

WHAT DIVORCING PARENTS SHOULD NOT DO

Divorce is often difficult and traumatic for parents, but because children are very sensitive to their parents' reactions, it is important for parents to avoid behaviors that will directly affect children in a negative way. Behaviors and actions to avoid are included in **Table 19-5**. Parents must also realize that in order to best help their children cope, they need to help themselves. Each parent needs to develop his or her own support system. Look to extended family, clergy or other community support groups, and friends for help with emotional needs. Many of these people are also frequently helpful for parents who require help with their parenting roles. Support people can help keep children in contact with family and friends and in normal school and extracurricular routines.

Many health and family professionals and divorce researchers agree that as long as parents are not physically or emotionally abusive, it is important for both parents to continue to have a role in their children's lives after the divorce. Unfortunately, in some

Table 19-5. Behaviors and Actions Divorced Parents Should Avoid

— *Hostility and verbal or physical aggression in front of children.* Watching parents fight is extremely difficult, and the psychological effects are long lasting.

— *Criticizing the other parent.* Most children love both of their parents and do not want to hear negative things about either of them.

— *Preventing or limiting visits with the other parent.* Children need contact with both of their parents, and this contact should be encouraged unless there is risk of physical, sexual, or emotional abuse.

— *Limiting phone or e-mail contact.* It is important to encourage a positive relationship between a child and each parent.

— *Lying or offering false hope.* It is important for children's well-being that they develop trust with their parents. Honesty is always the best policy.

— *Using children as messengers or spies.* It is imperative not to put them in the middle of parental struggles.

— *Asking children to keep secrets.* They will struggle over issues of loyalty.

— *Confiding in children and using them as emotional support in an effort to replace the void left by the missing spouse.* It will place undue emotional burden on children.

— *Asking children to take on adult responsibilities* (eg, chores or caring for younger siblings). Again, it is important not to place any further burdens on them.

— *Refusing to allow children to express anger and emotion.* It may potentially impede their adjustment process.

— *Unwillingness to recognize that the children's best interests may differ from the parents'.* It is extremely important to always make the children's best interests the highest priority.

Data from "Helping children survive divorce" by Sammons & Lewis.

instances, 1 parent does not maintain contact for a number of reasons, ranging from lack of self-confidence in his or her ability to care for children, to feelings of shame or inadequacy, to geographical distance. Parents rarely become uninvolved because they have absolutely no interest in their children; rather, loss of contact is more often a matter of circumstance. Therefore, the custodial parent needs to try to keep the lines of communication between children and the noncustodial parent open, allowing them the opportunity to have a relationship at a later time.

THE ISSUE OF CHILD CUSTODY

Divorce is the legal recognition of the end of marriage. Although the marriage is ending, in most cases, both parents will want to remain involved with and participate in the parenting of their children. Perhaps the most difficult decision that must be made during divorce proceedings involves child custody. Experts agree that the best interest of the child or children involved should receive first consideration in determining what type of custody should be granted. If the courts become involved in this decision, judges give greatest consideration to children's best interests, though the courts have, historically, not always been consistent when deciding what these "best interests" are. The "best interests" criteria should weigh each parent's mental and physical health status, any history of illegal behavior or of physically, sexually, or emotionally abusing the children, and how well each can care physically and emotionally for the children. Children's gender, race, and religion may also be taken into consideration. This information is obtained through testimony and reports provided by the parents themselves, mental health professionals, and others such as other relatives. Sometimes the children are questioned as well, though it is rare for a child to be asked to testify in court.

Sole custody, the traditional custodial arrangement in the United States, awards complete legal responsibility to 1 of the divorcing parents. In this arrangement, children live with that parent the majority of the time; the other parent has the right to scheduled visits. Mothers are usually appointed the custodian in sole custody arrangements. In recent years, however, judges have increased their sensitivity to fathers' rights and their ability to parent.

Joint custody is now becoming a much more popular type of arrangement. There are 2 types of joint custody: joint legal custody and joint physical custody. In *joint legal custody*, both parents share legal decision making responsibility. They must make all decisions together. With *joint physical custody*, a child lives with each parent for an equal amount of time. The child's schedule is created according to what is in his or her best interests, meaning that nothing prevents the child from continuing to attend his or her usual school and activities. The most common type of joint custody is joint legal custody. However, more and more parents are opting for both joint legal and physical custody.

In general, if there is no reason to suspect that either parent is abusive, child development experts recommend joint custody arrangements. This arrangement is more likely to ensure that both parents participate equally in parenting, which is very beneficial to the well-being of the child. In particular, children feel more secure when they see that their parents are reliable, capable of caring for them, and able to cooperate with one another in spite of their personal problems. Also, note that when a child requires medical care, the parent with legal custody must give consent for care. If the noncustodial parent seeks medical attention on behalf of the child, the custodial parent must usually provide written or verbal consent. Ask children's pediatricians for a description of office policies regarding consent for treatment. The American Bar Association is another very helpful resource for locating information on all divorce and custody issues, as well as for locating divorce lawyers (see "Where to Turn for Help").

PROFESSIONAL STUDY AND CONTROVERSY

When considering children's adjustment to divorce, remember that divorce is a process and not an event, particularly for them. The legal proceedings surrounding the divorce will often be insignificant in children's minds; it is the adjustments they need to make in everyday life that pose particular challenges. Early in the process, children may need to live in a new home, interact with new friends and caretakers, adjust to living without daily contact with one of their parents, and adapt to a new financial situation. Other challenges may occur later and include trouble accepting a parent's dating and sexual activities. Coping with a parent's remarriage and the stepfamily that may result can also be very difficult for children. Again, children are much more likely to make successful and positive adjustments when parents are honest, direct, and discreet.

As children get older, a periodic reassessment of custody and daily living arrangements is necessary. Preadolescents and adolescents have needs very different from those of toddlers and elementary school-aged children. Wallerstein's studies have found that adolescents may experience a phenomenon whereby a number of behavioral and emotional reactions to the separation may be reawakened, especially at times of subsequent loss, at anniversaries, with their advancing emotional and sexual maturity, and when the need to adjust to new and different family structures arises. Adolescents may require further discussion with their parents, pediatrician, or even a mental health professional to make a new and healthy adjustment.

CONCLUSION

Divorce is an increasingly common challenge for today's children. Parents and caregivers can help children work through their emotions and adjust to their new routines if they are honest, reassuring, and consistent. Parents who properly prepare their children for a divorce and its consequences and are able to work together will maintain healthy relationships with their children and help them form positive relationships as adults. **Table 19-6** contains list of dos and don'ts for parents to remember as they tell children about a pending divorce and begin rebuilding family life.

Table 19-6. Dos and Don'ts of Helping Children of Divorce

— Do tell children about the divorce before the separation takes place, and answer all of their questions honestly.

— Do reassure children that they are not responsible for the divorce and that both parents still love them very much.

— Do maintain discipline and keep routines as normal as possible.

— Do tell children's schools about the divorce.

— Do pay attention to children's behaviors and note any changes indicating that they may be having problems coping.

— Don't put children in the middle of the personal problems you have with your spouse. It is not their job to be spies, messengers, or pawns for displaying power and control.

— Do make a point to take care of yourself and form your own support systems so that you can continue to care for your children.

— Do put children's best interests first when negotiating custody.

— Don't expect children to adjust quickly; issues related to the divorce will need to be readdressed at various stages of development.

WHERE TO TURN FOR HELP

BOOKS FOR PARENTS

Benedek EP, Brown CF. *How To Help Your Child Overcome Your Divorce: A Support Guide for Families.* New York, NY: Newmarket Press; 1998.

Greydanus DE, ed-in-chief; Bashe P, for the American Academy of Pediatrics. *Caring for Your Teenager.* New York, NY: Bantam Books; 2003.

Schor EL, ed-in-chief; American Academy of Pediatrics. *Caring for Your School-Age Child: Ages 5–12.* New York, NY: Bantam Books; 2003.

Shelov SP, ed-in-chief; Hannemann RE, associate ed; American Academy of Pediatrics. *Caring for Your Baby and Young Child: Birth to Age 5.* New York, NY: Bantam Books; 2004.

Wallerstein J, Lewis J, Blakeslee S. The *Unexpected Legacy of Divorce*. New York, NY: Hyperion; 2000.

BOOKS FOR CHILDREN

Blakeslee Ives S, Fassler D, Lash M. *The Divorce Workbook: A Guide for Kids and Families*. Burlington, Vt: Waterfront Books; 1988.

Blume J. *It's Not the End of the World*. Scarsdale, NY: Bradbury Press; 1972.

Brown LK, Brown M. *Dinosaurs Divorce: A Guide for Changing Families*. Boston, Mass: Atlantic Monthly Press; 1986.

Danziger P. *The Divorce Express*. New York, NY: Delacorte Press; 1982.

Fassler D, Lash M, Blakslee Ives S. *Changing Families: A Guide for Kids and Grown-ups*. Burlington, Vt: Waterfront Books; 1988.

Holyoke N. *Help! A Girl's Guide to Divorce and Stepfamilies*. Middleton, WI: Pleasant Company Publications; 1999.

Kimball G. *How to Survive Your Parents' Divorce: Kids' Advice to Kids*. Chico, Calif: Equality Press; 1994.

Parsley BM. *The Choice Is Yours: A Teenager's Guide to Self-Discovery, Relationships, Values, and Spiritual Growth*. New York, NY: Simon & Schuster; 1992.

Rogers F, Judkis J. *Let's Talk About It: Divorce*. Pittsburgh, Pa: Family Communications Inc; 1996.

RESOURCES FOR GRANDPARENTS

Carson L. *The Essential Grandparent's Guide to Divorce: Making a Difference in the Family*. Deerfield Beach, Fla: Health Communications Inc; 1999.

Grandparents Rights Org

100 W. Long Lake Road, Suite 250
Bloomfield Hills, MI 48304
Phone: 248-646-1791
FAX: 248-646-9722

http://www.grandparentsrights.org

WEB SITES

American Academy of Child and Adolescent Psychiatry: Children and Divorce

http://www.aacap.org/publications/factsfam/divorce.htm

American Academy of Pediatrics: Divorce and Step Parenting

http://www.aap.org/healthtopics/divorce.cfm

American Bar Association

http://www.abanet.org/public.html

American Psychiatric Association: Healthy Minds, Healthy Lives

http://www.healthyminds.org

Bibliography

CHAPTER 1: BULLYING

Coloroso B. *The Bully, the Bullied, and the Bystander*. New York, NY: HarperResource; 2002.

Fekkes M, Pijpers FI, Verloove-Vanhorick SP. Bullying behavior and associations with psychosomatic complaints and depression in victims. *J Pediatr*. 2004;144:17-22.

Janssen I, Craig WM, Boyce WF, Pickett W. Associations between overweight and obesity with bullying behaviors in school-aged children. *Pediatrics*. 2004;113(5):1187-1194.

Juvonen J, Graham S, Schuster M. Bullying among young adolescents: the strong, the weak, and the troubled. *Pediatrics*. 2003;112(6):1231-1237.

Nansel TR, Overpeck M, Pilla RS, Ruan WJ, Simons-Morton B, Scheidt P. Bullying behaviors among US youth: prevalence and association with psychosocial adjustment. *JAMA*. 2001;285(16):2094-2100.

Nansel TR, Overpeck MD, Haynie DL, Ruan WJ, Scheidt PC. Relationships between bullying and violence among US youth. *Arch Pediatr Adolesc Med*. 2003;157(4):348-353.

Olweus D. *Bullying at School: What We Know and What We Can Do*. Malden, Mass: Blackwell Publishing; 1993. Understanding Children's Worlds series.

Spivak H, Prothrow-Stith D. The need to address bullying—an important component of violence prevention. *JAMA*. 2001;285(16):2131-2132.

CHAPTER 2: MEDIA VIOLENCE

American Academy of Pediatrics Committee on Public Education. Children, adolescents, and television. *Pediatrics*. 2001:107(2):423-426.

American Academy of Pediatrics Committee on Public Education. Media Violence. *Pediatrics*. 2001;108(5):1222-1226.

Bandura A, Ross D, Ross SA. Imitation of film-mediated aggressive models. *J Abnorm Soc Psychol*. 1963;66:3-11.

Bushman BJ, Anderson CA. Media violence and the American public: scientific fact versus media misinformation. *Am Psychol*. 2001;56(6-7):477-489.

Bushman BJ, Cantor J. Media ratings for violence and sex: implications for policy makers and parents. *Am Psychol*. 2003:58(2):130-141.

Centerwall BS. Television and violence: the scale of the problem and where to go from here. *JAMA*. 1992;267(22):3059-3063.

Dietz WH, Strasburger VC. Children, adolescents, and television. *Curr Probl Pediatr*. 1991;21(1):8-31.

Federal Communications Commission. Telecommunications Act of 1996. Los Angeles, Calif:1996; No 104-104, 110 Stat 56.

Kaiser Family Foundation (KFF). *Parents, Children, and the Television Ratings System: Two Kaiser Family Foundation Surveys*. Menlo Park, Calif: KFF; 1998.

National Institute of Mental Health. *Television and Behavior: Ten Years of Scientific Progress and Implications for the Eighties.* Vol 1. Rockville, Md: US Dept of Health & Human Services; 1982. DHHS Publication No ADM 82-1195.

Prothrow-Stith D, Wiessman M. *Deadly Consequences: How Violence is Destroying Our Teenage Population and a Plan to Begin Solving the Problem.* New York, NY: Harper Collins; July 1991.

Roberts DF, Foehr UG, Rideout VJ, Brodie M. *Kids & Media @ the New Millenium: A Comprehensive National Analysis of Children's Media Use.* Menlo Park, Calif: The Henry J. Kaiser Family Foundation; November 1999.

Sege R, Dietz W. Television viewing and violence in children: the pediatrician as agent for change. *Pediatrics.* 1994;94(4 pt 2):600-607.

Strasburger VC, Donnerstein E. Children, adolescents, and the media: issues and solutions. *Pediatrics.* 1999;103(1):129-139.

University of California Center for Communication and Social Policy. *National Television Violence Study I.* Thousand Oaks, Calif: Sage Publications; 1996.

University of California Center for Communication and Social Policy. *National Television Violence Study II.* Thousand Oaks, Calif: Sage Publications; 1997.

University of California Center for Communication and Social Policy. *National Television Violence Study III.* Thousand Oaks, Calif: Sage Publications; 1998.

Williams TM. *The Impact of Television: A Natural Experiment in Three Communities.* Orlando, Fla: Academic Press; 1986.

CHAPTER 3: ALCOHOL, DRUGS, AND ILLICIT SUBSTANCES

American Academy of Pediatrics. Alcohol use and abuse: a pediatric concern. *Pediatrics.* 2001;108(1):185-189.

Bogenschneider K. Has family policy come of age? A decade of review in the sate of US family policy in the 1990s. *J Marriage Fam.* 2000;62:1136-1159.

Drug Information Clearing House, Australian Drug Foundation. Fact Sheet: Club Drugs. Australian Drug Foundation Web site. Available at: http://www.druginfo.adf.org.au/article.asp?ContentID=club_drugs. Accessed January 16, 2006.

Hansen WB, Graham JW, Wolkenstein BH, Rohrbach LA. Program integrity as a moderator of prevention program effectiveness: results for fifth-grade students in the Adolescent Alcohol Prevention Trial. *J Studies Alcohol.* 1991;53(6):568-579.

Johnston LD, O'Malley PM., Bachman JG, Schulenberg JE. Teen drug use down but progress halts among youngest teens [press release]. University of Michigan News and Information Services. Ann Arbor, Mich: December 19, 2005. Available at: http://www.monitoringthefuture.org/pressreleases/05drugpr_complete.pdf. Accessed May 25, 2006.

Knight JR, Shrier LA, Bravender TD, et al. A new brief screen for adolescent substance use. *Arch Pediatr Adolesc Med.* 1999;153(6):591-596.

Levy S, Vaughan BL, Knight JR. Office based interventions for adolescent substance abuse. *Pediatr Clin North Am.* 2002;49(2):329-343.

Pride Surveys. 2002–2003 Pride surveys national summary. Pride questionnaire report for grades 6–12. Pride Surveys Web site. Available at: http://www.pridesurveys.com/customercenter/us03ns.pdf. Accessed May 25, 2005.

SADD National. *Contract for Life*. Marlborough, Mass: SADD, Inc; 2005. Available at: http://www.sadd.org/contract.htm#cfl. Accessed January 27, 2006.

Substance Abuse and Mental Health Services Administration Office of Applied Sciences. *Results from the 2004 National Survey on Drug Use and Health: National Findings*. Rockville, Md: US Dept of Health & Human Services; September 8, 2005. Available at: http://www.oas.samhsa.gov/NSDUH/2k4nsduh/2k4Results/2k4 Results.pdf. Accessed January 13, 2006. NSDUH Series H-28, DHHS Publication No SMA 05-4062.

Substance Abuse and Mental Health Services Administration Office of Applied Studies. *Overview of Findings from the 2002 National Survey on Drug Abuse and Health*. Rockville, Md: US Dept of Health & Human Services; September 2003. Available at: www.oas.samhsa.gov/nhsda/2k2nsduh/Overview/2k2Overview.htm. Accessed July 25, 2005. NHSDA Series H-21, DHHS Publication No SMA 03–3774.

The Weekly Reader National Survey on Drugs and Alcohol. Middletown, Conn: Field Publications; 1995.

US Department of Health and Human Services, Substance Abuse and Mental Health Services Administration. Opiates/narcotics: slang terms. SAMHSA Web site. Available at: http://store.health.org/catalog/slang.aspx?topic=57&h=drugs&m=slang. Accessed January 16, 2006.

US Department of Health and Human Services, Substance Abuse and Mental Health Services Administration. Heroin/morphine: slang terms. SAMHSA Web site. Available at: http://store.health.org/catalog/slang.aspx?topic=51&h=drugs&m=slang. Accessed January 16, 2006.

US Drug Enforcement Administration. *Drugs of Abuse*. Narcotics. Washington, DC: DEA; 2005. Available at: http://www.usdoj.gov/dea/pubs/abuse/4-narc.htm. Accessed January 16, 2006.

US Drug Enforcement Administration. DEA/USDOJ Cocaine fact sheet. DEA Web site. Available at: http://www.usdoj.gov/dea/concern/cocaine_factsheet.html. Accessed July 25, 2005.

US Drug Enforcement Administration. DEA/USDOJ Marijuana fact sheet. DEA Web site. Available at: http://www.usdoj.gov/dea/concern/marijuana_factsheet.html. Accessed July 25, 2005.

US Drug Enforcement Administration. DEA/USDOJ Methamphetamine & amphetamines fact sheet. DEA Web site. Available at: http://www.usdoj.gov/dea/concern/meth_factsheet.html. Accessed July 25, 2005.

US Drug Enforcement Administration. DEA/USDOJ Narcotics page. DEA Web site. Available at: http://www.usdoj.gov/dea/concern/narcotics.html. Accessed July 25, 2005.

US Drug Enforcement Administration. DEA/USDOJ Photo library. DEA Web site. Available at: http://www.usdoj.gov/dea/photo_library.html. Accessed July 25, 2005.

US Drug Enforcement Administration. Get it straight! What's up with cocaine and crack? DEA Web site. Available at: http://www.usdoj.gov/dea/pubs/straight/cocaine.htm. Accessed January 16, 2006.

US Drug Enforcement Administration. Get it straight! What's up with LSD? DEA Web site. Available at: http://www.usdoj.gov/dea/pubs/straight/lsd.htm. Accessed January 16, 2006.

US Drug Enforcement Administration. Get it straight! What's up with methamphetamine? DEA Web site. Available at: http://www.usdoj.gov/dea/pubs/straight/meth.htm. Accessed January 16, 2006.

US Drug Enforcement Administration. Get it straight! What's up with heroin? DEA Web site. Available at: http://www.usdoj.gov/dea/pubs/straight/heroin.htm. Accessed January 16 2006.

USDHHS and SAMHSA's National Clearinghouse for Alcohol and Drug Information (NCADI). Prevention online. Available at: http://www.health.org. Accessed February 22, 2006.

CHAPTER 4: TOBACCO AND SMOKING

Albers AB, Biener L. Adolescent participation in tobacco promotions: the role of psychosocial factors. *Pediatrics*. 2003;111(2):402-406.

American Psychiatric Association. *Diagnostic and Statistical Manual of Mental Disorders*. 4th ed, text revision. Arlington, Va: American Psychiatric Publishing; 2000.

Anderson HR, Cook DG. Passive smoking and sudden infant death syndrome: a review of the epidemiological evidence. *Thorax*. 1997;52(11):1003-1009.

Centers for Disease Control and Prevention. Incidence of cigarette smoking—United States, 1965-1996. *Morb Mortal Wkly Rep*. 1998;47(39):837-840.

Centers for Disease Control and Prevention. Reasons for tobacco use and symptoms of nicotine withdrawal among adolescent and young adult tobacco users, 1993. *Morb Mortal Wkly Rep*. 1994;43(41):745-750.

Center for Media Education. *Alcohol and Tobacco on the Web: New Threats to Youth*. Washington, DC: Center for Media Education; 1997. Available at: http://www.cme.org/publications/reports.html. Accessed May 19, 2005.

Center for Media Education. *Youth Access to Alcohol and Tobacco Web Marketing: The Filtering and Rating Debate*. Washington, DC: Center for Media Education; 1999. Available at: http://www.cme.org/publications/reports.html. Accessed May 19, 2005.

Colby SM, Tiffany ST, Shiffman S, Niaura RS. Are adolescent smokers dependent on nicotine? A review of the evidence. *Drug Alcohol Depend*. 2000;59(suppl 1):s83-s95.

Dalton MA, Sargent JD, Beach ML, et al. Effect of viewing smoking in movies on adolescent smoking initiation: a cohort study. *Lancet*. 2003;362:281-285.

Duncan B, Rees DI. Effect of smoking on depressive symptomatology: a reexamination of data from the National Longitudinal Study of Adolescent Health. *Am J Epidemiol*. 2005;162(5):461-470.

Evans N, Farkas A, Gilpin E, Berry C, Pierce JP. Influence of tobacco marketing and exposure to smokers on adolescent susceptibility to smoking. *J Natl Cancer Inst*. 1995;87(20):1538-1545.

Everett SA, Warren CW, Sharp D, Kann L, Husten CG, Crossett LS. Initiation of cigarette smoking and subsequent smoking behavior among US high school students. *Prev Med*. 1999;29(5):327-333.

Fiore MC, guideline panel chair. *Treating Tobacco Use and Dependence: Clinical Practice Guideline*. Rockville, Md: US Dept of Health & Human Services; June 2000.

Gilpin E, Choi WS, Berry C, Pierce JP. How many adolescents start smoking each day in the United States? *J Adolesc Health*. 1999;25(4):248-255.

Law KL, Stroud LR, LaGasse LL, Niaura R, Liu J, Lester BM. Smoking during pregnancy and newborn neurobehavior. *Pediatrics*. 2003;111(6 pt 1):1318-1123.

Monitoring the Future. *Cigarettes: Trends in 30-Day Use, Risk, Disapproval, and Availability—Eighth, Tenth, and Twelfth Graders*. Ann Arbor, Mich: Monitoring the Future; 2003. Available at: http://www.monitoringthefuture.org/data/03data/cfig03_1.pdf. Accessed July 25, 2005.

Monitoring the Future. *Smokeless Tobacco: Trends in 30-Day Use, Risk, Disapproval, and Availability—Eighth, Tenth, and Twelfth Graders*. Ann Arbor, Mich: Monitoring the Future; 2003. Available at: http://www.monitoringthefuture.org/data/03data/cfig03_2.pdf. Accessed July 25, 2005.

National Center for Chronic Disease Prevention and Health Promotion Office on Smoking and Health. *The Health Consequences of Smoking: A Report of the Surgeon General*. Washington, DC: US Dept of Health & Human Services; 2004.

National Center for Chronic Disease Prevention and Health Promotion Office on Smoking and Health. *Preventing Tobacco Use Among Young People: A Report of the Surgeon General*. Washington, DC: US Dept of Health & Human Services; 2004.

Pierce JP, Distefan JM, Jackson C, White MM, Gilpin EA. Does tobacco marketing undermine the influence of recommended parenting in discouraging adolescents from smoking? *Am J Prev Med*. 2002;23(2):73-81.

Rojas NL, Killen JD, Haydel KF, Robinson TN. Nicotine dependence among adolescent smokers. *Arch Ped Adolesc Med*. 1998;152(2):151-156.

Sargent JD, Dalton M. Does parental disapproval of smoking prevent adolescents from becoming established smokers? *Pediatrics*. 2001;108(6):1256-1262.

Schick S, Glantz S. Scientific analysis of second-hand smoke by the tobacco industry, 1929-1972. *Nicotine Tob Res*. 2005;7(4):591-612.

Substance Abuse and Mental Health Services Administration, Office of Applied Studies. *Overview of Findings From the 2002 National Survey on Drug Abuse and Health*. Rockville, Md: US Dept of Health & Human Services; September 2003. Available at: http://www.oas.samhsa.gov/nhsda/2k2nsduh/Overview/2k2Overview.htm. Accessed July 25, 2005. NSDUH Series H-21, DHHS Pub No SMA 03-3774.

Substance Abuse and Mental Health Services Administration, Office of Applied Studies. *Results of the 2004 National Survey on Drug Abuse and Health*. Rockville, Md: US Dept of Health & Human Services; September 8, 2005. Available at: http://www.oas.samhsa.gov/NSDUH/2k4nsduh/2k4Results/2k4Results.pdf. Accessed January 23, 2006. NSDUH Series H-28, DHHS Pub No SMA 05-4062.

Syed TS, Braverman PK, D'Amico F. Knowledge and attitudes of adolescents towards smoking cessation methods. *J Adolesc Health*. 2000;26:141.

Zolty B. The tobacco epidemic: a crisis of startling dimensions. World Health Organization Programme on Substance Abuse. 1998. Available at: http://www.who.int/archives//ntday/ntday98/ad98e_3.htm. Accessed May 19, 2005.

CHAPTER 5: INITIATION OF SEXUAL ACTIVITY

Alan Guttmacher Institute. Parents are youngster's top choice as source of health information. *Perspectives on Sexual and Reproductive Health* [journal online]. March/April 2002;34(2). Available at: http://www.guttmacher.org/pubs/journals/3411002.html. Accessed May 18, 2006.

Alan Guttmacher Institute. *Teenagers' Sexual and Reproductive Health: Developed Countries. Facts in Brief*. Alan Guttmacher Institute Web site. 2004. Available at: http://www.guttmacher.org/pubs/fb_teens.html. Accessed December 27, 2005.

Blum RW. *Mother's Influence on Teen Sex: Connections That Promote Postponing Sexual Intercourse*. Minneapolis: General Pediatrics and Adolescent Health, University of Minnesota; 2002. Robert Wood Johnson Foundation Monograph No 4. Available at: http://www.allaboutkids.umn.edu/kdwbvfc/fr_pub.htm. Accessed May 22, 2006.

Center for AIDS Prevention Studies. *Fact Sheet: Should We Teach Only Abstinence in Sexuality Education?* San Francisco, Calif: UCSF AIDS Research Institute; September 1997. Available at: http://caps.ucsf.edu/abstinence.html#10. Accessed May 24, 2006.

Centers for Disease Control. Youth risk behavior surveillance, 2003. *Morb Mortal Wkly Rep*. 2004;53(No SS 2).

Child Trends. Oral sex. Child Trends Data Bank Web site. Available at: http://www.childtrendsdtatabank.org/indicators/95OralSex.cfm. Accessed May 23, 2006.

Crosby RA, DiClemente RJ, Wingood GM, Lang DL, Harrington K. Infrequent parental monitoring predicts sexually transmitted infections among low-income African American female adolescents. *Arch Pediatr Adolesc Med*. 2003;157:169-173.

Denizet-Lewis B. Friends, friends with benefits and the benefits of the local mall. *New York Times*. May 30, 2004; sec 6:30.

Frost JJ, Jones RK, Woog V, Singh S, Darroch JE. *Teenage Sexual and Reproductive Behavior in Developed Countries: Country Report for the United States*. New York, NY: Alan Guttmacher Institute; November 2001. Occasional Report No 8. Available at: http://www.guttmacher.org/pubs/summaries/us_teens.pdf. Accessed May 22, 2006.

Gates GJ, Sonenstein SL. Heterosexual genital sexual activity among adolescent males: 1988 and 1995 [research note]. *Fam Plan Perspect* [journal online]. Nov/Dec 2000;32(6). Available at: http://www.guttmacher.org/pubs/journals/3229500.html. Accessed May 22, 2006.

Green JP, Foster G. *Sex, Drugs, and Delinquency in Urban and Suburban Public Schools*. New York, NY: Manhattan Institute for Policy Research; January 2004. Education Working Paper No 4. Available at: http://www.manhattaninstitute.org/html/ewp_04.htm. Accessed May 23, 2006.

Kaiser Family Foundation. Oral sex increasing "trend" among adolescents. *Daily Women's Health Policy: Public Health and Education* [daily e-mail news bulletin]. December 19, 2000. Available at: http://www.kaisernetwork.org/daily_reports/rep_index.cfm?hint=2&DR_ID=1770. Accessed May 24, 2006.

Kirby D. *Emerging Answers: Research Findings on Programs to Reduce Teen Pregnancy* (Summary). Washington, DC: National Campaign to Prevent Teen Pregnancy; 2001. Available at: http://www.teenpregnancy.org/product/pdf/emergingSumm.pdf. Accessed May 24, 2006.

Mosher WD, Chandra A, Jones J. Sexual behavior and selected health measures: Men and women 15-44 years of age, United States, 2002. Hyattsville, Md: National Center for Health Statistics; 2005. Advance Data from Vital and Health Statistics No 362. Available at: http://www.cdc.gov/nchs/products/pubs/pubd/ad/361-370/ad362.htm. Accessed May 23, 2006.

Pardini P. Federal law mandates "abstinence-only" sex ed: fundamentalists pushed stealth legislation. *Rethinking Schools* [serial online]. Summer 1998:12(4). Available at: http://www.rethinkingschools.org/archive/12_04/sexmain.shtml. Accessed May 24, 2006.

Sex bracelets. Sex Bracelets Web site. Available at: http://www.sex-bracelets.com. Accessed May 22, 2006.

Stepp LS. Study: half of all teens have had oral sex. *Washington Post.* September 16, 2005:A07. Available at: http://www.washingtonpost.com/wp-dyn/content/article/2005/09/15/AR2005091500915.html. Accessed May 24, 2006.

CHAPTER 6: PHYSICAL ABUSE AND NEGLECT

Administration for Children and Families. *What Everyone Can Do to Prevent Child Abuse.* Washington, DC: US Dept of Health & Human Services; 2003.

Akduman EI, Launis GD, Luisiri A, Silberstein MJ, Graviss ER. Skeletal and visceral radiological imaging. In: Giardino AP, Alexander R, eds. *Child Maltreatment: A Clinical Guide and Reference.* 3rd ed. St. Louis, Mo: GW Medical Publishing; 2005:13-36.

American Academy of Pediatrics Committee on Child Abuse and Neglect. The role of pediatricians in recognizing and intervening on behalf of abused women. *Pediatrics.* 1998;101(6):1091-1092.

American Academy of Pediatrics Division of Child Health Research. Executive summary of periodic survey of fellows #38: attitudes and counseling on corporal punishment in the home. July 1998. American Academy of Pediatrics Web site. Available at: http://www.aap.org/research/periodicsurvey/ps38exs1.htm. Accessed March 13, 2006.

American Academy of Pediatrics Section on Radiology. Diagnostic imaging of child abuse. *Pediatrics.* 1991;87(2):262-264.

Belsky J. Child maltreatment: an ecological integration. *Am Psychol.* 1980;35(4):320-335.

Berkowitz CD. Pediatric abuse. New patterns of injury. *Emerg Med Clin North Am.* 1995;13(2):321-341.

Briere J. Treating adult survivors of severe childhood abuse and neglect: further development of an integrated model. In: Myers JEB, Berlinger L, Briere J, Hendrix CT, Jenny C, Reid TA, eds. *The APSAC Handbook on Child Maltreatment.* 2nd ed. Thousand Oaks, Calif: Sage Publications; 2002:175-204.

Bronfenbrenner U. *The Ecology of Human Development: An Experiment by Nature and Design.* Cambridge, Mass: Harvard University Press; 1979.

Clark KD, Tepper D, Jenny C. Effect of a screening profile on the diagnosis of non-accidental burns in children. *Pediatr Emerg Care.* 1997;13(4):259-261.

Dubowitz H. Cost-effectiveness and the prevention of child maltreatment. *Child Abuse Neg.* 1990;14(2):177-1896.

Duhaime AC, Christian CW, Rorke LB, Zimmerman RA. Nonaccidental head injury in infants—the "shaken-baby syndrome." *N Engl J Med.* 1998;338(25):1822-1829.

Gabarino J, Brookhouser PE, Authier KJ. *Special Children, Special Risks: The Maltreatment of Children With Disabilities.* New York, NY: Aldine De Gruyter;1987.

Garbarino J, Crouter A. Defining the community context for parent-child relations: the correlates of child maltreatment. *Child Dev.* 1978;49(4):604-616.

Garbarino J, Eckenrode J. *Understanding Abusive Families: An Ecological Approach to Theory and Practice.* San Francisco, Calif: Jossey-Bass; 1997.

Giardino AP, Reece R. Child fatality review team. In: Giardino AP, Alexander R, eds. *Child Maltreatment: A Clinical Guide and Reference.* 3rd ed. St. Louis, Mo: GW Medical Publishing; 2005:806-852.

Goldman J, Salus MK, Wolcott D, Kennedy KY. *A Coordinated Response to Child Abuse and Neglect: The Foundation for Practice.* Washington, DC: Office on Child Abuse and Neglect, US Dept of Health & Human Services; 2003. Available at: http://www.nccanch.acf.hhs.gov/pubs/usermanuals/foundation/foundation.pdf. Accessed January 4, 2006.

Graham-Bermann SA. Child abuse in the context of domestic violence. In: Myers JEB, Berlinger L, Briere J, Hendrix CT, Jenny C, Reid TA, eds. *The APSAC Handbook on Child Maltreatment.* 2nd ed. Thousand Oaks, Calif: Sage Publications; 2002:119-130.

Grossman DC, Rauh MJ, Rivara FP. Prevalence of corporal punishment among students in Washington state schools. *Arch Pediatr Adolesc Med.* 1995;149(5):529-532.

Helfer RM. The etiology of child abuse. *Pediatrics.* 1973;51(suppl 4):777-779.

Hyman IA. *The Case Against Spanking: How to Discipline Your Child Without Hitting.* San Francisco, Calif: Jossey-Bass Publishers; 1997.

Kendall-Tackett K. *Treating the Lifetime Health Effects of Childhood Victimization.* Kingston, NJ: Civic Research Institute; 2003.

McCormick KF. Attitudes of primary care physicians toward corporal punishment. *JAMA.* 1992;267:3161-3165.

National Clearinghouse on Child Abuse and Neglect Information. *In Harm's Way: Domestic Violence and Child Maltreatment.* Washington, DC: Children's Bureau, Administration on Children, Youth, and Families, US Dept of Health & Human Services; 2001. Available at: http://www.calib.com/dvcps/facts/harmway.doc. Accessed: April 28, 2005. CD-37979.

Prevent Child Abuse America. Recognizing child abuse: what parents should know. Prevent Child Abuse America Web site. Available at: http://preventchildabuse.org/learn_more/parents/recognizing_abuse.pdf. Accessed March 14, 2006.

Prevent Child Abuse America. What you can do. Prevent Child Abuse America Web site. Available at: http://www.preventchildabuse.org/help/index.html. Accessed January 4, 2006.

Ricci LR. Initial medical treatment of the physically abused child. In: Reece RM, ed. *Treatment of Child Abuse: Common Ground for Mental Health, Medical, and Legal Practitioners.* Baltimore, Md: Johns Hopkins University Press; 2000:81-94.

Sedlak AJ, Broadhurst DD. *Third National Incidence Study of Child Abuse and Neglect* (NIS-3 Final Report). Washington, DC: US Dept of Health & Human Services; 1996. Contract No 105-94-1840.

Straus MA, Kantor GK. Stress and child abuse. In: Helfer RE, Kempe RS, eds. *The Battered Child.* 4th ed. Chicago, Ill: University of Chicago Press; 1987.

The National Center on Child Abuse and Neglect. *A Report on the Maltreatment of Children With Disabilities*. Washington, DC: US Dept of Health & Human Services; 1993. Report 105-89-16300.

Thomas D, Leicht C, Hughes C, Madigan A, Dowell K. *Emerging Practices in the Prevention of Child Abuse and Neglect*. Washington, DC: Office on Child Abuse and Neglect, US Dept of Health & Human Services; 2003.

Walter McDonald & Associates, Inc, and American Humane. *Child Maltreatment 2002: Summary of Key Findings*. Washington, DC: Administration for Children and Families, US Dept of Health & Human Services; 2004.

Widom CS. Does violence beget violence? A critical examination of the literature. *Psychol Bull*. 1989;106(1):3-28.

Wolraich ML, Aceves J, Feldman HM, et al, The American Academy of Pediatrics Committee on Psychological Aspects of Child and Family Health. The child in court: a subject review. *Pediatrics*. 1999;104(5 pt 1):1145-1148.

CHAPTER 7: SEXUAL ABUSE

Berkowitz CD. Medical consequences of child sexual abuse. *Child Abuse Negl*. 1998; 22(6):541-50, discussion 551-554.

Berlinger L, Elliott DM. Sexual Abuse of Children. In: Briere J, Berlinger L, Bulkley JA, Jenny C, Reid T, eds. *The APSAC Handbook on Child Maltreatment*. Thousand Oaks, Calif: Sage Publications; 1996:51-71.

Berlinger L. *Practice Guidelines: Psychosocial Evaluation of Suspected Sexual Abuse in Children*. 2nd ed. Chicago, Ill: American Professional Society on the Abuse of Children; 1997.

Centers for Disease Control and Prevention. Sexually transmitted diseases treatment guidelines 2002. *Morb Mortal Wkly Rep*. 2002;51(No RR-6):1-80.

Christian CW, Giardino AP. Forensic evidence collection. In: Finkel MA, Giardino AP, eds. *Medical Evaluation of Child Sexual Abuse: A Practical Guide*. Thousand Oaks, Calif: Sage Publications; 2002:131-158.

Davies SL, Glaser D, Kossoff R. Children's sexual play and behavior in pre-school settings: staff's perceptions, reports, and responses. *Child Abuse Negl*. 2000;24(10):1329-1343.

Ells M. *Forming a Multidisciplinary Team to Investigate Child Abuse: A Portable Guide to Investigating Child Abuse*. Washington, DC: US Dept of Justice; 1998.

Finkel M. The evaluation. In: Finkel M, Giardino AP, eds. *Medical Evaluation of Child Sexual Abuse: A Practical Guide*. 2nd ed. Thousand Oaks, Calif: Sage Publications; 2002:23-37.

Finkelhor D, Brown A. The traumatic impact of child sexual abuse: a conceptualization. *Am J Orthopsychiatry*. 1985;55(4):530-541.

Finkelhor D. Current information on the scope and nature of child abuse. *Future Child*. 1997;4:31-53.

Friederich WN. Sexual victimization and sexual behavior in children: a review of recent literature. *Child Abuse Neg*. 1993;17(1):59-66.

Gorey KM, Leslie DR. The prevalence of child sexual abuse: integrative review adjustment for potential response and measurement biases. *Child Abuse Negl.* 1997;21(4):391-398.

Heger A, Ticson L, Velasquea O, Bernier R. Children referred for possible sexual abuse: medical findings in 2384 children. *Child Abuse Neg.* 2002;26(6-7):645-659.

Heiman ML, Leiblum S, Cohen Esquilin C, Melendez Pallitto L. A comparative study of beliefs about "normal" childhood sexual behaviors. *Child Abuse Negl.* 1998;22:289-304.

Kendall-Tackett K, Williams L, Finkelhor D. Impact of sexual abuse on children: a review and synthesis of recent empirical studies. *Psychol Bull.* 1993;113(1):164-180.

Leventhal JM. Epidemiology of sexual abuse of children: old problems, new directions. *Child Abuse Negl.* 1998;22(6):481-491.

Lindblad F, Gustafsson PA, Larsson I, Lundin B. Preschoolers' sexual behavior at daycare centers: an epidemiological study. *Child Abuse Negl.* 1995;19(5):569-577.

Paolucci EO, Genuis ML, Violato C. A meta-analysis of the published research on the effects of child sexual abuse. *J Psychol.* 2001;135(1):17-36.

Paradise JE, Rostain AL, Nathnson M. Substantiation of sexual abuse charges when parents dispute custody or visitation. *Pediatrics.* 1988;81(6):835-839.

Saywitz KJ, Goodman GS, Lyon TD. Interviewing children in and out of court: current research and practice implications. In: Myers JEB, Berlinger L, Briere J, Hendrix CT, Jenny C, Reid TA, eds. *The APSAC Handbook on Child Maltreatment.* 2nd ed. Thousand Oaks, Calif: Sage Publications; 2002:349-378.

Sgroi SM, Blick LC, Porter FS. A conceptual framework for child sexual abuse. In: Sgroi SM, ed. *Handbook of Clinical Intervention in Child Sexual Abuse.* New York, NY: The Free Press; 1982:9-37.

Sgroi SM, Bunk BS. A clinical approach to adult survivors of child sexual abuse. In: Sgroi, SM, ed. *Vulnerable Populations.* Vol 1. New York, NY: Lexington Books; 1988.

The National Center on Child Abuse and Neglect. *A Report on the Maltreatment of Children With Disabilities.* Washington, DC: US Dept of Health & Human Services; 1993. Report 105-89-16300.

Walter McDonald & Associates, Inc, and American Humane. *Child Maltreatment 2002: Summary of Key Findings.* Washington, DC: Administration for Children and Families, US Dept of Health & Human Services; 2004.

CHAPTER 8: INTIMATE PARTNER VIOLENCE

American Academy of Pediatrics Committee on Child Abuse & Neglect. Role of the pediatrician in recognizing and intervening on behalf of abused women. *Pediatrics.* 1998;101(6):1091-1092.

American Bar Association, Commission on Domestic Violence. *Domestic Violence Safety Plan.* Chicago, Ill: American Bar Association; 1998. Available at: http://www.abanet.org/tips/dvsafety.html. Accessed January 30, 2006.

Appel AE, Holden GW. The co-occurrence of spouse and physical child abuse: a review and appraisal. *J Fam Psychol.* 1998;12(4):578-599.

Bragg HL. *Child Protection in Families Experiencing Domestic Violence*. Washington, DC: Children's Bureau, Office on Child Abuse & Neglect, US Dept of Health & Human Services; 2003. Available at: http://nccanch.acf.hhs.gov/pubs/usermanuals/domestic violence/domesticviolence.pdf. Accessed May 24, 2005.

Campbell JC, Webster D, Koziol-McLain J, et al. Risk factors for femicide in abusive relationships: results from a multisite case control study. *Am J Pub Health*. 2003;93(7): 1089-1097.

Council of Scientific Affairs, American Medical Association. Violence against women: relevance for medical practitioners. *JAMA*. 1992;267(23):3184-3190.

Edmunds C, Petersen D, Underwood T. V*iolence Against Women: A Review of Impact and Practices*. Topeka, Kan: Joint Center on Violence & Victim Studies; 2002. W7/CCU715003-05.

Fleury RE, Sullivan CM, Bybee DI. When ending the relationship does not end the violence: women's experience of violence by former partners. *Violence Against Women*. 2000;6:1363-1883.

Graham-Bermann SA, Seng J. Violence Exposure and traumatic stress symptoms as additional predictors of health problems in high-risk children. *J Pediatr*. 2005;146(3): 349-354.

Groves BM. *Children Who See Too Much: Lessons From the Child Witness to Violence Project*. Boston, Mass: Beacon Press; 2001.

Hughes HM. Psychological and behavioral correlates of family violence in child witnesses and victims. *Am J Orthopsychiatry*. 1988;58(1):77-90.

Jezl DR, Molidor CE, Wright TL. Physical, sexual, and psychological abuse in high school dating relationships: prevalence rates and self-esteem issues. *Child Adolesc Soc Work*. 1996;13(1):69-87.

Jonson-Reid M, Bivens L. Foster youth and dating violence. *J Interpersonal Violence*. 1999;14(2):1249-1262.

Klaus PA. *Crime and the Nation's Households, 2000. Bureau of Justice Statistics Bulletin with Trends, 1994-2000*. Washington, DC: US Dept of Justice, Bureau of Justice Statistics; 2002. NCJ 194107. Available at: http://www.ojp.usdoj.gov/bjs/pub/pdf/ cnh00.pdf. Accessed April 4, 2006.

Margolin G. Effects of domestic violence on children. In: Trickett PK, Schellenbach CJ, eds. *Violence Against Children in the Family and the Community*. Washington, DC: American Psychological Association; 1998:57-102.

McFarlane J, Greenberg L, Weltge A, Watson M. Identification of abuse in emergency room departments: effectiveness of a two-question screening tool. *J Emerg Nurs*. 1995; 21(5):391-394.

National Clearinghouse on Child Abuse and Neglect Information. *In Harm's Way: Domestic Violence and Child Maltreatment*. Washington, DC: Children's Bureau, Administration on Children, Youth, and Families, US Dept of Health & Human Services; 2001:10-13. Available at: http://nccanch.acf.hhs.gov. Accessed April 28, 2005. CD-37979.

Osofsky JD. Island of safety: assessing and treating young victims of violence. *Zero to Three Bulletin*. 1996:5-8.

Parkinson GW. Maternal domestic violence screening in an office-based pediatric practice. *Pediatrics*. 2001;108(3):e43.

Parsons LH, Zaccaro D, Well B, Stovall TG. Methods of and attitudes toward screening obstetrics and gynecology patients for domestic violence. *Am J Obstet Gynecol*. 1995; 173(2):381-386.

Price S, Baird K. Domestic violence in pregnancy: what midwives need to know. *Practising Midwife*. 2001;4(7):12-14.

Rennison CM, Welchans S. *Intimate Partner Violence*. Washington, DC: US Dept of Justice Office of Justice Programs; 2000:1-11. NCJ 178247.

Schoen C, Davis K, Collins K, Greenberg L, Des Roches C, Abrams M. *The Commonwealth Fund Survey of the Health of Adolescent Girls*. New York, NY: The Commonwealth Fund Committee on Women's Health; 1997.

Silverman JG, Raj A, Mucci LA, Hathaway JE. Dating violence against adolescent girls and associated substance use, unhealthy weight control, sexual risk behavior, pregnancy, and suicidality. *JAMA*. 2001;286(5):572-579.

Sinclair D. *Understanding Wife Assault: A Training Module for Counsellors and Advocates*. Toronto, Canada: Ontario Government Bookstore, Publications Services Section; 1985.

Soeken K, McFarlane J, Parker B. The abuse assessment screen. A clinical instrument to measure frequency, severity and perpetrator of abuse against women. In: Campbell JC, ed. *Beyond Diagnosis: Health Care Advocacy for Battered Women and Their Children*. Thousand Oaks, Calif: Sage Publications; 1997.

Straus MA, Gelles RJ; Smith C, ed. *Physical Violence in American Families: Risk Factors and Adaptations to Violence in 8,145 Families*. New Brunswick, NJ: Transaction Publishers; 1990.

Tjaden P, Thoennes N. *Extent, Nature, and Consequences of Intimate Partner Violence: Findings From the National Violence Against Women Survey*. Washington, DC: National Institute of Justice, US Dept of Justice; 2000. NCJ 181867.

Tjaden P, Thoennes N. *Full Report of the Prevalence, Incidence, and Consequences of Violence Against Women: Findings From the National Violence Against Women Survey*. Washington, DC: National Institute of Justice, US Dept of Justice; 2000. NCJ 183781.

Volpe JS. Effects of domestic violence on children and adolescents: an overview. The American Academy of Experts in Traumatic Stress Web site. 1996. Available at: http://www.aaets.org/article8.htm. Accessed March 7, 2006.

Wright RJ, Wright RO, Isaac NE. Response to battered mothers in the pediatric emergency department: a call for an interdisciplinary approach to family violence. *Pediatrics*. 1997;99(2):186-192.

Yates TM, Dodds MF, Sroufe LA, Egeland B. Exposure to partner violence and child behavior problems: a prospective study controlling for child physical abuse and neglect, child cognitive ability, socioeconomic status, and life stress. *Dev Psychopathol*. 2003; 15(1):199-218.

CHAPTER 9: RISKS OF THE INTERNET

Aftab P. Internet safety: what you always wanted to know about filtering software but were afraid to ask. Family Guide Book Web site. Available at: http://www.family guidebook.com/filtering.html. Accessed April 4, 2005.

Armagh DS, Battaglia NL, Lanning KV. *Use of Computers in the Sexual Exploitation of Children*. Washington, DC: Office of Juvenile Justice and Delinquency Prevention, US Dept of Justice; 2000. NCJ 170021.

Borzekowski DL, Rickert VI. Adolescent cybersurfing for health information: a new resource that crosses barriers. *Arch Pediatr Adolesc Med*. 2001;155(7):813-817.

Children's Partnership. *Internet Safety Guide: Safe Surfing for Kids*. Harrisburg: Commonwealth of Pennsylvania, The Governor's Community Partnership for Safe Children; 2001. Available at: http://www.cp.state.pa.us. Accessed October 4, 2001.

Cole JI, Suman M, Schramm P, et al. *The UCLA Internet Report: Surveying the Digital Future Year Three*. Los Angeles: University of California Los Angeles Center for Communications Policy; 2003:1-86.

CyberTipline. National Center for Missing & Exploited Children Web site. Available at: http://www.missingkids.com. Accessed March 28, 2005.

Digital chaperones for kids: which Internet filters protect the best? Which get in the way? *Consumer Reports*. March 2001:20-23.

Finkelhor D, Mitchell KJ, Wolak J. *Online Victimization: A Report on the Nation's Youth*. Alexandria, Va: Crimes Against Children Research Center, National Center for Missing & Exploited Children; 2000. Available at: http://www.ncmec.org/en_US/publications/NC62.pdf. Accessed January 9, 2006.

Fox S, Fallows D. *Internet Health Resources: Health Searches and Email Have Become Commonplace, but There Is Room for Improvement in Searches and Overall Internet Access*. Washington, DC: Pew Internet & American Life Project; 2003. Available at: http://www.pewinternet.org/PPF/r/95/report_display.asp. Accessed March 8, 2006.

Fox S, Lewis O. *Fear of Online Crime: Americans Support FBI Interception of Criminal Suspects' Email and New Laws to Protect Online Privacy*. Washington, DC: Pew Internet and & American Life Project; 2001. Available at: http://www.pewInternet.org/pdfs/PIP_Fear_of_crime.pdf. Accessed March 8, 2006.

Gallo D. Filtering tools, education, and the parent: ingredients for surfing safely on the information superhighway. *APSAC Advisor*. 1998;11(4):23-25.

Hansen D, Derry HA, Resnick PJ, Richardson CR. Adolescents searching for health information on the Internet: an observational study. *J Med Internet Res*. 2003;5(4):e25.

Home page. Partners Against Hate Web site. Available at: http://www.partnersagainsthate.org. Accessed April 20, 2005.

Huston P. Survey: few parents use filtering software. *ZDNet News* [serial online]. November 30, 1997. Available at: http://news.zdnet.com/2100-9595_22-505995.html. Accessed January 29, 2006.

Kaplan JE, Moss MP. *Investigating Hate Crimes on the Internet*. Lieberman ML, Wessler S, eds. Washington, DC: Partners Against Hate; September 2003. Available at: http://www. partnersagainsthate.org/publications/investigating_hc.pdf. Accessed April 20, 2005.

Lenhart A, Rainie L, Lewis O. *Teenage Life Online: The Rise of the Instant-Message Generation and the Internet's Impact on Friendships and Family Relationships*. Washington, DC: Pew Internet and & American Life Project; 2001. Available at: http://www.pewInternet.org/pdfs/PIP_Teens_Report.pdf. Accessed January 9, 2006.

Magid LJ. With the right tools, parents can keep kid surfers safe. *Los Angeles Times.* August 3, 1998: D3. Available at: http://www.safekids.com/Kids_safe.htm. Accessed January 9, 2006.

McLaughlin JF. Technophilia: a modern day paraphilia. Keene Police Department Web site. Available at: http://www.ci.keene.nh.us/police/technophilia.html. Accessed January 9, 2006.

Mitchell KJ, Finkelhor D, Wolak J. Risk factors for and impact of online sexual solicitation of youth. *JAMA.* 2001;285(23):3011-3014.

National School Boards Foundation. Research and guidelines for children's use of the Internet. National School Boards Foundation Web site. Available at: http://www.nsbf.org/safe-smart/full-report.htm. Accessed March 28, 2005.

Economic and Statistics Administration, National Telecommunications and Information Administration and Economic and Statistics Administration. *A Nation Online: How Americans are Expanding Their Use of the Internet.* Washington, DC: US Dept of Commerce; 2002:1-95.

Rideout VJ. *Generation RX.com: How Young People Use the Internet for Health Information.* Menlo Park, Calif: Henry J Kaiser Family Foundation; 2001. Available at: http://www.kff.org/entmedia/upload/Toplines.pdf. Accessed January 9, 2006.

Roberts DF, Foehr UG, Rideout VJ, Brodie M. *Kids & Media @ the New Millennium: A Comprehensive National Analysis of Children's Media Use.* Menlo Park, Calif: The Henry J. Kaiser Family Foundation; November 1999:1-83.

Sgroi SM, Blick LC, Porter FS. A Conceptual Framework for child sexual abuse. In: Sgroi, SM, ed. *Handbook of Clinical Intervention in Child Sexual Abuse.* New York, NY: Lexington Books; 1982:9-37.

Skinner H, Biscope S, Poland B, Goldberg E. How adolescents use technology for health information: Implications for health professionals from focus group studies. *J Med Internet Res.* 2003;5(4):e32.

Sullivan G. Raving on the Internet. *CMAJ.* 2000;162(13):1864.

Turow J, Nir L. *The Internet and the Family 2000: the View from Parents, the View from Kids.* Philadelphila: The Annenburg Public Policy Center of the University of Pennsylvania; 2000. Available at: http://www.asc.upenn.edu/usr/jturow/Adobe%20I&F%202000%20fixed.pdf. Accessed January 9, 2006.

Wax PM. Just a click away: recreational drug Web sites on the Internet. *Pediatrics.* 2002;109(6):e96.

CHAPTER 10: INJURY PREVENTION

American Academy of Pediatrics Committee on Injury, Violence, and Poison. Poison treatment in the home. *Pediatrics.* 2003;112(5):1182-1185.

American Academy of Pediatrics Committee on School Health. Health appraisal guidelines for day and resident camps. *Pediatrics.* 2000;105(3 pt 1):643-644.

American Academy of Pediatrics Committee on Sports Medicine and Fitness. Intensive training and sports specialization in young athletes. *Pediatrics.* 2000;106(1 pt 1):154-157.

American Academy of Pediatrics Committee on Sports Medicine and Fitness and Committee on Injury and Poison Prevention. Swimming programs for infants and toddlers. *Pediatrics.* 2000;105(4 pt 1):868-870.

American Veterinary Medical Association Task Force on Canine Aggression and Human-Canine Interactions. A community approach to dog bite prevention. *J Am Vet Med Assoc.* 2001;218(11):1732-1749.

Ashley P, Menkedick JR, Wooten MA. *Healthy Homes Issues: Injury.* Washington, DC: US Dept of Housing & Urban Development; 2002. Contract No C-OPC-21357. Available at: http://www.hud.gov/offices/lead/hhi/HHIInjury_3-29-2002.pdf. Accessed April 23, 2006.

Baker SP, Li G, Fowler C, Dannenberg AL. *Injuries to Bicyclists: A National Perspective.* Baltimore, Md: The Johns Hopkins Injury Prevention Center; 1993.

Bush D, González-Arroyo M, Stock L, et al. *Promoting Safe Work for Young Workers.* Washington, DC: US Dept of Health & Human Services; November 1999. Available at: http://www.cdc.gov/niosh/99-141.html. Accessed May 15, 2006. DHHS (NIOSH) Publication No 99-141.

Centers for Disease Control and Prevention. Human rabies prevention—1999 recommendations of the Advisory Committee on Immunization Practices (ACIP). *Morb Mortal Wkly Rep.* 1999;48(RR-1):1-21.

Centers for Disease Control and Prevention. Injury-control recommendations: bicycle helmets. *Morb Mortal Wkly Rep.* 1995;44(RR-1):1-16. Available at: http://wonder. cdc.gov/wonder/prevguid/m0036941/m0036941.asp. Accessed April 24, 2006.

Centers for Disease Control and Prevention. Nonfatal dog bite–related injuries treated in hospital emergency departments—United States, 2001. *Morb Mortal Wkly Rep.* 2003;52(26);605-610.

Cook PJ, Ludwig J. Guns in America: National survey on private ownership and use of firearms. *National Institute of Justice Research in Brief.* Washington, DC: US Dept of Justice; May 1997:1-12. NCJ 165476. Available at: http://www.ncjrs.gov/ pdffiles/165476.pdf. Accessed April 23, 2006.

Durbin DR, Elliot MR, Winston FK. Belt-positioning booster seats and reduction in risk of injuries among children in vehicle crashes. *JAMA.* 2003;289(21):2835-2840.

Everett Jones S, Brener ND, McManus T. Prevalence of school policies, programs, and facilities that promote a healthy physical school environment. *Am J Public Health.* 2003;93(9):1570-1575.

Gallagher SS, Finison K, Guyer B, Goodenough S. The incidence of injuries among 87,000 Massachusetts children and adolescents: results of the 1980-81 Statewide Childhood Injury Prevention Program Surveillance System. *Am J Public Health.* 1984;74(12):1340-1347.

Geller AL. Smart growth: a prescription for livable cities. *Am J Public Health.* 2003;93 (9):1410-1415.

Grossman DC. The history of injury control and the epidemiology of child and adolescent injuries. *Future Child.* 2000;10(1):23-52. Available at: http://www.future ofchildren.org/information2826/information_show.htm?doc_id=69735. Accessed April 23, 2006.

Haddon W Jr. A logical framework for characterizing highway safety phenomena and activity. *J Trauma.* 1972;12(3):193-207.

Humane Society of the United States. Selecting the right pet for your family and making the introduction. Human Society of the United States Web site. Available at: http://www.hsus.org/pets/pet_care/selecting_the_right_pet_for_your_family_and_makingthe_introduction.html. Accessed April 24, 2006.

Jackson RJ. The impact of the built environment on health: an emerging field. *Am J Public Health*. 2003;93(9):1382-1384.

Lavizzo-Mourey R, McGinnis JM. Making the case for active living communities [editorial]. *Am J Public Health*. 2003;93(9):1386-1388.

National Center for Health Statistics. Sports-related injuries cause 2.6 million visits annually by children and young adults to emergency rooms [press release]. Washington, DC: Centers for Disease Control and Prevention; March 5, 2001. Available at http://www.cdc.gov/nchs/pressroom/01news/sports.htm. Accessed April 28, 2006.

National Center for Injury Prevention and Control. Injuries among children and adolescents. Centers for Disease Control and Prevention Web Site. Available at: http://www.cdc.gov/ncipc/factsheets/children.htm. Accessed May 15, 2006.

National Center for Injury Prevention and Control. *Injury Fact Book 2001–2002*. Atlanta, Ga: Centers for Disease Control and Prevention; 2001. Available at: http://www.cdc.gov/ncipc/fact_book/Index.htm.

National SAFEKIDS Campaign (NSKC). *Playground Injury Fact Sheet*. Washington, DC: NSKC; 2004. Available at: http://www.preventinjury.org/PDFs/PLAYGROUND_INJURY.pdf. Accessed April 20, 2006.

NHTSA's National Center for Statistics and Analysis. *Traffic Safety Facts: 2004 Data*. Washington, DC: National Center for Statistics and Analysis; 2004. Available at: http://www-nrd.nhtsa.dot.gov/pdf/nrd-30/NCSA/TSF2004/809906.pdf. Accessed April 24, 2006.

Peter D. Hart Research Associates. Parents, kids, and guns: a nationwide survey. 1998. Brady Campaign to Prevent Gun Violence Web site. Available at: http://www.bradycampaign.org/facts/research/?page=hart98&menu=gvr. Accessed April 23, 2006.

Sacks JJ, Sinclair L, Gilchrist J, Golab G, Lockwood R. Breeds of dogs involved in fatal human attacks in the United States between 1979 and 1998. *J Am Vet Med Assoc*. 2000;217(6):836-840.

Tinsworth DK, McDonald JE. *Special Study: Injuries and Deaths Associated With Children's Playground Equipment*. Washington, DC: US Consumer Product Safety Commission; 2001. Available at: http://www.cpsc.gov/LIBRARY/playground.pdf. Accessed June 8, 2006.

US Consumer Product Safety Commission (CPSC). *Chromated Copper Arsenate (CCA)-Treated Wood Used in Playground Equipment*. Washington, DC: CPSC; 2003. Available at: http://www.cpsc.gov/phth/ccafact.html. Accessed April 28, 2006.

US Consumer Products Safety Commission (CPSC). Gear up, strap it on–helmets can save lives and reduce injuries [press release]. Washington, DC: CPSC; March 26, 2006. Available at: http://www.cpsc.gov/cpscpub/prerel/prhtml06/06122.html. Accessed April 24, 2006. Release No 06-122.

US Consumer Product Safety Commission (CPSC). Public playground safety checklist. Washington, DC: CPSC; 2004. Available at: http://www.cpsc.gov/CPSCPUB/PUBS/327.html. CSPC Document #327.

Washington RL, Bernhardt DT, Gomez J, et al, and the Committee on Sports Medicine and Fitness and Committee on School Health. Organized sports for children and preadolescents. *Pediatrics.* 2001;107(6):1459-1462.

Web-based Injury Statistics Query and Reporting System (WISQARS) [Database online]. Atlanta, Ga: National Center for Injury Control and Prevention (CDC Injury Center). Last Updated: March 30, 2006. Available at: http://webappa.cdc.gov/ncipc/wisqars. Accessed April 24, 2006.

CHAPTER 11: ENVIRONMENTAL HEALTH

Ambrose SE. *Undaunted Courage: Meriwether Lewis, Thomas Jefferson, and the Opening of the American West (Lewis & Clark Expedition).* New York, NY: Simon & Schuster; 1996:197.

American Academy of Pediatrics Committee on Environmental Health. Environmental tobacco smoke: a hazard to children. *Pediatrics.* 1997;99(4):639-642.

American Academy of Pediatrics Committee on Environmental Health. Screening for elevated blood levels. *Pediatrics.* 1998;101(6):1072-1078.

American Academy of Pediatrics Committee on Environmental Health. Ultraviolet light: a hazard to children. *Pediatrics.* 1999;104(2):328-333.

American Academy of Pediatrics Committee on Substance Abuse. Tobacco's toll: implications for the pediatrician. *Pediatrics.* 2001;107(4):794-798.

American Academy of Pediatrics. Keeping skin safe and healthy [press release]. Elk Grove Village, Ill: American Academy of Pediatrics; 2004. Available at: http//www.aap.org/advocacy/archives/tanning.htm. Accessed February 16, 2005.

Balk SJ. Resources for pediatricians: how do I answer questions from parents, patients, teachers, and others? *Pediatr Clin North Am.* 2001;48(5):1099-1111, viii.

Byers RK, Lord EE. Late effects of lead poisoning on mental development. *Am J Dis Child.* 1943;66(5):471-494.

Darling M, Ibbotson SH. Sun awareness and behavior in healthcare professionals and the general public. *Clin Exp Dermatol.* 2002;27(6):442-444.

Fu JM, Dusza SW, Halpern A. Sunless tanning. *J Am Acad Dermatol.* 2004;50(5):706-713.

Geller AC, Colditz G, Oliveria S, et al. Use of sunscreen, sunburning rates, and tanning bed use among more than 10 000 US children and adolescents. *Pediatrics.* 2002;109(6):1009-1014.

Gitterman BA, Bearer CF. A developmental approach to pediatric environmental health. *Pediatr Clin North Am.* 2001;48(5):1071-1083.

Goldman LR, Shannon MW, and the American Academy of Pediatrics Committee on Environmental Health. Technical report: mercury in the environment: implications for pediatricians. *Pediatrics.* 2001;108(1):197-205.

Goldman LR. The clinical presentation of environmental health problems and the role of the pediatric provider: what do I do when I see children who might have an environmentally related illness? *Pediatr Clin North Am.* 2001;48(5):1085-1098, vii.

Goldman RH. Information and educational resources for occupational and environmental health. In: Rose BD, ed. *UpToDate* [educational medical reference online]. Wellesley, Mass; 2006. Updated November 30, 2004.

Goldman RH. Overview of occupational and environmental health. In: Rose BD, ed. *UpToDate* [educational medical reference online]. Wellesley, Mass; 2006. Updated January 10, 2005.

Herbst AL, Ulfedler H, Poskanser DC. Adenocarcinoma of the vagina. Association of maternal stilbesterol therapy with tumor appearance in young females. *N Engl J Med.* 1971;284(15):878-881.

Kim JJ and the American Academy of Pediatrics Committee on Environmental Health. Ambient air pollution: health hazards to children. *Pediatrics.* 2004;114(6):1699-1707.

Lanphear BP, Wright RO, Dietrich KN. Environmental neurotoxins. *Pediatr Rev.* 2005; 26(6):191-197, quiz 198.

Monfrecola G, Fabbrocini G, Posteraro G, Pini G. What do young people think of the dangers of sunbathing, skin cancer, and sunbeds? A questionnaire survey among Italians. *Photodermatol Photoimmunol Photomed.* 2000;16(1):15-18.

Pirkle JL, Kaufmann RB, Brody DJ, Hickman T, Gunter EW, Paschal DC. Exposure of the US population to lead, 1991-1994. *Environ Health Perspect.* 1998;106(11):745-750.

Ramirez MA, Warthan MM, Uchida T, Wagner RF. Double exposure; natural and artificial ultraviolet radiation exposure in beachgoers. *South Med J.* 2003;96(7):652-655.

Randle HW. Suntanning: differences in perceptions throughout history. *Mayo Clin Proc.* 1997;72(5):461-466.

Stein J, Schettler T, Wallinga D, Valenti M. In harm's way: toxic threats to child development. *J Dev Behav Pediatr.* 2002;23(1 suppl):s13-s22.

Ugalde MR. Environmental toxicants and children—II. In: Rose BD, ed. *UpTo Date* [educational medical reference online]. Wellesley, Mass; 2006. Updated December 19, 2005.

Ugalde MR. Environtmental toxicants and children—I. In: Rose BD, ed. *UpTo Date* [educational medical reference online]. Wellesley, Mass; 2006. Updated December 19, 2005.

US Department of Health and Human Services, US Environmental Protection Agency. FDA and EPA announce the revised consumer advisory on methylmercury in fish [press release]. Washington, DC: US Department of Health and Human Services, US Environmental Protection Agency; 2004. Available at: http://www.fda.gov/bbs/topics/news/2004/NEW01038.html. Accessed February 16, 2005.

Weiss R. Study concludes Beethoven died from lead poisoning. *Washington Post.* December 6, 2005:A08.

Young AR. Tanning devices—fast track to skin cancer? *Pigment Cell Res.* 2004;17(1):2-9.

CHAPTER 12: EMERGENCY MEDICAL SITUATIONS

Leikin JB, Feldman BJ, eds. *American Medical Association Handbook of First Aid and Emergency Care.* New York, NY: Random House; 2000.

McCraig LF, Burt CW. *National Hospital Ambulatory Medical Care Survey: 2002 Emergency Department Summary.* Hyattsville, Md: National Center for Health Statistics; 2004. Advance Data from Vital and Health Statistics No 340. DHHS Publication No 2004-1250 04-0226.

Schwarz, MW. *5-Minute Pediatric Consult*. 4th ed. Philadelphia, Pa: Lippincott Williams & Wilkins; 2005.

CHAPTER 13: TERRORISM: DEALING WITH THREATS

American Academy of Pediatrics Committee on Environmental Health. Radiation disasters and children. *Pediatrics*. 2003;111(6 pt 1):1455-1466.

Centers for Disease Control and Prevention. Agents, diseases, and threats. CDC Web site. Available at: http://www.bt.cdc.gov/agent. Accessed October 31, 2005.

Centers for Disease Control and Prevention. Facts about ricin. Available at: http://www.bt.cdc.gov/agent/ricin/facts.asp. Accessed January 12, 2006.

Centers for Disease Control and Prevention. Recognition of illness associated with the international release of a biologic agent. *Morb Mortal Wkly Rep*. 2001;50:893-897. Available at: http://www.cdc.gov/mmwr/preview/mmwrhtml/mm5041a2.htm. Accessed January 12, 2006.

Centers for Disease Control and Prevention. Salmonellosis. CDC Web site. Available at: http://www.cdc.gov/ncidod/dbmd/diseaseinfo/salmonellosis_g.htm. Accessed October 31, 2005.

Centers for Disease Control and Prevention. Smallpox disease overview. Available at: http://www.bt.cdc.gov/agent/smallpox/overview/disease-facts.asp. Accessed January 12, 2006.

Christopher GW, Cieslak TJ, Pavlin JA, Eitzen EM. Biological warfare: a historical Perspective. *JAMA*. 1997;278(5):412-417.

Public Health Image Library [database online]. Washington, DC: Centers for Disease Control and Prevention; 1995. Available at: http://phil.cdc.gov/phil/home.asp. Accessed January 12, 2006.

Schonfeld DJ. Potential roles for pediatricians. *Pediatr Ann*. 2003;32(3):182-187.

CHAPTER 14: TATTOOING, PIERCING, AND BRANDING

American Academy of Pediatrics (AAP). Keeping skin safe and healthy [news release]. AAP Web site. Available at: http://www.aap.org/advocacy/archives/tanning.htm. Accessed May 23, 2006.

American Academy of Pediatrics (AAP). Summer safety tips—part 1. AAP Web site. Available at: http://www.aap.org/advocacy/releases/summertips.htm. Accessed May 17, 2006.

American Academy of Pediatrics Committee on Environmental Health. Ultraviolet light: a hazard to children. *Pediatrics*. 1999:104(2):328-333.

American Red Cross. Blood Donation Eligibility Guidelines. American Red Cross Web site. Available at: http://www.redcross.org/services/biomed/0,1082,0_557_,00.html#pie. Accessed February 24, 2006.

Armstrong ML, Murphy KP. Tattooing: another risk behavior warranting health education. *Appl Nurs Res*. 1997;10(4):181-189.

Armstrong ML, Owen DC, Roberts AE, Koch JR. College students and tattoos: influence of identity, family, and friends. *J Psychosoc Ment Health Serv*. 2002;40(10):20-29.

Armstrong ML, Stuppy DJ, Gabriel DC, Anderson RR. Motivation for tattoo removal. *Arch Dermatol*. 1996:132(4):412-416.

Braithwaite R, Robillard A, Woodring T, Stephens T, Arriola KJ. Tattooing and body piercing among adolescent detainees: relationship to alcohol and other drug use. *J Subst Abuse.* 2001;13(1-2):5-16.

Carroll L, Anderson R. Body piercing, tattooing, self-esteem, and body investment in adolescent girls. *Adolescence.* 2002;37(147):627-637.

Carroll ST, Riffenburgh RH, Roberts TA, Myhre EB. Tattoos and body piercings as indicators of adolescent risk-taking behaviors. *Pediatrics.* 2002;109(6):1021-1027.

Diary of a tongue splitter. Body Jewellery Shop Web site. Available at: http:// www. bodyjewelleryshop.com/body_piercing_information/tongue_splitting.cfm. Accessed March 13, 2006.

Forbes GB. College students with tattoos and piercings: motives, family experiences, personality factors and perceptions by others. *Psychol Rep.* 2001;89(3):774-786.

Geller AC, Colditz G, Oliveria S, et al. Use of sunscreen, sunburning rates, and tanning bed use among more than 10 000 US children and adolescents. *Pediatrics.* 2002;109(6): 1009-1014.

Houghton SJ, Durkin K, Parry E, Turbett Y, Odgers P. Amateur tattooing practices and beliefs among high school adolescents. *J Adolesc Health.* 1996;19(6):420-425.

Koenig LM, Carnes M. Body piercing: medical concerns with cutting edge fashion. *J Gen Intern Med.* 1999;14(6):379-385.

Larratt S. Tongue splitting FAQ, tongue lengthening FAQ. 2003. BME Zine Web site. Available at: http://www.bmezine.com/tsplitfaq.html. Accessed March 13, 2006.

Martel S, Anderson E. Decorating the human canvas: body art and your patients. *Contemp Pediatr.* 2002;19(8):86-101.

Monfrecola G, Fabbrocini G, Posteraro G, Pini D. What do young people think about the dangers of sunbathing, skin cancer and sunbeds? A questionnaire survey among Italians. *Photodermatol Photoimmunol Photomed.* 2000;16(1):15-18.

Olson AL, Dietrich AJ, Sox CH, Stevens MM, Winchell CW, Ahles TA. Solar protection of children at the beach. *Pediatrics.* 1997;99(6):e1.

Randle HW. Suntanning; differences in perceptions throughout history. *Mayo Clin Proc.* 1997;72(5):461-466.

Roberts TA, Ryan SA. Tattooing and high-risk behavior in adolescents. *Pediatrics.* 2002;110(6):1058-1063.

Schmidt RM, Armstrong ML. Tattooing and body piercing. In: Rose BD, ed. *UpToDate* [educational medical reference online]. Wellesley, Mass; 2006. Updated December 12, 2005.

CHAPTER 15: DEPRESSION AND SUICIDE

American Academy of Child and Adolescent Psychiatry. Practice parameter for the assessment and treatment of children and adolescents with suicidal behavior. *J Am Acad Child Adolesc Psychiatry.* 2001;40(suppl 7):24s-51s.

American Psychiatric Association. *Diagnostic and Statistical Manual of Mental Disorders: DSM-IV.* 4th ed. Washington, DC: American Psychiatric Association; 1994.

Bashe P, Greydanus DE, eds, and American Academy of Pediatrics. *Caring for Your Teenager*. New York, NY: Bantam Books; 2003.

Briggs-Gowan MJ, Horwitz SM, Schwab-Stone ME, Leventhal JM, Leaf PJ. Mental health in pediatric settings: distribution of disorders and factors related to service use. *J Am Acad Child Adolesc Psychiatry*. 2000;39(7):841-841.

Jellinek MS, Snyder JB. Depression and suicide in children and adolescents. *Pediatr Rev*. 1998;19(8):255-264.

National Mental Health Association (NMHA). Children's mental health statistics. NMHA Webs site. Available at: http://www.nmha.org/children/prevent/stats.cfm. Accessed May 16, 2006.

National Mental Health Association (NMHA). MHIC: mental illness and the family: mental health statistics. NMHA Web site. Available at: http://www.nmha.org/infoctr /factsheets/15.cfm. Accessed May 16, 2006.

Son SE, Kirchner JT. Depression in children and adolescents. *Am Fam Physician*. 2000;62:2297-2308, 2311-2312.

United States Food and Drug Administration. FDA public health advisory: suicidality in children and adolescents being treated with antidepressant medications [press release]. Washington, DC: US Department of Health and Human Services; October 15, 2005. Available at: http://www.fda.gov/cder/drug/antidepressants/SSRIPHA2004 10.htm. Accessed January 19, 2006.

Williams J, Klinepeter K, Palmes G, Pulley A, Meschan Foy J. Diagnosis and treatment of behavioral health disorders in pediatric practice. *Pediatrics*. 2004;114(3):601-606.

CHAPTER 16: AGGRESSIVE, DEFIANT, AND DELINQUENT BEHAVIOR

Alexander J, Barton C, Gordon D, et al. *Blueprints for Violence Prevention, Book Three: Functional Family Therapy*. Boulder, Colo: Center for the Study and Prevention of Violence; 1998. Fact Sheet available at: http:// www.colorado.edu/cspv/blueprints/ model/programs/FFT.html. Accessed November 8, 2003.

American Academy of Pediatrics (AAP). Running away from home. AAP Web site. Available at: http://www.aap.org/pubed/ZZZQ10MA79C.htm?&sub_cat=21. Accessed November 8, 2003.

American Academy of Pediatrics Committee on Public Education. Media violence. *Pediatrics*. 2001;108(5):1222-1226.

Borowsky IW, Ireland M, Resnick MD. Violence risk and protective factors among youth held back in school. *Ambul Pediatr*. 2002:2(6):475-484.

Calvert WJ. Neighborhood disorder, individual protective factors, and the risk of adolescent delinquency. *ABNF J*. 2002;13(6):127-135.

Farrow JA. Service delivery strategies for treating high-risk youth: delinquents, homeless, runaways, and sexual minorities. *NIDA A Res Monogr*. 1995;156:39-48.

Feldman J, Middleman AB. Homeless adolescents: common clinical concerns. *Semin Pediatr Infect Dis*. 2003;14(1):6-11.

Hawkins JD, Smith B, Catalano RF. Delinquent behavior. *Pediatr Rev*. 2002;23(11): 387-392.

Henggeler SW, Mihalic SF, Rone L, Thomas C, Timmons-Mitchell J. *Blueprints for Violence Prevention, Book Six: Multisystemic Therapy*. Boulder, Colo: Center for the Study of Prevention and Violence; 1998. Fact Sheet available at: http://www.colorado.edu/cspv/blueprints/model/programs/MST.html. Accessed November 8, 2003.

Hindeland RL, Dwyer WO, Leeming FC. Adolescent risk-taking behavior: a review of the role of parent involvement. *Curr Probl Pediatr*. 2001;31(3):67-83.

Kalb LM, Loeber R. Child disobedience and noncompliance: a review. *Pediatrics*. 2003;111(3):641-652.

Keating LM, Tomishima MA, Foster S, Alessandri M. The effects of a mentoring program on at-risk youth. *Adolescence*. 2002; 31(148):717-734.

Kurtz PD, Kurtz GL, Jarvis SV. Problems of maltreated runaway youth. *Adolescence*. 1991;26(103):543-555.

Rainey DY. Office-based care of adolescents part 1: creating a teen-friendly office. *Adolesc Health Update* [AAP News insert]. 2003;16(1):1-8.

Ryan SA, Rickert VI. Helping parents communicate with their teens part 2: challenging clinical situations. *Adolesc Health Update* [AAP News insert]. 1999;11(3):1-8.

Ryan SA. Helping parents communicate with their teens part 1: assessment and general strategies. *Adolesc Health Update* [AAP News insert]. 1999;11(2):1-8.

Sakuta T. Social factors leading to juvenile delinquency. *J Med*. 1996;45(4):287-295.

Schaffner L. Searching for connection: a new look at teenaged runaways. *Adolescence*. 1998;33(131):619-627.

Valois RF, MacDonal JM, Bretous L, Fischer MA, Drane JW. Risk factors and behaviors associated with adolescent violence and aggression. *Am J Health Behav*. 2002;26(6):454-464.

Vermeiren R. Psychopathology and delinquency in adolescents: a descriptive and developmental perspective. *Clin Psychol Rev*. 2003;23(2):277-328.

Webster-Stratton C, Taylor T. Nipping early risk factors in the bud: preventing substance abuse, delinquency, and violence in adolescence through interventions targeted at young children (0-8 years). *Prev Sci*. 2001;2(3):165-192.

CHAPTER 17: DISCIPLINE AND CORPORAL PUNISHMENT

Adams Larsen M, Tentis E. The art and science of disciplining children. *Pediatr Clin North Am*. 2003;50(4):817-840, viii-ix.

American Academy of Family Physicians. Tips for better parenting. *Am Fam Physician*. 1999:59:1591-1592.

Bauman LJ, Friedman SB. Corporal punishment. *Pediatr Clin North Am*. 1998;45(2):403-414.

Friedman SB, Schonberg SK, eds. The short- and long-term consequences of corporal punishment. Proceedings of a conference. *Pediatrics*. 1996;98(4 pt 2):i-vi, 803-860.

Graziano AM, Hamblen JL, Plante WA. Subabusive violence in child rearing in middle-class American families. *Pediatrics*. 1996;98(4 pt 2):845-848.

Hyman IA. *The Case Against Spanking: How to Discipline Your Child Without Hitting.* San Francisco, Calif: Jossey-Bass Publishers; 1997.

Kalb LM, Loeber R. Child disobedience and noncompliance: a review. *Pediatrics.* 2003; 111(3):641-652.

McCormick KF. Attitudes of primary care physicians toward corporal punishment. *JAMA.* 1992;267:3161-3165

Stein J, ed. *The Random House Dictionary of the English Language.* New York, NY: Random House; 1979.

Stein MT, Perrin EL, for the American Academy of Pediatrics and the Committee on Pyschosocial Aspects of Child and Family Health. Guidance for effective discipline [published correction appears in *Pediatrics.* 1998;102:433]. *Pediatrics.* 1998;101:723-728.

Straus MA. Spanking and the making of a violent society. *Pediatrics.*1996;98(4 pt 2):837-842.

Chapter 18: Selecting Childcare Providers

Adams G, Rohacek M. More than a work support? Issues around integrating child development goals into the child care subsidy system. *Early Child Res Q.* 2002;17: 418-440.

Alkon A, Ragland DR, Tschann JM, Genevro JL, Kaiser P, Boyce WT. Injuries in child care centers: gender-environment interactions. *Inj Prev.* 2000;6(3):214-218.

American Academy of Pediatrics Committee on Injury, Violence, and Poison Prevention. Poison treatment in the home. *Pediatrics.* 2003;112(5):1182-1185.

American Academy of Pediatrics, American Public Health Association, National Resource Center for Health and Safety in Childcare. *Caring for Our Children. The National Health and Safety Performance Standards. Guidelines for Out-of-Home Childcare Programs.* 2nd ed. Elk Grove Village, Ill: American Academy of Pediatrics/American Public Health Association; 2002.

Blank H, Shulman K, Ewan D. *Key Facts: Essential Information on Child Care, Early Education, and School Age Care—Overview.* Washington, DC: Children's Defense Fund; 1999.

Brooks-Gunn J, Han W, Waldfogel J. Maternal employment and child cognitive outcomes in the first three years of life: the NICHD Study of Early Child Care. *Child Dev.* 2002;73(4):1052-1072.

Campbell FA, Ramey CT, Pungello E, Sparling J, Miller-Johnson S. Early childhood education: outcomes as a function of different treatments. *Appl Dev Sci.* 2002;6:42-57.

Centers for Disease Control and Prevention. National estimates of 10 leading causes of nonfatal injury treated in emergency departments in the United States, 2002. Available at: ftp://ftp.cdc.gov/pub/ncipc/10LC-2001/GIF/101c-nonfatal.gif. Accessed April 12, 2006.

Cohen HJ. Child care for children with special needs. *Pediatrics.* 1994;94(6 pt 2):1055-1059.

Consumer Products Safety Commission. *Home Playground Equipment-Related Deaths and Injuries.* Washington, DC: US CSPC; July 2001. Available at: http://www.cpsc.gov/ LIBRARY/playground.pdf. Accessed April 12, 2006.

Consumer Products Safety Commission. Requirements for full size baby cribs, 16 C.F.R. Part 1508. Washington, DC: US CPSC Office of Compliance; January 2001. Available at: http://www.cpsc.gov/BUSINFO/regsumcrib.pdf. Accessed April 12, 2006.

Consumer Products Safety Commission. Safety Hazards in child care settings. US CSPC Web site. April 1999. Available at: http://www.cpsc.gov/library/ccstudy.html. Accessed April 4, 2006.

Cryer D, Clifford R, eds. *Early Childhood Education and Care in the USA*. Baltimore, Md: Brookes Publishing Company; 2003.

Dye JL. *Fertility of American Women: June 2004*. Washington, DC: US Census Bureau; December 2005:20-555. Current Population Reports. Available at: http://www.census.gov/prod/2005pubs/p20-555.pdf. Accessed April 4, 2006.

Galinsky E, Howes C, Kontos S, Shinn M. The study of children in family child care and relative care—key findings and policy recommendations. *Young Child*. 1994;50: 58-61.

Gergen PJ, Fowler JA, Maurer KR, Davis WW, Overpeck MD. The burden of environmental tobacco smoke exposure on the respiratory health of children 2 months through 5 years of age in the United States: Third National Health and Nutrition Examination Survey, 1988 to 1994. *Pediatrics*. 1998;101(2):e8.

Helburn S, ed. *Cost, Quality and Child Outcomes in Child Care Centers. Technical Report*. Denver, Colo: Department of Economics, Center for Research in Economic and Social Policy, University of Colorado; 1995.

Helburn S, Howes C. Child care cost and quality. *Future Child*. 1996 Summer-Fall;6(2):62-82.

Holferth SL. Child care in the United States today. *Future Child*. 1996 Summer-Fall;6(2):41-61.

Johnson JO. *Who's Minding the Kids? Child Care Arrangements: Winter 2002*. Washington, DC: US Census Bureau; October 2005:70-101. Current Population Reports. Available at: http://www.census.gov/prod/2005pubs/p70-101.pdf. Accessed April 25, 2006.

Landrigan PJ, Claudio L, Markowitz SB, et al. Pesticides and inner-city children: exposures, risk and prevention. *Environ Health Perspect*. 1999;107(Suppl 3):431-437.

Li DK, Pitetti DB, Willinger M, et al. Infant sleeping position and the risk of sudden infant death syndrome in California, 1997-2000. *Am J Epidemiol*. 2003;157(5): 446-455.

Magnuson K, Waldfogel J. Early childhood care and education: effects on ethnic and racial gaps in school readiness. *Future Child*. 2005;15(1):169-196.

Moon RY, Patel KM, Shaefer SJ. Sudden infant death syndrome in child care settings. *Pediatrics*. 2000;106(2 pt1):295-300.

National Association for the Education of Young Children. Teacher-child ratios within group size. 2005. NAEYC Web site. Available at: http://www.naeyc.org/accreditation/performance_criteria/teacher_child_ratios.html. Accessed April 25, 2006.

National Institute of Child Health and Human Development Early Child Care Research Network. Child care and common communicable illnesses: results from the

National Institute of Child Health and Human Development Study of Early Child Care. *Arch Pediatr Adolesc Med.* 2001;155(4):481-488.

National Resource Center for Health and Safety in Child Care and Early Education. Individual states' child care licensure regulations. NRC Web site. Available at: http://nrc.uchsc.edu/STATES/states.htm. Accessed April 4, 2006.

National SAFEKIDS Campaign (NSKC). *Playground Injury Fact Sheet.* Washington, DC: National SAFEKIDS Campaign; 2004. Available at: http://www.preventinjury. org/PDFs/PLAYGROUND_INJURY.pdf. Accessed April 12, 2006.

NICHD Early Child Care Research Network. Child-care structure, process, outcome: direct and indirect effects of child-care quality on young children's development. *Psychol Sci.* 2002;13(3):199-206.

NICHD Early Child Care Research Network. Does the amount of time in child care predict socioemotional adjustment during the transition to kindergarten? *Child Dev.* 2003:74(4):976-1005.

Peisner-Feinberg ES, Burchinal MR, Clifford RM, et al. The relation of preschool childcare quality to children's cognitive and social development trajectories through second grade. *Child Dev.* 2001;72(5):1534-1553.

Ramey CT, Campbell FA, Burchinall M, Skinner ML, Gardner DM, Ramey SL. Persistent effects of early childhood education on high-risk children and their mothers. *Appl Dev Sci.* 2000;4:2-14.

Rivara FP, DiGiuseppi C, Thompson RS, Calonge N. Risk of injury to children less than 5 years of age in day care versus home settings. *Pediatrics.* 1989;84(6):1011-1016.

Rivara FP, Sacks JJ. Injuries in child care, an overview. *Pediatrics.* 1994;94(6 pt 2):1031-1033.

Schulman K. *The High Cost of Quality Child Care Puts Quality Care Out of Reach for Many Families.* Washington, DC: Children's Defense Fund; December 2000. Available at: http://www.childrensdefense.org/earlychildhood/childcare/highcost.pdf. Accessed February 2, 2006.

Snow CW, Teleki JK, Cline DM, Dunn K. Is day care safe? A review of research on accidental injuries. *Day Care Early Educ* (now *Early Child Educ J*). 1992;19(3):28-31.

US Environmental Protection Agency. Integrated pest management in schools. EPA Web site. Available at: http://www.epa.gov/pesticides/ipm/index.htm. Accessed April 25, 2006.

US General Accounting Office. *Child Care: State Efforts to Enforce Safety and Health Requirements.* United States General Accounting Office report to congressional requestors. Washington, DC: US General Accounting Office; January 2000. GAO/HEHS-00-28.

Vandivere S, Tout K, Zaslow M, Calkins J, Capizzano J. *Unsupervised Time: Family and Child Factors Associated With Self-Care.* Washington, DC: The Urban Institute; November 2003. Occasional Paper No 71. Available at: http://www.urban. org/UploadedPDF/310894_OP71.pdf. Accessed April 25, 2006.

Zoritch B, Roberts I, Oakley A. Day care fore pre-school children. *Cochrane Database Syst Rev.* 2000;(2):CD000564. Update in: *Cochrane Database Syst Rev.* 2000;(3): CD000564.

CHAPTER 19: DIVORCE AND CUSTODY ISSUES

American Academy of Pediatrics Committee on Psychosocial Aspects of Child and Family Health. The pediatrician's role in helping children and families deal with separation and divorce. *Pediatrics.* 1994:94(1):119-121.

Cohen GJ and the Committee on Psychological Aspects of Child and Family Health, for the American Academy of Pediatrics. Helping children and families deal with divorce and separation. *Pediatrics.* 2002;11(5):1019-1023.

Emery RE. *Marriage, Divorce, and Children's Adjustment.* 2nd ed. Thousand Oaks, Calif: Sage Publications; 1999. Developmental Clinical Psychology and Psychiatry, No 14.

Emery RE, Laumann-Billings L. Practical and emotional consequences of parental divorce. *Adolesc Med.* 1998;9(2):271-282, vi.

Healey JM Jr, Malley JE, Stewart AJ. Children and their fathers after parental separation. *Am J Orthopsychiatry.* 1990;60(4):531-543.

Hofferth SL. Updating children's life course. *J Marriage Fam.* 1985;47(1):93-115.

Kelly JB. Current research on children's postdivorce adjustment: no simple answers. *Fam Concil Courts Rev.* 1993;31(1):29-43.

Kreider RM. *Household Economic Studies: Number, Timing, and Duration of Marriages and Divorces: 2001.* Washington, DC: US Dept of Commerce, US Census Bureau; February 2005. Current Population Reports, P70-97.

McCormick CB, Kennedy JH. Father-child separation, retrospective and current views of attachment relationship with father, and self-esteem in late adolescence. *Psychol Rep.* 2000;86(3):827-834.

Sammons WAH, Lewis J. Helping children survive divorce. *Contemp Pediatr.* 2001; March:103-114.

Wallerstein JS. Children of divorce: the psychological tasks of the child. *Am J Orthopsychiatry.* 1983;53(2):230-243.

Wallerstein JS, Johnston JR. Children of divorce: recent findings regarding long-term effects and recent studies of joint and sole custody. *Pediatr Rev.* 1990;11(7):197-204.

Wallerstein JS, Kelly JB. *Surviving the Breakup: How Parents and Children Cope With Divorce.* New York, NY: BasicBooks; 1980.

Wallerstein J, Lewis J, Blakeslee S. *The Unexpected Legacy of Divorce.* New York, NY: Hyperion; 2000.

Willemsen E, Willemsen M. The best interest of the child: a child's right to have stable relationships must be central to custody decisions. *Issues in Ethics.* 2000;11(1). Available at: http://www.scu.edu/ethics/publications/iie/v11n1/custody.html. Accessed June 5, 2006.

Wolrach ML, Aceves J, Feldman HM, et al, and the Committee on Psychosocial Aspects of Child and Family Health for the American Academy of Pediatrics. The child in court: a subject review. *Pediatrics.* 1999;104(5):1145-1148.